ANTIFUNGAL PROPERTIES IN HERBS

Aditi Gupta

ABSTRACT

The fungal organism is a eukaryotic, microscopic, heterotrophic, unicellular or multicellular with inflexible cell wall compiled with chitin, glucan, and/or cellulose with a plethora of organelles.

The fungi, a eukaryotic organism causing infection to the human beings are a growing serious public health concern. Diseases caused by fungi which have clinical significance are characterized as primary infections or opportunistic infections. Primary infections are seen in healthy population those who are not exposed to endemic fungi, whereas opportunistic infections are seen commonly in immunosuppressed individuals.

Superficial fungal infections begin to occur from a pathogen that is restricted to the stratum corneum, with or without tissue involvement. Some fungi can generate keratinase with specific metalloproteinase enzymes, which causes to allow them to metabolize and grow on keratin-based constituents such as skin, nail, and hair. The organisms caused dermatosis belongs to the genus Trichophyton, Microsporum, or Epidermophyton which colloquially referred to as Tinea.

The Plants that have therapeutic beneficiaries or exert pharmacological actions on human beings are generally called as medicinal plants which are rich in naturally synthesizable and accumulative secondary metabolites like alkaloids, cyanogenic glycosides, flavonoids, glycosides, lactones, quinines, resins, terpenes, saponins, sterols, tannins, volatile oils, etc.

Soleshine is the formulation containing indigenous plants that are of medicinal importance manufactured and marketed by Rumi Herbals Pvt Ltd, Chennai. In this formulation, the plants used as an ingredients are the most common and essential plants which are Neem and Henna.

The *in-silico* approach is a method of drug discovery which used to be performed on computer applications or via computer simulations currently used in this modern era.

Reverse pharmacology can be defined as a new discipline of science which deals with the integrating documented experimental hits, into lead molecule by trans-disciplinary exploratory studies and finally developed as drug candidates.

The standard assay used for anti-microbial tests is being carried out by Disc Diffusion Method where the 5%DMSO is vehicle control and

Clotrimazole as a standard. The 10 μl of the sample extract (1 mg per ml) was taken with the help of micropipette and placed over the SDA inoculated Petri dish plate.

The antifungal activity was screened by considering the Zone of Inhibition (ZOI) that means by measuring the area where the extracts inhibit the growth of organisms; thus the experiment was repeated with all the four organisms, i.e., Trichophyton spp., Microsporum spp., Epidermophyton spp., Candida spp. separately, the ZOI was evaluated with the help of digital dial caliper.

The Minimum Inhibitory Concentration (MIC) was performed by the Resazurin Microtitre Indicator method. Resazurin was observed as an indicator to know the cell viability in mammalian cell cultures. The irreversible reaction of Resazurin to Resorfurin is based on the proportionality to the aerobic reaction.

The various extracts of *A. indica* and *L. inermis* like hexane, benzene, ethyl acetate, methanol, and aqueous tested for ZOI in a concentration of 50 mcg, 100 mcg, 250 mcg, 500 mcg on three dermatophytes and Candida spp. for six times which subjected for statistical analysis with SPSS version 20 where it was found that aqueous extract has maximum zone of inhibition with both *A. indica* and *L. inermis*.

The synergistic activity was observed by combining the aqueous extract of *A. indica* and aqueous extract of *L. inermis* with 1:1 ratio concentrations against dermatophytes and *C. albicans.*

In the second section, the proteins are selected which are vital in the fungal organisms' metabolic function that were docked with the ligands (secondary metabolites present in plants).

Homology modelling is a computational approach for 3D protein structure modelling and prediction that means the 3D structure is fabricated by aligning a target protein sequence with known template structures and validated with Ramachandran plot.

The various proteins selected for the study were 1, 3-Beta glucan synthase, Chitin synthase, Chitinase, Deuterolysin, Fungalysin, Homoserine dehydrogenase, Lumazine synthase, Phosphoribosylaminoimidazole carboxylase, Protein elongation factor 3, Sulphite reductase.

The plants *A. indica* and *L. inermis* are abundant with well known secondary metabolites that are useful for different ailments common in human beings. The azadirachtin, nimbin, and nimonol are the secondary metabolites which are of having anti-microbial properties are selected from

A. indica for the *in-silico* analysis. The lawsone, lawsoniaside, scopoletin, stigmasterol are the secondary metabolites present in *L. inermis* also known for its anti-microbial activity are selected.

The selected secondary metabolites were subjected for quick docking with web tool iGEMDOCK software (version 2.0). Autodock Vina, the interactive molecular graphics program for calculating and displaying the possible docking modes of the protein-ligand pair for accurate docking.

Physicochemical, medicinal, drug-likeness, and toxicity profile was retrieved with different software's for all the derivatives.

The available antifungal drugs in modern medicine are not only toxic to the fungal organism but also to the host. The safest fungicidal drug is in need without untoward effects is the need of the study.

Finally concluded that totally 09 molecules were chosen as best from the derivatives of lawsoniaside (*L.inermis*) and azadirachtin (*A.indica*) as these are showing more negativity which implies that these are excellent ligands for all the drug targets in fungal organism and sulphite reductase is an enzyme observed as suitable drug target as it allows to bind all the derivatives of the ligands of *A.indica* and *L.inermis*.

TABLE OF CONTENTS

LIST OF FIGURES

LIST OF TABLES

95	The canonical SMILE, IUPAC name, Physicochemical properties, Hydrophilicity, Lipophilicity, Pharmacokinetics, Druglikeliness, Medicinal Chemistry, and Toxicity profile showing the secondary metabolite of *A. indica*, Derivative, Nimbin Derivative 63	227
96	The canonical SMILE, IUPAC name, Physicochemical properties, Hydrophilicity, Lipophilicity, Pharmacokinetics, Druglikeliness, Medicinal Chemistry, and Toxicity profile showing the secondary metabolite of *A. indica*, Derivative, Nimbin Derivative 107	228
97	The canonical SMILE, IUPAC name, Physicochemical properties, Hydrophilicity, Lipophilicity, Pharmacokinetics, Druglikeliness, Medicinal Chemistry, and Toxicity profile showing the secondary metabolite of *A. indica*, Derivative, Nimonol Derivative 1	229
98	The canonical SMILE, IUPAC name, Physicochemical properties, Hydrophilicity, Lipophilicity, Pharmacokinetics, Druglikeliness, Medicinal Chemistry, and Toxicity profile showing the secondary metabolite of *A. indica*, Derivative, Nimonol Derivative 17	230
99	The canonical SMILE, IUPAC name, Physicochemical properties, Hydrophilicity, Lipophilicity, Pharmacokinetics, Druglikeliness, Medicinal Chemistry, and Toxicity profile showing the secondary metabolite of *A. indica*, Derivative, Nimonol Derivative 60	231
100	The canonical SMILE, IUPAC name, Physicochemical properties, Hydrophilicity, Lipophilicity, Pharmacokinetics, Druglikeliness, Medicinal Chemistry, and Toxicity profile showing the secondary metabolite of *A. indica*, Derivative, Nimonol Derivative 96	232
101	The canonical SMILE, IUPAC name, Physicochemical properties, Hydrophilicity, Lipophilicity, Pharmacokinetics, Druglikeliness, Medicinal Chemistry, and Toxicity profile showing the secondary metabolite of *A. indica*, Derivative, Nimonol Derivative 136	233
102	The canonical SMILE, IUPAC name, Physicochemical properties, Hydrophilicity, Lipophilicity, Pharmacokinetics, Druglikeliness, Medicinal Chemistry, and Toxicity profile showing the secondary metabolite of *L. inermis*, Derivative, Lawsone Derivative 1	234

LIST OF ABBREVIATIONS

AI – *Azadirachta indica*

ALT – Alanine transaminase

ARAPD – 5-amino-6-(D-ribitylamino)-, 4(1H,3H)-pyrimidinedione

ASA – Aspartate semialdehyde

AST – Aspartate transaminase

CADD – Computer Aided Drug Designing

CHO – Chinese Hamster Ovary

CHS – Chitin Synthase

CMC – Chronic Mucocutaneous Candidiasis

CMI – Cell Mediated Immunity

COX - Cyclooxygenase

CPDB – Carcinogenic Potency Database

DEN – Diethylnitrosamine

DHBP – 3,4-dihydroxy-2-butanone-4phosphate

DMRL – 6,7-dimethyl-8-ribityllumazine

DMSO – DimethylSulphoxide

EC – Enzyme Commission

EF – Elongation Factor

FAD – Flavin Adenine Dinucleotide

FMD – Flavin Mononucleotide

GC-MS – Gas Chromatography – Mass Spectrometry

GGT – Gamma Glutamyl Transpeptidase

HSD – Homoserine Dehydrogenase

HSP – Heat Shock Protein

IUPAC - International Union of Pure and Applied Chemistry

LDH – Lactate Dehydrogenase

LI – *Lawsonia inermis*

LOX – Lipoxygenase

MIC – Minimum Inhibitory Concentration

NMR – Nuclear Magnetic Resonance

OPC – Oropharyngeal Candidiasis

PBS – Phosphate Buffer Solution

PDB – Protein Data Bank

PMN – Polymorphonuclear neutrophil

QSAR – Quantitative structure–activity relationship

QSPR – QuantitativeStructure-Property Relationship

RCSB – Research Collaboratory for Structural Bioinformatics

RVVC – Recurrent Vulvovaginal Candidiasis

SDA – Sabouraud Dextrose Agar

SOD – Superoxide Dismutase

SR – *Shorea robusta*

SRBE – *Shorea robusta* Bark Extract

TPSA – Topological Polar Surface Area

VMC oil – Vepa Madhurani Castor oil

GLC – Gas Liquid Chromatography

GPx – Glutathione Peroxidase

GR – Glutathione reductase

GSH – Reduced Glutathione

HERG – Human Ether-a-go-go Related Gene

HIV – Human Immunodeficiency Virus

HONV – 5-hydroxy-4-oxo-l-norvaline

HRBC – Human Red Blood Cell

VVC – Vulvovaginal Candidiasis

ZOI – Zone Of Inhibition

NOMENCLATURE

Fraction Csp3

- The ratio of sp3 hybridized carbons over the total carbon count of the molecule (Fraction Csp3) should be at least 0.25

Molar refractivity

- Molar refractivity (A) is a measure of the total polarizability of a mole of a substance

TPSA – Topological Polar Surface Area: TPSA optimal range between 20 and 130 $^0A^2$.

Solubility Class (Log S Scale)

- Insoluble <-10 < Poorly soluble < -6, < Moderately soluble <-4, < Soluble <-2< Very soluble <0 <Highly
- iLOGP (for implicit log P) is an in-house physics-based methods relying on Gibbs free energy of solvation calculated by GB/SA in water and n-octanol
- XLOGP3 values are obtained through the command-line Linux program (version 3.2.2, courtesy of CCBG, Shanghai Institute of Organic Chemistry) including the knowledge-based corrections.
- WLOGP is our own implementation of the atomistic method developed by Wildman and Crippen.
- MLOGP values are computed through an in-house implementation of Moriguchi's topological method.
- SILICOS-IT is the log Po/w estimation returned by executing the FILTER-IT program
- Consensus log Po/w value, which is the arithmetic mean of the five predictive values mentioned above
- Skin permeability coefficient (Kp) is linearly correlation with molecular size and lipophilicity. The more negative the log Kp (with Kp in cm/s), the less skin permeable of the molecule.

Lipinski rule:

- No more than 5 hydrogen bond donors (the total number of nitrogen–hydrogen and oxygen–hydrogen bonds)
- No more than 10 hydrogen bond acceptors (all nitrogen or oxygen atoms)
- A molecular mass less than 500 daltons
- An octanol-water partition coefficient log P not greater than 5

Ghose Filter

- calculated log P is between -0.4 and 5.6
- molecular weight is between 160 and 480
- molar refractivity is between 40 and 130
- total number of atoms is between 20 and 70[2].

Veber Rule

- Rotatable Bond Count $<= 10$
- tPSA $<= 140$

Egan rule

- $-1 \leq \log P \leq 5.8$
- tPSA $\leq$ 130 A° 2

Muegge filter

- $200 \leq MW \leq 600$
- $-2 \leq XLOG\ P \leq 5$
- tPSA ≤ 150
- Num. Rings ≤ 7
- Num. Carbon >4
- Num. Heteroatoms >1
- Num. Rotatable bonds ≤ 15
- H-Bond acceptors ≤ 10
- H-Bond donators $\leq$ 5

Bioavailability Score

- Probability of F >10 % in rats

PAINS - **P**an-**A**ssay **IN**terference compounds: PAINS is a tool to enhance reproducibility and reliability of true hit identification

Brenk - Brenk is purely knowledge-based with a compilation of chemical moities known to be toxic, unstable, dye and so on.

Leadlikeness

- $250 \leq MW \leq 350$
- $XLOGP \leq 3.5$
- Num. rotatable bonds ≤ 7

Synthetic accessibility: from 1 (very easy) to 10 (very difficult) based on 1024 fragmental contributions (FP2) modulated by size and complexity penaties, trained on 12'782'590 molecules and tested on 40 external molecules ($r2 = 0.94$)

CHAPTER 1

INTRODUCTION

1. INTRODUCTION

The fungal organism is a eukaryotic, microscopic, heterotrophic, unicellular or multicellular with inflexible cell wall compiled with chitin, glucan, and/or cellulose with a plethora of organelles. Fungi are ubiquitously found in air, soil, plants, and water even as a part of lichens growing on a rock. Multitudinous species of fungal organisms are in free-living in the environment and are pathogenic to plants but with engrossment is to a few species that are pathogenic for vertebrates and invertebrate individuals. It is a known fact that any fungus capable of growing at 37°C has the potential to cause infections in debilitated or immunocompromised individuals. Some of the elite fungal organisms are adapted as commensals, but most pathogens are accidental hosts. Out of all fungal species a selected bit of species can cause disease but majority are opportunistic, and the healthy humans who have an intact immune system are disease free.

Fungi are not plants, but these are microorganisms that are a distinct group of highly evolved organisms. These are discrete from both plant and animal kingdom, which vary with all other groups in several significant aspects. First, fungal cells are composed of stringent and robust cell wall comprising a complete structure of the protein called chitin and glucan. These protein cell components are the hallmark features juxtaposed with other animals, which made of without cell walls, and the plants which composed of cellulose as the primary cell wall component. Second, fungi are heterotrophic which describes that they are parasitic due to the absence of green pigment chlorophyll and they cannot synthesize their organic food as plants through photosynthesis. The fungal organism lives entrenched in food material or medium and obtains its food by secreting specific enzymes which aid in external digestion and also by imbibing the nutrients that are sapped out from the medium. The fungal organism possesses a different form of nutritional habit which was considered as one of the salient features that lead to beingcategorized under a separate kingdom. Third, the fungal organism was relatively more straightforward in its structure when compared with any other creature that is due to the indiscrimination between the cells and tissues. The fundamental structural unit of fungi is either a string of tube-like filamentous cell called hyphae or a self-subsistent single cell. Many fungal pathogens affect humans and animals by invading various tissues with continuous growth. The dimorphic class of fungal pathogens usually changes from multicellular hyphae to a single-celled budding form in the natural environment. The most multicellular fungi, in their vegetative stage, consists of a lump of branching hyphae are called mycelium. Each hypha has a stiffened cell wall which can increase their length to form an apical growth. In the early stages of fungi, the hypha looks aseptate, i.e., without cross-walls, but in advanced groups, the hyphae can become septate with more or less thickened cross walls. The single cell of fungal organisms propagates by budding out similar cells from its surface. The buds are produced by detaching from the parent or remain tagged themselves to it, and it can produce another bud which is the way for the generation of a stream of cells.

Fungi, which do not produce hyphae with a loose arrangement of budding cells, will be characterized as yeasts. Fourth, fungal organisms' reproduction will also be through conidia or spores by microscopic propagation. Fungi which produce conidia by asexual reproduction are identical to parent except only in case of occasional mutation. Asexual conidia are generally familiar, short-lived and produced enormously to disperse the fungi to new habitats. Most of the fungi are capable of sexual reproduction. When they are homothallic, that form reproductive structures within individual colonies, however, heterothallic fungi do not form reproductive structures unless two different mating organism strains reach together to contact. In some species, the sexual spores which are produced by meiosis are borne singly on specialized generative cells.

The fungi, a eukaryotic organism causing infection to human beings are a growing serious public health concern. Diseases caused by fungi which have clinical significance are characterized as primary infections or opportunistic infections. Primary infections are seen in healthy population those who are not exposed to endemic fungi, whereas opportunistic infections are seen commonly in immunosuppressed individuals (1). The medical services and devices utilized, lead to an increased in the number of susceptible hosts. The most common and deadly fungal infections like candidiasis, zygomycosis (mucormycosis), cryptococcosis, aspergillosis, and pneumocystosis (2). From 1980, there has been a dramatic acceleration in the occurrence of dangerous fungal infections, mainly by an increase in the individuals those are at deadly risk which is owed to the acquired immune deficiency syndrome (AIDS) and much of this increase, by other factors, such as the indiscriminate use of immunosuppressive agents (3). The infections caused by invasive fungal species in solid-organ transplanted individuals are 53% candidiasis, 19% aspergillosis, 8% non-Aspergillus molds, 8% cryptococcosis, 5% endemic fungi, and 2% zygomycosis (4).

Superficial fungal infections begin to occur from a pathogen that is restricted to the stratum corneum, with or without tissue involvement.

Some fungi can generate keratinase with specific metalloproteinase enzymes, which causes to allow them to metabolize and grow on keratin-based constituents such as skin, nail, and hair. The organisms caused dermatosis belongs to the genus Trichophyton, Microsporum, or Epidermophyton which colloquially referred to as Tinea. Tinea is derived from a Latin word for worm or grub because the infections are initially being believed to be caused by worm-like parasites (5). Different technical terms are in use concerning where the affected — *Tinea corporis* or ringworm of epidermis, *Tinea cruris* or jock itch affected in the groin, *Tinea unguum* affected to nails, *Tinea capitis* or ringworm of the scalp, *Tinea barbae* affected to beard and *Tinea manuum* affected to hands (6).

1.1 Polyherbal formulation

The Plants that have therapeutic beneficiaries or exert pharmacological actions on human beings are generally cognominate as medicinal plants which are rich in naturally synthesizable and accumulative secondary metabolites like alkaloids, cyanogenic glycosides, flavonoids, glycosides, lactones, quinines, resins, terpenes, saponins, sterols, tannins, volatile oils, etc. These medicinal plants are available in India and used traditionally as these are rich sources of one or other secondary metabolites. The crude drugs that are plenty, cheaper, and with null or trivial untoward effects have been frequently prescribed to patients of all ages. The multiple actions and therapeutic uses of these indigenous plant products or drugs are sufficiently prescribed in classical literature in many medicinal plant volumes and pharmacopeias (7).

Soleshine is the formulation containing indigenous plants that are of medicinal importance manufactured and marketed by Rumi Herbals Pvt

Ltd, Chennai. In this formulation, the plants used as ingredients are the most common and essential plants which are Neem and Henna. The aqueous extracts of leaves of these plants are prepared by soaking the leaves in cold water for 24 hours, for which the hot water extraction will be done, which is the condensed aqueous extraction. To this above extraction, castor oil will be added which is named as VMC oil. In the process of launching a fresh batch the molten resin of sal tree, sesame oil, paraffin wax, and petroleum jelly will be added, thereby the final product of Soleshine will be packed and marketed that can be used for soothing the sole, to prevent scaling, cracking of skin/foot, and to cure fungal infection of hair/ groin/ fingers/ toes, so forth which was presented in figure 1 and figure 2.

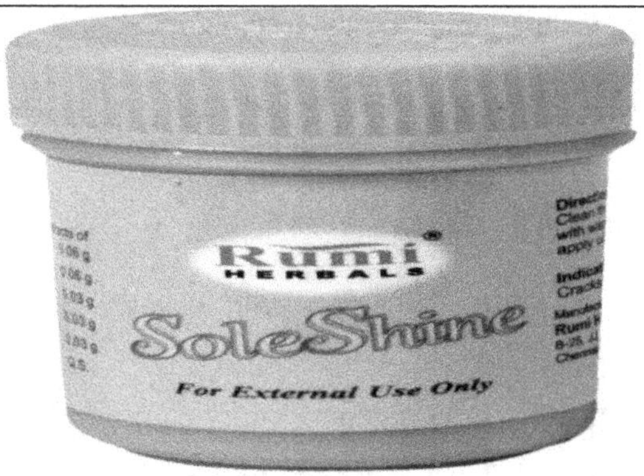

Figure 1: The Polyherbal preparation used in this research which was manufactured by Rumi Herbals Pvt Ltd, Chennai.

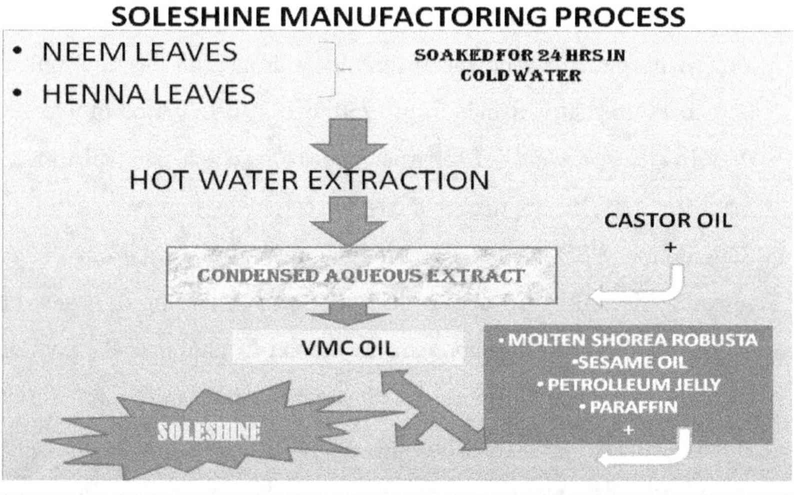

Figure 2: The methodology used by the manufacturer for the preparation of formulation SOLESHINE.

1.2 *In-silico* method of Drug Designing

The *In-silico* approach is a method of drug discovery which used to be performed on computer applications or via computer simulations currently used in this modern era (8).

The Drug discovery and drug development is a very robust, laborious, long-delayed process where many factors are involved for achieving a good and reliable therapeutic agent and may need to encounter many hindrances like the absence of effectiveness, unexpected adverse events, erratic pharmacokinetics, etc. The expenditure incurred in the process has been magnified ominously during the past few years. The previous reports showing the expenditure on drug development has been accumulated from 4 million USD in 1962 to over 350 million USD in 1996 along with the enhancement of time for a drug from the lead molecule to post-marketing surveillance from 1960 to 1980 as a period of 9 to 13 years (9). In the purview of pharmaceutical research and pharmaceutical manufacturers, the approximate cost for complete drug discovery is around 880 million USD and takes a minimum of 14 years from the earliest research hit molecule stage to the successful marketing of a new drug in 2001 (10). The *in-silico* approach is a boon to minimize the cost of drug discovery, in which it needs to identify the target and validate it simultaneously identify the hit molecule or lead compound and optimization is done through computer simulation methods. In the arena of computer-aided drug design (CADD), which includes *in-silico* method of drug discovery, needs the integrity of scholars of different fields in joint research such as biology, biophysics, structural biology, and computational scientists (11). In this modern *in-silico* computational drug design, the various field researchers combine and conglomerate each other with

(12)modern techniques such as QSAR/QSPR, structure-based design, bioinformatics, cheminformatics, combinatorial library design, and the multiple biological and chemical databases with the aid of online, web-based, offline tools. This cutting-edge technology is based on designing small molecules or ligands and macromolecules with preferred specificity (13).

The incidence and prevalence of fungal diseases globally was estimates as approximately a billion people with skin, nail and hair fungal infections, and many 10's of millions are infected with mucosal candidiasis and above 150 million people are gruesome with serious fungal diseases.

The current existing antifungal drugs are of different classes that are targeting the fungal organism but unfortunately which are prone for diverse untoward events to the host. The selective target is in legwork to avoid these adverse effects which is the need or lacunae of this study.

Hence this study was conceived to try and develop after accomplishing the good results in pilot study through obtaining the sequential extracts of the major plants used in the formulation and finally derived the structure activity relative molecules of the active principles responsible for their mechanism of antifungal activity with the aid of many software's that can be a promising investigational new drug molecules which will be bind and dock with the endogenous constituents of the fungal organism that hampers the metabolic function which leads to death of the organism.

CHAPTER 2

AIM AND OBJECTIVE

2. AIM AND OBJECTIVE

- To establish the anti fungal properties of individual plants present in a poly herbal preparation.
- To prove the synergistic action of combination of different plants present in a poly herbal preparation.
- To know the MIC (minimum inhibitory concentration) against fungi of individual plants in a poly herbal preparation.
- To find active principles present in the different plants in polyherbal preparation by molecular docking method.
- To prepare the derivatives of the active principles by *in-silico* method and to find its antifungal activity by molecular docking method.

CHAPTER 3

REVIEW OF LITERATURE

3. REVIEW OF LITERATURE

3.1 Reverse pharmacology

Reverse pharmacology can be defined as a new discipline of science which deals with the integrating documented experimental hits, into lead molecule by trans-disciplinary exploratory studies and finally developed as drug candidates.

In a statement by Sir Peter B Medawar "A synthetic discovery is always the first recognition of an event, a phenomenon, a process, or a state of affairs not previously recognized or known" which is being followed by the highest demand, cornerstone, cutting-edge technological discoveries of science came under this heading (14). The pharmaceutical industry has conventionally been a vibrant, innovative, and highly successful in the global market (15). A concourse of dramatic development in medicinal chemistry, molecular biology, genetics, and the cognate fields of spectroscopy, chromatography, and crystallography led to the discovery and development of novel therapeutic drugs for all ailments. To ease this process, the eminent researchers launched a significant effort to improve the integration of discovery techniques, chemical sourcing for route selection or delivery of active pharmaceutical ingredients. The pharmaceutical industry has incredible growth due to the industry's strategy of focusing efforts on the evolution of wonderful drugs. Expenses incurred by research and development has been raised enormously but failed to market most efficacious agents. To speed up the screening process of individual molecular targets, a high throughput screening of drugs implemented. A new chemical entity navigates a path from laboratories to clinics, involving target identification, lead identification, lead optimization, pre-clinical studies and then four phases of clinical trials. The drug discovery and development is extremely time-consuming, the complex and capital demanding procedure makes pharmaceutical industries "target rich" but "lead poor" (16). Therefore, surrogative and interdependent approaches in therapeutics are becoming popular options.

The concept of reverse pharmacology is considered for the Polyherbal preparation, Soleshine which contains many traditional components like phytochemicals with known clinical activity.

3.2 General aspects of mycology

Fungi are a non-motile, ubiquitous, eukaryotic, microorganism. Approximately 50,000 species of fungal organisms are found and out of which 400 species are clinically significant. However, just about 50 species are enough to cause approximately 90 percent of lethal fungal diseases.

Mycology is a separate branch of medical microbiology involved with all aspects of diseases in mammals caused by the pathogenic fungal organism. Mycoses are the fungal diseases of human beings and lower animals. These mycotic infections are a broad spectrum ranging from superficial skin diseases to deep-seated, multiorgan disseminated diseases.

The brief history about the mycotic infections involving humans started between 1837 and 1841 when Gruby and Remak discovered *Tinea favosa* as the first human mycotic disease, Agostino Bassi, an Italian lawyer and farmer in 1835 discovered the mycotic nature of silkworms known as muscardine. He was the first person who demonstrated the fungus which causes an infectious disease. Unacquainted of the observations of Remak and Schonlein, Gruby outlined the clinical and microscopic characteristics of *Tinea favosa* and established the infectious nature of a disease. Gruby in 1844 isolated a fungi endothrix hair invasion as *Herpes (Trichophyton) tonsurans*. The European researchers recognized the relationship between the fungal organism and the disease in human beings which was the groundwork for the evolution of medical mycology. In the late 19th century, Raimond Jacques Sabouraud had precipitated and standardized the various observations considering the position of pathogenic fungi in dermatophytic infections, and his contribution marked the transition from the study of the dermatophytosis to that of systemic mycoses. In the year between 1894 and 1919, the Discovery of the dimorphic fungi and establishment of their dimorphic nature was observed and acknowledged the fungal organism as the etiologic agent of disease, inclusive of systemic diseases. In 1926, Columbia University first time started the establishment of a research center and training sessions in medical mycology. In the formative years of history of medical mycology, the growth of laboratory diagnostic tests and classification of a separate branch was taken place. The advent of anti-fungal drugs and immunotherapy was between 1950 and 1969. The first anti-fungal drug nystatin and amphotericin B was discovered around 1950. In the same year, the establishment of a relationship between opportunistic fungal infections and antibiotic policy and in 1960 it was recognized the interrelation between immunotherapy with opportunistic fungal infections. Around 1975, the discovery of high quality rapid diagnostic tests like an immunodiagnostic test for severe systemic infections like coccidioidomycosis and histoplasmosis, fluorescent antibodies in tissues, identification of fungal antigens and metabolites, yeast identification systems, exoantigen test improvement were established. Elevated prevalence of fungal infections among AIDS patients and a more significant number of cancer patients and transplant recipients was between

1980 and 1994. During the same period, the genomic-based or DNA-based methods are discovered for more authentic, swift diagnostic laboratory tests and reliable epidemiological tools.

The taxonomy of the mycology is based on their morphology of fungal organism which is classified as molds, yeasts, dimorphic fungi, and dermatophytes. Molds usually sprout as a filamentous structure, yeasts like single cells and dermatophytes are of multicellular that causes diseases on skin, hair, nails like keratin-rich tissues. Dimorphic fungi as the name suggest appearing in both forms, as yeast or as mycelia which are carbon heterotrophs. The saprophytic fungi or saprobic organisms imbibe carbon compounds from dead organic material whereas biotrophic fungi (parasites or symbionts) nourished by living on a host. Some of the fungal organism can endure in both saprophytic and biotrophic forms. The hypha and yeast are the two necessary morphological forms in fungal organisms. The hypha is usually 2–10 μm in width and is the fundamental element of filamentous fungi with branches, and tubular structures. The Mycelium is the web-like structure of hyphae which may be substrate mycelia that penetrate the nutrients (specialized for nutrition), while the aerial mycelia develop up on the nutrient medium (for asexual propagation).

The fungal thallus is the totality of the mycelia and is also called colony while the yeast is the necessary element of the single-celled fungal organism which is circular to oval in shape and 3 – 10 μm in diameter. The chain of elongated several yeast cells resembles true hyphae that are called pseudohyphae. The Dimorphic species can develop either as yeast or mycelium-based on the environmental conditions. Dimorphic pathogenic fungal organisms are existing as yeast cells when these are in the parasitic stage but emerge as mycelium at the saprophytic stage.

Systemic mycoses are the pathogenic fungi that are acquired through inhalational and begin as a pulmonary infection that spreads via systemic circulation to the other regions of the body which is common because of one of the four pathogenic fungal organisms, Ascomycota spp., Histoplasma spp., Blastomyces spp., Coccidioides spp., or Paracoccidioides spp. The Opportunistic fungi do not typically affect healthy individuals because of the lack of genes that are involved in virulence and make those organisms invasive actively. However, the opportunistic mycotic infections are limited to those individuals affected with reduced immunity. Owing to the growing number of AIDS patients, opportunistic fungal infections have become significant in morbidity and mortality. The common opportunistic fungal organisms are Pneumocystis spp., Candida spp., Aspergillus spp., Cryptococcus spp., and Mucor spp.

Superficial, Cutaneous, and Subcutaneous Mycoses are the most commonly reported fungal diseases localized at sites at or near the surface of the body through environmental exposure and more frequently via person to person contact which are not life-threatening, but they often cause chronic, recurring infections and diseases. Superficial mycoses are the fungal infections confined to outer, dead layers of skin, nails, or hair which are composed of keratin. In individuals who have AIDS, these superficial fungi can spread to cover significant areas of skin or become systemic.

Dermatophytosis are the infections caused by dermatophytes, which are contagious that grow only on skin, nails, and hair. In olden days these infections are called as ringworms as these produce circular, scaly patches that resemble like a worm lying below the surface of the skin. These dermatophytes are colloquially called as tinea, which is from Latin for "worm." Dermatophytes use keratin as a nutrient and grow only in dead tissue. The Spores and bits of hyphae are continuously shed from infected patients, making recurrent infections.

The three genera of ascomycetes belong to dermatophytosis, Trichophyton species, Epidermophyton species, and Microsporum species. The *Malassezia furfur* is a dimorphic basidiomycete group that is a typical member of the microbiota of the skin which feeds on the skin's oil and causes common, a chronic superficial infection known as *Pityriasis versicolor*.

The Cutaneous and subcutaneous fungal infections are Chromoblastomycosis and Phaeohyphomycosis are caused by dark-pigmented ascomycetes. Another genus of Ascomycota is mycetomas which are tumor-like appearance while *Sporothrix schenckii* belongs to dimorphic ascomycete which causes a subcutaneous infection usually limits to arms or legs are called as sporotrichosis.

The successful oral treatment of experimental *Microsporum canis* infections in guinea pigs with griseofulvin, by Gentles in 1958, opened new avenues in the therapy of the dermatophytosis, especially ringworm of the scalp.

Epidermophyton genus: This genus is characterized by the presence of numerous; broadly clavate, nearly smooth-walled, thin to thick walls with one to nine septa of macroconidia and in this genus microconidia are usually absent. There is only a single acknowledged in this genus as *E. floccosum* which is anthropophilic that is specially adapted to cause open-ended human infection. This species attaches skin, nails, and very rarely hair.

Microsporum genus: The species of this genus usually produce both macroconidia and microconidia. The essential distinguishing feature is the presence of rough walls that are as asperulate, echinulate, or verrucose with textures ranging from sping to warty in macroconidia. The macroconidia vary in shape from egg-shaped (obovate) to cylindro-fusiform. They may have thin to thick cell walls and 1-15 septa depending upon the species. The roughness of the cell wall may not be readily apparent in some isolates or species. This organism may require particular media to induce its formation.

Similarly, special media may be required for conidial production. Microconidia are typically clavate (club-shaped). On microscopic examination, one should also note the composition and formation of both types of conidia. Members of this genus commonly attack skin and hair but rarely the nails.

Trichophyton genus: The species of this genus are typical which produce smooth-walled macroconidia and microconidia. The macroconidia may range in shape from elongate to pencil shaped, clavate, fusiform or cylindro-fusiform. They are multiseptate and may be thin or thick walled. Microconidia are usually produced in greater abundance than macroconidia, and their shape varies from pyriform, clavate, spherical to elongate. They are produced along the hyphae singly or in clusters and are sessile or borne on short stalks. Their organization on fertile hyphae is one of the essential factors for their recognition. Members of this genus attack nails, skin, as well as hair. For many Trichophyton species, particular media may be compulsory to stimulate conidial formation. Some species induce few or no conidia regardless of the growth conditions.

3.3 Superficial candidiasis

Superficial candidiasis encompasses the infections of cutaneous or mucocutaneous tissues. *Candida albicans* is the causative organism in the preponderance of infections. Others are *Candida tropicalis*, *Candida glabrata*, *Candida parapsilosis*, *Candida stellatoidea*, *Candida dubliniensis*, and *Candida krusei* which can be acute, chronic or recurrent. The Candida spp. and in particular, *Candida albicans* is pervasive and dimorphic fungal organisms that are part of the normal microflora of healthy individuals. However, they are also opportunistic pathogens that can rapidly transform from harmless mucosal commensals to a profusely pathogenic organism of the same tissues with relative morbidity and even mortality under appropriate conditions. Superficial candidiasis can include skin, oropharyngeal, gastrointestinal, vaginal and conjunctival tissue infections. Cutaneous candidiasis is typically seen as erythematous patches on the thigh and buttocks or as superficial infections on the hands in persons who frequently wear plastic gloves.

Mucocutaneous infections may be chronic or recurrent and are distinct form is classified as the disorder known as chronic mucocutaneous candidiasis (CMC). These infections affect a variety of mucosal tissues, skin, and nails.

Oropharyngeal candidiasis (OPC) implicates infections of the buccal mucosa, gingiva, and tongue which can be atrophic with erythematous lesions or pseudomembranous (thrush) with characteristic white lesions. Oesophagitis is the most common form of gastrointestinal candidiasis. The second most common site of gastrointestinal candidiasis is the stomach. Vaginitis affects infections of the vaginal lumen and may involve vulva as well. An estimation of 75 percent of all women will encounter at least one episode of acute vulvovaginal candidiasis (VVC). A distinct population of a woman (5-10 percent) will experience recurrent vulvovaginal candidiasis (RVVC). Conjunctivitis caused by C. albicans affects the mucous membrane of the eye, while keratitis infects the cornea.

The common superficial candida infections are summarized as Cutaneous and Mucocutaneous. Immune-mediated defense mechanisms that insulate against *C. albicans* infections include natural resistance and acquired immunity. The comparative contributions of these two systems, however, differ depending upon the site at which *C.albicans* enters the host. Innate host defenses (polymorphonuclear leukocytes, macrophages) are heavily involved in protecting the systemic circulation. While antibodies (IgA, IgG) appear to play a role at both systemic and mucosal sites, and cell-mediated immunity (CMI) (T-Cells, important cytokines) conserves primarily mucosal tissues. Concerning mucosal tissues, historically there was no differentiation between different anatomical sites, there is now accumulating documentation that not all mucosal tissues are created equal to protect host defenses.

3.4 Pathology of dermatophytes

The pathogenesis of dermatophytosis is dependent on fungi as well as the host. Mostly the pathology is dependent on the host immune system which is helpful for the elimination of pathogen. The tissue of the host is contributing the nutrition for the growth of fungi and establishment of infection will contribute the pathology.

During infection and tissue damage which is caused by the fungi or the metabolic products of the pathogen leads to an inflammatory response in the pathogenesis of dermatophytosis (17,18). The fungal species colonize in host tissue compromises surface molecules that are responsible for attachment, secreted enzymes contributed to nutritional sources, metabolic adjustments to metabolize, thermotolerance, and dimorphism, through which an individual fungal species reorganize amid mycelia and yeast rely upon the environment (18). The adhesion proteins expressed as cell surface approves for a rapid extension to host tissues and the *Matrix Extracellularis* which prevents the expulsion. When it gets adapted to the host tissue, it acts as a scavenger for nutrients to survive. The number of enzymes produced by the fungi includes proteases like collagenolytic and elastolytic enzymes, lipases, nucleotidases, and mucolytic enzymes (19,20). Owing to the adverse effects of the antifungal agents or under stressful circumstances like nutrition shortage, oxidative or osmotic stress may lead to hampering the metabolic pathways.

The fungi can overcome the deficiency in metabolic pathways by utilizing the different substances for energy and contribute to progress infection and inflammatory process (21). Fungal infection affects not only the skin but also invade the lungs, liver, spleen, kidneys, and nervous system. The infections caused by the fungi are not severe or emergency, but they cause a decreased quality of life (22). The species causing dermatomycosis include dermatophytes and non-dermatophytic molds and yeasts like *C. albicans* and *Malassezia furfur* but the dermatophytes being more rampant (17). Dermatophytes precipitate superficial infections in both healthy and immunocompromised individuals but the deep and deadly infection caused by immunosuppression (23). The lesions caused by the dermatophytic fungi are usually round erythematous and itchy due to inflammatory mediators and the metabolites produced by fungi (17). The dermatophytic fungi can surmount the natural barriers of the host like acidic nature of the skin, inhibitory molecules such as fatty acids and anti-microbial peptides, the phagocytic cells and exuviations of skin (24–26). Usually, 3-4 hours will take after the invasion of the dermatophytic fungal conidia to show adherence (27), and it takes one day to germinate the conidia. It almost takes two-three days to spread all over the skin (28).

The fibril-like structures present in the *Trichophyton mentagrophytes* are responsible for the adhesion of the fungi to host tissue (29). In a study where the Chinese hamster ovary (CHO) epithelial cells possess galactose and mannose residues which interact with surface glycoproteins that are expressed in *Trichophyton rubrum* and *T. mentagrophytes* (30).

The protein, subtilisin (Sub3) family belongs to an enzyme protease was secreted in *Microsporum canis* was responsible for the adhesion to reestablish feline epidermis which informs that proteases also play a role in the attachment (31). The pneumonia-causing pathogenic fungi *Coccidioides immitis* cell was expresses the immunodominant antigen SOWgp tangled in virulence by serving the pathogenic fungi attached to the *Matrix Extracellularis* (ECM) (32). The same immunodominant antigen SOWgp is upregulated in *T.rubrum* which causes *in-vitro* nail and keratin growth that indicates the involvement of SOWgp in dermatophytic pathology (33). Keratinocytes are the first cells encountered in the dermatophytic infection and are play an important role in innate host defense (24). Keratinocytes infected with *Arthroderma beuhamiae* expresses proinflammatory genes which cause to secrete cytokines to produce various inflammatory cells in the epidermis while infection, tissue remodeling and wound healing. However, in the case of *Trichophyton tonsurans* keratinocytes cause to induce limited expression of pro-inflammatory proteins and limited secretion of cytokines (34). In some studies on dermatophytes causing organisms like *Trichophyton schoenleinii*, *Microsporum canis* and *T.rubrum* shows the absolve of pro-inflammatory cytokine IL-1B in macrophages and dendritic cells, by activating NLRP3 inflammasome (35–37). Activation of pro-inflammatory cytokines and mobilize inflammatory cells in fungal infections are controlled by the inflammasome which is an intracellular protein complex (38). Changes in the metabolism of fungi permit the adaptation to the host environment, acquiring energy and locomotion. The glyoxylate cycle is used to see in fungi is required for fungal viability (39). The genes coding for glyoxylate cycle, malate synthase, and isocitrate lyase in *A. benhamiae* are upregulated in Guinea pigs even during infection (40). When the fungi affixed to the host skin, nail or hair surfaces, the pathogen senses the host tissue and scavenges nutrients for their endurance. The hydrolytic enzymes which are secreted by fungi are helpful for hydrolysis of macromolecules which may also use as an energy source and the other substances like glyoxylate, isocitrate, malate, the genes coding proteases are also upregulated in *T.rubrum* and *A.benhamiae* (40,41). The ability to sense and acknowledge the pathogenic fungi is based on the pH of the environment.

This sensing ability is dependent on PacC/Pal signal cell cross-talk cascade composed of different genes like *PalA, PalB, PacC, PalC, PalF, PalH,* and *PalI*(26). These all genes are helpful to mediate some metabolic changes in filamentous, pathogenic, and model fungi are ruling the reaction to variation in the pH. One study infers that the existence of all these genes involves in PacC/PalI signal transducing mechanism cascade (26). The incubation of *T. rubrum* at either basic or acidic medium causes to up-regulate of some genes which were identified on successful experiments of suppression of subtractive hybridization (42). This incubation of *T. rubrum* at either acidic or alkaline pH, several genes displays various transcription factors in PacC background which implies PacC has a variety of metabolic functions. The selection of novel genes attuned by the transcriptional regulators like *PacC* genes gives new molecular-level facts. Heat shock proteins (HSP) are the molecular chaperones that play a role in a myriad of functions. This HSP plays a significant role in standardization and correct folding of nascent polypeptides, for assessment of protein complexes and transport and categorizing of proteins into cellular compartments and also in cell cycle control (43) and apoptosis (44). In yeast, the expression of HSP genes is based on two responsive elements. Those are HSE, it is bound by transcription factor HSF1P (45,46) and STRE, and it is bound by transcription factor Msn2/4p (47,48). At the time of pathogen entered the host tissue, the heat shock proteins are released into the extracellular environment in response to stressful conditions. This activation may be to alert the host for the potentially damaging situation (43,49). The infections caused by bacteria as well as fungi are observed that there is an elevation of HSP in the respective hosts (49,50). The formation of *C. albicans* biofilm also depends on HSP (51). It was found out that in the degradation of keratin, the three genes encoding HSP 70 in *A.benhamiae*(40) and HSP30 in *T.rubrum* are observed (24,41,52).

It was observed that the three genes HSP 60, HSP 70, and HSP 78 are expressed in *in-vitro* human nails infection studies. The HSP 90 protein is constitutively present and increases further under stressful conditions. It is hypothesized that some chemicals produced endogenously by pathogens are used to antagonize HSP 90 ATPase activity. In *ex-vivo* experiments in nail infections, it was seen the role of HSP 90 in *T. rubrum* pathogenicity.

HSP 90 inhibition by 17-AAG (17-allylamino-17-demethoxy geldanamycin) vitiate the fungal virulence which suggests the role of HSP in pathogenicity (53). It is also observed the role of HSP 90 proteins in *C. albicans* and *Candida glabrata* (54,55).

3.5 Taxonomical features of dermatophytes

In the early 19th Century, Robert Remak founded the unique microscopic skeletons which are formerly identified with fungal species and nomenclature as *Achorion schoenleinii.* Later after the discovery of *Microsporum audouinii* and *Herpes (Trichophyton) tonsurans* from cases of human *Tinea capitis*, the dermatophytes are classified into four genera, Achorion spp., Epidermophyton spp., Microsporum spp., and Trichophyton spp. based on the combination and permutation of clinical presentation, cultural and microscopic manifestations, and the genus Achorion (i.e., *Trichophyton schoenleinii*, *T. mentagrophytes sensu stricto*, *Microsporum gallinae*, and *M. gypseum*) group apparent as favus-like diseases. After a while, from vegetative structures and conidia (i.e., fungi imperfecti), the first taxonomic classification was revised, and the genus Achorion was removed and established just three genera (i.e., Microsporum, Trichophyton, and Epidermophyton), and also the number of species was truncated to 19. Eventually, the identification of the organisms was filtered on nutritional and physiological characters, which led to the consolidation of *T.tonsurans* character and the identification of *T. equinum.* The discovery of the teleomorphic state of dermatophytes (perfect or sexual state), imported the concept of biological species, further interrelating the taxonomy of dermatophytes. With the opinion of the teleomorphic state, the genus *Microsporum* was initially classified as *Nannizzia* and after that combined into *Arthroderma* in which also *Chrysosporium*, *Keratinomyces*, and *Trichophyton* are included. By anamorphic characters, the genus *Epidermophyton*, *Microsporum*, *Trichophyton*, *Keratinomyces*, and *Chrysosporium* (the last two comprises as non-pathogenic fungi) are recognized. The genus *keratinomyces* was synonymously called as *Trichophyton* by Ajello in 1968. The appearance of micro and macroconidia of anamorphic characters of *keratinomyces* closely associated with *Trichophyton* genus. As on the date, dermatophytes are classified as zoophilic, geophilic, and anthropophilic species positioned on their growth on animals, in the soil, or humans respectively. Even though the taxonomy based on phylogeny was not wholly accepted like the *T. mentagrophytes* is identical to the variety of quinckeanum species which is very hardly isolated now, but the *T. interdigitale* and the species of *Arthroderma benhamiae* can be discriminated by molecular tools but not morphological characters (*T. mentagrophytes var. granulosum*).

3.6 Neem

The *Azadirachta indica* also commonly called neem, which is a native of India and acclimatized in most of the tropical and subtropical geographical and climatic zones with great medicinal importance. In India, it is habitat to Burma and found in all over the states. The taxonomical classification of this important plant belongs to the Kingdom: Plantae; Order: Rutales; Suborder: Rutinae; Family: Meliaceae; Subfamily: Melioideae; Tribe: Melieae; Genus: Azadirachta; Species: Indica. In English, it is called a Neem tree, Margosa tree. In Ayurveda, it has many names like Nimba, Nimbaka, Arishta, Arishtaphala, Pichumarda, Pichumanda, Pichumandaka, Tiktaka, Sutiktak, Paaribhadra. In Unani, as Aazaad-Darakht-e-Hindi. In Siddha/Tamil called as Vemmu, Veppu, Veppan, Arulundi.

In the extracted portion of various parts of neem plant exhibits myriad of biologically active compounds, including triterpenoids, alkaloids, phenolic compounds, flavonoids, carotenoids, ketones, and steroid. Among these constituents, the most biologically effective one is azadirachtin (56) which is a compound that belongs to the C-seco limonoids under classified as tetranortriterpenes (57).

A. indica has the myriad of complex secondary metabolites which includes nimbin, nimbidin, nimbolide, and limonoids and such types of ingredients may play an essential role in many diseases even pharmacogenetic and pharmacogenomic polymorphic individuals(58). Other constituents like Quercetin and Beta-sitosterol was recognized as first polyphenolic flavonoid compounds isolated from freshly obtained leaves of neem are well known to have antifungal and antibacterial activity (59). The 38 different constituents like n- Hentriacontane, n-Nonacosane, n-Pentacosane, 2-Methoxy-5,40-dimethylbenzenebutanal, Methyl octadecanoate acid was observed in the extracted portion of flowers of *A. indica* and analyzed the insecticidal activity (60). *A. indica* shows pharmacotherapeutic role in health care management due to the abundant source of various types of active ingredients. The appropriate molecular mechanism in various ailments is beyond the level of understanding. However, the probable mechanism can be due to the abundant availability of antioxidants like molecules and other beneficial secondary compounds like azadirachtin, nimbolinin, nimbin, nimbidin, nimbidol, salannin, and quercetin. It is hypothesized that the antimicrobial activity of the neem can be through bacterial cell wall breakdown. Azadirachtin is a tetranortriterpenoid and/or limonoid compound present in seeds which is the critical component answerable for the anti-feedant and toxic effects as an insecticide (61). The ethanolic extract of *A. indica* leaves exhibits antibacterial action *in-vitro* against both *Staphylococcus aureus* and Methicillin-Resistant*Staphylococcus aureus* (MRSA) with the highest zone of inhibition noted at cent percent concentration (62). Neem portrayed a role as free radical scavenger due to the abundant supply of antioxidants. Azadirachtin and nimbolide showed dose-dependent oxygen radical absorbance action and reductive potential in the following order: nimbolide > azadirachtin > ascorbate (63). The secondary metabolites of Neem show an active role in handling cancer through the reorganization of cell signaling pathways. *A. indica* also modulates the function of various tumour suppressor genes (e.g., p53, pTEN), angiogenesis (VEGF), transcription factors (e.g., NF- kB), and apoptosis (e.g., bcl2, bax) genes. Neem also acts as an anti-inflammatory by regulation of pro-inflammatory enzyme activities including cyclooxygenase I and II (COX), and lipoxygenase (LOX) enzyme.

3.7 Biological activity of some secondary metabolites of neem

A vast myriad of compounds have been sequestered from different parts of neem plant; the tetranortriterpenoids have been observed intensely for their antibiotic, antitumor, insecticidal, antibacterial and antifungal activities. The methanolic extract of neem bark exhibits antimalarial activity against *Plasmodium falciparum*. The aqueous extract of leaves of *A. indica* exhibits anti-ulcer and anti-inflammatory activity. The water-soluble portion of alcoholic extract of leaves ameliorates the hyperglycemia in glucose-fed and also adrenaline induced hyperglycaemic rodents and in healthy control rats and also streptozotocin-induced diabetic rats. A volatile fraction of the neem oil was disclosed as spermicidal in a dose of 25 mg per ml for *Homo sapiens* sperm to maintain contraception.

The same volatile oil is also inhibiting the virulence of human immunodeficiency virus (HIV). Neem oil was observed as toxic to mitochondria in mice and declared as a highly toxic compound on heavy doses.

Nimbidin, the major bitter constituent extracted from the seed kernels of A. indica, manifests various biological/ physiological/ pharmacological activities. The crude principle of A. indica has some tetranortriterpenes, including nimbin, nimbinin, nimbidinin, nimbolide, andnimbidic acid (64,65). Nimbidin and the sodium salt of it possess a significant concentration-dependent anti-inflammatory activity against carrageenin-induced acute rat paw edema and formalin-induced rheumatoid arthritis (66,67). Anti-pyretic action has also been observed and confirmed with nimbidin. Hypoglycaemic effects are demonstrated by the oral administration of nimbidin in fasting rabbits (68). A significant anti-ulcer effect was observed with nimbidin in preventing drug-induced acetylsalicylic acid, indomethacin, stress or serotonin-induced gastric lesions as well as histamine-induced duodenal ulcers (69,70). Nimbidin can also subdue basal as well as histamine and carbachol (cholinergic drug) induced gastric acid secretion and possibly by inhibiting H_2 receptors' antihistaminic action (71). The spermicidal activity of nimbidin and nimbin was established in rats as well as human beings in 1959 (72). Nimbidin also manifests anti-fungal activity by obstructing the growth of *Tinea rubrum* (73). In *an in-vitro* analysis, it inhibits the viability of *Mycobacterium tuberculosis* and is also observed as bactericidal (73). The diuretic activity is found with a salt preparation of nimbidin called sodium nimbidinate in dogs (74). Nimbolide has been observed as anti-malarial by inhibiting the virulence of *Plasmodium falciparum*. Nimbolide also exhibits antibacterial activity against *S. aureus* and *S. coagulase* (75). Gedunin is segregated from neem seed oil that has been proclaimed to exist both antifungal and antimalarial (76) activities. Azadirachtin, highly oxygenated C-secomeliacins obtained from neem seed and showing strong anti-feedant activity (77), and has been demonstrated to have anti-malarial property by inhibiting the growth and development of the malarial parasite. (78). Mahmoodin, a deoxygedunin sequestered from seed oil which was observed to have antimicrobial activity against pathogenic microorganisms especially bacteria in human beings. Condensed tannins from the bark of *A. indica* contains many secondary metabolites like gallic acid, (+) gallocatechin, (–) epicatechin, (+) catechin and epigallocatechin, of which gallic acid, (–) epicatechin and catechin are very creditworthy in suppressing the production of chemiluminescence by mobilize human polymorphonuclear neutrophil (PMN) cells (79), which specifies that these compounds constrain the oxidative burst of PMN during inflammatory conditions. The three tricyclic diterpenoids named as margolone, margolonone and isomargolonone sequestered from neem stem bark are ascertained to be active against Klebsiella spp., Staphylococcus spp. and Serratia spp. (80). Sulfur-containing compounds such as cyclic trisulphide and tetrasulphidecharacterized from the steam distillation of fresh, matured leaves of *A. indica* has been found to possess antifungal action against *Trichophyton mentagrophytes* (81). Several polysaccharides available in neem exhibit diversified biological effects. A polysaccharide extracted from the bark of *A. indica* exhibits inhibition of carrageenan-induced inflammation in the mouse (82). Two water-soluble polysaccharides GIa and GIb sequestered from the bark of *Melia azadirachta*, exhibited strong anti-tumor effect with complete regression of the tumor on the administration of a daily dose of 50 mg per kg for four days from 24 hours after subcutaneous inoculation of Sarcoma-180 cells in mice (83). Two more polysaccharides named as GIIa and GIIIa are extracted from the bark of *M. azadirachta* which exhibit a significant anti-inflammatory effect in mice' carrageenin-induced oedema (84). Two polymers quarantined from an aqueous extract of neem bark demonstrated anti-complement activity by peptidoglycan of lower molecular weight observed as NB-II which was raised to be more potent (85,86). Some sequestered active ingredients especially phytosterol fraction from the lipid factor of neem fruits illustrates the antiulcer activity in stress-induced gastric mucosal lesions (87).

3.8 Henna

Lawsonia inermis Linn (Lythraceae) is a perennial plant commonly known as Henna (88), or mignonette tree (89) belongs to Kingdom: Plantae; Division: Angiospermae; Class: Dicotyledoneae; Order: Myrtales; Family: Lythraceae; Genus: Lawsonia; Species: inermis (90)having different vernacular names in India viz., In Ayurveda it called as Madayanti, Madayantikaa, Mendika, Ranjaka. In Unani, it is Hinaa, Mehndi. In Siddha, it is called as Marithondi, Marudum; as Mehndi in Hindi; as Mendika, Rakigarbha in Sanskrit; Mailanchi in Malayalam; Muruthani in Tamil; Benjati in Oriya; Mayilanchi in Kannada and Mehedi in Bengali. It is indigenous to North Africa and South East Asia and frequently cultivated as an ornamental plant throughout India, Persia, and along the African coast of the Mediterranean Sea. *L. inermis* is a plant of complete flowers with an average height of 5 meters, a habitat of South Asia, Africa, and an oasis of Sahara desert also even in northern regions of Australia. The Leaves of henna plant are entire, opposite, sub-sessile, mostly oval in shape and smooth in texture. Leaves grow a length of approximately 2–3 cm and a width of 1–2 cm (88). Henna plant is profusely branched with brownish-grey barks (91). The phytochemistry of leaves contain naphthoquinones, in particularly lawsone, coumarins (laxanthone, I, II and III), flavonoids, luteolin, and luteolin-7-O-glucoside, acacetin-7-O-glucoside; beta-sitosterol-3-O-glucoside; all parts of the plant is rich in tannins (92). The henna plant also shows to contain mannite, tannic acid, mucilage, gallic acid, and naphthoquinone (93–95).

The ether and alcohol extracted leaves of henna render hennatannic acid. Flowers produce an essential oil approximately 0.01-0.02 % with brownish color, strong fragrance and consists of a nitrogenous compound, alpha and beta ionones; and a resin. Seeds also present 5.0 % of proteins, 33.62 % of carbohydrates, 33.5 % of fibers, 10 % of fatty oils which is composed of arachidic acid, behenic acid, linoleic acid, oleic acid, palmitic acid, and stearic acid. The unsaponified matter consists of waxes and coloring matter. The root consists of a red coloring matter (96).

3.9 Sal tree resin

Shorea robusta Gaertn. is colloquially called as sal or shala tree, belonging to the family Dipterocarpaceae (97). It is a habitat of Eastern districts of Madhya Pradesh extending further to the Eastern Ghats of Andhra Pradesh, and well diffused in various districts from Himachal Pradesh to Assam, Tripura, West Bengal, Bihar, and Orissa. In English, it is called a Sal tree, Oleoresin as Sal Dammer or Bengal Dammer. In Ayurveda, it is called Shaala, Saalasaara, Dhuupa-vriksha. (Substitute: *Vateria indica*.) In Siddha/ Tamil it is known as Kungiliyam, Venkungiliyam (resin) (92). Sal tree is used not only in the Ayurvedic system but also used in Unani medicine (98). The resin of *S. robusta* is a rough, brittle with faint resinous, balsamic odour and is ubiquitously employed as incense in various religious ceremonies as it emits copious white fumes (99). Synergistic activity was observed in a combination of oleoresin with cows' ghee to suppress the burning sensation of haemorrhoids, pain, and swelling (100). The tannins present in various parts of the plant such as bark, young leaves, twigs/leaves, and powder dust as 7-12%, 20%, 22%, and 12%, respectively. The aqueous extract of bark possesses 39.6 % of tannins with a trans/non-trans ratio of 0.73 which are of pyrogallol type. Oleanolic acid, another secondary metabolite has also been extracted from the bark of the Sal tree. The oleoresin of the aerial parts has been reported to be a component of ointments to heal wounds, burns, pains, skin diseases and to control diarrhea and dysentery (101–104). The biological activity of entire plant parts was observed in many diseases like skin allergies, diarrhea, and dysentery. The fruits of *S. robusta* are showed to be useful in burning sensation, dermopathy, seminal weakness, and tubercular ulcers (105). The exudation of *S. robusta* consists of astringent, carminative, and stomachic properties. It has adhered to aid in vitiated conditions of pitta, wounds, ulcers, neuralgia, burns, bone fractures, hyperpyrexia, diarrhea, bacterial as well as amoebic dysentery, splenomegaly, obesity, and burning sensation of the eyes (105). In Unani medicine, the resin is in use of various ailments like menorrhagia, splenomegaly and for relieving eye irritation. In Ayurvedic medicine, it is mixed with honey or sugar for the treatment of bacterial dysentery and anal fissures, bleeding piles. It is also given in sexually transmitted diseases like gonorrhea and to aid in digestive disorders (106). According to Siddha practitioners, this oleoresin is used for ulcers, wounds and menopausal disorders (106). Earlier many research in experimental animal studies confirmed its antibacterial (107), anti-aging (97), analgesic, anti-inflammatory (108) and wound healing (106) effects. The anti-ulcer property of *S. robusta* does not have scientific evidence but by the traditional practitioners used this to heal ulcers and it was decided that the gastroprotective potential of the *S. robusta* is a target for ethnobotanical scientists. It is having numerous secondary metabolites of medicinal importance such as ursolic acid, alpha-amyrenone, alpha-amyrin, and beta-amyrin (104,109). The bark is rich with ursolic acid and oleanane, shoreaphenol (101,110). The seeds of *S. robusta* contain hopeaphenol, leucoanthocyanidin, and 3, 7-dihydroxy-8-methoxyflavone7-O-α-l-rhamnopyranosyl-(1→4)-α-l-rhamnonopyrano-syl (1→6)-β-d-glucopyranoside (111) and the heartwood contains germacrene-D. (100). The presence of various secondary metabolites of interest like β-amyrin, friedelin, β-sitosterol, pheophytin-α, and dihydroxyisoflavone from matured and developed leaves was reported in different literature (112).

3.10 Pharmacological properties of *S. robusta*

The 70% ethanolic extract in 30, 100 and 300 mg per kg intraperitoneal injection observed as significant central and peripheral analgesic activity by elevation in reaction time in the hot plate and tail flick tests (106). The methanolic and aqueous leaf extract on intraperitoneal administration in 200 and 400 mg per kg Sal tree shows analgesic activity in rats and mice in acetic acid-induced writhing and tail flick tests (98). The 70 % ethanolic extract of Sal tree oleoresin was studied using Brewer's yeast-induced pyrexia test in rats (113). The aqueous extract of leaves of *S. robusta* with a dose of 100, 200 and 500 mcg per ml was taken in Human Red Blood Cell (HRBC) membrane stabilization model and heat-inducedhaemolytic method for the anti-inflammatory activity which 500 mcg per ml was observed the good result (114). The methanolic and aqueous extract was observed significant effect with 200 and 400 mg per kg intraperitoneally and per oral in carrageenan and dextran-induced paw method and cotton-pellet-induced granuloma model (98,115,116). The aqueous extract of floral parts of *S. robusta* was prepared with cold water maceration which was employed for antibacterial activity with a well-diffusion method which showed significant inhibition of growth of Gram-positive bacteria viz. *Staphylococcus aureus* and *Bacillus subtilis* and Gram-negative bacteria viz. *Klebsiella pneumoniae* and *Serratia marcescens*. The phytochemical compounds present in *S. robusta* are revealed as tannins, flavonoids, cardiac glycosides, and steroids are involved in the antibacterial activity (113). The aqueous, methanol, petroleum, and benzene extract of oleoresin of *S. robusta* are tested for antimicrobial activity in which the aqueous extracts of *S. robusta* showed significant activity against *B.coagulans*, *E.coli*, *B.cereus* and moderate inhibition on *S. typhi* and *B. subtilis* and less activity was observed against *P. vulgaris* and *P. fluorescence*. In ethanolic extracts, there was significant activity against *S. aureus*, *S. epidermidis*, and *E. coli*, moderate inhibition on *C. albicans* and *B.coagulans*. The Petroleum ether extract gives an activity against *E.coli*, *A. flavus*, and *C. albicans* and the benzene extract observed against *B. licheniformis*, *B. cereus*, and *A. flavus* organisms where it can be concluded as *S. robusta* resin have a robust and broad-spectrum antimicrobial activity (117). The antioxidants in plants and plant products are cardinal in the suppression of tumorigenesis where the antioxidants in several natural and synthetic compounds are observed to have anticancer effects. Administration of diethylnitrosamine (DEN) to male wistar rats led to increasing the biomarkers present as serum enzymes like aspartate transaminase (AST), alanine transaminase (ALT), lactate dehydrogenase (LDH), and gamma-glutamyl transpeptidase (GGT). The lipid peroxide levels are inflated with a subsequent decrease in the tissue antioxidant levels like superoxide dismutase (SOD), catalase (CAT), reduced glutathione (GSH), glutathione peroxidase (GPx), and glutathione reductase (GR) while the *S. robusta* bark resin extract (SRBE) supplementation at 500 mg per kg body weight significantly attenuated these enzymes (118). The 10 and 30 % w/w ethanolic extract of *S. robusta* was employed externally in the excised and incised wounds and observed as a concentration-dependent expedition in wound contraction and accelerated hydroxyproline content and tensile strength in rat models that can be stated the demonstration of wound healing activity of *S. robusta* resin (106).

3.11 Castor oil

Castor oil is technically called as *Ricinus communis* Linn is a plant which commonly found in tropical and temperate geographical and climatic zones of the world (119,120). It belongs to the Family Euphorbiaceae and Habitat of Andhra Pradesh, Maharashtra, Karnataka, and Orissa. In English, it is called as Castor seed; in Ayurveda known as Eranda, Chitrabija, Triputi, Tribija, Vaataari, Chanchu, Manda, Uruvaka, Gandharva-hastaa, Panchaangula, Vardhamaana, Uttaanpatraka, Vyaaghrapuchha, Chitraa; In Unani as Bedanjeer, Arand; and Siddha/Tamil as Ammanakku (92). The *R. communis* is popular for the castor seeds commonly known as 'palm of Christ,' Jada (Oriya), Verenda (Bengali), Endi (Hindi), Errandi (Marathi), Diveli (Gujarati). The plant is a fast-growing, perennial shrub or a soft wood which is up to 6 meters or more. The leaves look like a green or reddish, about 30-60 cm in diameter which is of 5-12 deep lobes with coarsely toothed segments altering in pigmentation. The flowers are monoicous and about 30-60 cm long. The seeds are of different in size and colour which are oval, somewhat compressed, 8-18 mm long and 4-12 mm broad. Castor seeds have a wart-likeprocess called a caruncle (121). The Phytochemical constituents of *R.communis* are the presence of steroids, saponins, alkaloids, flavonoids, and glycosides. The dried leaves of castor oil witnessed the availability of two alkaloids, ricinine with 0.55 % and N-demethylricinine with 0.016 % and flavones glycosides like kaempferol-3-O-β-D-xylopyranoside, kaempferol-3-O-β-D-glucopyranoside, quercetin-3-O-β-D-xylopyranoside, quercetin-3-O-β-D-glucopyranoside, kaempferol-3-β-D-rutinoside, and quercetin-3-O-β-rutinoside. The major phenolic compounds obtained from leaves of castor oil plant are monoterpenoids (1, 8-cineole, camphor, and α-pinene) and sesquiterpenoid (β-caryophyllene), ellagic acid, epicatechin, gallic acid, gentisic acid, quercetin, and rutin. The compound Indole-3-acetic acid is isolated from the roots of *R. communis* (122). The seeds contain 45% of fixed oil, which consist glycosides of ricinoleic acid, isoricinoleic acid, stearic acid, and dihydroxystearic acid and also lipases and a ricinine (123). The chromatographic analysis shows the presence of 1.2 % palmitic acid; 0.7% stearic acid; 0.3 % arachidic acid; 0.2 % hexadecenoic acid; 3.2 % oleic acid; 3.4 % linoleic acid; 89.4 % ricinoleic acid and also witness the presence of dihydroxy stearic acid (124). The stem of *R. communis* contains ricinine and in the ether extract of seeds contains some compounds like ergot-5-en-3-ol, stigmasterol, Y-stigmasterol, fucosterol, and probucol. The GC-MS analysis of castor bean oil proves the presence of compounds like 31.71% of alpha-thujone, 30.98% of 1,8-cineole, 16.88% of alpha-pinene, 12.92 % of camphor, and 7.48% of camphene. (125). Lupeol and 30-Norlupan-3β-ol-20-one were found to obtain from the coat of castor bean (126).

3.12 Sesame oil

Sesame oil is botanically called as *Sesamum indicum* Linn. It has a Synonym as *Sesamum orientale* Linn belongs to a Family Pedaliaceae which is a habitat of Uttar Pradesh, Madhya Pradesh, Rajasthan, Orissa, Gujarat, Andhra Pradesh, Tamil Nadu, and Maharashtra. In English, it is called Sesame, Gingelly; in Ayurveda as Tila, Snehphala; in Unani as Kunjad, Til; in Siddha as Ellu (seed), Nallennai (oil) (92). It is an annual plant with branching stem of 50-100 cm tall with opposite leaves of 10 cm long and with an entire margin (127).

The seeds of *S. indicum* have a very high level of approximately 2.5 % of furofuran lignans mainly sesamin, sesamolin, and sesaminol glucosides. Another phenolic compounds sesamol and sesaminol are generated from sesamin and sesamolin which are used to prevent elevated blood pressure, lowering cholesterol level and increase HDL by the abundant availability of tocopherol. The sesamum seeds contain phytosterols which are used in many clinical conditions. Sesame oil is mostly accumulated with triglycerides of 40 % singly unsaturated oleic acid and 45 % doubly unsaturated linoleic acid. The shelf life of sesame oil is due to the presence of powerful antioxidants and absence of triply unsaturated fatty acids. A new anthraquinone derivative called as anthrasesamone F was obtained from the seeds of *S. indicum* with a structure (Z)-6,7-dihydroxyl 2-(6-hydroxy-4-methyl-3pentenyl) anthraquinone (128). The Root of *S. indicum* was reported to have hydroxysesamone, 2,3-epoxysesamone and a chlorinated red napthaquinone pigment (chlorosesamone) which is showing fungicidal activity (129). Three anthraquinones are procured from roots as anthrasesamone A, B, and C. Two more anthraquinone derivatives are obtained from the roots as anthrax sesamone D and E (130). 2-Geranyl-1, 4-naphthaquinone is sequestered from the root culture of *S. indicum* (131). In the mass spectroscopy and NMR spectroscopy, it observes new lignin, sesaminol diglucoside which is isolated from defatted sesame seed flour. Another two phenylethanoid glycosides and three triglycerides having the same sugar sequence are isolated from aqueous extract. The lignans pinoresinol and lariciresinol are found in Sesamum seeds (132).

3.13 1, 3-Beta Glucan synthase

1,3-Beta Glucan synthase also called as callose synthase with Enzyme Commission no 2.4.1.34. It is a glycosyltransferase enzyme involved in the generation of beta-glucan in fungi by utilizing the products of disaccharides, oligosaccharides, and polysaccharides. The glycosyl transferase catalyzes the substitution of sugar moieties from functionally active donor molecules to a specific acceptor molecule, forming glycosidic bonds. 1, 3-β Glucan synthase is a multi-subunit enzyme which is helpful in fungal cell wall construction, a division of septum, and ascospore wall assembly (133). Glucan is a polysaccharide of the fungal cell wall with the majority of around 60 % of dry weight (134,135). Polymers of Glucan are compiled of recurring glucose residues that are congregated into chains through different chemical linkages. Typically, fungal cell wall contains around 65-90% 1, 3-β Glucan synthase and also found beta 1, 6-, mixed beta 1,3- and 1,4-, alpha-1,3- and alpha-1-4-linked glucans (136–138). The 1, 3- β glucan serves as the essential structural component to which other cell wall constituents will attach covalently. According to some studies, Beta-1, 3 and Beta-1, 6 glucans are present in *S. cerevisiae* and *C. albicans* (139). Recent studies have shown that beta-1, 6 glucan was absent in filamentous fungi like *N.crassa* and *A.fumigatus* (140,141). Glucan synthase catalyzes the configuration of elongated linear chains of Glucan each consists of approximately 1500 glucose residues conjoined via Beta-1,3 linkages within each long Glucan chain, the 6 carbon positions of approximately 40-50 glucose residues became sites at which additional beta-1,3 glucans are affixed to generate a branched structure (141,142). The ramified glucans can be cross-linked together and to chitin and mannoproteins to cater to the cell wall with mechanical support and integrity (143). The genes encoding the constituents of 1, 3-β Glucan synthase machinery, are recognized in *S. cerevisiae* which carries two known catalytic subunits and one regulatory protein (144). The *S. cerevisiae FKS1* and *FKS2* genes encode two functionally obsolete catalytic subunits of the Glucan synthase complex, but the genetic analysis has expressed the involvement of each in Glucan synthesis and cell wall formation. The disturbance occurred on any reason in either *FKS1* or *FKS2* gene may lead to the mutation that leads to a slow growth rate and cell wall defects (145,146). The simultaneous deletion of *FKS1* and *FKS2* is appeared to be lethal. This observation with the catalytic subunits showing overlapping functions and exemplifies the grandness of 1, 3-Beta glucan production for the survival of yeast. Disruptions of the *S. cerevisiae RHO1* gene which encodes the Rho1 GTPase regulatory subunit exhibited that it is indispensable for survival. The inhibition of 1, 3-β glucan synthase leads to the inhibition of synthesis of cell wall component; glucan leads to loss of integrity of cell wall and disrupting the cell wall formation and forbids the growth of the fungal organism. The subclass of anti-fungal agents known as echinocandins has been formulated for clinical uses that known to bind to the catalytic sub-unit of Glucan synthase.

3.14 Chitin synthase

Chitin synthase is a glycosyltransferase enzyme with Enzyme Commission no: 2.4.1.16 that require UDP-N-acetyl glucosamine as a substrate with another, 1, 4-(N-acetyl-beta-D-glucosaminyl to produce 1,4-(N-acetyl-beta-D-glucosaminyl which is called as chitin, a cell component of 60% (147). Approximately 2% (w/w) of chitin of the total cell wall is present in *S. cerevisiae* which is confined specifically at the bud scars as a polysaccharide consisting of around 190 N-acetyl glucosamine residues which are diffused in the lateral walls where it is covalently linked to (1, 3)-β-glucan and (1, 6)-β-glucan (148,149). Chitin synthases are the integral membrane proteins with the substrate of UDP-N-acetyl glucosamine and which are of three types are identified in *S. cerevisiae*. On experiments on gene-disruption, Cabib et al. concluded that Chitin synthase 2 (*CHS2*) is crucial for vegetative growth, whereas chitin synthase 1 (*CHS1*) is not essential (150,151).

A third chitin synthase, *CHS3*, must be accountable for chitin synthase activity. On cloning and disruption of the genes for *CHS3* observed as Chitin synthase 3 is important for chitin dispersed in the bud ring and the lateral wall, whereas *CHS2* catalyzes the synthesis of chitin (152,153). Genes homologous to *CHS1* and *CHS2* have been identified in other fungi, like *C. albicans, A. nidulans, A. fumigatus*, and *S. pombe* (154,155). Depletion or overexpression of Chitin Synthase 1 (*CHS1*) did not show marked errors during vegetative growth, but the formation of ascospore was powerfully affected which indicates that the gene is required for sporulation (155). The function of chs2+ is unknown clearly but is upregulated during meiosis (156), and therefore may also play a role in sporulation.

3.15 Chitinase

Chitinases are glycosyl hydrolases, (157) with Enzyme Commission no: 3.2.2.14, present in many organisms like bacteria, fungi, yeasts, plants, actinomycetes, arthropods and humans. Chitinases can metabolize chitin into a small molecules chitooligomers which are widely used in industrial, agricultural, activation of elicitor-induced genes, and anti-tumor agent (158). Chitinases are a variety of group of enzymes that exhibit variations in their molecular structure, substrate specificity, and catalytic mechanism (159). It is essential to study the substrate specificity to reveal the relationship with physiological roles which are metabolized to novel products of industrial use (160). According to Yamanaka et al., 1994, and Sandor et al., 1998, the fungal cell wall Chitinases activity can be finding out based on the role in filamentous fungal sporulation where the inhibitors, demethylallosamidin or allosamidin led to the blockade of chitinase enzyme activity leads to fragmentation of hyphae into arthroconidia (161,162). The antitumor activity was observed by the metabolic products of chitin like chitohexose and chitoheptaose. N-acetylhexosaminidase has used an anti-fungal drug target in a study by Horsch et. al. (163).

3.16 Deuterolysin

Deuterolysin is formerly called as neutral proteinase II with enzyme commission no: 3.4.24.39 which contains 1 gm atom of zinc per molecule of an enzyme of single chain amino acid residues with a molecular weight of 19.018 Daltons includes three disulphide bonds (164,165). This deuterolysin belongs to the M35 family of metalloendopeptidase. Metalloendopeptidases are biologically significant proteinases used for processing proteins thereby known as proteolytic enzymes (166,167). Hooper (168) explained the scheme about zinc binding site which was extended to classify zinc metalloproteinases into distinct families such as gluzincins, metzincins, inverzincins, the carboxypeptidase family and the DD-carboxypeptidase family. Deuterolysin as of now has an unknown zinc-binding motif, aspzincin, defined as the "HEXXH+D" motif with an aspartic acid residue as the third ligand (165). Deuterolysin has been found in certain molds belonging to the genera Aspergillus and Penicillium. The biological role of deuterolysin was probably to utilize the substrate in their environment. Deuterolysin shows unique thermal stability. It is mostly unstable on exposure to 65-75°C for 10 minutes but regains stability beyond this temperature, and it is relatively stable at 100°C (169,170).

3.17 Fungalysin

Fungalysin is a metalloprotease that belongs to M 36 group of thermolysin family. This enzyme can disintegrate the proteins of *Matrix Extracellularis* like elastin and collagen by the secreted fungal peptidases, and they act as virulence factors in fungal diseases. Fungalysin was first discovered in *A. fumigates*, but their role in non-pathogenic fungi is unknown (171,172). Fungalysin was nominated as a unique family among zinc-dependent peptidases that with low sequence similarity to known bacterial peptidases (173).

The metalloprotease enzymes utilize co-ordination to a zinc metal for their action. The zinc metal provides a substantial electrophilic "Pull" to assist in an attack by a water molecule. This fungalysin metalloprotease native enzyme has a water molecule embedded to the fourth tetrahedral site. This water molecule may be displaced upon coordination of the substrate carbonyl to the metal atom, but it is believed to remain at the active site. It has been advised that it may remain coordinated to the metal atom at least in the transition state.

3.18 Homoserine dehydrogenase

The homoserine dehydrogenase is an enzyme involved in the catalysis of aspartate semialdehyde (ASA) to homoserine with an enzyme commission no: 1.1.1.3 of oxidoreductase family. The metabolic pathway was presented in figure 3, of aspartate shows the involvement of storage of asparagine and the synthesis of aspartate related amino acids (174). Homoserine dehydrogenase is helpful to catalyze the intermediate step of nitrogen and carbon storage and utilization pathway (175). In fungi, the essential amino acids like methionine, threonine, and isoleucine are used to synthesize by this pathway with the help of homoserine dehydrogenase which is the safest and novel target as it is not present in mammals (176).

3.19 Lumazine synthase

Lumazine synthase is also known as 5-amino-6-(D-ribitylamino) uracil butanedione-transferase(177), an enzyme involved in riboflavin (vitamin B_2) synthesis with EC no: 2.5.1.78. Riboflavin is a coenzyme/cofactor as flavin mononucleotide (FMD) and flavin adenine dinucleotide (FAD) that are essential for the activity of numerous metabolic enzymes involved in the electron chain reaction. Plants, fungi, and microorganisms produce riboflavin while mammals it is from exogenous (178–180). Lumazine synthase executes a crucial role in the penultimate step of the biosynthetic pathway of riboflavin which catalyzes the condensation of 5-amino-6-(D-ribitylamino)-, 4(1H,3H)-pyrimidinedione(ARAPD) with 3,4-dihydroxy-2-butanone-4phosphate (DHBP) yielding one molecule each of 6,7-dimethyl-8-ribityllumazine

(DMRL) and orthophosphate (177). In the following step, two molecules of DMRL dismutate yielding riboflavin and ARAPD. Riboflavin synthase is helpful in the above-said reaction (181,182). The product ARAPD which formed in the subsequent reaction is reutilized as a substrate for lumazine synthase. The enzyme designed as heavy riboflavin synthase with a molecular weight of 1MD a characterized by two subunits, alpha, and beta. The alpha subunit is of 23,500 Daltons molecular weight while 16,000 Daltons for the beta (183,184). The alpha subunit of the enzyme formation of 5-amino-6-ribitylamino-2,4-(1H,3H)pyrimidine-dione from 6, 7-dimethyl-8-ribityl-lumazine which caused to form riboflavin and thereby named riboflavin synthase (184). The beta subunit acts as a catalyzing the biosynthesis of 6, 7-dimethyl-8-ribityl-lumazine from 5-amino-6-ribitylamino-2,4-(1H,3H)pyrimidine-dione, the precursor molecule with the help of (3S)-3,4-dihydroxy-2butanone-4-phosphate (185,186) thus the beta subunit is called as Lumazine synthase. The metabolic pathway is presented in figure 4.

3.20 Phosphoribosylaminoimidazole carboxylase

Phosphoribosylaminoimidazole carboxylase (AIR carboxylase) is an enzyme involved in nucleotide biosynthesis and in particular in purine biosynthesis with enzyme commission no: 4.1.1.21. It is helpful in the catalyzes of the conversion of 5'-phosphoribosyl-5-aminoimidazole into 5'-phosphoribosyl-4-carboxy-5-aminoimidazole as given in the reaction:

5-aminoimidazole ribonucleotide+CO_2 $\leftrightarrow$ 5'-phosphoribosyl-4-carboxy-5-aminoimidazole + $2H^+$

Since 1940, purine metabolism has been an essential biochemical pathway in the discovery of drugs (187–189). The enzymes involved in the purine biosynthesis pathway have been useful as newer and reliable drug targets.

The purine and pyrimidine biosynthetic pathways of an organism are linked to its virulence (190–193). The antifungal drug Flucytosine has already expressed the unique enzymes in the pyrimidine pathway in a fungal organism (194) which is effectively inhibiting the growth. The association between decreased virulence and purine auxotrophy in bacteria and fungi is also well documented. As early as 1950, Bacon et al. (195)reported that *Salmonella typhi* strains carrying a mutation in the purine biochemical pathway was less virulent with the wild-type strain in rodents. This reduction in the virulence of purine auxotrophs has also been found in *Salmonella typhimurium*(193), *Salmonella dublin*(193), *Klebsiella pneumoniae*(196), *Bacillus anthracis*(197), *Yersinia pestis*(198,199), and *C. albicans*(191,192). The association of reduced virulence and a purine or pyrimidine auxotrophy presumably implicates from the incompetence of the organism to multiply sufficiently in the host environment, reflecting the limited availability of nutrients or the incompetence to use exogenous metabolites from the host (200,201). The metabolic pathway is presented in figure 5.

3.21 Protein elongation factor

Elongation factors are a set of endogenous proteins that are used in protein synthesis in the cell cycle and elongation in some cells. Elongation is a very rapid step in the process of translation with a rate of two amino acids per second in eukaryotes. Elongation factors are responsible for curbing the accuracy in the translation process at this speed.

The ribosomes in the body require two factors in the process of the reactions of the elongation cycle. Elongation factor 1α is responsible for the codon dependent selection of the related aminoacyl-tRNA at the ribosomal A site and elongation factor 2 for the translocation. The third elongation factor (EF-3) is said to be essential for the elongation cycle in the fungal organism. (202). EF1α and EF2 belong to GTPase superfamily which is characterized by common structural motifs, and they can alternate between conformational states with GDP or GTP. (203). Elongation factor 3 is a ribosome-dependent ATPase, which accepts GTP and ITP as substrates and pyrimidine nucleotides. (204). The S. cerevisiae Elongation factor 3 is a single polypeptide chain of 1044 amino acids (204). The function of Elongation Factor 3 is unique with the other two which is dependent on 40 S subunit of the ribosome. The monoclonal antibody against it blocks *in-vitro* translation of poly (U) as natural mRNA and also associated with polysomes rather than ribosomes. It is evident that the elongation factor 3 is helpful to stimulate the binding of aminoacyl-tRNA to the A site but in the presence of catalytic amounts of EF1α with deacetylated tRNA. Moreover, the ATP-dependent activity of EF3 is for deacetylation of tRNA from E site at A site occupation (204).

3.22 Sulphite reductase

Sulphite reductase is an enzyme belongs to oxidoreductase family which is involved in sulfate metabolism/sulfate assimilation pathway with enzyme commission no: 1.8.99.1 that catalyzes the reduction of sulfite to hydrogen sulfide and water (205,206)by utilizing the electrons with the aid of a dissociable molecule, NADPH, bounded flavins, or ferredoxins. (207).

SO_3^{2-} (sulfite) + electron donor↔ H_2S (hydrogen sulfide) + oxidized donor + 3 H_2O

The sulfate assimilation pathway is not needed for fungal organisms as the fungal organisms can utilize the methionine available from the environment. In the process of synthesis of cysteine and methionine in fungi requires cellular uptake and reduction of sulfate to sulfide. The sulfate assimilation pathway is the mechanism involved the interference of amino acid transport and cellular regulation of amino acid metabolism in the fungal organism. A sulphite reductase, a complex enzyme containing both a sirohaem and an iron-sulphur cluster, carries out the six-electron reduction of sulphite to sulphide (208). It is now clear that in yeast, sulphide is incorporated into a four-carbon chain yielding homocysteine. (209). Homocysteine synthase is helpful to catalyze the synthesis of homocysteine from O-acetyl homoserine and sulphide(210). In *S. cerevisiae*, methionine and cysteine both acquire their sulphur from homocysteine while, in eubacteria, the sulphur atom of methionine is derived from cysteine (211). An aliphatic amino acid with an azoxy side chain drug, Azoxybacillin which is obtained from *Bacillus cereus* is known to inhibit the induction of five enzymes in the SA pathway (212). The inhibition of expression of sulfite reductase by azoxybacillin should involve two steps: (I) restraint of factors that are responsible for the transcription of the genes for the expression of sulfite reductase activity, and (II) interference with the posttranscriptional process required for the expression of sulfite reductase activity.

Hence the literature explains that the secondary metabolites present in the plants and plant products are responsible for the antifungal activity. Based on this the present study was designed to retrieve the secondary metabolites which are helpful to hamper the metabolic functions of the fungal organism by using various software by in-silico / docking method.

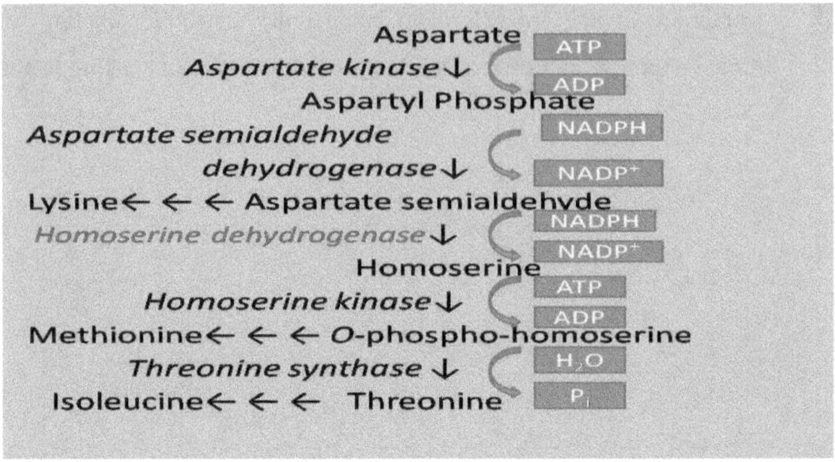

Figure 3:The metabolic pathway of homoserine dehydrogenase

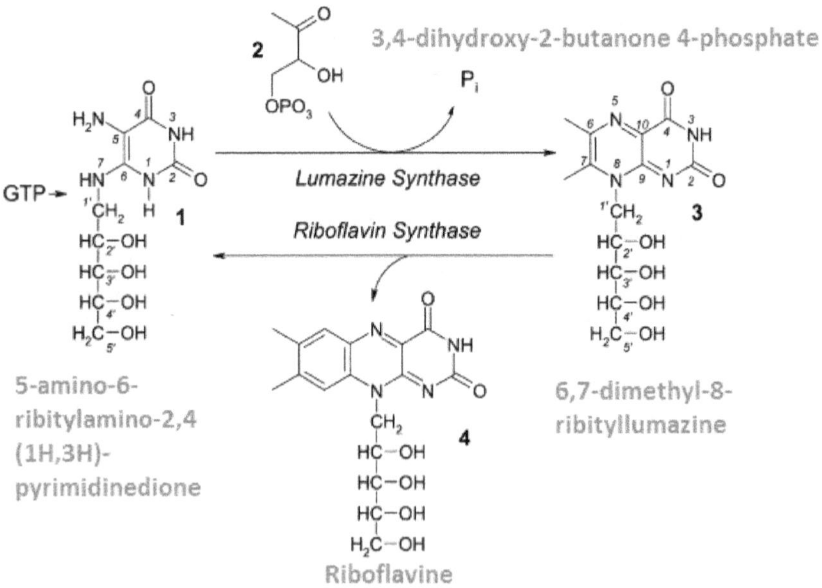

Figure 4: The metabolic pathway of Lumazine synthase

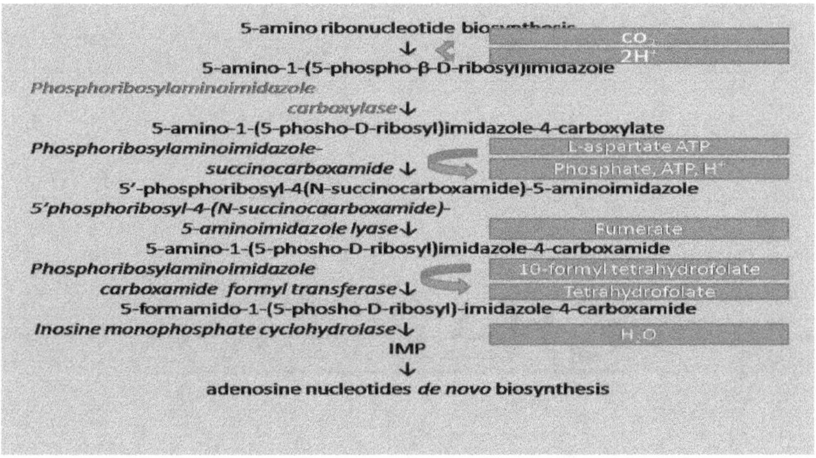

Figure 5: The metabolic pathway of Phosphoribosylaminoimidazole carboxylase

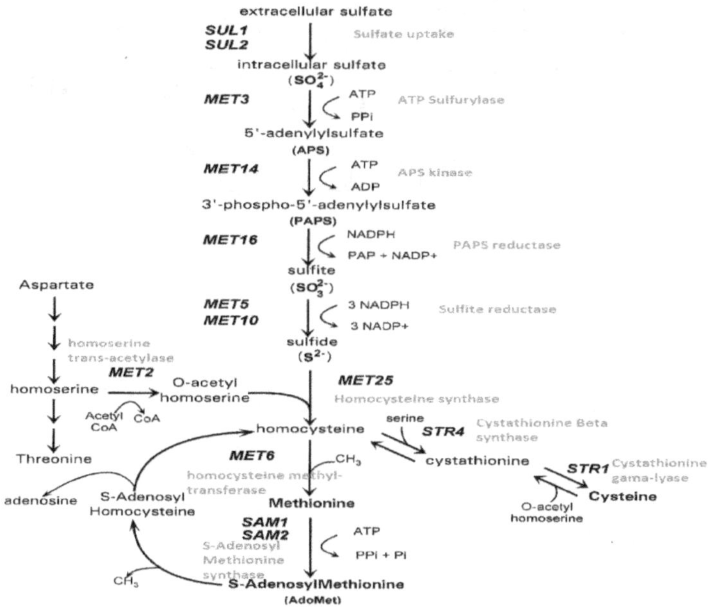

Figure 6: The metabolic pathway of Sulphite reductase

CHAPTER 4

ANTI-FUNGAL ACTIVITY OF THE INDIVIDUAL PLANT EXTRACTS AND IN COMBINATION

4. ANTI-FUNGAL ACTIVITY OF THE INDIVIDUAL PLANT EXTRACTS AND IN COMBINATION

4.1 Aim and objective

1. To study the antifungal activity of different extracts of *Azadirachta indica*, *Lawsonia inermis*, *Shorea robusta, Ricinus communis,* and *Sesamum indicum.*

2. To determine the Minimum Inhibitory Concentration (MIC) of different extracts of *A.indica, L. inermis*, *S. robusta.*

3. To study the synergistic anti-fungal activity between the various plant's extracts.

4.2 Materials and Methods

The research work was carried in the central research lab, Tagore Medical College and Hospital, Chennai, with prior approval of experimental protocol approved by the Research Committee (RC)-approval no RC 001/March 2016 and Institutional Ethical Committee (IEC) - 25/March 2016.

4.2.1 Collection of Plant Material and Preparation of Extracts

The plant material, the leaves of *A.indica* and *L. inermis* were collected from the local area of Rajamahendravaram, Andhra Pradesh, and it was authenticated by Mr. Y.V.V.V. Ramana, lecturer in botany, and preserved in the laboratory of the botany department, SKVT College, Rajamahendravaram, Andhra Pradesh. The fresh leaves are plucked, washed, dried in shaded sunlight which was later milled into a fine, coarse powder. The powder obtained from both the plant leaves (approximately 3 kg each) was extracted using different solvents from non-polar to polar, i.e., hexane, benzene, ethyl acetate, methanol, with a Soxhlet apparatus and aqueous extract was with cold maceration. The extracts are filtered and condensed at room temperature, and they are kept for storage at 4°C, the resin of *S. robusta*, castor oil, sesame oil, and Clotrimazole was purchased from Sigma Labs.

4.2.2 Sequential extraction of medicinal plants

The sequential extraction of the medicinally essential plants or its plant products/material using a method called a Soxhlet extraction method. Soxhlet extractor is a designed tool piece of laboratory apparatus which was invented by Franz Von Soxhlet in 1879. Usually, the solid powdered medicinal plant material containing an unknown active principle is kept inside the thimble made from thick filter paper, which is loaded into the main chamber of the apparatus. The soxhlet apparatus is placed upon the flask containing the extraction solvent and connected to the condenser. The solvent is heated towards upwards; the vapor generated by the solvent travels up to a distillation arm and passes into the chamber present in the thimble of solid material. The condenser helps to make sure that the solvent vapours cool down and drips into the chamber where the solid medicinal plant material placed, the thimble which slowly fills with warm solvent. Some of the compounds which are to be extracted will be dissolved in the warm solvent. Whenever the soxhlet chamber is about to get full, the filled chamber immediately gets transferred by a siphon present as a sidearm, with the solvent running back down to the distillation flask. The same step is subjected to repeat for many times, throughout hours or long days. During each step, the portion of the non-volatile compound will dissolve in the solvent. After repeated steps, the desired concentrated component is available in the distillation flask. The highlight of the Soxhlet apparatus extraction system is that at rather many batches of warm solvent being passed through the sample; the one batch of solvent is recycled. After completing the extraction, the solvent is ejected to yield extracted compound by using an apparatus rotary evaporator. The undissolved proportion of the extracted material will remain in the thimble which is usually discarded.

The aqueous extraction is with cold maceration process in which the finely powdered plant material is kept in a stoppered container with the solvent and assigned to stand at normal room temperature for 3 days with frequent agitation to dissolve the soluble matter. The mixture then is strained, the marc (the damp solid material) is pressed, and the combined liquids are settled down by filtration or decantation after standing.

4.2.3 Procurement of Microorganisms

The microorganisms which are used in this research were procured from the Microbial Type Culture Collection and Genebank (MTCC), Chandigarh. The antifungal activity was screened in clinically significant dermatophytes and the *Candida albicans* (MTCC code: 3017) species. The three dermatophytes used for screening are *Trichophyton rubrum* (MTCC code: 7859), *Microsporum gypseum* (MTCC code: 4524), and *Epidermophyton floccosum* (MTCC code: 7880).

4.3 Determination of Antifungal Activity

4.3.1 Disc Diffusion Method

The standard assay used for anti-microbial tests is being carried out by Disc Diffusion Method by using 100 μl of a suspension containing 104 spores per ml of fungi spread on Sabouraud Dextrose Agar (SDA). The discs of 6 mm in diameter of Whatman filter paper was taken and impregnated in the Petri dish with a capacity of 15-18 μl where the SDA was poured and subjected it to cool.

The 10 μl of the sample extract (1 mg per ml) was taken with the help of micropipette and placed over the SDA inoculated Petri dish plate. The 5% Dimethyl Sulfoxide (DMSO) was taken as vehicle control and 2% Clotrimazole (1mg per ml) as a positive control. Different concentrations of the extract are taken and placed in the different places of the Petri dish plates. The inoculated Petri dishes are incubated at 37°C for 72 hours. The antifungal activity was screened by considering the ZOI that means by measuring the area where the extracts inhibit the growth of organisms; thus the experiment was repeated with all the four organisms, i.e., Trichophyton spp., Microsporum spp., Epidermophyton spp., Candida spp. separately, the ZOI was evaluated with the help of digital dial caliper.

After a 72 hour incubation period, the ZOI was noted down, and the same experiment was repeated for another five times. The mean value was obtained with an average of 6 values, and it was subjected to statistics. Table 1 shows the average value of results obtained as a ZOI of various extracts in various concentrations for plant *A.indica*. Table 2 shows the average value of results obtained for *L. inermis* in various concentrations with various extracts. Table 3 shows the average value of results obtained for *S. robusta* in various concentrations with various extracts.

4.3.2 Principle

The disc diffusion technique is a method which does not demand homogenous dispersion of solids in water. It is an agar-overlay method using a disc, hole or cylinder kept as a reservoir which should contain the sample that to be tested is exposed to contact with the inoculated medium for incubation of 72 hours. After incubation, the diameter of the apparent growth inhibition area appeared around the reservoir (inhibition diameter) implies as inhibition of growth which is to be measured. This method was developed to monitor the amount of bacterial or fungal organism growth inhibition with crude extracts. To get the best results, the inoculated system should be preserved at low temperature before incubation, which enhances diffusion through the culture medium and this exhibits an increase in the inhibition diameter. This technique can also be used for obtaining biograms. The disc diffusion method was the most often employed in research because of the absence of a relation between the diffusion power and anti-microbial activity. The essential feature of this method is keeping the filter paper or Whatman paper with the antimicrobial agent on the surface of agar instantaneously after inoculation with the microorganism tested. Direct application of discs to plates seeded with the clinical material is not recommended because of errors with inoculum, control and mixed cultures. A great scientist Bauer et al. initially standardized this disc diffusion method technique in 1966 (213) and by Ericson and Sherris in 1971 (214).

4.4 Minimum Inhibitory Concentration (MIC)

The MIC was performed by the Resazurin Microtitre Indicator method. Resazurin chemically is 7-hydroxy-3H-Phenoxazin-3-one 10-oxide, and it is usually in blue, and it is an indicator dye to impose the oxidation-reduction reactions in viable cells. The chemical formula of Resazurin is $C_{12}H_7NO_4$ and is irreversibly reduced to pink colour which is the metabolite Resorfurin, the reduced form of Resazurin. The resazurin is commercially available as Resazurin sodium salt. This dye itself is a weak fluorescent (215). The solution made with distilled water has highest values that estimated as Kreft's dichromaticity index (216) which means by increasing or decreasing the concentration of the sample, the Resazurin solution has substantial changes in perceived color. Resazurin was initially used to quantify the bacterial contamination present in milk by Pesch and Simmert in 1929 (217) and also observed as an indicator to know the cell viability in mammalian cell cultures (218). The irreversible reaction of Resazurin to Resorfurin is based on the proportionality to the aerobic reaction (219). Resazurin is manufactured by a method called acid-catalyzed condensation between the compounds resorcinol and 4-nitrosorcinol followed by oxidation of the intermediate product with manganese oxide. This crude product when treated with an excess amount of sodium carbonate yields Resazurin sodium.

4.4.1 Principle

The Resazurin within the cell undergoes a reduction in mitochondria with the help of nicotinamide adenine dehydrogenase, flavin adenine dinucleotide dehydrogenase, flavin mononucleotide dehydrogenase, and cytochromes. The cytosolic and microsomal enzymes can reduce Resazurin. Moreover, the extent of mitochondrial reduction is similar to cytosolic reduction by NADPH: Quinine oxidoreductase, flavin reductase, and cytochromes. The red Resorfurin is excreted from the cells to the medium which results in an apparentcolour change from blue to pink. The rate of reduction is based on color change which is quantified colorimetrically or fluorometrically which reflects the number of viable cells. This Resazurin is very sensitive and depends on cell type and the incubation time is linear with a range of 50-5000 cells in 96 well plate. The maximum absorbance for Resazurin/Resorfurin is 605/573 nm, whereas the maximum peak of excitation/emission spectrum for Resorfurin is 579/584 nm.

4.4.2 Resazurin assay

4.4.2.1 Optimizing the experimental parameters is the first step earlier to start the assay like setting the incubation period, a number of cells, quantity of dye to be used which is a crucial and unique step where the resazurin is reduced to Resorfurin. The incubation time is pre-determined as 4 hours, and 10 percent solution is standard for 1,000 – 1,00,000 cells per well. It is better to perform the screening in different cell densities with a minimum of three concentrations of resazurin with different incubation times. Incubating cells for too long period results in false positive by the formation of a non-fluorescent colorlesshydroresorfin secondary reduction of pink colored fluorescent product.

4.4.2.2 By naturally, the Resazurin can be reduced by natural anti-oxidants like vitamin C, Cysteine, Dithionate, Dithiothreitol. Different culture medium shows different incubation time. Selection of culture medium correlates with incubation time is a prerequisite step.

4.4.2.3 Depending on the manufacturer, Alamar Blue (Resazurin) can be stored at -20° C, 4°C or at room temperature. The stability can be more on storage at lower temperatures.

4.4.2.4 Both the resazurin and its product Resorfurin are photosensitive. These compounds can be stored in an amber coloured bottle to avoid false positive results which protect from light.

4.4.2.5 It is recommended to prepare the resazurin solution on the day of the experiment. In case it requires the storage the solution should be wrapped in an aluminum foil and store at 4°C to avoid degradation on exposure to sunlight during transportation.

4.4.2.6 The oxidation-reduction reactions can be temporarily ceased and stabilized for a day by incubating the dye by adding 50 μl of 3% Sabouraud Dextrose Agar (SDA) Solution in Phosphate Buffer Solution (PBS) per 100 ml at pH 7.4 which stacked away at ambient temperature wrapped in an aluminum foiled paper.

4.4.2.7 Resazurin is known as a non-toxic for a short-period exposure. On continuous impinge of cells with Resazurin may affect the reduction rate and viability of cells.

4.4.2.8 Directly adding Alamar blue dye in longtime experiments may result in false positive as the protein content of the cells quenches the fluorescent dye. A freshly prepared solution in required concentration and aliquoting into different concentrations is recommended for every time which should be washed with the PBS solution before starting the experiment.

4.5 Results

4.5.1 Antifungal Activity of Plant extracts by Disc Diffusion Method

The antifungal activity of different extracts of *A. indica* tested by disc diffusion method in which Dimethyl Sulfoxide (DMSO) considered as vehicle control and Clotrimazole as standard.

The various extracts of *A. indica* like hexane, benzene, ethyl acetate, methanol, and aqueous in a concentration of 50 mcg, 100 mcg, 250 mcg,

500 mcg are observed on three dermatophytes and Candida spp. for six times, the average with standard deviation was presented in table 1 which was observed as significant in inhibition of growth and is statistically significant.

The aqueous extract of *A. indica* shown a maximum ZOI for Trichophyton spp. as 7.10 mm at 50 mcg per ml, 7.80 mm at 100 mcg per ml, 8 mm at 250 mcg per ml, 8.15 mm at 500 mcg per ml, Microsporum spp. as 7.12 mm at 50 mcg per ml, 8.76 mm at 100 mcg per ml, 9.34 mm at 250 mcg per ml, 10.69 mm at 500 mcg per ml, Epidermophyton spp. as 6.30 mm at 50 mcg per ml, 7.58 mm at 100 mcg per ml, 7.79 mm at 250 mcg per ml, 7.95 mm at 500 mcg per ml and Candida spp. is 7.08 mm at 50 mcg per ml, 7.43 mm at 100 mcg per ml, 11.58 mm at 250 mcg per ml, 12.24 mm at 500 mcg per ml but the hexane extract is 13.15 mm ZOI at 500 mcg per ml against Trichophyton spp. The vehicle control, DMSO did not show any inhibition in any of the organism tested. The Clotrimazole was 19.30 mm against Trichophyton spp., 20.15 mm against Microsporum spp., 21.58 mm against Epidermophyton spp., 19.99 mm against Candida spp. The values obtained from six repeated times of the same experiment was subjected to statistical analysis with SPSS version 20 software for ANOVA and Wilks Lambda P value which is highly significant at $P<0.001$.

The antifungal activity of different extracts of *L.inermis* tested by disc diffusion method in which DMSO considered as vehicle control and Clotrimazole was standard.

The various extracts of *L. inermis* like hexane, benzene, ethyl acetate, methanol, and aqueous in a concentration of 50 mcg, 100 mcg, 250 mcg, 500 mcg are observed on three dermatophytes and Candida spp. for six times, the average with standard deviation was presented in table 2 which was observed as significant in inhibition of growth and is statistically significant.

The aqueous extract of *L. inermis* shown as a maximum ZOI in Trichophyton spp. 6.06 mm at 50 mcg per ml, 7.60 mm at 100 mcg per ml, 8.12 mm at 250 mcg per ml, 10.04 mm at 500 mcg per ml, Microsporum spp. as 6.44 mm at 50 mcg per ml, 7.16 mm at 100 mcg per ml, 8.42 mm at 250 mcg per ml, 10.28 mm at 500 mcg per ml, Epidermophyton spp., 6.56 mm at 50 mcg per ml, 6.86 mm at 100 mcg per ml, 8.31 mm at 250 mcg per ml, 10.49 mm at 500 mcg per ml and Candida spp. 8.67 mm at 50 mcg per ml, 9.40 mm at 100 mcg per ml, 10.80 mm at 250 mcg per ml, 11.25 mm at 500 mcg per ml but the benzene extract was 10.65 mm ZOI at 500 mcg per ml against Microsporum spp. The vehicle control, DMSO does not show any inhibition in any organism. The Clotrimazole as 19.30 mm against Trichophyton spp., 20.15 mm against Microsporum spp., 21.58 mm against Epidermophyton spp., 19.99 mm against Candida spp. The values obtained from six repeated times of the same experiment was subjected to statistical analysis with SPSS version 20 software for ANOVA and Wilks Lambda P value which is highly significant at $P<0.001$.

The antifungal activity of different extracts of *S.robusta* tested by disc diffusion method in which DMSO considered as vehicle control and Clotrimazole was standard.

The various extracts of *S. robusta* like hexane, benzene, ethyl acetate, methanol, and aqueous in a concentration of 50 mcg, 100 mcg, 250 mcg, 500 mcg are observed on three dermatophytes and Candida spp. for six times, the average with standard deviation was presented in table 3 which was observed as significant in inhibition of growth and is statistically significant.

The antifungal activity *S. robusta* is not established with any extract due to the absence of a zone of inhibition. However, the aqueous extract was shown activity against Candida spp. as 6.03 mm in 50 mcg per ml, 6.22 mm in 100 mcg per ml, 6.30 mm in 250 mcg per ml, 6.55 mm in 500 mcg per ml. The antifungal activity is not observed with castor oil, sesame oil as the ZOI was not detected in any of the dermatophytes as well as Candida spp.

All extracts of *A.indica* and *L. inermis* were observed as having significant antifungal activity but the aqueous extract showed the maximum zone of inhibition.

4.5.2 Synergistic activity

The synergistic activity was observed by combining the aqueous extract of *A.indica* and aqueous extract of *L. inermis* with 1:1 ratio against dermatophytes and Candida spp. in 10 mcg, 20 mcg, 50 mcg, 100 mcg, 250 mcg, 500 mcg concentrations tested for Zone of Inhibition (ZOI) which, the average with standard deviation of six-time repeated values were presented in table 4, the convincing values obtained as 10 mcg per ml as 8.3 mm zone of inhibition; 20 mcg per ml as 14.13 mm; 50 mcg per ml as 17.01 mm; 100 mcg per ml as 20.82 mm; 250 mcg per ml as 11.73 mm; 500 mcg per ml as 13.87 mm against Trichophyton spp. In Microsporum spp., the mean as 7.95 mm at 10 mcg per ml; 8.83 mm at 20 mcg per ml; 10.12 mm at 50 mcg per ml; 11.41 mm at 100 mcg per ml; 11.52 mm at 250 mcg per ml; 13.44 mm at 500 mcg per ml. For Epidermophyton spp., the average ZOI is 8.04 mm at 10 mcg per ml; 10.32 mm at 20 mcg per ml; 12.49 mm at 50 mcg per ml; 13.99 mm at 100 mcg per ml; 12.77 mm at 250 mcg per ml; 14.64 mm at 500 mcg per ml. and against Candida spp., the mean value as 8.01 mm at 10 mcg per ml; 8.62 mm at 20 mcg per ml; 8.93 mm at 50 mcg per ml; 11.06 mm at 100 mcg per ml; 12.76 mm at 250 mcg per ml; 14.04 mm at 500 mcg per ml. The values which shown above are the six repeated times of the same experiment and was subjected to statistical analysis with SPSS version 20 software for ANOVA and Wilks Lambda P value which is highly significant at $P<0.001$.

The synergism of aqueous extract of *A. indica*, aqueous extract of *L. inermis*, an aqueous extract of *S. robusta* in a 1:1:1 ratio against dermatophytes and Candida spp. in 10 mcg, 20 mcg, 50 mcg, 100 mcg, 250 mcg, 500 mcg concentrations which was presented in table 5. The average with standard deviation of the six experimental values against dermatophytes and Candida spp. was 10 mcg per ml as 7.17 mm zone of inhibition; 20 mcg per ml as 8.08 mm; 50 mcg per ml as 9.54 mm; 100 mcg per ml as 10.57 mm; 250 mcg per ml as 13.95 mm; 500 mcg per ml as 15.85 mm against Trichophyton spp. In Microsporum spp., the mean values are 7.44 mm at 10 mcg per ml; 8.85 mm at 20 mcg per ml; 10.82 mm at 50 mcg per ml; 12.79 mm at 100 mcg per ml; 12.05 mm at 250 mcg per ml; 13.80 mm at 500 mcg per ml. For Epidermophyton spp., the average ZOI is 6.81 mm at 10 mcg per ml; 7.34 mm at 20 mcg per ml; 9.94 mm at 50 mcg per ml; 10.65 mm at 100 mcg per ml; 15.05 mm at 250 mcg per ml; 16.25 mm at 500 mcg per ml. and against Candida spp. 6.91 mm at 10 mcg per ml; 8.09 mm at 20 mcg per ml; 11.02 mm at 50 mcg per ml; 13.67 mm at 100 mcg per ml; 13.14 mm at 250 mcg per ml; 13.62 mm at 500 mcg per ml. The values obtained from six repeated times of the same experiment was subjected to statistical analysis with SPSS version 20 software for ANOVA and Wilks Lambda P value which is highly significant at $P<0.001$.

In regards to synergistic activity the combination of aqueous extract of *A.indica* and *L. inermis* in 1:1 concentration was observed as having maximum zone of inhibition than 1:1:1 ratio of *A.indica*, *L. inermis*, and *S.robusta*.

4.5.3 Determination of Minimum Inhibitory Concentration (MIC)

The MIC of various extracts of *A. indica* against dermatophytes and Candida spp. was presented in table 6 which showed that the aqueous extract of neem leaves required the minimum concentration of 125 mcg per ml against Trichophyton spp. and Microsporum spp., 250 mcg per ml against Epidermophyton spp. and 62.5 mcg per ml against Candida spp. to inhibit their growth.

The MIC of various extracts of *L. inermis* against dermatophytes and Candida spp. presented in table 6 which showed that the aqueous extract of henna leaves required the minimum concentration of 125 mcg per ml against Trichophyton spp., Microsporum spp., Epidermophyton spp. and Candida spp.

The MIC of various extracts of *S. robusta* against dermatophytes and Candida spp. presented in table 6 which showed as all the extracts require above 500 mcg per ml of concentration to inhibit the growth against Trichophyton spp., Microsporum spp., Epidermophyton spp. and Candida spp. however, 250 mcg per ml for Hexane extract and Ethyl acetate extract against Trichophyton spp., 250 mcg per ml for benzene extract against

Epidermophyton spp., and 125 mcg per ml of Hexane extract against Candida spp. to inhibit their growth.

Regarding minimum inhibitory concentration (MIC) it was observed that the aqueous extract of *A. indica* and aqueous extract of *L. inermis* showed significant minimum concentration required to inhibit the growth of fungal organism.

Table 1: The effect of various extracts of *A. indica* on different organisms in different concentrations.

EXTRACT	ORGANISM	ZONE OF INHIBITION(mm)					
		50 mcg/ml	100 mcg/ml	250 mcg/ml	500 mcg/ml	Vehicle Control mcg/ml	Std mcg/ml
HEAI	Trichophyton spp.	6.93±0.01	7.28±0.05	10.28±0.04	13.14±0.01	0.00	19.30±0.02
	Microsporum spp.	6.34±0.04	6.73±0.01	6.99±0.01	7.93±0.01	0.00	20.15±0.01
	Epidermophyton spp.	6.90±0.04	7.48±0.01	8.29±0.02	8.44±0.01	0.00	21.58±0.01
	Candida spp.	0.00	0.00	0.00	0.00	0.00	19.99±0.02
BEAI	Trichophyton spp.	6.46±0.01	7.64±0.02	7.48±0.01	10.68±0.00	0.00	19.30±0.02
	Microsporum spp.	6.19±0.01	7.37±0.02	7.70±0.01	10.54±0.02	0.00	20.15±0.01
	Epidermophyton spp.	6.35±0.01	6.54±0.02	7.08±0.06	6.66±0.01	0.00	21.58±0.01
	Candida spp.	0.00	6.53±0.03	6.74±0.01	7.77±0.01	0.00	19.99±0.02
EAEAI	Trichophyton spp.	6.06±0.01	6.55±0.02	6.87±0.01	8.32±0.01	0.00	19.30±0.02
	Microsporum spp.	6.26±0.02	7.53±0.04	7.94±0.01	8.42±0.01	0.00	20.15±0.01
	Epidermophyton spp.	6.55±0.05	7.86±0.04	8.13±0.03	7.42±0.03	0.00	21.58±0.01
	Candida spp.	0.00	0.00	7.24±0.01	9.65±0.02	0.00	19.99±0.02
MEAI	Trichophyton spp.	6.52±0.01	7.46±0.02	8.13±0.12	8.43±0.01	0.00	19.30±0.02
	Microsporum spp.	6.53±0.02	8.93±0.02	9.97±0.01	10.30±0.06	0.00	20.15±0.01
	Epidermophyton spp.	6.06±0.02	6.84±0.02	7.23±0.02	7.42±0.02	0.00	21.58±0.01
	Candida spp.	0.00	6.82±0.01	7.41±0.01	8.16±0.02	0.00	19.99±0.02
AQEAI	Trichophyton spp.	7.13±0.02	7.80±0.01	8.03±0.03	8.14±0.01	0.00	19.30±0.02
	Microsporum spp.	5.93±0.01	8.74±0.02	9.34±0.01	10.69±0.02	0.00	20.15±0.01
	Epidermophyton spp.	6.33±0.05	7.57±0.02	7.83±0.09	7.95±0.02	0.00	21.58±0.01
	Candida spp.	7.07±0.01	7.42±0.01	11.57±0.02	12.23±0.02	0.00	19.99±0.02

Table 2: The effect of various extracts of *L. inermis* on different organisms in different concentrations

EXTRACT	ORGANISM	ZONE OF INHIBITION(mm)					
		50 mcg/ml	100 mcg/ml	250 mcg/ml	500 mcg/ml	Vehicle Control mcg/ml	Std mcg/ml
HELI	Trichophyton spp.	6.06±0.01	6.92±0.02	7.70±0.01	10.57±0.03	0.00	19.30±0.02
	Microsporum spp.	6.24±0.02	6.24±0.02	6.71±0.01	7.46±0.02	0.00	20.15±0.01
	Epidermophyton spp.	6.11±0.01	6.25±0.01	6.95±0.02	8.70±0.01	0.00	21.58±0.01
	Candida spp.	0.00	6.06±0.01	6.15±0.01	6.35±0.02	0.00	19.99±0.02
BELI	Trichophyton spp.	6.28±0.01	6.32±0.01	6.39±0.03	6.57±0.01	0.00	19.30±0.02
	Microsporum spp.	6.18±0.02	6.35±0.02	8.69±0.04	10.66±0.02	0.00	20.15±0.01
	Epidermophyton spp.	6.31±0.01	6.52±0.01	6.93±0.00	6.96±0.01	0.00	21.58±0.01
	Candida spp.	0.00	6.32±0.01	6.61±0.05	7.60±0.02	0.00	19.99±0.02
EAELI	Trichophyton spp.	6.32±0.02	6.47±0.01	6.52±0.01	6.72±0.01	0.00	19.30±0.02
	Microsporum spp.	6.12±0.01	6.67±0.01	8.27±0.01	10.30±0.01	0.00	20.15±0.01
	Epidermophyton spp.	6.24±0.01	6.43±0.01	6.60±0.15	6.86±0.02	0.00	21.58±0.01
	Candida spp.	6.18±0.01	6.37±0.01	6.85±0.01	7.13±0.01	0.00	19.99±0.02
MELI	Trichophyton spp.	6.22±0.01	6.33±0.01	6.42±0.01	6.83±0.01	0.00	19.30±0.02
	Microsporum spp.	6.22±0.01	6.55±0.01	7.75±0.40	9.11±1.22	0.00	20.15±0.01
	Epidermophyton spp.	6.26±0.01	6.31±0.01	6.61±0.01	6.89±0.11	0.00	21.58±0.01
	Candida spp.	0.00	6.46±0.01	7.02±0.01	7.42±0.01	0.00	19.99±0.02
AQELI	Trichophyton spp.	6.06±0.01	7.60±0.01	8.13±0.01	10.04±0.03	0.00	19.30±0.02
	Microsporum spp.	6.44±0.02	7.16±0.01	8.43±0.01	10.38±0.21	0.00	20.15±0.01
	Epidermophyton spp.	6.57±0.01	6.85±0.02	8.32±0.01	10.47±0.01	0.00	21.58±0.01
	Candida spp.	8.67±0.01	9.41±0.01	10.81±0.01	11.25±1.06	0.00	19.99±0.02

Table 3: The effect of various extracts of *S. robusta* on different organisms in different concentrations

EXTRACT	ORGANISM	ZONE OF INHIBITION(mm)					
		50 mcg/ml	100 mcg/ml	250 mcg/ml	500 mcg/ml	Vehicle Control mcg/ml	Std mcg/ml
HESR	Trichophyton spp.	0.00	0.00	0.00	0.00	0.00	19.30±0.02
	Microsporum spp.	0.00	0.00	0.00	0.00	0.00	20.15±0.01
	Epidermophyton spp.	0.00	0.00	0.00	0.00	0.00	21.58±0.01
	Candida spp.	6.58±0.01	8.06±0.01	10.16±0.02	10.75±0.01	0.00	19.99±0.02
BESR	Trichophyton spp.	0.00	0.00	0.00	0.00	0.00	19.30±0.02
	Microsporum spp.	0.00	0.00	0.00	0.00	0.00	20.15±0.01
	Epidermophyton spp.	0.00	0.00	0.00	0.00	0.00	21.58±0.01
	Candida spp.	0.00	6.60±0.01	7.62±0.01	10.04±0.01	0.00	19.99±0.02
EAESR	Trichophyton spp.	0.00	0.00	0.00	0.00	0.00	19.30±0.02
	Microsporum spp.	0.00	0.00	0.00	0.00	0.00	20.15±0.01
	Epidermophyton spp.	0.00	0.00	0.00	0.00	0.00	21.58±0.01
	Candida spp.	6.26±0.01	6.57±0.01	7.94±0.01	7.16±0.01	0.00	19.99±0.02
MESR	Trichophyton spp.	0.00	0.00	0.00	0.00	0.00	19.30±0.02
	Microsporum spp.	0.00	0.00	0.00	0.00	0.00	20.15±0.01
	Epidermophyton spp.	0.00	0.00	0.00	0.00	0.00	21.58±0.01
	Candida spp.	0.00	6.77±0.01	7.30±0.01	8.61±0.02	0.00	19.99±0.02
AQESR	Trichophyton spp.	0.00	0.00	0.00	0.00	0.00	19.30±0.02
	Microsporum spp.	0.00	0.00	0.00	0.00	0.00	20.15±0.01
	Epidermophyton spp.	0.00	0.00	0.00	0.00	0.00	21.58±0.01
	Candida spp.	6.04±0.01	6.25±0.01	6.30±0.01	6.54±0.01	0.00	19.99±0.02

Table 4: **The effect of aqueous extract of *A. indica* + aqueous extract of *L. inermis* on different organisms in different concentrations**

EXTRACT	ORGANISM	ZONE OF INHIBITION(mm)							
		10 mcg/ml	20 mcg/ml	50 mcg/ml	100 mcg/ml	250 mcg/ml	500 mcg/ml	Vehicle Control mcg/ml	Std mcg/ml
AQEAI + AQELI	Trichophyton spp.	8.23±0.02	14.13±0.02	17.01±0.01	20.82±0.02	11.73±0.02	13.87±0.03	0.00	19.30±0.02
	Microsporum spp.	7.95±0.05	8.83±0.03	10.12±0.01	11.41±0.03	11.52±0.02	13.44±0.04	0.00	20.15±0.01
	Epidermophyton spp.	8.04±0.02	10.32±0.02	12.49±0.02	13.99±0.02	12.77±0.04	14.64±0.06	0.00	21.58±0.01
	Candida spp.	8.01±0.02	8.62±0.19	8.93±0.08	11.06±0.01	12.76±0.03	14.04±0.02	0.00	19.99±0.02

Table 5: **The effect of aqueous extract of *A. indica* + aqueous extract of *L. inermis* + aqueous extract of *S. robusta* on different organisms in different concentrations.**

EXTRACT	ORGANISM	ZONE OF INHIBITION(mm)							
		10 mcg/ml	20 mcg/ml	50 mcg/ml	100 mcg/ml	250 mcg/ml	500 mcg/ml	Vehicle Control mcg/ml	Std mcg/ml
AQEAI + AQELA + AQESR	Trichophyton spp.	7.17±0.05	8.08±0.04	9.54±0.03	10.57±0.04	13.95±0.04	15.85±0.03	0.00	19.30±0.02
	Microsporum spp.	7.44±0.02	8.85±0.02	10.82±0.03	12.79±0.24	12.05±0.03	13.80±0.04	0.00	20.15±0.01
	Epidermophyton spp.	6.81±0.04	7.34±0.04	9.94±0.03	10.65±0.03	15.05±0.02	16.25±0.04	0.00	21.58±0.01
	Candida spp.	6.91±0.02	8.09±0.06	11.02±0.02	13.67±0.04	13.14±0.02	13.62±0.02	0.00	19.99±0.02

Table 6: The average values of Minimum Inhibitory Concentration (MIC) of various extracts on different organisms

EXTRACT	FUNGAL ORGANISM			
	Trichophyton spp. (mcg/ml)	Microsporum spp. (mcg/ml)	Epidermophyton spp. (mcg/ml)	Candida spp. (mcg/ml)
HEAI	500	500	500	250
BEAI	500	500	500	500
EAEAI	500	250	500	500
MEAI	500	500	500	500
AQEAI	125	125	250	62.5
HELI	250	500	500	250
BELI	250	500	500	500
EAELI	250	500	500	500
MELI	250	500	500	500
AQELAI	125	125	125	125
HESR	250	>500	>500	125
BESR	>500	>500	250	>500
EAESR	>500	>500	>500	>500
MESR	>500	>500	>500	>500
AQESR	>500	>500	>500	>500
Std	50	20	10	10

Abbreviations: HEAI – Hexane extract of *Azadirachta indica*, BEAI – Benzene extract of *Azadirachta indica,* EAEAI – Ethyl Acetate extract of *Azadirachta indica*, MEAI – Methanol extract of *Azadirachta indica*, AQEAI – Aqueous extract of *Azadirachta indica*, HELI – Hexane extract of *Lawsonia inermis*, BELI – Benzene extract of *Lawsonia inermis*, EAEAI – Ethyl Acetate extract of *Lawsonia inermis*, MEAI – Methanol extract of *Lawsonia inermis,* AQEAI – Aqueous extract of *Lawsonia inermis,* HESR – Hexane extract of *Shorea robusta,* BESR – Benzene extract of *Shorea robusta,* EAESR – Ethyl Acetate extract of *Shorea robusta,* MESR – Methanol extract of *Shorea robusta*, AQESR – Aqueous extract of *Shorea robusta,* Std – Standard.

4.6 Discussion

The Soleshine, a polyherbal preparation is a formulation of medicinal plants with *A. indica*, *L. inermis*, *S. robusta*, *S. indicum*, *R. communis* used for soothing the soles, cracks, etc. The two common plants, *A. indica*, *L. inermis*, are used as anti-microbial agents that are in use since centuries. The disc-diffusion method is used to evaluate the anti-fungal activity with sequential extracts with non-polar to polar solvents. The activity of extracts is tested against dermatophytes and Candida spp. The minimum concentration expected to inhibit the growth of an organism is evaluated by Resazurin assay method where the colour change infers the viability of cells.

The *A. indica*, an indigenous plant is well known for use in human ailments. According to Saradhajyothi, and Subbarao, the neem leaves have an excellent antifungal activity which confirms the presence of high potential of compounds by which it can be a rationale to include the essential drug list in primary health care (219). In a study, by Patil RC, Kulkarni CP, and Ashu Pandey, the petroleum ether extract exhibited a powerful fungal growth inhibitory action against *C. albicans* and *A.niger*, but with a moderate activity against *A. fumigatus*, *M. gypseum* and mild action against *T. rubrum* (221). According to Puvan Arul Arumugam, the aqueous extract of *A. indica* Malaysian leaves shows maximum activity against *A. niger*(222). In a study by Mahmoud et al, the ethanolic extract and ethyl acetate extract showed 20 % more suppression in the growth than the aqueous extract against Aspergillus spp., and Candida spp. (223). In this research it was observed as the aqueous extract of *A. indica* shows a potential anti-fungal activity on comparison with the standard drug, Clotrimazole. The other extracts tested also have the antifungal activity, but the maximum ZOI observed at 500 mcg per ml with the aqueous extract. The average minimum inhibitory concentration of aqueous extract of *A. indica* is 62.5 mcg per ml against Candida spp.; 125 mcg per ml against Trichophyton spp., and Microsporum spp.; 250 mcg per ml against Epidermophyton spp.

The *L. inermis* is commonly called as Henna which is used not only as decorative and fungicidal in the palm and sole common in a winter season. In another study by Fariba Berenji, the aqueous extract is more effective on Malassezia spp. affected on the skin and called as *Pityriasis versicolor* and folliculitis under certain conditions than the methanolic and chloroform extracts (224). In a study by Demet Yigit, the *L. inermis* extract was shown as 35.4 % highest, 38 % moderate and 26.5 % resistant activity in Candida isolates from patients. In research by N.C. Sowjanya, the aqueous extract of *Allium sativum*, *Ocimum sanctum, A. indica*, *L. inermis*, and *Murraya koenigii* in a 5% and 10% concentration shown the inhibition of growth of fungi in a day by day observation. Out of which *A. sativum* was maximum onthe third day itself (225). In this research it was observed as the aqueous extract of *L. inermis* shows the highest efficiency as the ZOI is more with a comparison of other organic extracts.

The MIC of aqueous extract of *L. inermis* was 125 mcg per ml of SDA broth solution while others are 500 mcg per ml. According to Kavitha Sagar, the minimum inhibitory concentration at 2,500 mcg per ml in methanol, alcohol, acetone, ethyl acetate, chloroform, petroleum ether extract was 58 %, 70 %, 55 %, 58 %, 85 %, 47 % respectively against *Trichophyton tonsurans* while 40 %, 50 %, 50 %, 60 %, 40 %, 85 % respectively against *Trichophyton mentagrophytes*, while 10 %, 0 %, 26%, 0 %, 10 %, 20 % respectively against *Trichophyton rubrum*, while 10 %,

30 %, 30 %, 60 %, 60 %, 20 % respectively against *Microsporum gypseum*, and 0 %, 26 %, 44 %, 50 %, 67 %, 50 % respectively against *Epidermophyton floccosum* (226). In a study by Neetu Jain, the Minimum Inhibitory Concentration (MIC) of *essential oil obtained from L. inermis* was ranging from 0.025 to 1.5 μl per ml against dermatophytes and other fungi. The MIC of the fractions studied which are ranging from 0.3 to <4 μl per ml. in which *T. rubrum* was found to be susceptible, and *C. albicans* was resistant(227).

In this research it was observed as the resin of *S. robusta* is not showing antifungal activity in dermatophytes in any concentration, but the hexane extract and aqueous extract of resin were observed activity against Candida spp. only. In a study by Wani TA, the ethanolic extract *S. robusta* of 10 % and 30 % w/w on local application demonstrated an acceleration of dose-dependent excised wound infections and increased hydroxyproline and tensile strength in albino rats after 12 days treatment (106). The aqueous extract, methanolic extract, petroleum ether extract and benzene extract of oleoresin of *S.robusta* observed inhibition while the aqueous extract exhibits substantial activity against *B.coagulans*, *E.coli*, *B.cereus* and moderate activity on *S. typhi* and *B.subtilis* and mild inhibition on *P.vulgaris* and *P.fluorescence*(117). In a study by Murthy and Wani, the bactericidal activity was observed on aqueous extract of floral parts of *S. robusta* on Gram-negative bacteria like *K. pneumonia* and *S.marcescens* and Gram-positive like *S.aureus*, *B.subtilis*, with penicillin (106,116,117).

In this study, it was observed as castor oil and sesame oil did not show any activity in any concentration against dermatophytes as well as Candida spp. In a study by Islam, petroleum ether and acetone extracts of castor bean seeds have excellent activity against dermatophytic and pathogenic bacteria like *S. progenies*, *S. aureus* and *K. pneumonia*, *E.coli* (228). The hexane and methanol extract of roots of castor oil at 200 mg per ml exhibit antimicrobial activity by well diffusion method against microorganisms like *E. coli, S. aureus, P. aeruginosa, S. typhi, P. vulgaris, B. subtilis, C. albicans*, and *A. niger*(229). In a study by Mohamed Saleem TS, the sesame oil observed as a best bactericidal with a ZOI of 15-25 mm which is almost near to standard antibiotic Kanamycin with 19-40 mm and also shown as a maximum ZOI against *Salmonella typhi* (230). According to Anand, the sesame oil was observed to have antibacterial activity against *S.mutans, L.acidophilus*(231). In a study by Fukuda, the antioxidants present in sesame oil have been found to enhance wound healing by preventing oxidative damage and promote the healing process(232,233). *S. indicum* seeds and oil both promote wound healing in experimental models on rats. The gel prepared from seeds or oil directly applied topically or peroral administration significantly accelerates the breaking strength, wound contraction and period of epithelialization of incision, excision, and burn wounded rodent models (234).

The synergistic activity observed in the combination of aqueous extract of *A. indica*, aqueous extract of *L. inermis* in 1:1 ratio of different strength was accelerated in a dose-dependently as it exhibits nearly 80 % equal to standard drug Clotrimazole. However, it was found that the combination of aqueous extract of *A. indica*, aqueous extract of *L. inermis* with aqueous extract of *S. robusta* in 1:1:1 ratio was little less than the combination of neem and henna. In a study by Kamal A Salih, the effect of Fresh Ginger Extract has effects on *C.albicans*, but black seeds do not have effects on Candida spp., synergism on a combination of both Black seeds with Fresh Ginger Extract, however, less effect than individual Fresh

Ginger Extract but more effect than Fluconazole (235). According to Kianoush Khosravi-Darani, the addition of Honey to Mint extract, Ginger extract, Zataria extract, and ginger starch increases antibacterial and anti-candidal properties of honey, which shows synergism(236).

4.7 Conclusion

Fungi are ubiquitous with many thousands of various fungal species on Earth; however, just 300 species of them are of clinical importance (237). Fungal diseases are often caused by a fungal organism that is present commonly in the global environment which lives outdoors in the soil and on the plants as well as trees and in indoor surfaces and on the skin of mammals. Many of the fungal species are not as deadly but sometimes may cause illness. Naturally obtaining trench of medicinally essential plants is in need as an alternative for the fungal ailments as these are distant to untoward effects to the host and the drug resistance is familiar with the currently available drugs. In the polyherbal preparation, *A. indica*, *L. inermis* has observed an excellent anti-fungal activity. The other ingredients present in the polyherbal formulation are helpful to avoid or eradicate the secondary infections as the *S. robusta*, castor oil, and sesame oil are not exhibiting activity in fungal organisms. It was also proven that the mixture of more than one ingredient in this formulation exhibits synergism. The antifungal activity of *A. indica* was observed in all the sequential extracts, but the aqueous extract was the maximum zone of inhibition. Moreover, also the antifungal activity of *L. inermis* exhibits in all the extracts of this study but the maximum ZOI was with the aqueous extract. The minimum concentration required to inhibit the growth of a fungal organism is observed with aqueous extract of *A. indica* and *L. inermis*.

The literature shows that the biological actions showed by the plants are because of the hidden secondary metabolites. The secondary metabolites are the real-time chemical compounds that are showing the antimicrobial activity. In the plant *A. indica*, the most common secondary metabolites assumed to be effective against fungi are azadirachtin, nimbin, nimonol from the literature show these have an anti-microbial effect. In *L. inermis*, the most common secondary metabolites are lawsone, lawsoniaside, scopoletin, and stigmasterol where these are creditworthy for their antifungal activity. These secondary metabolites are taken further to equip as a ligand for targeting some of the proteins as targets where they hamper the metabolic functions of the fungal organism in an *in-silico* study.

CHAPTER 5

ANTI-FUNGAL ACTIVITY OF THE SECONDARY METABOLITES OF *Azadirachta indica* AND *Lawsonia inermis* – AN *IN-SILICO* STUDY

5. ANTI-FUNGAL ACTIVITY OF THE SECONDARY METABOLITES OF *Azadirachta indica* AND *Lawsonia inermis* – AN *in-silico* STUDY

5.1 Aim and Objective

The aqueous extract of *A. indica* and *L. inermis* are present in polyherbal preparation exhibits a maximum zone of inhibition (ZOI) with disc diffusion method. The secondary metabolites which are common in these plants are taken further to know the target and modulate the target to hamper the metabolic functions of an organism with the following aim and objective.

1. To identify the secondary compounds from *A. indica* and *L. inermis* herbs for anti-fungal activity by molecular docking method.
2. To prepare the derivatives of the active principles by *in-silico* method and to find its antifungal activity by molecular docking method.

5.2 Materials and Methods

5.2.1 Preparation of protein by homology modelling

The 3D structure of a protein which is a drug target for *in-silico* drug discovery will be downloaded from the RCSB database, protein data bank. The Proteins where their 3D structures are not characterized or identified can be modeled by using homology modelling by using the structure of a protein which can be obtained by its amino acid sequence. The Homology modelling is also called as comparative modelling will be employed for those which the protein 3D is not available. Homology modelling is a computational approach for 3D protein structure modelling and prediction that means the 3D structure is fabricated by aligning a target protein sequence with known template structures. The modelled structure with above 40 % similarity with the template would be considered as a reliable target. If any of the sequences has its known structure, then the modelled structure can be superposed onto the unknown protein of a high degree of confidence.

Homology modelling is a multi-step procedure that involves six steps:

5.2.1.1Template selection

The template or sequence of similarity can be intensively searched by using BLAST and align with the known structures that obtained from Protein Data Bank (PDB) which is the most extensive database. BLAST allows scanning a query sequence with the available sequence from a database and identifying the best sequence with a high degree of identity. To get a good model, the aligned protein sequence should possess a minimum of 40 % sequence identity with high resolution and the aptest cofactors. The protein sequence which was obtained from PDB whose tertiary structure which is to predict can be called as the target sequence.

5.2.1.2 Sequence alignment

The sequence of similarity of each and every line is compiled with its E-value (Expected value) that is near closer to 0 is designed as a high degree of similarity. The E-value accounts the representation of hits one can "expect" when searching through a database of a particular size. The sequences which categorized under safe zone are supposed to be an excellent structure.

5.2.1.3 Backbone model building

Once the most favorable alignment of the template achieved, the corresponding coordinate residues from the template proteins can be copied onto the target proteins. When the two aligned residues are identical, coordinates of the side chain atoms are transcribed along with the preeminent chain atoms. If multiple templates selected, then the average coordinate values of the templates are taken into consideration. The backbone building from the aligned regions can be done using modelling tools such as Modeller.

5.2.1.4 Loop modelling

Whenever the sequence of the protein aligned, there are often regions generated by insertions and deletions leading to the establishment of gaps in the aligned sequence. These gaps are safe to shift the insertion and deletions of the alignment, out of helices or strands and placing them in loops or coils by loop modelling, which is less authentic which may cause an error. The two important main techniques are in use to avoid the problem which is Database searching method and energy based method. In the database searching method, the methodology of a searching database involves finding loops from known available protein structures and superposing them on the stem regions of the target protein which can be done by some specialized programmes like FREAD and CODA.

5.2.1.5 Side chain refinement

Whenever the core atoms are constructed by the previous step now the existence of side chains should be fixed. It is essential in appraising protein-ligand interactions at active sites and protein-protein interactions at the contact intersection. A side chain for the homology can be built by searching for every possible confirmation in torsion angle that has the lowest interaction energy with adjacent atoms in amino acid. A rotamer library is used in all the agreeable side-chain torsion angles derive from known protein crystal structures.

5.2.1.6 Model refinement and model evaluation

This step is essential to minimize energy on the entire model, which resolves the relative position of atoms so that the confirmation of the molecule has minimum possible energy potential. The main aim of energy minimization is to make the protein free of steric collisions by inhibiting the altering of the structure. In the above loop and side chain modelling steps, the energy calculations are applied to enhance the model. Refinement of modelled protein can be done by molecular dynamic stimulation which propels atoms by implementing various stimulation conditions like heating, cooling, considering water molecules, thus having fortuitous to find the very compatible structure. The final model is to be analyzed for psi-phi angles, chirality, bond lengths, close contactness and also the stereochemical properties. A successful model can depend upon the selection of the template and the validation of the model by Ramachandran plot. The homology model was obtained for all the proteins that are used like 1,3 beta-glucan synthase (238), Chitin synthase (239), Chitinase (240), Deuterolysin, Fungalysin, Glutamine fructose, Homoserine dehydrogenase (241), Lumazine synthase, Phosphoribosylaminoimidazole carboxylase (242), Protein elongation factor (243–245), Sulphite reductase (212)drug targets was chosen and validated with the Ramachandran plot for this homology modeled targets in the in-silico study.

Modeller is a procedure for comparative protein structure modelling by the achievement of spatial restraints which can be described as "Modeling by the satisfaction of restraints" uses a set of restriction obtained from the alignment, and the model is procured by deprecation of these restrictions.

5.3 Identification and Preparation of ligand for *In-silico* docking

The plants *A. indica* and *L. inermis* are with abundant and well known secondary metabolites that are useful for various ailments common in human beings. The azadirachtin, nimbin, and nimonol are the secondary metabolites which are of having antimicrobial properties selected from *A.indica* for the *in-silico* analysis. The lawsone, lawsoniaside, scopoletin, stigmasterol are the secondary metabolites known for its antimicrobial activity present in *L. inermis* are also selected. The .sdf file of these secondary metabolites was obtained from the PubChem database which is the prerequisite step for docking with the target. The .sdf file obtained from PubChem compound database is converted into a .pdb format with an online web tool OPENBABEL as this is the only acceptable format for docking.

5.4 Protein-ligand interaction

Docking is defined as that which anticipates the elected orientation of one compound to another compound when they are constrained to each other to form a stable complex. Molecular docking can be referred to as a "lock and key" model. The protein that targeted appears as a lock and the small molecule as a key which depicts the best-fit acclimatization between the ligand to a particular protein. The selected secondary metabolites are the ligands that are subjected for quick docking with web tool iGEMDOCK software (version 2.0) which is set a default for docking accuracy settings as 150 population size and 70 generations. AutoDock Vina (246) is a docking online tool, which is used to anticipate the performance of ligands and aids to accomplish the docking of small molecules to a set of grids which depicts the target, once docking accomplishes the result can apprehend in the 3D view. It is usually displayed in a hierarchically based on the binding affinity.

5.5 Lead-likeliness properties

A small molecule pharmacologically calling as a ligand is an organic compound which has a low molecular weight that may act as a substrate or inhibitor. Any new compound that is called as a lead compound or Hit molecule which acts as a future therapeutic agent should possess certain properties like physicochemical characteristics, medicinal properties, and drug-likeness which can be attained by another online web tool SwissADME for all the selected ligands obtained from *A. indica* and *L. inermis*. Lipinski's rule (247,248) also called the rule of five (RO5) is helpful for evaluation of the drug-likeness or to reap up to a chemical compound with a specific pharmacological or physiological activities which show the properties that may be active in enteral or parenteral administration.

5.6 Structure Activity Relativity

The selected ligands from *A. indica* and *L. inermis* are submitted for the derivatives with the aid of SwissADME, online web tool. The derivatives which are called as structure active relative agents that are well designed for their diversity in the spectrum of the pharmacological actions of the compound.

5.7 Toxicity

The toxicity contour of the chosen ligand was noticed with admetSAR, a free online web server. This software provides the possible toxicity incurred with the compounds with the values suggesting the safety for host or not. The various parameters like acute oral toxicity, acute rat toxicity, fish toxicity, honey bee toxicity, AMES toxicity, Human ether-a-go-go-related gene inhibition (HERG), carcinogenicity, tetra hymenapyriformis toxicity, biodegradation, and will be assessed to find out the toxicity.

5. 8 Results

5.8.1 Homology modelling

The proteins selected as drug targets for the *in-silico* study are checked for their 3D structure in RCSB – protein data bank, but the proteins' 3D structure is not available. Homology modelling is the alternative method to generate the 3D structure by Easy Modellar and which was validated by the Ramachandran plot. For the homology modelling, the prerequisite is the primary structure which was obtained from the UniProtKB database in a FASTA sequence, and the template for the protein was collected from the Protein Data Bank (PDB) database. The various proteins selected for the study are 1, 3-Beta glucan synthase (Uniprot accession no: P38631), Chitin synthase (Uniprot accession no: P29465), Chitinase (Uniprot accession no: P40954), Deuterolysin (Uniprot accession no: COIPP1), Fungalysin (Uniprot accession no: Q8NIB6), Homoserine dehydrogenase (Uniprot accession no: P31116), Lumazine synthase (Uniprot accession no: P50861), Phosphoribosylaminoimidazole carboxylase (Uniprot accession no: P27616), Protein elongation factor 3

(Uniprot accession no: P16521), Sulphite reductase (Uniprot accession no: Q59109). The templates used for generating homology model for the proteins 1,3-Beta glucan synthase (template RCSB accession code: FKS1), Chitin synthase (template RCSB accession code: 4WJW), Chitinase (template RCSB accession code: 4TX6), Deuterolysin (template RCSB accession code: 1EB6), Fungalysin (template RCSB accession code: 4K90), Homoserine dehydrogenase (template RCSB accession code: 1TVE), Lumazine synthase (template RCSB accession code: 1EJB), Phosphoribosylaminoimidazole carboxylase (template RCSB accession code: 2CNQ), Protein elongation factor 3 (template RCSB accession code: 6CNF), Sulphite reductase (template RCSB accession code: 3OR2). The homology modeling was performed with the help of software called MODELLER version: 9.0 using EasyModeller as the graphical user interface. The query sequence obtained from the UniProtKB database and the template obtained from the PDB database of the selected proteins are submitted and processed to generate the 3D structures. The obtained 3D structures of the chosen protein are validated before proceeding for further step.

5.8.2 Validation of drug targets

The generated 3D structures from the homology modeling are validated with the help of Ramachandran plot which was presented from figure 7 to figure 16 for each drug target. The Ramachandran plot depicts that in the selected proteins, the amino acids are clustered tightly in the most-favoured regions with very few outliers. The Ramachandran plot (249) is a way to anticipate the dihedral angles, namely ψ (psi) and φ (phi), of a protein backbone (250). It depicts the given protein is devoid of steric hindrances that occur between adjacent atoms of amino acids within the protein structure, ψ (psi) and φ (phi) values are usually restricted within the specific areas of the plot to form helices and sheets for ordered structure.

The values obtained from Ramachandran plot, Procheck server which analyze the stereo chemical trait of a protein structure for the proteins like 1,3-Beta-glucan synthase protein structure contained 87.5% amino acid residues in the favoured region, 6.9% in the allowed region, and 5.6% in the disallowed region; for chitin synthase the values are 88.8 % favoured region, 7.6 % in allowed region, and 3.6 % in disallowed region; for chitinase, the favoured, allowed, and disallowed regions are 91.6%, 6.1%, and 2.3%, respectively. In the case of deuterolysin it shows as 92.0 % in favored region, 6.4 % in allowed region, and 5 % in disallowed region; for fungalysin was 96.9% favoured, 2.3% allowed, and 0.8% disallowed; for homoserine dehydrogenase as 93.1 % favoured region, 5.4 % in allowed region, and 1.5 % in disallowed region; for lumazine synthase as 93.8% favoured, 3.6% allowed, and 2.6% disallowed; for Phosphoribosylaminoimidazole carboxylase as 98.2 % favoured region, 1.7 % in allowed region, and 0.1 % in disallowed region; protein elongation factor exhibits as 95.3 % favoured region, 3.9 % in allowed region, and 0.8 % in disallowed region; and sulphite reductase as 93.3 % favoured region, 5.3 % in allowed region, and 1.4 % in disallowed region.

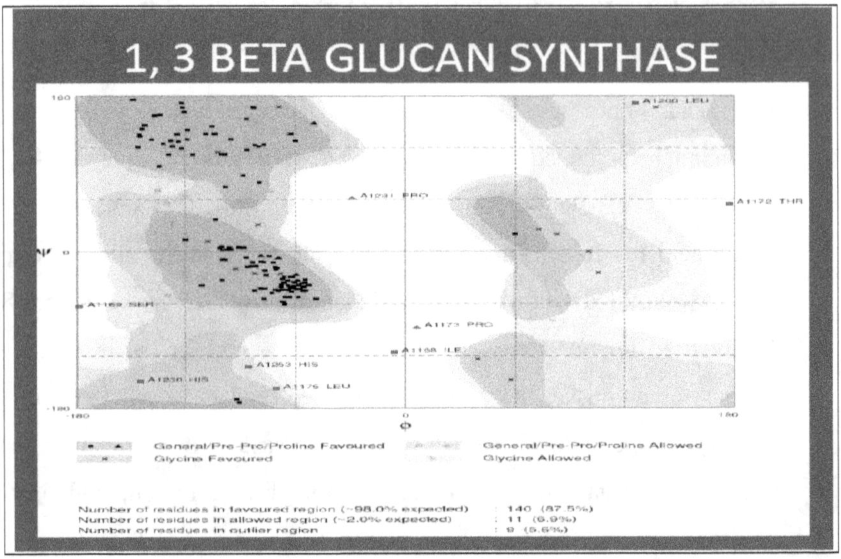

Figure 7: The Ramachandran Plot showing for the targeted protein – 1, 3 Beta Glucan Synthase

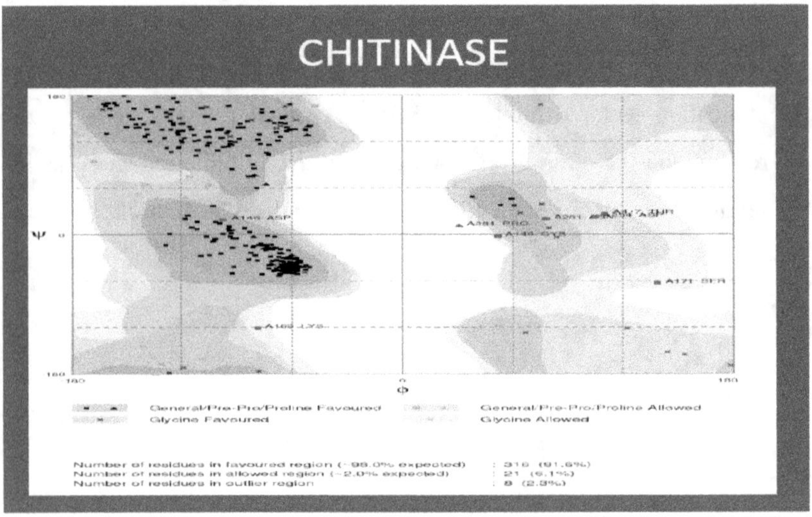

Figure 8: The Ramachandran Plot showing for the targeted protein – Chitinase

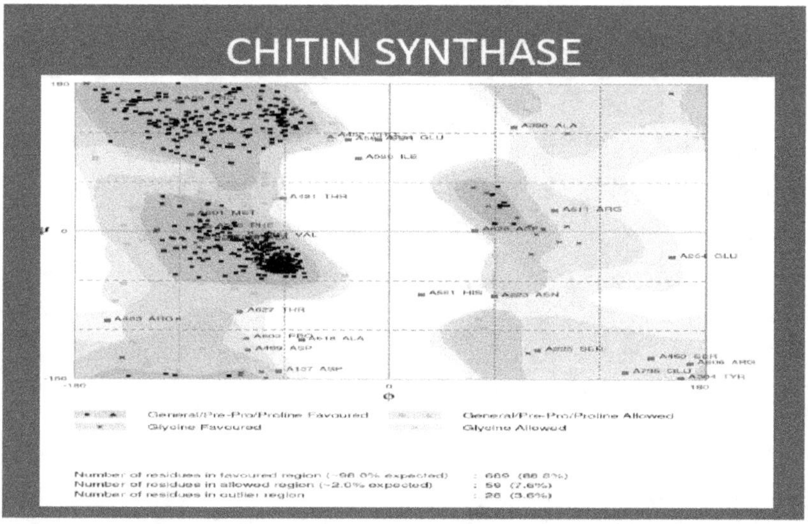

Figure 9: **The Ramachandran Plot showing for the targeted protein – Chitin Synthase**

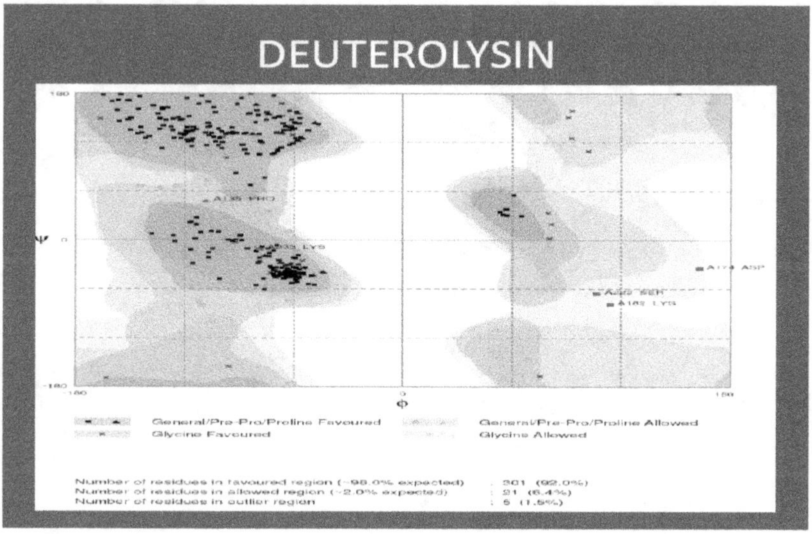

Figure 10: **The Ramachandran Plot showing for the targeted protein – Deuterolysin**

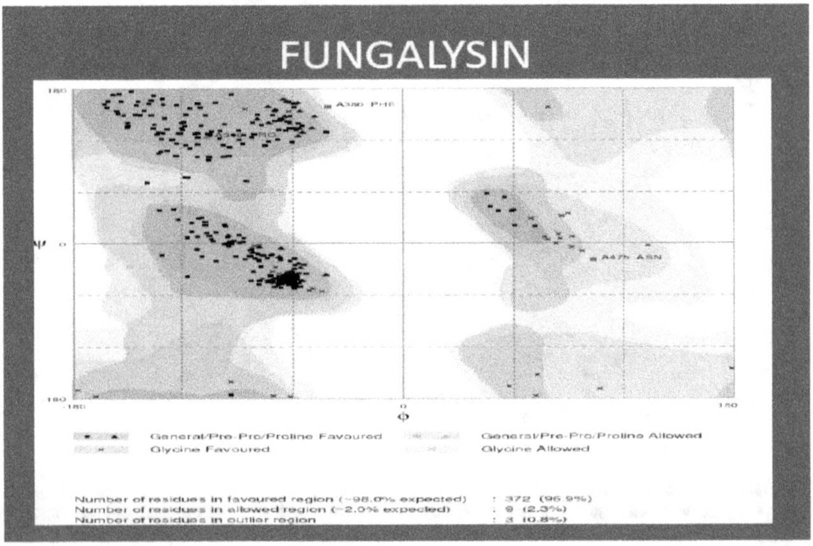

Figure 11: The Ramachandran Plot showing for the targeted protein – Fungalysin

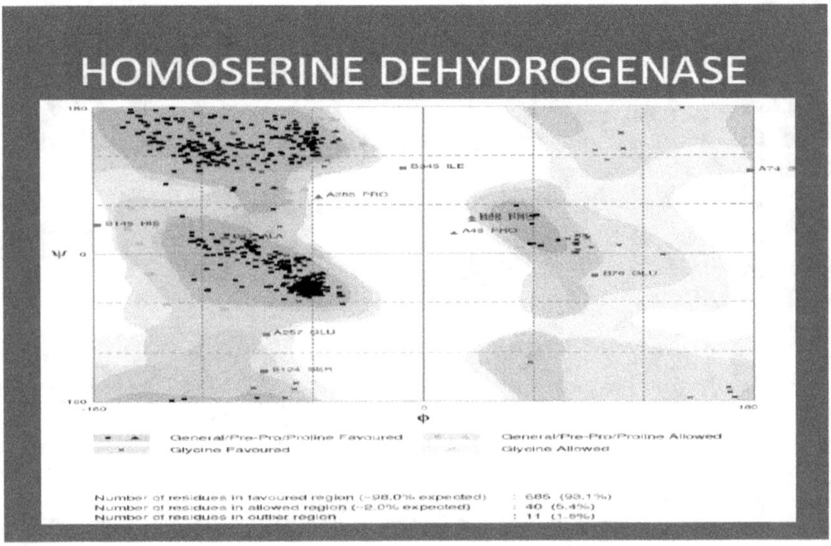

Figure 12: The Ramachandran Plot showing for the targeted protein – Homoserine dehydrogenase

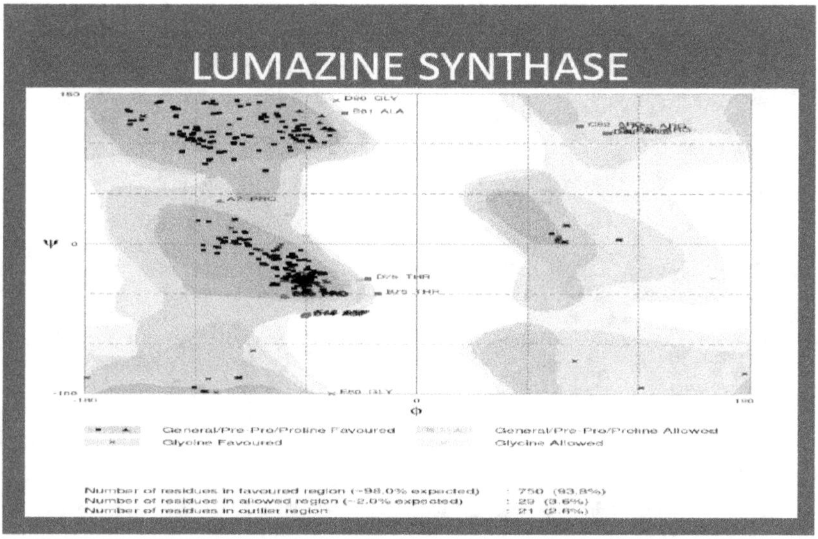

Figure 13: The Ramachandran Plot showing for the targeted protein – Lumazine Synthase

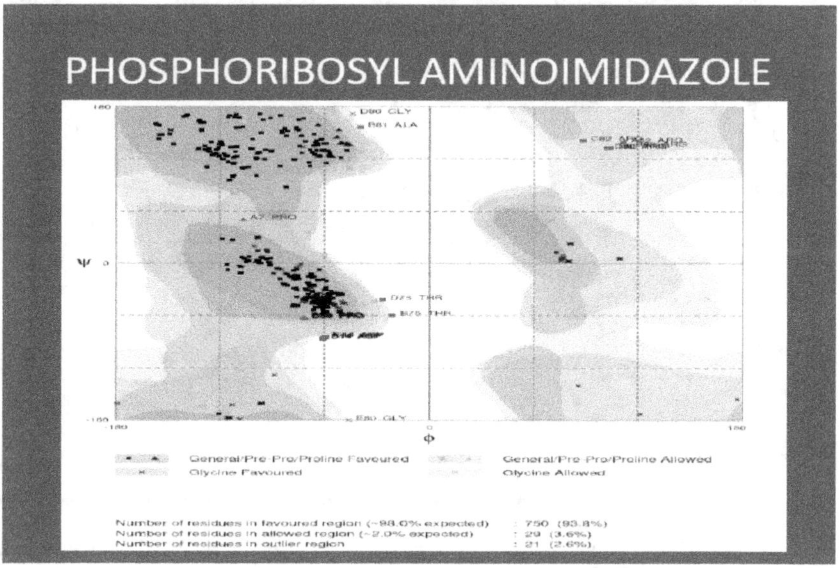

Figure 14: The Ramachandran Plot showing for the targeted protein – Phosphoribosylaminoimidazole carboxylase.

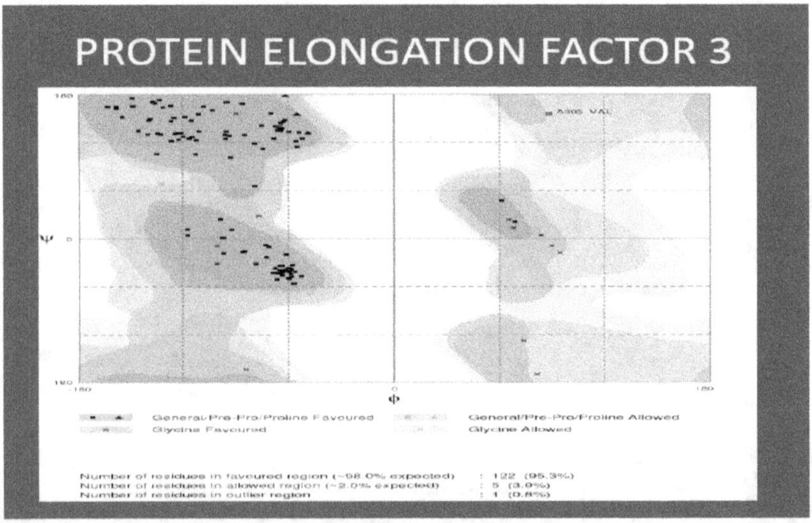

Figure 15: **The Ramachandran Plot showing for the targeted protein – Protein elongation factor 3**

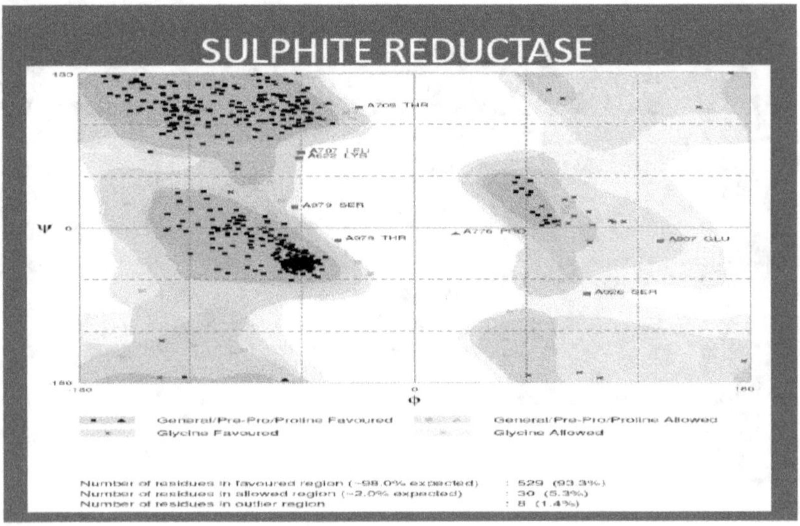

Figure 16: **The Ramachandran Plot showing for the targeted protein – Sulphite Reductase**

5.8.3 Preparation of ligand for docking

The secondary metabolites, azadirachtin, nimbin, nimonol, lawsone, lawsoniaside, scopoletin, and stigmasterol, which are known for their antimicrobial activity from neem and henna plant, are selected as ligands in *in-silico* study. The prerequisite file format of these ligands is a .pdb file for proceeding molecular docking. However, the obtained format file for these ligands was .sdf format from the PubChem compound database. These .sdf files are converted into .pdb file format by using a chemical toolbox named OPENBABEL software which was designed to speak many chemical languages.

5.8.4 Molecular docking

The selected target proteins, namely 1,3-Beta-glucan synthase, chitin synthase, chitinase, deuterolysin, fungalysin, homoserine dehydrogenase, lumazine synthase, Phosphoribosylaminoimidazole carboxylase, protein elongation factor 3, and sulphite reductase are docked with azadirachtin, nimbin, nimonol, lawsone, lawsoniaside, scopoletin, and stigmasterol by iGEMDOCK 2.0 and Autodock Vina. The classical azole group of antifungal drug, Clotrimazole, was also included to analyze the values for comparison in the docking study.

The energy values and the binding affinities between the ligand and protein are presented in table 7-16.

The energy values obtained with iGEMDOCK 2.0 for the selected drug targets with selected secondary metabolites of neem and henna plant are 1,3-Beta Glucan synthase with azadirachtin was -219.317 Kcal per mol while with stigmasterol was +359.819 and with Clotrimazole was -

128.424, the binding affinity was -13.3,-9.8,-7.1 respectively which was presented in table 7.

The energy values of chitin synthase are with nimbin as -189.149 kcal per mol, for lawsoniaside as +251.281, for stigmasterol as +536.619, and with Clotrimazole as -134.833, while the binding affinity as -14.2, -10.4, -10.2, and 8.5 respectively which was presented in table 8.

The energy values of Chitinase are with azadirachtin as -209.02, lawsoniaside as +453.67 stigmasterol as -14.06, Clotrimazole was -143.803 kcal per mol and binding affinity are -17.6, -11.4, -13.8, and -10.1 respectively which was presented in table 9.

The energy values of deuterolysin with azadirachtin shows as -176.069, lawsoniaside as +79.576, stigmasterol was +237.541, and Clotrimazole was -126.689 kcal per mol and binding affinity of these was -13.1, -9.1, -10.1, -7.6 respectively which was presented in table 10.

The energy values of Fungalysin with azadirachtin was -166.152, lawsoniaside was +66.1007, stigmasterol was +517.875, and Clotrimazole was -105.115 kcal per mol and the binding affinity was -11.6, -9.2, -10.1, -7.9 respectively which was presented in table 11.

The energy values of homoserine dehydrogenase with azadirachtin was -178.717, nimonol as -176.259, lawsoniaside was +343.906, and Clotrimazole was -139.49 kcal per mol, while the binding affinity was -15.8, -17.1, -11.8, and -7.1 respectively which was presented in table 12.

The energy values of Lumazine synthase with azadirachtin was -197.211, stigmasterol was +436.404, and Clotrimazole was -115.185 kcal per mol, while the binding affinity was -14.4, -13.2, and -8.1 respectively which was presented in table 13.

The energy values of Phosphoribosylaminoimidazole carboxylase with azadirachtin shows as -187.813, stigmasterol was +73.504, and Clotrimazole was -121.516 kcal per mol and binding affinity of these was -15.9, -11.3, -8.6 respectively which was presented in table 14.

The energy values of protein elongation factor 3 with nimbin shows as -153.42, lawsoniaside was +512.481, and Clotrimazole was -115.573 kcal per mol and binding affinity of these was -10, -7.1, -6.3 respectively which was presented in table 15.

The energy values of sulphite reductase with azadirachtin shows as -168.194, lawsoniaside was +104.201, and Clotrimazole was -135.168 kcal per mol and binding affinity of these was -14.4, -9.7, -7.9 respectively which was presented in table 16.

Table 7: The results of quick docking and accurate docking performed with a software iGEMDOCK 2.0 and Autodock Vina between the selected drug target, 1, 3 β Glucan synthasewith selected secondary metabolites of neem and henna as ligands

S no	Drug targets or Protein with Ligand	Quick docking energy values with iGEMDOCK 2.0			Binding affinity with Autodock Vina
		Total Energy (Kcal/mol)	VDW (Kcal/mol)	H Bond (Kcal/mol)	Binding Affinity
1	1,3 β Glucan synthase + azadirachtin	-219.317	-197.687	-21.6302	-13.3
2	1,3 β Glucan synthase + nimbin	-180.669	-174.365	-6.3048	-14.3
3	1,3 β Glucan synthase + nimonol	-149.955	-147.879	-2.0762	-13.2
4	1,3 β Glucan synthase + lawsone	-84.4344	-71.5045	-12.9299	-7.2
5	1,3 β Glucan synthase + lawsoniaside	78.3044	89.5371	-11.2327	-9.9
6	1,3 β Glucan synthase + scopoletin	-87.7434	-70.0445	-17.6989	-6.7
7	1,3 β Glucan synthase + stigmasterol	359.819	359.819	0	-9.8
8	1,3 β Glucan synthase + clotrimazole	-128.424	-124.853	-3.5713	-7.1

Table 8: The results of quick docking and accurate docking performed with a software iGEMDOCK 2.0 and Autodock Vina between the selected drug target, Chitin synthase and selected secondary metabolites of neem and henna as ligands

S no	Drug targets or Protein with Ligand	Quick docking energy values with iGEMDOCK 2.0			Binding affinity with Autodock Vina
		Total Energy (Kcal/mol)	VDW (Kcal/mol)	H Bond (Kcal/mol)	Binding Affinity
1	Chitin synthase + azadirachtin	-159.869	-147.288	-12.5813	-14.7
2	Chitin synthase + nimbin	-189.149	-172.924	-16.2253	-14.2
3	Chitin synthase + nimonol	-137.841	-134.341	-3.5	-14.2
4	Chitin synthase + lawsone	-91.0095	-78.6229	-12.3866	-8.5
5	Chitin synthase + lawsoniaside	251.281	275.861	-24.5795	-10.4
6	Chitin synthase +scopoletin	-84.5797	-68.72	-15.8597	-8
7	Chitin synthase + stigmasterol	536.619	535.762	0.85736	-10.2
8	Chitin synthase + clotrimazole	-134.833	-131.333	-3.5	-8.5

Table 9: The results of quick docking and accurate docking performed with a software iGEMDOCK 2.0 and Autodock Vina between the selected drug target, Chitinase and selected secondary metabolites of neem and henna as ligands.

S no	Drug targets or Protein with Ligand	Quick docking energy values with iGEMDOCK 2.0			Binding affinity with Autodock Vina
		Total Energy (Kcal/mol)	VDW (Kcal/mol)	H Bond (Kcal/mol)	Binding Affinity
1	Chitinase + azadirachtin	-209.854	-191.128	-18.7257	-17.6
2	Chitinase + nimbin	-169.097	-160.783	-8.31389	-17
3	Chitinase + nimonol	-149.348	-144.348	-5	-17.1
4	Chitinase + lawsone	-91.6454	-75.8358	-15.8096	-9
5	Chitinase + lawsoniaside	453.67	479.227	-25.5564	-11.4
6	Chitinase + scopoletin	-92.8269	-69.7604	-23.0664	-9.7
7	Chitinase + stigmasterol	-14.0681	-14.0681	0	-13.8
8	Chitinase + clotrimazole	-143.803	-140.303	-3.5	-10.1

Table 10: The results of quick docking and accurate docking performed with a software iGEMDOCK 2.0 and Autodock Vina between the selected drug target, Deuterolysin and selected secondary metabolites of neem and henna as ligands.

S no	Drug targets or Protein with Ligand	Quick docking energy values with iGEMDOCK 2.0			Binding affinity with Autodock Vina
		TotalEnergy (Kcal/mol)	VDW (Kcal/mol)	H Bond (Kcal/mol)	Binding Affinity
1	Deuterolysin + azadirachtin	-176.069	-158.044	-18.0245	-13.1
2	Deuterolysin + nimbin	-153.137	-140.226	-12.9108	-13.6
3	Deuterolysin + nimonol	-133.185	-129.685	-3.5	-14.6
4	Deuterolysin + lawsone	-86.9537	-74.4921	-12.4617	-7.6
5	Deuterolysin + lawsoniaside	79.5765	90.7356	-11.1591	-9.1
6	Deuterolysin + scopoletin	-88.8193	-78.9968	-9.82247	-7.1
7	Deuterolysin + stigmasterol	237.541	237.541	0	-10.1
8	Deuterolysin + clotrimazole	-126.689	-119.689	-7	-7.6

Table 11: The results of quick docking and accurate docking performed with a software iGEMDOCK 2.0 and Autodock Vina between the selected drug target, Fungalysin and selected secondary metabolites of neem and henna as ligands.

S no	Drug targets or Protein with Ligand	Quick docking energy values with iGEMDOCK 2.0			Binding affinity with Autodock Vina
		Total Energy (Kcal/mol)	VDW (Kcal/mol)	H Bond (Kcal/mol)	Binding Affinity
1	Fungalysin + azadirachtin	-166.152	-133.387	-32.7654	-11.6
2	Fungalysin + nimbin	-131.43	-111.374	-20.0558	-12.5
3	Fungalysin + nimonol	-120.025	-118.69	-1.33427	-13.9
4	Fungalysin + lawsone	-78.8417	-65.0134	-13.8283	-7.9
5	Fungalysin + lawsoniaside	66.1007	71.6984	-5.59768	-9.2
6	Fungalysin + scopoletin	-85.1649	-62.7076	-22.4572	-7.5
7	Fungalysin + stigmasterol	517.875	519.376	-1.50145	-10.1
8	Fungalysin + clotrimazole	-105.115	-100.119	-4.99543	-7.9

Table 12: The results of quick docking and accurate docking performed with a software iGEMDOCK 2.0 and Autodock Vina between the selected drug target, Homoserine dehydrogenase and selected secondary metabolites of neem and henna as ligands.

S no	Drug targets or Protein with Ligand	Quick docking energy values with iGEMDOCK 2.0			Binding affinity with Autodock Vina
		Total Energy (Kcal/mol)	VDW (Kcal/mol)	H Bond (Kcal/mol)	Binding Affinity
1	Homoserine dehydrogenase + azadirachtin	-178.717	-152.067	-26.6493	-15.8
2	Homoserine dehydrogenase + nimbin	-172.356	-169.099	-3.25651	-16.7
3	Homoserine dehydrogenase + nimonol	-176.259	-159.633	-16.6261	-17.1
4	Homoserine dehydrogenase + lawsone	-105.487	-78.8391	-26.6481	-8
5	Homoserine dehydrogenase + lawsoniaside	343.906	357.139	-13.2326	-11.8
6	Homoserine dehydrogenase + scopoletin	-107.231	-84.0977	-23.1337	-7.8
7	Homoserine dehydrogenase + stigmasterol	126.99	129.448	-2.45724	-12.6
8	Homoserine dehydrogenase + clotrimazole	-139.49	-132.78	-6.71053	-7.1

Table 13: The results of quick docking and accurate docking performed with a software iGEMDOCK 2.0 and Autodock Vina between the selected drug target, Lumazine synthase and selected secondary metabolites of neem and henna as ligands.

S no	Drug targets or Protein with Ligand	Quick docking energy values with iGEMDOCK 2.0			Binding affinity with Autodock Vina
		Total Energy (Kcal/mol)	VDW (Kcal/mol)	H Bond (Kcal/mol)	Binding Affinity
1	Lumazine synthase + azadirachtin	-197.211	-168.881	-28.3306	-14.4
2	Lumazine synthase + nimbin	-159.724	-144.839	-14.8856	-14.7
3	Lumazine synthase + nimonol	-148.514	-141.16	-7.35391	-13.8
4	Lumazine synthase + lawsone	-96.0307	-63.8257	-32.2049	-8.3
5	Lumazine synthase + lawsoniaside	131.482	140.72	-9.23823	-10.8
6	Lumazine synthase + scopoletin	-91.7861	-74.443	-17.3431	-7.9
7	Lumazine synthase + stigmasterol	436.404	441.189	-4.78576	-13.2
8	Lumazine synthase + clotrimazole	-115.185	-109.823	-5.36169	-8.1

Table 14: The results of quick docking and accurate docking performed with a software iGEMDOCK 2.0 and Autodock Vina between the selected drug target, Phosphoribosylaminoimidazole carboxylase and selected secondary metabolites of neem and henna as ligands.

S no	Drug targets or Protein with Ligand	Quick docking energy values with iGEMDOCK 2.0			Binding affinity with Autodock Vina
		Total Energy (Kcal/mol)	VDW (Kcal/mol)	H Bond (Kcal/mol)	Binding Affinity
1	Phosphoribosyl + azadirachtin	-187.813	-181.939	-5.8739	-15.9
2	Phosphoribosyl + nimbin	-155.021	-141.023	-13.9979	-15.7
3	Phosphoribosyl + nimonol	-155.899	-144.277	-11.6215	-15.4
4	Phosphoribosyl + lawsone	-81.9317	-70.8643	-11.0674	-8
5	Phosphoribosyl + lawsoniaside	-31.0004	-27.7392	-3.26127	-10.7
6	Phosphoribosyl + scopoletin	-93.6627	-76.3733	-17.2894	-7.5
7	Phosphoribosyl + stigmasterol	73.5044	77.0044	-3.5	-11.3
8	Phosphoribosyl + clotrimazole	-121.516	-117.209	-4.30768	-8.6

Table 15: The results of quick docking and accurate docking performed with a software iGEMDOCK 2.0 and Autodock Vina between the selected drug target, Protein elongation factor 3 and selected secondary metabolites of neem and henna as ligands.

S no	Drug targets or Protein with Ligand	Quick docking energy values with iGEMDOCK 2.0			Binding affinity with Autodock Vina
		Total Energy (Kcal/mol)	VDW (Kcal/mol)	H Bond (Kcal/mol)	Binding Affinity
1	Protein Elongation Factor 3 + azadirachtin	-132.45	-114.957	-17.4929	-10.4
2	Protein Elongation Factor 3 + nimbin	-153.42	-143.173	-10.2467	-10
3	Protein Elongation Factor 3 + nimonol	-116.231	-107.07	-9.16076	-10.9
4	Protein Elongation Factor 3 + lawsone	-72.8893	-65.922	-6.96726	-5.6
5	Protein Elongation Factor 3 + lawsoniaside	512.481	524.642	-12.161	-7.1
6	Protein Elongation Factor 3 + scopoletin	-75.0842	-65.0983	-9.9859	-9.2
7	Protein Elongation Factor 3 + stigmasterol	238.744	238.744	0	-10.8
8	Protein Elongation Factor 3 + clotrimazole	-115.573	-112.073	-3.5	-6.3

Table 16: The results of quick docking and accurate docking performed with a software iGEMDOCK 2.0 and Autodock Vina between the selected drug target, Sulphite reductase and selected secondary metabolites of neem and henna as ligands.

S no	Drug targets or Protein with Ligand	Quick docking energy values with iGEMDOCK 2.0			Binding affinity with Autodock Vina
		Total Energy (Kcal/mol)	VDW (Kcal/mol)	H Bond (Kcal/mol)	Binding Affinity
1	Sulphite reductase + azadirachtin	-168.194	-138.575	-29.619	-14.4
2	Sulphite reductase + nimbin	-143.362	-136.408	-6.95443	-13.4
3	Sulphite reductase + nimonol	-128.922	-125.422	-3.5	-13.3
4	Sulphite reductase + lawsone	-90.0447	-67.1004	-22.9443	-7.8
5	Sulphite reductase + lawsoniaside	104.201	128.893	-24.692	-9.7
6	Sulphite reductase + scopoletin	-94.5167	-74.858	-19.6586	-7.2
7	Sulphite reductase + stigmasterol	-39.2956	-39.2956	0	-8.9
8	Sulphite reductase + clotrimazole	-135.168	-127.74	-7.42791	-7.9

The docking pose of these ligands with various drug targets (proteins) was analyzed and retrieved with Pymol software tool which was presented from figure 17 to figure 26.

The docking pose of drug target, 1, 3 Beta Glucan synthase with selected secondary metabolites, Azadirachtin, Nimbin, and Nimonol from *A. indica* and Lawsone, Lawsoniaside, Scopoletin, and Stigmasterol from *L. inermis* was presented in figure 17.

The docking pose of drug target, chitinase with selected secondary metabolites, Azadirachtin, Nimbin, and Nimonol from *A. indica* and Lawsone, Lawsoniaside, Scopoletin, and Stigmasterol from *L. inermis* was presented in figure 18.

The docking pose of drug target, chitin synthase with selected secondary metabolites, Azadirachtin, Nimbin, and Nimonol from *A. indica* and Lawsone, Lawsoniaside, Scopoletin, and Stigmasterol from *L. inermis* was presented in figure 19.

The docking pose of drug target, Deuterolysin with selected secondary metabolites, Azadirachtin, Nimbin, Nimonol from *A. indica* and Lawsone, Lawsoniaside, Scopoletin, and Stigmasterol from *L. inermis* was presented in figure 20.

The docking pose of drug target, Fungalysin with selected secondary metabolites, Azadirachtin, Nimbin, Nimonol from *A. indica* and Lawsone, Lawsoniaside, Scopoletin, and Stigmasterol from *L. inermis* was presented in figure 21.

The docking pose of drug target, Homoserine dehydrogenase with selected secondary metabolites, Azadirachtin, Nimbin, and Nimonol from

A. indica and Lawsone, Lawsoniaside, Scopoletin, and Stigmasterol from *L. inermis* was presented in figure 22.

The docking pose of drug target, Lumazine synthase with selected secondary metabolites, Azadirachtin, Nimbin, and Nimonol from *A. indica* and Lawsone, Lawsoniaside, Scopoletin, and Stigmasterol from *L. inermis* was presented in figure 23.

The docking pose of drug target, Phosphoribosylaminoimidazole carboxylase with selected secondary metabolites, Azadirachtin, Nimbin, and Nimonol from *A. indica* and Lawsone, Lawsoniaside, Scopoletin, and Stigmasterol from *L. inermis* was presented in figure 24.

The docking pose of drug target, Protein elongation factor 3 with selected secondary metabolites, Azadirachtin, Nimbin, and Nimonol from *A. indica* and Lawsone, Lawsoniaside, Scopoletin, and Stigmasterol from *L. inermis* was presented in figure 25.

The docking pose of drug target, Sulphite reductase with selected secondary metabolites, Azadirachtin, Nimbin, and Nimonol from *A. indica* and Lawsone, Lawsoniaside, Scopoletin, and Stigmasterol from *L. inermis* was presented in figure 26.

The docking poses are analyzed by software's that the amino acid residues involved in between protein and ligand interactions are evaluated.

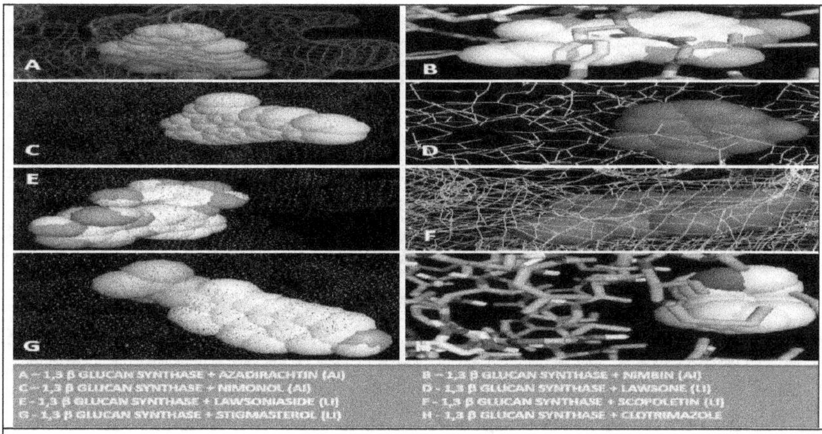

Figure 17: **The docking poses of 1, 3 β Glucan Synthase with secondary metabolites of *A. indica* and *L. inermis* like Azadirachtin, Nimbin, Nimonol, Lawsone, Lawsoniaside, Scopoletin, Stigmasterol, and with the standard drug Clotrimazole.**

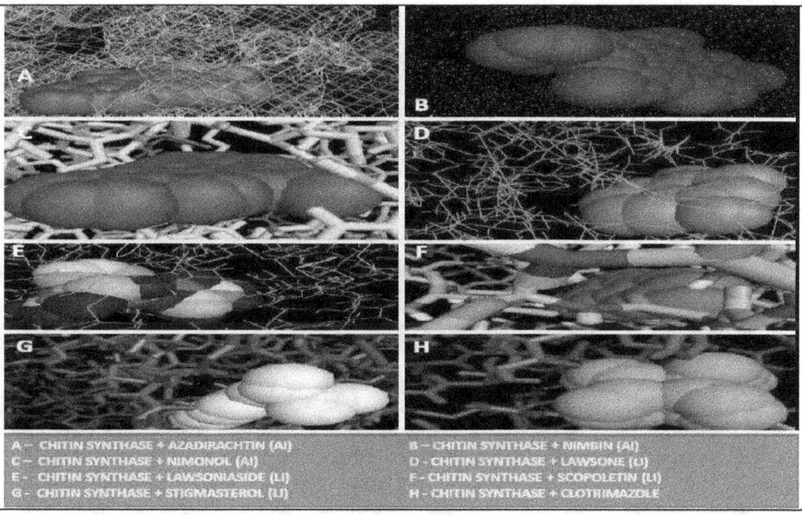

Figure 18: **The docking poses of Chitin Synthase with secondary metabolites of *A. indica* and *L. inermis* like Azadirachtin, Nimbin, Nimonol, Lawsone, Lawsoniaside, Scopoletin, Stigmasterol, and with the standard drug Clotrimazole.**

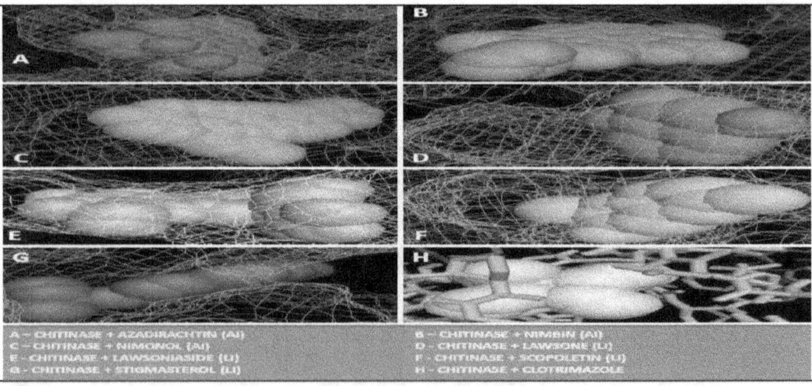

Figure 19: **The docking poses of Chitinase with secondary metabolites of *A.indica* and *L. inermis* like Azadirachtin, Nimbin, Nimonol, Lawsone, Lawsoniaside, Scopoletin, Stigmasterol, and with the standard drug Clotrimazole.**

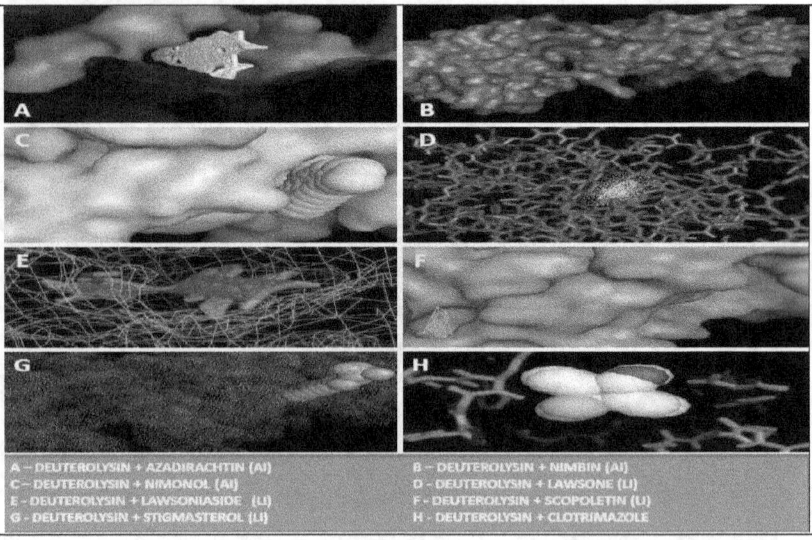

Figure 20: **The docking poses of Deuterolysin with secondary metabolites of *A. indica* and *L. inermis* like Azadirachtin, Nimbin, Nimonol, Lawsone, Lawsoniaside, Scopoletin, Stigmasterol, and with the standard drug Clotrimazole.**

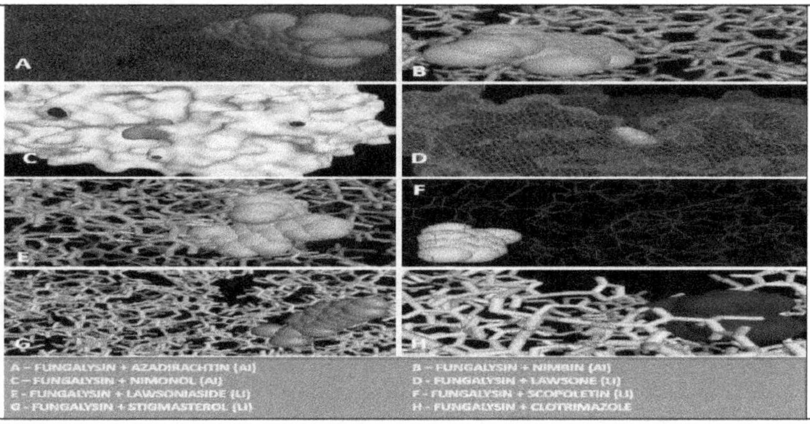

Figure 21: **The docking poses of Fungalysin with secondary metabolites of *A. indica* and *L. inermis* like Azadirachtin, Nimbin, Nimonol, Lawsone, Lawsoniaside, Scopoletin, Stigmasterol, and with the standard drug Clotrimazole.**

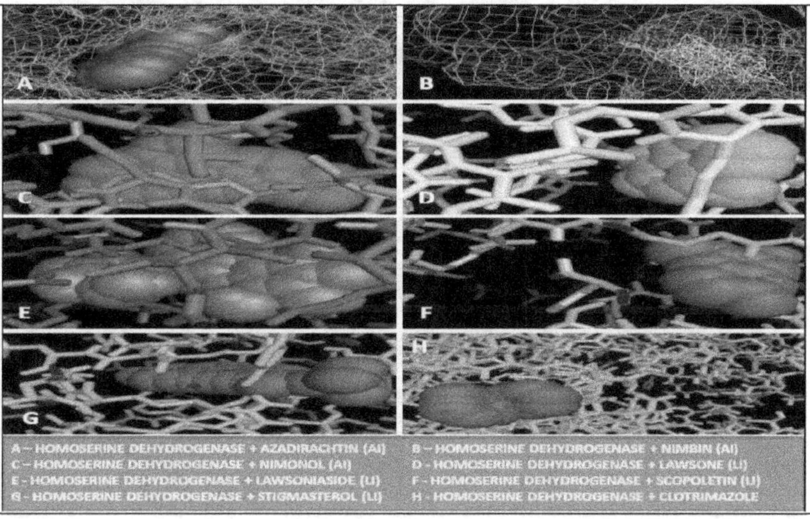

Figure 22: **The docking poses of Homoserine dehydrogenase with secondary metabolites of *A. indica* and *L. inermis* like Azadirachtin, Nimbin, Nimonol, Lawsone, Lawsoniaside, Scopoletin, Stigmasterol, and with the standard drug Clotrimazole.**

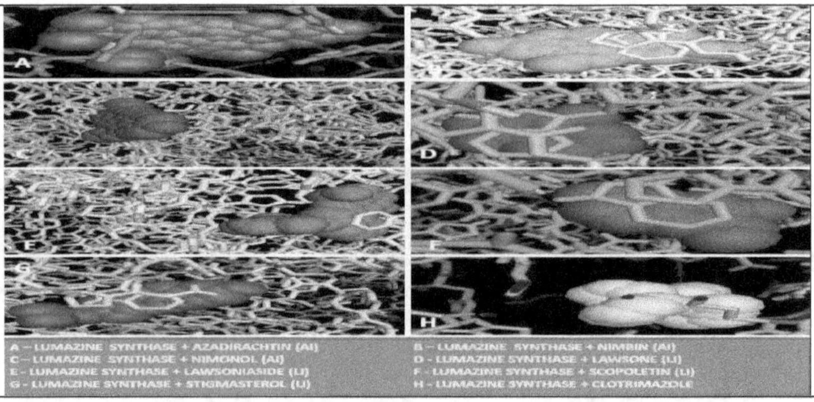

Figure 23: **The docking poses of Lumazine Synthase with secondary metabolites of *A.indica* and *L.inermis* like Azadirachtin, Nimbin, Nimonol, Lawsone, Lawsoniaside, Scopoletin, Stigmasterol, and with the standard drug Clotrimazole.**

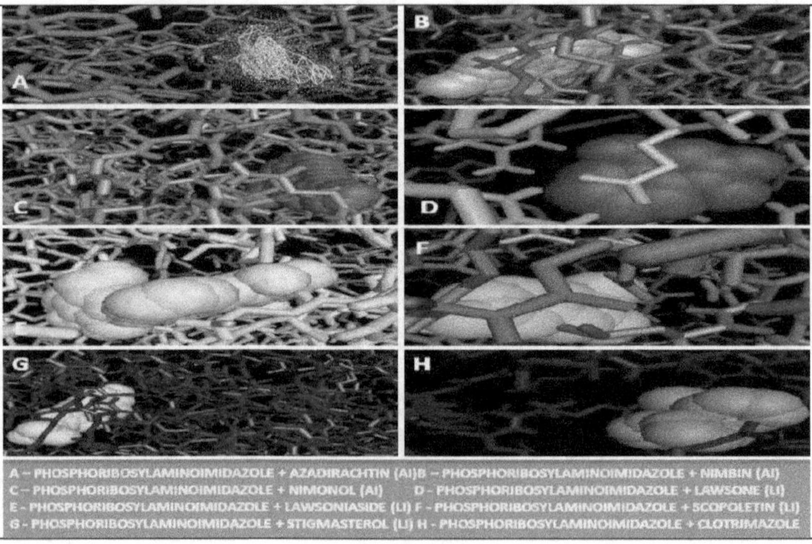

Figure 24: **The docking poses of Phosphoribosylaminoimidazole with secondary metabolites of *A. indica* and *L. inermis* like Azadirachtin, Nimbin, Nimonol, Lawsone, Lawsoniaside, Scopoletin, Stigmasterol, and with the standard drug Clotrimazole.**

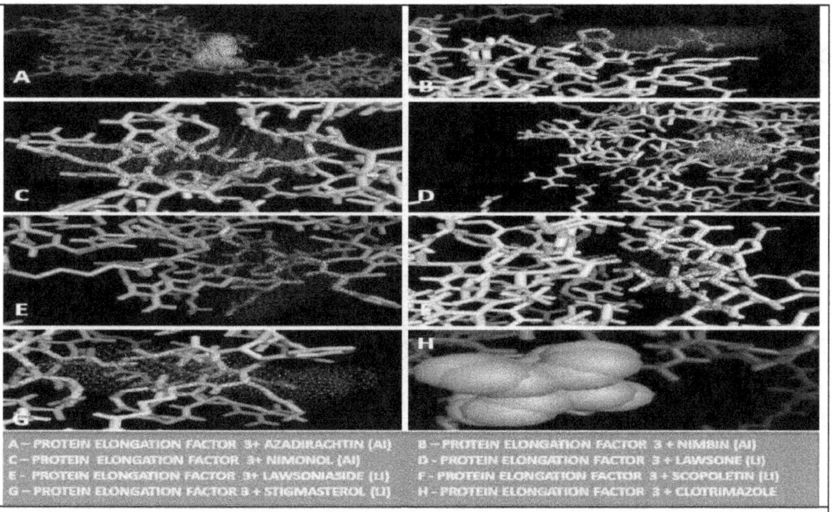

Figure 25: **The docking poses of Protein Elongation Factor 3 with secondary metabolites of *A.indica* and *L. inermis* like Azadirachtin, Nimbin, Nimonol, Lawsone, Lawsoniaside, Scopoletin, Stigmasterol, and with the standard drug Clotrimazole.**

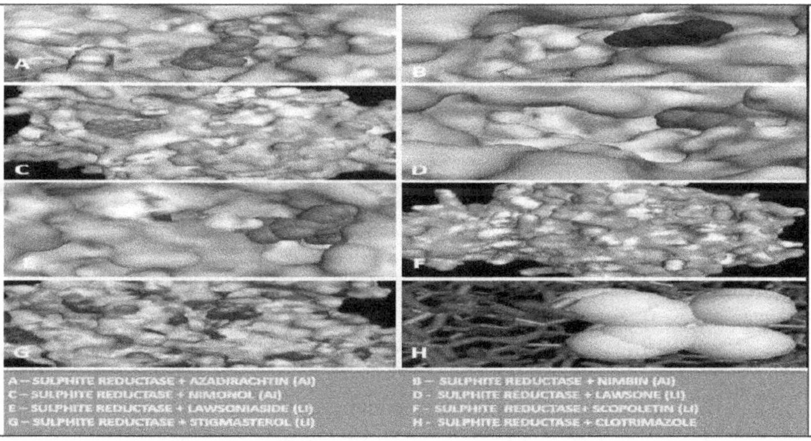

Figure 26: **The docking poses of Sulphite reductase with secondary metabolites of *A. indica* and *L. inermis* like Azadirachtin, Nimbin, Nimonol, Lawsone, Lawsoniaside, Scopoletin, Stigmasterol, and with the standard drug Clotrimazole.**

5.8.5 Properties of ligands

The properties of the selected secondary metabolites for molecular docking which comprises the Physicochemical properties, Lipophilicity, Hydrophilicity, Pharmacokinetics, Drug likeliness, Medicinal properties, and Toxicity profile are the pre-requisite for selection of a compound as a Hit or Lead compound. Normally, SwissADME (251), a free web tool is used to derive the properties of a ligand. The specifications required in the properties as mentioned earlier are the chemical formula, molecular weight, number of heavy atoms, number of heavy aromatic atoms of the ligand.

The PubChem compound database consists of all the details of the compound. The PubChem id of Azadirachtin is 5281303; lawsone is 6755; lawsoniaside is 189451; nimbin is 108058; nimonol is 73356511; scopoletin is 5280460; stigmasterol is 5280794 and Clotrimazole is 2812.

For saturation of a molecule, the ratio of sp3 hybridized carbons over the total carbon count of the molecule is known as Fraction Csp3 which should be at least 0.25. For flexibility of the molecule, not more than 9 rotatable bonds are acceptable.

Molar refractivity will be between 40 to 130 which is a measure of the total polarizability of a mole of a compound, and this relies on the temperature, refraction index, and ligands' pressure.

The polar surface area of the ligand is calculated by TPSA where the phosphorus and sulfur are considered as polar atoms which need to be between 20 and 130 $^{o}A^{2}$.

The Lipophilicity of the ligand is the partition coefficient between n-octanol and water (log $P_{o/w}$). XLOGP3 which is an atomistic method,

WLOGP is the purely atomistic method; MLOGP is an original model of topological method depending on a linear relationship. SILICOS-IT is a hybrid method trusting on 27 fragments and 7 topological descriptors. The iLOGP is free energies of solvation in n-octanol and water. iLOGP was the standard to predict the Lipophilicity of a drug like small molecule.

The water solubility of a drug molecule can be predicted by three parameters which are needed for a molecule to be hydrophilic which significantly facilitates the drugs to ease in handling and formulation and targeting oral administration challenges the property influencing absorption. Also, the drug meant to use for the non-enteral route of administration will be highly water soluble. The water solubility factor includes ESOL model and Ali model and SILICOS-IT model, the Log S scale as insoluble; if <-10 it is poorly soluble; if <-6 it is moderately soluble; if<-4 it is soluble; if<-2 it is very soluble; if 0 it is highly soluble.

In the pharmacokinetic profile of this software, it renders the gastrointestinal absorption of a small molecule, whether it is a substrate for efflux pump, the influence of Cytochrome P450 enzymes and acceptance for topical application.

Another parameter is drug-likeness which is a five star filter to adopt a compound as a drug like compound as these are the Lipinski (248)(Pfizer) filter, the Ghose (252) (Amgen), the Veber (253)(GSK), the Egan (254)(Pharmacia), and the Muegge (255) (Bayer) methods.

In the medicinal chemistry portfolio, the two filters PAINS and Brenk are helpful to evaluate the promiscuous compounds in which the filter PAINS is helpful for a molecule containing sub-structures showing a strong response in assays regardless of the targeted protein leads to yield a false positive biological output that fragments are assayed by Brenk. On application of these two filters and other physicochemical filters is to construct the screening libraries and detect that most of the compounds satisfy criteria for lead likeness.

The Synthetic accessibility score ranges from 1 to 10 as very easy to very difficult based on the difficulty in synthesis.

The toxicity profile of a small molecule was measured by the parameters like Human ether-a-go-go-related gene (hERG)(256) is a gene related to the significant portion of transport protein, ion gated protein which conducts potassium (K^+) ions out of the cardiac myocyte, and this current is very vital in repolarisation – depolarization of the cell membrane during the cardiac action potential which finally helpful in detection of delayed ventricular repolarization (QT interval prolongation).

AMES toxicity is a parameter of detecting the possible mutations in the DNA by any of the agent or compound administered. The Mutations identified by performing AMES test (257) in the compounds are of possible carcinogens, in early studies demonstrates the 90% of carcinogenicity (258), and in other later research, the possibility was fallen up to a range of 50–70%.

Acute oral toxicity is another parameter to evaluate the toxicity in which it is characterized as four categories in which the category I consist of substances with LD50 values ≤ 50 mg per kg. Category II consists of substances with LD50 values > 50 mg per kg but less than 500 mg per kg. Category III includes substances with LD50 values > 500 mg per kg but less than 5000 mg per kg. Category IV consists of substances with LD50 values > 5000 mg per kg.

The carcinogenicity profile was based on the Carcinogenic Potency Database (CPDB) which is characterized into three classes as Danger, Warning, and Non-required based on the TD50 values. Carcinogenic compounds with TD50 less than or equal to 10 mg per kg body weight per day are designated as Danger, those with TD50 more than 10 mg per kg body weight per day are designated as Warning, and non-carcinogenic chemicals are designed as Non-required.

TPT is one of the parameters to evaluate the environmental toxicity. For a substance with the pIGC50 more than -0.5 was nominated as TPT, otherwise as non-TPT. The pIGC50 is called as the negative logarithm of 50% growth inhibitory concentration. Fish toxicity can be assessed as the compound which the value LC50 > 0.5 mmol per L are designed as high acute Fat Head Minnow Toxicity (FHMT) substance, whereas it was nominated as a low acute FHMT compound.

The synthetic accessibility of Clotrimazole is 2.70, while for scopoletin is 2.62 which depicts as efficiently synthesize as these are near to 1 in the range of 1-10 as easy to hard for synthesis.

PAINS and Brenk filters for the ligands depicts as of no violation for Clotrimazole and lawsoniaside, but scopoletin and stigmasterol have 1 violation in Brenk filter which predicts as a false positive signal or promiscuous compounds.

The bioavailability score of Clotrimazole was 0.55 while for nimonol, nimbin, stigmasterol, and scopoletin also are 0.55 but lawsone as 0.56.

Clotrimazole and nimonol follows the drug-likeness filters while nimbin with 1 violation (mw>500) in Lipinski and 3 violations in Ghose

(MW > 480, MR >130, no of atoms >70) filter, lawsone observes as 1 violation in Ghose (no of atoms <20) and Muegge (mw<200) filter, for scopoletin 1 violation (mw<200) in Muegge filter while for stigmasterol shows 1 violation in Lipinski's rule, 3 in Ghose, 1 in Egan, and 2 in Muegge filter.

Clotrimazole, nimonol, nimbin, lawsone, scopoletin, are highly absorbable through gastrointestinal, while azadirachtin, lawsoniaside, stigmasterol are low. Clotrimazole, lawsone, and scopoletin crossblood-brain barrier others do not.

Clotrimazole, azadirachtin, and nimonol are a substrate for P-gp while other ligands are not.

Clotrimazole was influenced by Cytochrome P450 enzyme while only stigmasterol was a CYP2C9 inhibitor and all others are not inhibitors.

Clotrimazole showed as moderately soluble for Log S (ESOL) and Log S (Ali) while poorly soluble for Log S (SILICOS-IT), but stigmasterol was poorly soluble for Log S (ESOL) and Log S (Ali) while moderately soluble for Log S (SILICOS-IT) and in scopoletin, and nimbin was observed as soluble and moderately soluble for all three respectively. The lawsoniaside was very soluble for Log S (ESOL) and soluble for Log S (Ali) and Log S (SILICOS-IT). While the lawsone was observed as very soluble for Log S (ESOL) and Log S (Ali) but only soluble for Log S (SILICOS-IT). The nimonol was observed as moderately soluble for Log S (ESOL) and Log S (SILICOS-IT) while poorly soluble for Log S (Ali). The azadirachtin was showed as moderately soluble for Log S (ESOL) and Log S (Ali) while soluble for Log S (SILICOS-IT).

The Lipophilicity of the Clotrimazole can be predicted by many factors like Log $P_{o/w}$ (iLogP), Log $P_{o/w}$ (XLOGP3), Log $P_{o/w}$ (WLOGP), Log $P_{o/w}$ (MLOGP), Log $P_{o/w}$ (SILICOS - IT), and consensus Log $P_{o/w}$ which for Clotrimazole was 4.64, nimonol showed as 4.17 and stigmasterol was 6.98, but lawsoniaside was -1.79.

The TPSA of Clotrimazole was 17.82 $^oA^2$, while stigmasterol was 20.23 $^oA^2$ and azadirachtin was 215.34 $^oA^2$ those less than 70 are shown as good penetrable into the brain while less than 140 are good intestinal absorbable.

Molar refractivity of Clotrimazole was 101.84 and lawsone was 46.39 and scopoletin showed as 51.

The toxicity of these ligands was also detected as all of them are non-toxic. The values obtained on the subjection of these SMILES to the admetSAR online tool are predicted as these are in the normal range.

All the ligands are shown as non-inhibitor for HERG-inhibition toxicity profile, but it was an inhibitor for Clotrimazole.

AMES toxicity as observed as AMES toxic for lawsone, but others are non-AMES toxic.

Acute oral toxicity was exhibited as IV category for lawsoniaside, III for azadirachtin, nimbin, nimonol, scopoletin, and Clotrimazole but II category for lawsone.

Nimbin was observed as a danger for carcinogenicity (Three class) but non-required for others including Clotrimazole.

5.8.6 The interaction of a protein with derivatives of ligands

The structure-activity related molecules are derived from the parent compounds (ligands) with the help of SwissADME online tool to a maximum number of derivatives. These ligands are subjected to the SwissADME tool where here retrieved azadirachtin 105 derivatives; nimbin with 124 derivatives; nimonol of 144 derivatives; lawsone with 112 derivatives; lawsoniaside of 191 derivatives; scopoletin of 140 derivatives and stigmasterol with 193 derivatives. Out of these derivatives, the most best-suited one in each was selected for docking with iGEMDOCK 2.0, software to elucidate the protein-ligand interactions and atomic positions or compound properties which were presented from table 17 to table 86 and the general properties are from table 87-121.

The molecular docking of a selected drug target with the selected ligand derivative was performed with the help of iGEMDOCK 2.0 software for screening, integrating docking, post-analysis, and visualization of docked poses, where the quick docking was set as a default with 150 population size and 70 generations to integrate the values that insinuate the total energy, Van der Waals force, H bond for protein-ligand interactions and atomic composition between the bonded compounds which was displayed from table 17 to table 86. The total energy values, Van der Waals forces, and H-bond between the ligand derivatives with various drug targets are the determining endpoints.

The azadirachtin with 1,3 beta glucan synthase interaction observed that the total energy between them as -217.317 Kcal/mol, Van der Waals force between them as -197.687 Kcal/mol, and H-bond between them as -21.6302 Kcal/mol while with the derivative of azadirachtin 56 (SAR 3) with IUPAC name: 4,11-dimethyl(1S,4S,5R,6S,7S,8R,11S,12R,14S,15R)-12-ethoxy-4,7-dihydroxy-6 [(1S,2S,6S,8S,9R,11S)-2-hydroxy-11-methyl-5,7,10-trioxatetracyclo[6.3.1.$0^{2,6}$.$0^{9,11}$]dodec-3-en-9-yl]-6-methyl-14-{[(2E)-2-methylbut-2-enoyl]oxy}-3,9-dioxatetracyclo[6.6.1.$0^{1,5}$.$0^{11,15}$]pentadecane-4,11-dicarboxylate shows as -143.1 Kcal/mol as total energy, -119.845 Kcal/mol as Van der Waals force and H-bond as -23.2549 Kcal/mol which was presented in table 17.

The azadirachtin with chitin synthase interaction observed that the total energy between them as -159.869 Kcal/mol, Van der Waals force between them as -147.288 Kcal/mol, and H-bond between them as -12.5813 Kcal/mol while with the derivative of azadirachtin 19 (SAR 2) with IUPAC name: 4,11-dimethyl (1S,4S,5R,6S,7S,8R,11S,12R,14S,15R)-12-(acetyloxy)-4,7-dihydroxy-6-[(1S,2S,6R,8S,9R,11S)-2-hydroxy-11-methyl-5,10-dioxa-7-azatetracyclo[6.3.1.$0^{2,6}$.$0^{9,11}$]dodec-3-en-9-yl]-6-methyl-14-{[(2E)-2-methylbut-2-enoyl]oxy}-3,9-dioxatetracyclo[6.6.1.$0^{1,5}$.$0^{11,15}$]pentadecane-4,11-dicarboxylate shows as -172.283 Kcal/mol as total energy, -145.991 Kcal/mol as Van der Waals force and H-bond as -26.2919 Kcal/mol which was presented in table 18.

The azadirachtin with chitinase interaction observed that the total energy between them as -209.854 Kcal/mol, Van der Waals force between them as -191.128 Kcal/mol, and H-bond between them as -18.7257 Kcal/mol while with the derivative of azadirachtin 19 (SAR 2) with IUPAC name: 4,11-dimethyl (1S,4S,5R,6S,7S,8R,11S,12R,14S,15R)-12-(acetyloxy)-4,7-dihydroxy-6-[(1S,2S,6R,8S,9R,11S)-2-hydroxy-11-methyl-5,10-dioxa-7-azatetracyclo[6.3.1.$0^{2,6}$.$0^{9,11}$]dodec-3-en-9-yl]-6-methyl-14-{[(2E)-2-methylbut-2-enoyl]oxy}-3,9-dioxatetracyclo[6.6.1.$0^{1,5}$.$0^{11,15}$]pentadecane-4,11-dicarboxylate shows as -

204.849 Kcal/mol as total energy, -183.776 Kcal/mol as Van der Waals force and H-bond as -21.0725 Kcal/mol which was presented in table 19.

The azadirachtin with Deuterolysin interaction observed that the total energy between them as -176.069 Kcal/mol, Van der Waals force between them as -158.044 Kcal/mol, and H-bond between them as -18.0245 Kcal/mol while with the derivative of azadirachtin 56 (SAR 3) with IUPAC name: 4,11-dimethyl (1S,4S,5R,6S,7S,8R,11S,12R,14S,15R)-12-ethoxy-4,7-dihydroxy-6-[(1S,2S,6S,8S,9R,11S)-2-hydroxy-11-methyl-5,7,10-trioxatetracyclo[6.3.1.$0^{2,6}$.$0^{9,11}$]dodec-3-en-9-yl]-6-methyl-14-{[(2E)-2-methylbut-2-enoyl]oxy}-3,9-dioxatetracyclo[6.6.1.$0^{1,5}$.$0^{11,15}$]pentadecane-4,11-dicarboxylate shows as -176.641 Kcal/mol as total energy, -150.119 Kcal/mol as Van der Waals force and H-bond as -26.5219 Kcal/mol which was presented in table 20.

The azadirachtin with Fungalysin interaction observed that the total energy between them as -166.152 Kcal/mol, Van der Waals force between them as -133.387 Kcal/mol, and H-bond between them as -32.7654 Kcal/mol while with the derivative of azadirachtin 58 (SAR 4) with IUPAC name: 4,11-dimethyl (1S,4S,5R,6S,7S,8R,11S,12R,14S,15R)-12-(ethanimidoyloxy)-4,7-dihydroxy-6-[(1S,2S,6S,8S,9R,11S)-2-hydroxy-11-methyl-5,7,10-trioxatetracyclo[6.3.1.$0^{2,6}$.$0^{9,11}$]dodec-3-en-9-yl]-6-methyl-14-{[(2E)-2-methylbut-2-enoyl]oxy}-3,9-dioxatetracyclo[6.6.1.$0^{1,5}$.$0^{11,15}$]pentadecane-4,11-dicarboxylate shows as -164.763 Kcal/mol as total energy, -124.717 Kcal/mol as Van der Waals force and H-bond as -40.0461 Kcal/mol which was presented in table 21.

The azadirachtin with homoserine dehydrogenase interaction observed that the total energy between them as -178.717 Kcal/mol, Van der

Waals force between them as -152.067 Kcal/mol, and H-bond between them as -26.6493 Kcal/mol while with the derivative of azadirachtin 81 (SAR 5) with IUPAC name: 4,11-dimethyl (1S,4S,5R,6S,7S,8R,11S,12R,14S,15R)-12-(acetyloxy)-14-{[(2Z)-2-(bromomethyl)but-2-enoyl]oxy}-4,7-dihydroxy-6-[(1S,2S,6S,8S,9R,11S)-2-hydroxy-11-methyl-5,7,10-trioxatetracyclo[6.3.1.0^{2,6}.0^{9,11}]dodec-3-en-9-yl]-6-methyl-3,9-dioxatetracyclo[6.6.1.0^{1,5}.0^{11,15}]pentadecane-4,11-dicarboxylate shows as -226.658 Kcal/mol as total energy, -189.755 Kcal/mol as Van der Waals force and H-bond as -36.9027 Kcal/mol which was presented in table 22.

The azadirachtin with lumazine synthase interaction observed that the total energy between them as -197.211 Kcal/mol, Van der Waals force between them as -168.881 Kcal/mol, and H-bond between them as -28.3306 Kcal/mol while with the derivative of azadirachtin 81 (SAR 5) with IUPAC name: 4,11-dimethyl (1S,4S,5R,6S,7S,8R,11S,12R,14S,15R)-12-(acetyloxy)-4,7-dihydroxy-6-[(1S,2S,6R,8S,9R,11S)-2-hydroxy-11-methyl-5,10-dioxa-7-azatetracyclo[6.3.1.0^{2,6}.0^{9,11}]dodec-3-en-9-yl]-6-methyl-14-{[(2E)-2-methylbut-2-enoyl]oxy}-3,9-dioxatetracyclo[6.6.1.0^{1,5}.0^{11,15}]pentadecane-4,11-dicarboxylate shows as -171.633 Kcal/mol as total energy, -135.127 Kcal/mol as Van der Waals force and H-bond as -36.5057 Kcal/mol which was presented in table 23.

The azadirachtin with phosphoribosylaminoimidazole interaction observed that the total energy between them as -187.813 Kcal/mol, Van der Waals force between them as -181.939 Kcal/mol, and H-bond between them as -5.8739 Kcal/mol while with the derivative of azadirachtin 02 (SAR 1) with IUPAC name: 4,11-dimethyl (1S,4S,5R,6S,7S,8R,11S,12R,14S,15R)-12-(acetyloxy)-4,7-dihydroxy-6-

[(1S,2S,6R,8S,9R,11S)-2-hydroxy-11-methyl-7,10-dioxatetracyclo[6.3.1.0^{2,6}.0^{9,11}]dodec-3-en-9-yl]-6-methyl-14-{[(2E)-2-methylbut-2-enoyl]oxy}-3,9-dioxatetracyclo[6.6.1.0^{1,5}.0^{11,15}]pentadecane-4,11-dicarboxylate shows as -181.62 Kcal/mol as total energy, -136.741 Kcal/mol as Van der Waals force and H-bond as -44.8791 Kcal/mol which was presented in table 24.

The azadirachtin with protein elongation factor 3 interaction observed that the total energy between them as -132.45 Kcal/mol, Van der Waals force between them as -114.957 Kcal/mol, and H-bond between them as -17.4929 Kcal/mol while with the derivative of azadirachtin 56 (SAR 3) with IUPAC name: 4,11-dimethyl (1S,4S,5R,6S,7S,8R,11S,12R,14S,15R)-12-ethoxy-4,7-dihydroxy-6-[(1S,2S,6S,8S,9R,11S)-2-hydroxy-11-methyl-5,7,10-trioxatetracyclo[6.3.1.0^{2,6}.0^{9,11}]dodec-3-en-9-yl]-6-methyl-14-{[(2E)-2-methylbut-2-enoyl]oxy}-3,9-dioxatetracyclo[6.6.1.0^{1,5}.0^{11,15}]pentadecane-4,11-dicarboxylate shows as -141.14 Kcal/mol as total energy, -116.132 Kcal/mol as Van der Waals force and H-bond as -25.0077 Kcal/mol which was presented in table 25.

The azadirachtin with sulphite reductase interaction observed that the total energy between them as -168.194 Kcal/mol, Van der Waals force between them as -138.575 Kcal/mol, and H-bond between them as -29.619 Kcal/mol while with the derivative of azadirachtin 56 (SAR 3) with IUPAC name: 4,11-dimethyl (1S,4S,5R,6S,7S,8R,11S,12R,14S,15R)-12-ethoxy-4,7-dihydroxy-6-[(1S,2S,6S,8S,9R,11S)-2-hydroxy-11-methyl-5,7,10-trioxatetracyclo[6.3.1.0^{2,6}.0^{9,11}]dodec-3-en-9-yl]-6-methyl-14-{[(2E)-2-methylbut-2-enoyl]oxy}-3,9-dioxatetracyclo[6.6.1.0^{1,5}.0^{11,15}]pentadecane-4,11-dicarboxylate shows as -

187.527 Kcal/mol as total energy, -151.95 Kcal/mol as Van der Waals force and H-bond as -35.577 Kcal/mol which was presented in table 26.

The nimbin with 1, 3 β Glucan Synthase interaction observed that the total energy between them as -180.669 Kcal/mol, Van der Waals force between them as -174.365 Kcal/mol, and H-bond between them as -6.3048 Kcal/mol while with the derivative of nimbin 63 (SAR 4) with IUPAC name: methyl (1S,2R,3R,4R,8R,9S,10R,13R,15R)-2-(acetyloxy)-13-(furan-3-yl)-9-(2-methoxy-2-oxoethyl)-4,8,10,12-tetramethyl-7-oxo-16-oxatetracyclo[8.6.0.0^{3,8}.0^{11,15}]hexadeca-5,11-diene-4-carboxylate shows as -165.653 Kcal/mol as total energy, -159.587 Kcal/mol as Van der Waals force and H-bond as -6.06566 Kcal/mol which was presented in table 27.

The nimbin with chitin synthase interaction observed that the total energy between them as -189.149 Kcal/mol, Van der Waals force between them as -172.924 Kcal/mol, and H-bond between them as -16.2253 Kcal/mol while with the derivative of nimbin 41 (SAR 2) with IUPAC name: methyl (1S,2R,3R,4S,8R,9S,10R,13R,15R)-2-(acetyloxy)-13-(furan-3-yl)-9-(2-methoxy-2-oxoethyl)-4,5,8,10,12-pentamethyl-7-oxo-16-oxatetracyclo[8.6.0.0^{3,8}.0^{11,15}]hexadeca-5,11-diene-4-carboxylate shows as -156.099 Kcal/mol as total energy, -134.315 Kcal/mol as Van der Waals force and H-bond as -21.785 Kcal/mol which was presented in table 28.

The nimbin with chitinase interaction observed that the total energy between them as -169.097 Kcal/mol, Van der Waals force between them as -160.783 Kcal/mol, and H-bond between them as -8.31389 Kcal/mol while with the derivative of nimbin 41 (SAR 2) with IUPAC name: methyl (1S,2R,3R,4S,8R,9S,10R,13R,15R)-2-(acetyloxy)-13-(furan-3-yl)-9-(2-methoxy-2-oxoethyl)-4,5,8,10,12-pentamethyl-7-oxo-16-

oxatetracyclo[8.6.0.$0^{3,8}$.$0^{11,15}$]hexadeca-5,11-diene-4-carboxylate shows as -168.806 Kcal/mol as total energy, -157.158 Kcal/mol as Van der Waals force and H-bond as -11.6484 Kcal/mol which was presented in table 29.

The nimbin with deuterolysin interaction observed that the total energy between them as -153.137 Kcal/mol, Van der Waals force between them as -140.226 Kcal/mol, and H-bond between them as -12.9108 Kcal/mol while with the derivative of nimbin 1 (SAR 1) with IUPAC name: ethyl (1S,2R,3R,4R,8R,9S,10R,13R,15R)-2-(acetyloxy)-13-(furan-3-yl)-9-(2-methoxy-2-oxoethyl)-4,8,10,12-tetramethyl-7-oxo-16-oxatetracyclo[8.6.0.$0^{3,8}$.$0^{11,15}$]hexadeca-5,11-diene-4-carboxylate shows as -149.349 Kcal/mol as total energy, -131.628 Kcal/mol as Van der Waals force and H-bond as -17.7213 Kcal/mol which was presented in table 30.

The nimbin with fungalysin interaction observed that the total energy between them as -131.43 Kcal/mol, Van der Waals force between them as -111.374 Kcal/mol, and H-bond between them as -20.0558 Kcal/mol while with the derivative of nimbin 50 (SAR 3) with IUPAC name: methyl (1S,2R,3R,4R,8R,9S,10R,13R,15R)-2-(acetyloxy)-13-(furan-3-yl)-9-(2-methoxy-2-oxoethyl)-4,6,8,10,12-pentamethyl-7-oxo-16-oxatetracyclo[8.6.0.$0^{3,8}$.$0^{11,15}$]hexadeca-5,11-diene-4-carboxylate shows as -137.746 Kcal/mol as total energy, -118.294 Kcal/mol as Van der Waals force and H-bond as -19.4515 Kcal/mol which was presented in table 31.

The nimbin with homoserine dehydrogenase interaction observed that the total energy between them as -172.36 Kcal/mol, Van der Waals force between them as -169.099 Kcal/mol, and H-bond between them as -3.25651 Kcal/mol while with the derivative of nimbin 41 (SAR 2) with IUPAC name: methyl (1S,2R,3R,4S,8R,9S,10R,13R,15R)-2-(acetyloxy)-

13-(furan-3-yl)-9-(2-methoxy-2-oxoethyl)-4,5,8,10,12-pentamethyl-7-oxo-16-oxatetracyclo[8.6.0.0^{3},^{8}.0^{11},^{15}]hexadeca-5,11-diene-4-carboxylate shows as -146.099 Kcal/mol as total energy, -128.346 Kcal/mol as Van der Waals force and H-bond as -17.7527 Kcal/mol which was presented in table 32.

The nimbin with lumazine synthase interaction observed that the total energy between them as -159.724 Kcal/mol, Van der Waals force between them as -144.839 Kcal/mol, and H-bond between them as -14.8856 Kcal/mol while with the derivative of nimbin 107 (SAR 5) with IUPAC name: methyl (1S,2R,3R,4R,8R,9S,10R,13R,15R)-2-(acetyloxy)-13-(furan-3-yl)-9-(2-methoxy-2-oxoethyl)-4,8,10,12,14-pentamethyl-7-oxo-16-oxatetracyclo[8.6.0.0^{3},^{8}.0^{11},^{15}]hexadeca-5,11-diene-4-carboxylate shows as -173.198 Kcal/mol as total energy, -149.197 Kcal/mol as Van der Waals force and H-bond as -24.0014 Kcal/mol which was presented in table 33.

The nimbin with phosphoribosylaminoimidazole carboxylase interaction observed that the total energy between them as -155.021 Kcal/mol, Van der Waals force between them as -141.023 Kcal/mol, and H-bond between them as -13.9979 Kcal/mol while with the derivative of nimbin 107 (SAR 5) with IUPAC name: methyl (1S,2R,3R,4R,8R,9S,10R,13R,15R)-2-(acetyloxy)-13-(furan-3-yl)-9-(2-methoxy-2-oxoethyl)-4,8,10,12,14-pentamethyl-7-oxo-16-oxatetracyclo[8.6.0.0^{3},^{8}.0^{11},^{15}]hexadeca-5,11-diene-4-carboxylate shows as -168.921 Kcal/mol as total energy, -147.439 Kcal/mol as Van der Waals force and H-bond as -21.4817 Kcal/mol which was presented in table 34.

The nimbin with protein elongation factor 3 interaction observed that the total energy between them as -153.42 Kcal/mol, Van der Waals force between them as -143.173 Kcal/mol, and H-bond between them as -10.2467 Kcal/mol while with the derivative of nimbin 1 (SAR 1) with IUPAC name: ethyl (1S,2R,3R,4R,8R,9S,10R,13R,15R)-2-(acetyloxy)-13-(furan-3-yl)-9-(2-methoxy-2-oxoethyl)-4,8,10,12-tetramethyl-7-oxo-16-oxatetracyclo[8.6.0.0^{3},^{8}.0^{11},^{15}]hexadeca-5,11-diene-4-carboxylate shows as -129.258 Kcal/mol as total energy, -113.308 Kcal/mol as Van der Waals force and H-bond as -15.9503 Kcal/mol which was presented in table 35.

The nimbin with sulphite reductase interaction observed that the total energy between them as -143.362 Kcal/mol, Van der Waals force between them as -136.408 Kcal/mol, and H-bond between them as -6.95443 Kcal/mol while with the derivative of nimbin 107 (SAR 5) with IUPAC name: methyl (1S,2R,3R,4R,8R,9S,10R,13R,15R)-2-(acetyloxy)-13-(furan-3-yl)-9-(2-methoxy-2-oxoethyl)-4,8,10,12,14-pentamethyl-7-oxo-16-oxatetracyclo[8.6.0.0^{3},^{8}.0^{11},^{15}]hexadeca-5,11-diene-4-carboxylate shows as -133.98 Kcal/mol as total energy, -103.817 Kcal/mol as Van der Waals force and H-bond as -30.1629 Kcal/mol which was presented in table 36.

The nimonol with 1, 3 Beta Glucan synthase interaction observed that the total energy between them as -149.955 Kcal/mol, Van der Waals force between them as -147.879 Kcal/mol, and H-bond between them as -2.0762 Kcal/mol while with the derivative of nimonol 96 (SAR 4) with IUPAC name: (1R,3bR,4S,5R,5aS,9aR,9bR,11aS)-1-(furan-3-yl)-5-hydroxy-3b,6,6,9a,11a-pentamethyl-1H,2H,3bH,4H,5H,5aH,6H,7H,9aH,9bH,10H,11H,11aH-cyclopenta[a]phenanthren-4-yl acetate shows as -140.671 Kcal/mol as total energy, -134.643 Kcal/mol as Van der Waals force and H-bond as -6.02776 Kcal/mol which was presented in table 37.

The nimonol with chitin synthase interaction observed that the total energy between them as -137.841 Kcal/mol, Van der Waals force between them as -134.341 Kcal/mol, and H-bond between them as -3.5 Kcal/mol while with the derivative of nimonol 136 (SAR 5) with IUPAC name: (1R,3bR,4S,5R,5aR,9aS,9bR,11aS)-1-(furan-3-yl)-5-hydroxy-3b,6,6,9a,9b,11a-hexamethyl-7-oxo-1H,2H,3bH,4H,5H,5aH,6H,7H,9aH,9bH,10H,11H,11aH-cyclopenta[a]phenanthren-4-yl acetate shows as -173.153 Kcal/mol as total energy, -154.118 Kcal/mol as Van der Waals force and H-bond as -19.0353 Kcal/mol which was presented in table 38.

The nimonol with chitinase interaction observed that the total energy between them as -149.348 Kcal/mol, Van der Waals force between them as -144.348 Kcal/mol, and H-bond between them as -5 Kcal/mol while with the derivative of nimonol 17 (SAR 2) with IUPAC name: (1R,3bR,4S,5R,5aR,9aR,9bR,11aS)-5-hydroxy-3b,6,6,9a,11a-pentamethyl-7-oxo-1-(1H-pyrrol-3-yl)-1H,2H,3bH,4H,5H,5aH,6H,7H,9aH,9bH,10H,11H,11aH-cyclopenta[a]phenanthren-4-yl acetate shows as -149.912 Kcal/mol as total energy, -136.26 Kcal/mol as Van der Waals force and H-bond as -13.6529 Kcal/mol which was presented in table 39.

The nimonol with deuterolysin interaction observed that the total energy between them as -133.185 Kcal/mol, Van der Waals force between them as -129.685 Kcal/mol, and H-bond between them as -3.5 Kcal/mol while with the derivative of nimonol 96 (SAR 4) with IUPAC name: (1R,3bR,4S,5R,5aS,9aR,9bR,11aS)-1-(furan-3-yl)-5-hydroxy-3b,6,6,9a,11a-pentamethyl-1H,2H,3bH,4H,5H,5aH,6H,7H,9aH,9bH,10H,11H,11aHcyclopenta[a]phenanthren-4-yl acetate shows as -151.926 Kcal/mol as total energy, -142.432 Kcal/mol as Van der Waals force and H-bond as -9.49364 Kcal/mol which was presented in table 40.

The nimonol with fungalysin interaction observed that the total energy between them as -120.025 Kcal/mol, Van der Waals force between them as -118.69 Kcal/mol, and H-bond between them as -1.33427 Kcal/mol while with the derivative of nimonol 60 (SAR 3) with IUPAC name: (1R,3bR,4S,5R,5aR,9aR,9bR,11aS)-1-(furan-3-yl)-5-hydroxy-3,3b,6,6,9a,11a-hexamethyl-7-oxo-1H,2H,3bH,4H,5H,5aH,6H,7H,9aH,9bH,10H,11H,11aH-cyclopenta[a]phenanthren-4-yl acetate shows as -132.549 Kcal/mol as total energy, -124.143 Kcal/mol as Van der Waals force and H-bond as -8.40529 Kcal/mol which was presented in table 41.

The nimonol with homoserine dehydrogenase interaction observed that the total energy between them as -176.259 Kcal/mol, Van der Waals force between them as -159.633 Kcal/mol, and H-bond between them as -16.6261 Kcal/mol while with the derivative of nimonol 60 (SAR 3) with IUPAC name: (1R,3bR,4S,5R,5aR,9aR,9bR,11aS)-1-(furan-3-yl)-5-hydroxy-3,3b,6,6,9a,11a-hexamethyl-7-oxo-1H,2H,3bH,4H,5H,5aH,6H,7H,9aH,9bH,10H,11H,11aH-cyclopenta[a]phenanthren-4-yl acetate shows as -179.557 Kcal/mol as total energy, -166.112 Kcal/mol as Van der Waals force and H-bond as -13.4448 Kcal/mol which was presented in table 42.

The nimonol with lumazine synthase interaction observed that the total energy between them as -148.514 Kcal/mol, Van der Waals force between them as -141.16 Kcal/mol, and H-bond between them as -7.35391

Kcal/mol while with the derivative of nimonol 136 (SAR 5) with IUPAC name: (1R,3bR,4S,5R,5aR,9aS,9bR,11aS)-1-(furan-3-yl)-5-hydroxy-3b,6,6,9a,9b,11a-hexamethyl-7-oxo-1H,2H,3bH,4H,5H,5aH,6H,7H,9aH,9bH,10H,11H,11aH-cyclopenta[a]phenanthren-4-yl acetate shows as -156.615 Kcal/mol as total energy, -146.955 Kcal/mol as Van der Waals force and H-bond as -9.65985 Kcal/mol which was presented in table 43.

The nimonol with phosphoribosylaminoimidazole carboxylase interaction observed that the total energy between them as -155.899 Kcal/mol, Van der Waals force between them as -144.277 Kcal/mol, and H-bond between them as -11.6215 Kcal/mol while with the derivative of nimonol 96 (SAR 4) with IUPAC name: (1R,3bR,4S,5R,5aS,9aR,9bR,11aS)-1-(furan-3-yl)-5-hydroxy-3b,6,6,9a,11a-pentamethyl-1H,2H,3bH,4H,5H,5aH,6H,7H,9aH,9bH,10H,11H,11aH-cyclopenta[a]phenanthren-4-yl acetate shows as -140.355 Kcal/mol as total energy, -123.872 Kcal/mol as Van der Waals force and H-bond as -16.4826 Kcal/mol which was presented in table 44.

The nimonol with protein elongation factor 3 interaction observed that the total energy between them as -153.42 Kcal/mol, Van der Waals force between them as -143.173 Kcal/mol, and H-bond between them as -10.2467 Kcal/mol while with the derivative of nimonol 17 (SAR 2) with IUPAC name: (1R,3bR,4S,5R,5aR,9aR,9bR,11aS)-5-hydroxy-3b,6,6,9a,11a-pentamethyl-7-oxo-1-(1H-pyrrol-3-yl)-1H,2H,3bH,4H,5H,5aH,6H,7H,9aH,9bH,10H,11H,11aH-cyclopenta[a]phenanthren-4-yl acetate shows as -129.298 Kcal/mol as total energy, -118.52 Kcal/mol as Van der Waals force and H-bond as -10.778 Kcal/mol which was presented in table 45.

The nimonol with sulphite reductase interaction observed that the total energy between them as -128.922 Kcal/mol, Van der Waals force between them as -125.422 Kcal/mol, and H-bond between them as -3.5 Kcal/mol while with the derivative of nimonol 17 (SAR 2) with IUPAC name: (1R,3bR,4S,5R,5aR,9aR,9bR,11aS)-5-hydroxy-3b,6,6,9a,11a-pentamethyl-7-oxo-1-(1H-pyrrol-3-yl)-1H,2H,3bH,4H,5H,5aH,6H,7H,9aH,9bH,10H,11H,11aH-cyclopenta[a]phenanthren-4-yl acetate shows as -146.079 Kcal/mol as total energy, -131.472 Kcal/mol as Van der Waals force and H-bond as -14.6067 Kcal/mol which was presented in table 46.

The lawsone with 1, 3 Beta Glucan Synthase interaction observed that the total energy between them as -84.4344 Kcal/mol, Van der Waals force between them as -71.5045 Kcal/mol, and H-bond between them as -12.9299 Kcal/mol while with the derivative of lawsone 87 (SAR 4) with IUPAC name: 4-hydroxy-2-imino-1,2-dihydronaphthalen-1-one shows as -84.1084 Kcal/mol as total energy, -78.0642 Kcal/mol as Van der Waals force and H-bond as -6.04421 Kcal/mol which was presented in table 47.

The lawsone with chitin synthase interaction observed that the total energy between them as -91.0095 Kcal/mol, Van der Waals force between them as -78.6229 Kcal/mol, and H-bond between them as -12.3866 Kcal/mol while with the derivative of lawsone 101 (SAR 5) with IUPAC name: 4-hydroxy-1-imino-1,2-dihydronaphthalen-2-one shows as -93.5276 Kcal/mol as total energy, -78.7206 Kcal/mol as Van der Waals force and H-bond as -14.8069 Kcal/mol which was presented in table 48.

The lawsone with chitinase interaction observed that the total energy between them as -91.6454 Kcal/mol, Van der Waals force between them as -75.8358 Kcal/mol, and H-bond between them as -15.8096 Kcal/mol while with the derivative of lawsone 1 (SAR 1) with IUPAC name: 4-hydroxy-8-methyl-1,2-dihydronaphthalene-1,2-dione shows as -96.6913 Kcal/mol as total energy, -72.5408 Kcal/mol as Van der Waals force and H-bond as -24.1504 Kcal/mol which was presented in table 49.

The lawsone with deuterolysin interaction observed that the total energy between them as -86.9537 Kcal/mol, Van der Waals force between them as -74.4921 Kcal/mol, and H-bond between them as -12.4617 Kcal/mol while with the derivative of lawsone 87 (SAR 4) with IUPAC name: 4-hydroxy-2-imino-1,2-dihydronaphthalen-1-one shows as -89.8203 Kcal/mol as total energy, -73.5112 Kcal/mol as Van der Waals force and H-bond as -16.309 Kcal/mol which was presented in table 50.

The lawsone with Fungalysin interaction observed that the total energy between them as -78.8417 Kcal/mol, Van der Waals force between them as -65.0134 Kcal/mol, and H-bond between them as -13.8283 Kcal/mol while with the derivative of lawsone 101 (SAR 5) with IUPAC name: 4-hydroxy-1-imino-1,2-dihydronaphthalen-2-one shows as -88.6353 Kcal/mol as total energy, -65.4454 Kcal/mol as Van der Waals force and H-bond as -23.1899 Kcal/mol which was presented in table 51.

The lawsone with homoserine dehydrogenase interaction observed that the total energy between them as -105.487 Kcal/mol, Van der Waals force between them as -78.8391 Kcal/mol, and H-bond between them as -26.6481 Kcal/mol while with the derivative of lawsone 1 (SAR 1) with IUPAC name: 4-hydroxy-8-methyl-1,2-dihydronaphthalene-1,2-dione shows as -109.496 Kcal/mol as total energy, -83.244 Kcal/mol as Van der Waals force and H-bond as -26.2517 Kcal/mol which was presented in table 52.

The lawsone with lumazine synthase interaction observed that the total energy between them as -96.0307 Kcal/mol, Van der Waals force between them as -63.8257 Kcal/mol, and H-bond between them as -32.2049 Kcal/mol while with the derivative of lawsone 71 (SAR 3) with IUPAC name: 4-hydroxy-3-methyl-1,2-dihydronaphthalene-1,2-dione shows as -102.582 Kcal/mol as total energy, -70.2286 Kcal/mol as Van der Waals force and H-bond as -32.3535 Kcal/mol which was presented in table 53.

The lawsone with phosphoribosylaminoimidazole carboxylase interaction observed that the total energy between them as -81.9317 Kcal/mol, Van der Waals force between them as -70.8643 Kcal/mol, and H-bond between them as -11.0674 Kcal/mol while with the derivative of lawsone 1 (SAR 1) with IUPAC name: 4-hydroxy-8-methyl-1,2-dihydronaphthalene-1,2-dione shows as -97.7377 Kcal/mol as total energy, -85.8562 Kcal/mol as Van der Waals force and H-bond as -11.8814 Kcal/mol which was presented in table 54.

The lawsone with protein elongation factor 3 interaction observed that the total energy between them as -72.8893 Kcal/mol, Van der Waals force between them as -65.922 Kcal/mol, and H-bond between them as -6.96726 Kcal/mol while with the derivative of lawsone 1 (SAR 1) with IUPAC name: 4-hydroxy-8-methyl-1,2-dihydronaphthalene-1,2-dione shows as -72.7794 Kcal/mol as total energy, -59.5533 Kcal/mol as Van der

Waals force and H-bond as -13.2262 Kcal/mol which was presented in table 55.

The lawsone with sulphite reductase interaction observed that the total energy between them as -90.0447 Kcal/mol, Van der Waals force between them as -67.1004 Kcal/mol, and H-bond between them as -22.9443 Kcal/mol while with the derivative of lawsone 1 (SAR 1) with IUPAC name: 4-hydroxy-8-methyl-1,2-dihydronaphthalene-1,2-dione shows as -94.9317 Kcal/mol as total energy, -66.9371 Kcal/mol as Van der Waals force and H-bond as -27.9946 Kcal/mol which was presented in table 56.

The lawsoniaside with 1,3 Beta Glucan Synthase interaction observed that the total energy between them as +78.3044 Kcal/mol, Van der Waals force between them as +89.5371 Kcal/mol, and H-bond between them as -11.2327 Kcal/mol while with the derivative of lawsoniaside 182 (SAR 5) with IUPAC name: (2S,3R,4S,5S,6R)-4,5-dihydroxy-2-[(3-hydroxy-4-{[(2S,3R,4S,5S,6R)-3,4,5-trihydroxy-6-(hydroxymethyl)oxan-2-yl]oxy}naphthalen-1-yl)oxy]-6-(hydroxymethyl)oxan-3-yl hypofluorite shows as -145.626 Kcal/mol as total energy, -139.343 Kcal/mol as Van der Waals force and H-bond as -6.28282 Kcal/mol which was presented in table 57.

The lawsoniaside with chitin synthase interaction observed that the total energy between them as +251.281 Kcal/mol, Van der Waals force between them as +275.861 Kcal/mol, and H-bond between them as -24.5795 Kcal/mol while with the derivative of lawsoniaside 1 (SAR 1) with IUPAC name: (2S,3R,4S,5S,6R)-2-[(2-hydroxy-5-methyl-4-{[(2S,3R,4S,5S,6R)-3,4,5-trihydroxy-6-(hydroxymethyl)oxan-2-

yl]oxy}naphthalen-1-yl)oxy]-6-(hydroxymethyl)oxane-3,4,5-triol shows as -131.024 Kcal/mol as total energy, -106.427 Kcal/mol as Van der Waals force and H-bond as -24.5973 Kcal/mol which was presented in table 58.

The lawsoniaside with chitinase interaction observed that the total energy between them as +453.67 Kcal/mol, Van der Waals force between them as +479.227 Kcal/mol, and H-bond between them as -25.5564 Kcal/mol while with the derivative of lawsoniaside 151 (SAR 4) with IUPAC name: (2R,3S,4S,5R,6S)-2-[(aminooxy)methyl]-6-[(3-hydroxy-4-{[(2S,3R,4S,5S,6R)-3,4,5-trihydroxy-6-(hydroxymethyl)oxan-2-yl]oxy}naphthalen-1-yl)oxy]oxane-3,4,5-triol shows as -157.473 Kcal/mol as total energy, -136.212 Kcal/mol as Van der Waals force and H-bond as -21.2614 Kcal/mol which was presented in table 59.

The lawsoniaside with deuterolysin interaction observed that the total energy between them as +79.5765 Kcal/mol, Van der Waals force between them as +90.7356 Kcal/mol, and H-bond between them as -11.1591 Kcal/mol while with the derivative of lawsoniaside 151 (SAR 4) with IUPAC name: (2R,3S,4S,5R,6S)-2-[(aminooxy)methyl]-6-[(3-hydroxy-4-{[(2S,3R,4S,5S,6R)-3,4,5-trihydroxy-6-(hydroxymethyl)oxan-2-yl]oxy}naphthalen-1-yl)oxy]oxane-3,4,5-triol shows as -141.325 Kcal/mol as total energy, -78.6451 Kcal/mol as Van der Waals force and H-bond as -62.6802 Kcal/mol which was presented in table 60.

The lawsoniaside with fungalysin interaction observed that the total energy between them as +66.1007 Kcal/mol, Van der Waals force between them as +71.6984 Kcal/mol, and H-bond between them as -5.59768 Kcal/mol while with the derivative of lawsoniaside 182 (SAR 5) with IUPAC name: (2S,3R,4S,5S,6R)-4,5-dihydroxy-2-[(3-hydroxy-4-

{[(2S,3R,4S,5S,6R)-3,4,5-trihydroxy-6-(hydroxymethyl)oxan-2-yl]oxy}naphthalen-1-yl)oxy]-6-(hydroxymethyl)oxan-3-yl hypofluorite shows as -120.284 Kcal/mol as total energy, -83.9387 Kcal/mol as Van der Waals force and H-bond as -36.3452 Kcal/mol which was presented in table 61.

The lawsoniaside with homoserine dehydrogenase interaction observed that the total energy between them as +343.906 Kcal/mol, Van der Waals force between them as +357.139 Kcal/mol, and H-bond between them as -13.2326 Kcal/mol while with the derivative of lawsoniaside 75 (SAR 2) with IUPAC name: (2S,3R,4S,5S,6R)-4,5-dihydroxy-2-[(2-hydroxy-4-{[(2S,3R,4S,5S,6R)-3,4,5-trihydroxy-6-(hydroxymethyl)oxan-2-yl]oxy}naphthalen-1-yl)oxy]-6-(hydroxymethyl)oxan-3-yl hypofluorite shows as -121.477 Kcal/mol as total energy, -86.5718 Kcal/mol as Van der Waals force and H-bond as -34.9054 Kcal/mol which was presented in table 62.

The lawsoniaside with lumazine synthase interaction observed that the total energy between them as +131.482 Kcal/mol, Van der Waals force between them as +140.72 Kcal/mol, and H-bond between them as -9.23823 Kcal/mol while with the derivative of lawsoniaside 1 (SAR 1) with IUPAC name: (2S,3R,4S,5S,6R)-2-[(2-hydroxy-5-methyl-4-{[(2S,3R,4S,5S,6R)-3,4,5-trihydroxy-6-(hydroxymethyl)oxan-2-yl]oxy}naphthalen-1-yl)oxy]-6-(hydroxymethyl)oxane-3,4,5-triol shows as -160.986 Kcal/mol as total energy, -130.842 Kcal/mol as Van der Waals force and H-bond as -30.144 Kcal/mol which was presented in table 63.

The lawsoniaside with phosphoribosylaminoimidazole carboxylase interaction observed that the total energy between them as -31.0004

Kcal/mol, Van der Waals force between them as -27.7392 Kcal/mol, and H-bond between them as -3.26127 Kcal/mol while with the derivative of lawsoniaside 182 (SAR 5) with IUPAC name: (2S,3R,4S,5S,6R)-4,5-dihydroxy-2-[(3-hydroxy-4-{[(2S,3R,4S,5S,6R)-3,4,5-trihydroxy-6-(hydroxymethyl)oxan-2-yl]oxy}naphthalen-1-yl)oxy]-6-(hydroxymethyl)oxan-3-yl hypofluorite shows as -166.142 Kcal/mol as total energy, -129.958 Kcal/mol as Van der Waals force and H-bond as -36.1842 Kcal/mol which was presented in table 64.

The lawsoniaside with protein elongation factor 3 interaction observed that the total energy between them as +512.481 Kcal/mol, Van der Waals force between them as +524.642 Kcal/mol, and H-bond between them as -12.161 Kcal/mol while with the derivative of lawsoniaside 124 (SAR 3) with IUPAC name: (2S,3R,4S,5S,6R)-2-[(3-hydroperoxy-4-{[(2S,3R,4S,5S,6R)-3,4,5-trihydroxy-6-(hydroxymethyl)oxan-2-yl]oxy}naphthalen-1-yl)oxy]-6-(hydroxymethyl)oxane-3,4,5-triol shows as -125.268 Kcal/mol as total energy, -91.7771 Kcal/mol as Van der Waals force and H-bond as -33.491 Kcal/mol which was presented in table 65.

The lawsoniaside with sulphite reductase interaction observed that the total energy between them as +104.201 Kcal/mol, Van der Waals force between them as +128.893 Kcal/mol, and H-bond between them as -24.692 Kcal/mol while with the derivative of lawsoniaside 124 (SAR 3) with IUPAC name: (2S,3R,4S,5S,6R)-2-[(3-hydroperoxy-4-{[(2S,3R,4S,5S,6R)-3,4,5-trihydroxy-6-(hydroxymethyl)oxan-2-yl]oxy}naphthalen-1-yl)oxy]-6-(hydroxymethyl)oxane-3,4,5-triol shows as -174.222 Kcal/mol as total energy, -122.808 Kcal/mol as Van der Waals force and H-bond as -51.4136 Kcal/mol which was presented in table 66.

The scopoletin with 1, 3 Beta Glucan Synthase interaction observed that the total energy between them as -87.7434 Kcal/mol, Van der Waals force between them as -70.0445 Kcal/mol, and H-bond between them as -17.6989 Kcal/mol while with the derivative of scopoletin 114 (SAR 4) with IUPAC name: 7-(aminooxy)-6-methoxy-2H-chromen-2-one shows as -88.8804 Kcal/mol as total energy, -81.6147 Kcal/mol as Van der Waals force and H-bond as -7.26574 Kcal/mol which was presented in table 67.

The scopoletin with chitin synthase interaction observed that the total energy between them as -84.5797 Kcal/mol, Van der Waals force between them as -68.72 Kcal/mol, and H-bond between them as -15.8597 Kcal/mol while with the derivative of scopoletin 60 (SAR 3) with IUPAC name: 7-hydroxy-6-methoxy-3-sulfanyl-2H-chromen-2-one shows as -101.356 Kcal/mol as total energy, -80.0042 Kcal/mol as Van der Waals force and H-bond as -21.3519 Kcal/mol which was presented in table 68.

The scopoletin with chitinase interaction observed that the total energy between them as -92.8269 Kcal/mol, Van der Waals force between them as -69.7604 Kcal/mol, and H-bond between them as -23.0664 Kcal/mol while with the derivative of scopoletin 44 (SAR 2) with IUPAC name: 4-amino-7-hydroxy-6-methoxy-2H-chromen-2-one shows as -101.045 Kcal/mol as total energy, -82.2182 Kcal/mol as Van der Waals force and H-bond as -18.8269 Kcal/mol which was presented in table 69.

The scopoletin with deuterolysin interaction observed that the total energy between them as -88.8193 Kcal/mol, Van der Waals force between them as -78.9968 Kcal/mol, and H-bond between them as -9.82247 Kcal/mol while with the derivative of scopoletin 44 (SAR 2) with IUPAC name: 4-amino-7-hydroxy-6-methoxy-2H-chromen-2-one shows as -

87.7408 Kcal/mol as total energy, -65.1847 Kcal/mol as Van der Waals force and H-bond as -22.5561 Kcal/mol which was presented in table 70.

The scopoletin with fungalysin interaction observed that the total energy between them as -85.1649 Kcal/mol, Van der Waals force between them as -62.7076 Kcal/mol, and H-bond between them as -22.4572 Kcal/mol while with the derivative of scopoletin 44 (SAR 2) with IUPAC name: 4-amino-7-hydroxy-6-methoxy-2H-chromen-2-one shows as -93.6776 Kcal/mol as total energy, -64.1106 Kcal/mol as Van der Waals force and H-bond as -29.567 Kcal/mol which was presented in table 71.

The scopoletin with homoserine dehydrogenase interaction observed that the total energy between them as -107.231 Kcal/mol, Van der Waals force between them as -84.0977 Kcal/mol, and H-bond between them as -23.1337 Kcal/mol while with the derivative of scopoletin 127 (SAR 5) with IUPAC name: 6-ethoxy-7-hydroxy-2H-chromen-2-one shows as -103.514 Kcal/mol as total energy, -73.1225 Kcal/mol as Van der Waals force and H-bond as -30.3916 Kcal/mol which was presented in table 72.

The scopoletin with lumazine synthase interaction observed that the total energy between them as -91.7861 Kcal/mol, Van der Waals force between them as -74.443 Kcal/mol, and H-bond between them as -17.3431 Kcal/mol while with the derivative of scopoletin 114 (SAR 4) with IUPAC name: 7-(aminooxy)-6-methoxy-2H-chromen-2-one shows as -96.5144 Kcal/mol as total energy, -70.9017 Kcal/mol as Van der Waals force and H-bond as -25.6127 Kcal/mol which was presented in table 73.

The scopoletin with phosphoribosylaminoimidazole carboxylase interaction observed that the total energy between them as -93.6627 Kcal/mol, Van der Waals force between them as -76.3733 Kcal/mol, and

H-bond between them as -17.2894 Kcal/mol while with the derivative of scopoletin 44 (SAR 2) with IUPAC name: 4-amino-7-hydroxy-6-methoxy-2H-chromen-2-one shows as -101.672 Kcal/mol as total energy, -79.4941 Kcal/mol as Van der Waals force and H-bond as -22.1776 Kcal/mol which was presented in table 74.

The scopoletin with protein elongation factor 3 interaction observed that the total energy between them as -75.0842 Kcal/mol, Van der Waals force between them as -65.0983 Kcal/mol, and H-bond between them as -9.9859 Kcal/mol while with the derivative of scopoletin 44 (SAR 2) with IUPAC name: 4-amino-7-hydroxy-6-methoxy-2H-chromen-2-one shows as -82.9808 Kcal/mol as total energy, -69.5038 Kcal/mol as Van der Waals force and H-bond as -13.477 Kcal/mol which was presented in table 75.

The scopoletin with sulphite reductase interaction observed that the total energy between them as -94.5167 Kcal/mol, Van der Waals force between them as -74.858 Kcal/mol, and H-bond between them as -19.6586 Kcal/mol while with the derivative of scopoletin 44 (SAR 2) with IUPAC name: 4-amino-7-hydroxy-6-methoxy-2H-chromen-2-one shows as -107.662 Kcal/mol as total energy, -80.2991 Kcal/mol as Van der Waals force and H-bond as -27.3627 Kcal/mol which was presented in table 76.

The stigmasterol with 1, 3 Beta Glucan Synthase interaction observed that the total energy between them as +359.819 Kcal/mol, Van der Waals force between them as +359.819 Kcal/mol, and H-bond between them as 0 Kcal/mol while with the derivative of stigmasterol 181 (SAR 5) with IUPAC name: (1R,3aS,3bS,7S,9aR,9bS,11aS)-1-[(3E)-1-amino-5-ethyl-6-methylhept-3-en-2-yl]-9a,11a-dimethyl-1H,2H,3H,3aH,3bH,4H,6H,7H,8H,9H,9aH,9bH,10H,11H,11aHcyclopenta[a]phenanthren-7-ol shows as -123.805 Kcal/mol as total energy, -121.305 Kcal/mol as Van der Waals force and H-bond as -2.5 Kcal/mol which was presented in table 77.

The stigmasterol with chitin synthase interaction observed that the total energy between them as +536.619 Kcal/mol, Van der Waals force between them as +535.762 Kcal/mol, and H-bond between them as 0.85736 Kcal/mol while with the derivative of stigmasterol 181 (SAR 5) with IUPAC name: (1R,3aS,3bS,7S,9aR,9bS,11aS)-1-[(3E)-1-amino-5-ethyl-6-methylhept-3-en-2-yl]-9a,11a-dimethyl-1H,2H,3H,3aH,3bH,4H,6H,7H,8H,9H,9aH,9bH,10H,11H,11aH-cyclopenta[a]phenanthren-7-ol shows as -143.725 Kcal/mol as total energy, -138.261 Kcal/mol as Van der Waals force and H-bond as -5.46416 Kcal/mol which was presented in table 78.

The stigmasterol with chitinase interaction observed that the total energy between them as -14.0681 Kcal/mol, Van der Waals force between them as -14.0681 Kcal/mol, and H-bond between them as 0 Kcal/mol while with the derivative of stigmasterol 16 (SAR 1) with IUPAC name: (1R,3aS,3bS,7S,9aR,9bS,11aR)-1-[(3E)-7-amino-5-ethyl-6-methylhept-3-en-2-yl]-9a,11a-dimethyl-1H,2H,3H,3aH,3bH,4H,6H,7H,8H,9H,9aH,9bH,10H,11H,11aH-cyclopenta[a]phenanthren-7-ol shows as -148.059 Kcal/mol as total energy, -136.305 Kcal/mol as Van der Waals force and H-bond as -11.7533 Kcal/mol which was presented in table 79.

The stigmasterol with deuterolysin interaction observed that the total energy between them as +237.541 Kcal/mol, Van der Waals force between them as +237.541 Kcal/mol, and H-bond between them as 0 Kcal/mol while with the derivative of stigmasterol 16 (SAR 1) with IUPAC name: (1R,3aS,3bS,7S,9aR,9bS,11aR)-1-[(3E)-7-amino-5-ethyl-6-methylhept-3-en-2-yl]-9a,11a-dimethyl-1H,2H,3H,3aH,3bH,4H,6H,7H,8H,9H,9aH,9bH,10H,11H,11aH-cyclopenta[a]phenanthren-7-ol shows as -146.112 Kcal/mol as total energy, -138.643 Kcal/mol as Van der Waals force and H-bond as -7.46839 Kcal/mol which was presented in table 80.

The stigmasterol with fungalysin interaction observed that the total energy between them as +517.875 Kcal/mol, Van der Waals force between them as +519.376 Kcal/mol, and H-bond between them as -1.50145 Kcal/mol while with the derivative of stigmasterol 44 (SAR 2) with IUPAC name: (1R,3aS,3bS,7S,9aR,9bS,11aR)-1-[(3E)-6-amino-5-ethyl-6-methylhept-3-en-2-yl]-9a,11a-dimethyl-1H,2H,3H,3aH,3bH,4H,6H,7H,8H,9H,9aH,9bH,10H,11H,11aH-cyclopenta[a]phenanthren-7-ol shows as -115.637 Kcal/mol as total energy, -108.292 Kcal/mol as Van der Waals force and H-bond as -7.34529 Kcal/mol which was presented in table 81.

The stigmasterol with homoserine dehydrogenase interaction observed that the total energy between them as +126.99 Kcal/mol, Van der Waals force between them as +129.448 Kcal/mol, and H-bond between them as -2.45724 Kcal/mol while with the derivative of stigmasterol 16 (SAR 1) with IUPAC name: (1R,3aS,3bS,7S,9aR,9bS,11aR)-1-[(3E)-7-amino-5-ethyl-6-methylhept-3-en-2-yl]-9a,11a-dimethyl-1H,2H,3H,3aH,3bH,4H,6H,7H,8H,9H,9aH,9bH,10H,11H,11aH-cyclopenta[a]phenanthren-7-ol shows as -115.686 Kcal/mol as total energy, -104.859 Kcal/mol as Van der Waals force and H-bond as -10.8265 Kcal/mol which was presented in table 82.

The stigmasterol with lumazine synthase interaction observed that the total energy between them as +436.404 Kcal/mol, Van der Waals force between them as +441.189 Kcal/mol, and H-bond between them as -4.78576 Kcal/mol while with the derivative of stigmasterol 145 (SAR 4) with IUPAC name: (1R,3aS,3bS,7S,9aR,9bS,11aR)-4-amino-1-[(3E)-5-ethyl-6-methylhept-3-en-2-yl]-9a,11a-dimethyl-1H,2H,3H,3aH,3bH,4H,6H,7H,8H,9H,9aH,9bH,10H,11H,11aH-cyclopenta[a]phenanthren-7-ol shows as -120.585 Kcal/mol as total energy, -113.831 Kcal/mol as Van der Waals force and H-bond as -6.75424 Kcal/mol which was presented in table 83.

The stigmasterol with phosphoribosylaminoimidazole carboxylase interaction observed that the total energy between them as +73.5044 Kcal/mol, Van der Waals force between them as +77.0044 Kcal/mol, and H-bond between them as -3.5 Kcal/mol while with the derivative of stigmasterol 44 (SAR 2) with IUPAC name: (1R,3aS,3bS,7S,9aR,9bS,11aR)-1-[(3E)-6-amino-5-ethyl-6-methylhept-3-en-2-yl]-9a,11a-dimethyl-1H,2H,3H,3aH,3bH,4H,6H,7H,8H,9H,9aH,9bH,10H,11H,11aH-cyclopenta[a]phenanthren-7-ol shows as -164.044 Kcal/mol as total energy, -156.046 Kcal/mol as Van der Waals force and H-bond as -7.99889 Kcal/mol which was presented in table 84.

The stigmasterol with protein elongation factor 3 interaction observed that the total energy between them as +238.744 Kcal/mol, Van der Waals force between them as +238.744 Kcal/mol, and H-bond between them as 0 Kcal/mol while with the derivative of stigmasterol 44 (SAR 2) with IUPAC name: (1R,3aS,3bS,7S,9aR,9bS,11aR)-1-[(3E)-6-amino-5-ethyl-6-methylhept-3-en-2-yl]-9a,11a-dimethyl-

1H,2H,3H,3aH,3bH,4H,6H,7H,8H,9H,9aH,9bH,10H,11H,11aH-cyclopenta[a]phenanthren-7-ol shows as -120.361 Kcal/mol as total energy, -116.009 Kcal/mol as Van der Waals force and H-bond as -4.35265 Kcal/mol which was presented in table 85.

The stigmasterol with sulphite reductase interaction observed that the total energy between them as -39.2956 Kcal/mol, Van der Waals force between them as -39.2956 Kcal/mol, and H-bond between them as 0 Kcal/mol while with the derivative of stigmasterol 181 (SAR 5) with IUPAC name: (1R,3aS,3bS,7S,9aR,9bS,11aS)-1-[(3E)-1-amino-5-ethyl-6-methylhept-3-en-2-yl]-9a,11a-dimethyl-1H,2H,3H,3aH,3bH,4H,6H,7H,8H,9H,9aH,9bH,10H,11H,11aH-cyclopenta[a]phenanthren-7-ol shows as -133.042 Kcal/mol as total energy, -124.431 Kcal/mol as Van der Waals force and H-bond as -8.611 Kcal/mol which was presented in table 86.

Table 17: The results of derivatives of Azadirachtin, a secondary metabolite of *A. indica*, with 1,3 β Glucan synthase obtained from quick docking by using iGEMDOCK 2.0.

Sno	Protein + Ligand derivative	1,3 β Glucan synthase with azadirachtin derivatives (IUPAC name)	Total Energy (Kcal per mol)	V D W (Kcal per mol)	H. Bond (Kcal per mol)
1	1,3 β Glucan synthase-Azadirachtin structure Derivative 02(SAR 1)	4,11-dimethyl (1S,4S,5R,6S,7S,8R,11S,12R,14S,15R)-12-(acetyloxy)-4,7-dihydroxy-6-[(1S,2S,6R,8S,9R,11S)-2-hydroxy-11-methyl-7,10-dioxatetracyclo[6.3.1.0^{2,6}.0^{9,11}]dodec-3-en-9-yl]-6-methyl-14-{[(2E)-2-methylbut-2-enoyl]oxy}-3,9-dioxatetracyclo[6.6.1.0^{1,5}.0^{11,15}]pentadecane-4,11-dicarboxylate	-239.777	-225.809	-13.9683
2	1,3 β Glucan synthase-Azadirachtin structure Derivative 19(SAR 2)	4,11-dimethyl (1S,4S,5R,6S,7S,8R,11S,12R,14S,15R)-12-(acetyloxy)-4,7-dihydroxy-6-[(1S,2S,6R,8S,9R,11S)-2-hydroxy-11-methyl-5,10-dioxa-7-azatetracyclo[6.3.1.0^{2,6}.0^{9,11}]dodec-3-en-9-yl]-6-methyl-14-{[(2E)-2-methylbut-2-enoyl]oxy}-3,9-dioxatetracyclo[6.6.1.0^{1,5}.0^{11,15}]pentadecane-4,11-dicarboxylate	-173.747	-170.247	-3.5
3	1,3 β Glucan synthase-Azadirachtin structure Derivative 56(SAR 3)	4,11-dimethyl (1S,4S,5R,6S,7S,8R,11S,12R,14S,15R)-12-ethoxy-4,7-dihydroxy-6-[(1S,2S,6S,8S,9R,11S)-2-hydroxy-11-methyl-5,7,10-trioxatetracyclo[6.3.1.0^{2,6}.0^{9,11}]dodec-3-en-9-yl]-6-methyl-14-{[(2E)-2-methylbut-2-enoyl]oxy}-3,9-dioxatetracyclo[6.6.1.0^{1,5}.0^{11,15}]pentadecane-4,11-dicarboxylate	-143.1	-119.845	-23.2549
4	1,3 β Glucan synthase-Azadirachtin structure Derivative 58(SAR 4)	4,11-dimethyl (1S,4S,5R,6S,7S,8R,11S,12R,14S,15R)-12-(ethanimidoyloxy)-4,7-dihydroxy-6-[(1S,2S,6S,8S,9R,11S)-2-hydroxy-11-methyl-5,7,10-trioxatetracyclo[6.3.1.0^{2,6}.0^{9,11}]dodec-3-en-9-yl]-6-methyl-14-{[(2E)-2-methylbut-2-enoyl]oxy}-3,9-dioxatetracyclo[6.6.1.0^{1,5}.0^{11,15}]pentadecane-4,11-dicarboxylate	-173.873	-168.185	-5.68824
5	1,3 β Glucan synthase-Azadirachtin structure Derivative 81(SAR 5)	4,11-dimethyl (1S,4S,5R,6S,7S,8R,11S,12R,14S,15R)-12-(acetyloxy)-14-{[(2Z)-2-(bromomethyl)but-2-enoyl]oxy}-4,7-dihydroxy-6-[(1S,2S,6S,8S,9R,11S)-2-hydroxy-11-methyl-5,7,10-trioxatetracyclo[6.3.1.0^{2,6}.0^{9,11}]dodec-3-en-9-yl]-6-methyl-3,9-dioxatetracyclo[6.6.1.0^{1,5}.0^{11,15}]pentadecane-4,11-dicarboxylate	-243.297	-236.12	-7.17628

Table 18: The results of derivatives of Azadirachtin, a secondary metabolite of *A. indica*, with Chitin synthase obtained from quick docking by using iGEMDOCK 2.0.

S no	Protein + Ligand derivative	Chitin synthasewith azadirachtin derivatives (IUPAC name)	Total Energy (Kcal per mol)	V D W (Kcal per mol)	H. Bond (Kcal per mol)
1	Chitin synthase - Azadirachtin structure Derivative 02(SAR 1)	4,11-dimethyl (1S,4S,5R,6S,7S,8R,11S,12R,14S,15R)-12-(acetyloxy)-4,7-dihydroxy-6-[(1S,2S,6R,8S,9R,11S)-2-hydroxy-11-methyl-7,10-dioxatetracyclo[6.3.1.0^{2},^{6}.0^{9},^{11}]dodec-3-en-9-yl]-6-methyl-14-{[(2E)-2-methylbut-2-enoyl]oxy}-3,9-dioxatetracyclo[6.6.1.0^{1},^{5}.0^{11},^{15}]pentadecane-4,11-dicarboxylate	-197.148	-178.537	-18.6107
2	Chitin synthase - Azadirachtin structure Derivative 19(SAR 2)	4,11-dimethyl (1S,4S,5R,6S,7S,8R,11S,12R,14S,15R)-12-(acetyloxy)-4,7-dihydroxy-6-[(1S,2S,6R,8S,9R,11S)-2-hydroxy-11-methyl-5,10-dioxa-7-azatetracyclo[6.3.1.0^{2},^{6}.0^{9},^{11}]dodec-3-en-9-yl]-6-methyl-14-{[(2E)-2-methylbut-2-enoyl]oxy}-3,9-dioxatetracyclo[6.6.1.0^{1},^{5}.0^{11},^{15}]pentadecane-4,11-dicarboxylate	-172.283	-145.991	-26.2919
3	Chitin synthase - Azadirachtin structure Derivative 56(SAR 3)	4,11-dimethyl (1S,4S,5R,6S,7S,8R,11S,12R,14S,15R)-12-ethoxy-4,7-dihydroxy-6-[(1S,2S,6S,8S,9R,11S)-2-hydroxy-11-methyl-5,7,10-trioxatetracyclo[6.3.1.0^{2},^{6}.0^{9},^{11}]dodec-3-en-9-yl]-6-methyl-14-{[(2E)-2-methylbut-2-enoyl]oxy}-3,9-dioxatetracyclo[6.6.1.0^{1},^{5}.0^{11},^{15}]pentadecane-4,11-dicarboxylate	-177.906	-160.918	-16.9886
4	Chitin synthase - Azadirachtin structure Derivative 58(SAR 4)	4,11-dimethyl (1S,4S,5R,6S,7S,8R,11S,12R,14S,15R)-12-(ethanimidoyloxy)-4,7-dihydroxy-6-[(1S,2S,6S,8S,9R,11S)-2-hydroxy-11-methyl-5,7,10-trioxatetracyclo[6.3.1.0^{2},^{6}.0^{9},^{11}]dodec-3-en-9-yl]-6-methyl-14-{[(2E)-2-methylbut-2-enoyl]oxy}-3,9-dioxatetracyclo[6.6.1.0^{1},^{5}.0^{11},^{15}]pentadecane-4,11-dicarboxylate	-163.707	-148.847	-14.8604
5	Chitin synthase - Azadirachtin structure Derivative 81(SAR 5)	4,11-dimethyl (1S,4S,5R,6S,7S,8R,11S,12R,14S,15R)-12-(acetyloxy)-14-{[(2Z)-2-(bromomethyl)but-2-enoyl]oxy}-4,7-dihydroxy-6-[(1S,2S,6S,8S,9R,11S)-2-hydroxy-11-methyl-5,7,10-trioxatetracyclo[6.3.1.0^{2},^{6}.0^{9},^{11}]dodec-3-en-9-yl]-6-methyl-3,9-dioxatetracyclo[6.6.1.0^{1},^{5}.0^{11},^{15}]pentadecane-4,11-dicarboxylate	-163.793	-135.222	-28.5711

Table 19: The results of derivatives of Azadirachtin, a secondary metabolite of *A. indica*, with Chitinase obtained from quick docking by using iGEMDOCK 2.0.

S no	Protein + Ligand derivative	Chitinasewith azadirachtin derivatives (IUPAC name)	Total Energy (Kcal per mol)	V D W (Kcal per mol)	H. Bond (Kcal per mol)
1	Chitinase - Azadirachtin structure Derivative 02(SAR1)	4,11-dimethyl (1S,4S,5R,6S,7S,8R,11S,12R,14S,15R)-12-(acetyloxy)-4,7-dihydroxy-6-[(1S,2S,6R,8S,9R,11S)-2-hydroxy-11-methyl-7,10-dioxatetracyclo[6.3.1.$0^{2,6}$.$0^{9,11}$]dodec-3-en-9-yl]-6-methyl-14-{[(2E)-2-methylbut-2-enoyl]oxy}-3,9-dioxatetracyclo[6.6.1.$0^{1,5}$.$0^{11,15}$]pentadecane-4,11-dicarboxylate	-204.084	-185.468	-18.6157
2	Chitinase - Azadirachtin structure Derivative 19(SAR 2)	4,11-dimethyl (1S,4S,5R,6S,7S,8R,11S,12R,14S,15R)-12-(acetyloxy)-4,7-dihydroxy-6-[(1S,2S,6R,8S,9R,11S)-2-hydroxy-11-methyl-5,10-dioxa-7-azatetracyclo[6.3.1.$0^{2,6}$.$0^{9,11}$]dodec-3-en-9-yl]-6-methyl-14-{[(2E)-2-methylbut-2-enoyl]oxy}-3,9-dioxatetracyclo[6.6.1.$0^{1,5}$.$0^{11,15}$]pentadecane-4,11-dicarboxylate	-204.849	-183.776	-21.0725
3	Chitinase - Azadirachtin structure Derivative 56(SAR 3)	4,11-dimethyl (1S,4S,5R,6S,7S,8R,11S,12R,14S,15R)-12-ethoxy-4,7-dihydroxy-6-[(1S,2S,6S,8S,9R,11S)-2-hydroxy-11-methyl-5,7,10-trioxatetracyclo[6.3.1.$0^{2,6}$.$0^{9,11}$]dodec-3-en-9-yl]-6-methyl-14-{[(2E)-2-methylbut-2-enoyl]oxy}-3,9-dioxatetracyclo[6.6.1.$0^{1,5}$.$0^{11,15}$]pentadecane-4,11-dicarboxylate	-194.033	-178.277	-15.7561
4	Chitinase - Azadirachtin structure Derivative 58(SAR 4)	4,11-dimethyl (1S,4S,5R,6S,7S,8R,11S,12R,14S,15R)-12-(ethanimidoyloxy)-4,7-dihydroxy-6-[(1S,2S,6S,8S,9R,11S)-2-hydroxy-11-methyl-5,7,10-trioxatetracyclo[6.3.1.$0^{2,6}$.$0^{9,11}$]dodec-3-en-9-yl]-6-methyl-14-{[(2E)-2-methylbut-2-enoyl]oxy}-3,9-dioxatetracyclo[6.6.1.$0^{1,5}$.$0^{11,15}$]pentadecane-4,11-dicarboxylate	-206.225	-188.823	-17.4017
5	Chitinase - Azadirachtin structure Derivative 81(SAR 5)	4,11-dimethyl (1S,4S,5R,6S,7S,8R,11S,12R,14S,15R)-12-(acetyloxy)-14-{[(2Z)-2-(bromomethyl)but-2-enoyl]oxy}-4,7-dihydroxy-6-[(1S,2S,6S,8S,9R,11S)-2-hydroxy-11-methyl-5,7,10-trioxatetracyclo[6.3.1.$0^{2,6}$.$0^{9,11}$]dodec-3-en-9-yl]-6-methyl-3,9-dioxatetracyclo[6.6.1.$0^{1,5}$.$0^{11,15}$]pentadecane-4,11-dicarboxylate	-206.663	-190.026	-16.6372

Table20: The results of derivatives of Azadirachtin, a secondary metabolite of *A. indica*, with Deuterolysin obtained from quick docking by using iGEMDOCK 2.0.

S no	Protein + Ligand derivative	Deuterolysinwith azadirachtin derivatives (IUPAC name)	Total Energy (Kcal per mol)	V D W (Kcal per mol)	H. Bond (Kcal per mol)
1	Deuterolysin - Azadirachtin structure Derivative 02(SAR 1)	4,11-dimethyl (1S,4S,5R,6S,7S,8R,11S,12R,14S,15R)-12-(acetyloxy)-4,7-dihydroxy-6-[(1S,2S,6R,8S,9R,11S)-2-hydroxy-11-methyl-7,10-dioxatetracyclo[6.3.1.$0^{2,6}$.$0^{9,11}$]dodec-3-en-9-yl]-6-methyl-14-{[(2E)-2-methylbut-2-enoyl]oxy}-3,9-dioxatetracyclo[6.6.1.$0^{1,5}$.$0^{11,15}$]pentadecane-4,11-dicarboxylate	-164.408	-144.581	-19.8266
2	Deuterolysin - Azadirachtin structure Derivative 19(SAR 2)	4,11-dimethyl (1S,4S,5R,6S,7S,8R,11S,12R,14S,15R)-12-(acetyloxy)-4,7-dihydroxy-6-[(1S,2S,6R,8S,9R,11S)-2-hydroxy-11-methyl-5,10-dioxa-7-azatetracyclo[6.3.1.$0^{2,6}$.$0^{9,11}$]dodec-3-en-9-yl]-6-methyl-14-{[(2E)-2-methylbut-2-enoyl]oxy}-3,9-dioxatetracyclo[6.6.1.$0^{1,5}$.$0^{11,15}$]pentadecane-4,11-dicarboxylate	-166.072	-165.282	-0.7903
3	Deuterolysin - Azadirachtin structure Derivative 56(SAR 3)	4,11-dimethyl (1S,4S,5R,6S,7S,8R,11S,12R,14S,15R)-12-ethoxy-4,7-dihydroxy-6-[(1S,2S,6S,8S,9R,11S)-2-hydroxy-11-methyl-5,7,10-trioxatetracyclo[6.3.1.$0^{2,6}$.$0^{9,11}$]dodec-3-en-9-yl]-6-methyl-14-{[(2E)-2-methylbut-2-enoyl]oxy}-3,9-dioxatetracyclo[6.6.1.$0^{1,5}$.$0^{11,15}$]pentadecane-4,11-dicarboxylate	-176.641	-150.119	-26.5219
4	Deuterolysin - Azadirachtin structure Derivative 58(SAR 4)	4,11-dimethyl (1S,4S,5R,6S,7S,8R,11S,12R,14S,15R)-12-(ethanimidoyloxy)-4,7-dihydroxy-6-[(1S,2S,6S,8S,9R,11S)-2-hydroxy-11-methyl-5,7,10-trioxatetracyclo[6.3.1.$0^{2,6}$.$0^{9,11}$]dodec-3-en-9-yl]-6-methyl-14-{[(2E)-2-methylbut-2-enoyl]oxy}-3,9-dioxatetracyclo[6.6.1.$0^{1,5}$.$0^{11,15}$]pentadecane-4,11-dicarboxylate	-170.542	-154.402	-16.1404
5	Deuterolysin - Azadirachtin structure Derivative 81(SAR 5)	4,11-dimethyl (1S,4S,5R,6S,7S,8R,11S,12R,14S,15R)-12-(acetyloxy)-14-{[(2Z)-2-(bromomethyl)but-2-enoyl]oxy}-4,7-dihydroxy-6-[(1S,2S,6S,8S,9R,11S)-2-hydroxy-11-methyl-5,7,10-trioxatetracyclo[6.3.1.$0^{2,6}$.$0^{9,11}$]dodec-3-en-9-yl]-6-methyl-3,9-dioxatetracyclo[6.6.1.$0^{1,5}$.$0^{11,15}$]pentadecane-4,11-dicarboxylate	-201.776	-188.616	-13.1598

Table21: **The results of derivatives of Azadirachtin, a secondary metabolite of *A. indica*, with Fungalysin obtained from quick docking by using iGEMDOCK 2.0.**

S no	Protein + Ligand derivative	Fungalysinwith azadirachtin derivatives (IUPAC name)	Total Energy (Kcal per mol)	V DW (Kcal per mol)	H. Bond (Kcal per mol)
1	Fungalysin - Azadirachtin structure Derivative 02(SAR1)	4,11-dimethyl (1S,4S,5R,6S,7S,8R,11S,12R,14S,15R)-12-(acetyloxy)-4,7-dihydroxy-6-[(1S,2S,6R,8S,9R,11S)-2-hydroxy-11-methyl-7,10-dioxatetracyclo[6.3.1.$0^{2,6}$.$0^{9,11}$]dodec-3-en-9-yl]-6-methyl-14-{[(2E)-2-methylbut-2-enoyl]oxy}-3,9-dioxatetracyclo[6.6.1.$0^{1,5}$.$0^{11,15}$]pentadecane-4,11-dicarboxylate	-159.203	-127.176	-32.0274
2	Fungalysin - Azadirachtin structure Derivative 19(SAR 2)	4,11-dimethyl (1S,4S,5R,6S,7S,8R,11S,12R,14S,15R)-12-(acetyloxy)-4,7-dihydroxy-6-[(1S,2S,6R,8S,9R,11S)-2-hydroxy-11-methyl-5,10-dioxa-7-azatetracyclo[6.3.1.$0^{2,6}$.$0^{9,11}$]dodec-3-en-9-yl]-6-methyl-14-{[(2E)-2-methylbut-2-enoyl]oxy}-3,9-dioxatetracyclo[6.6.1.$0^{1,5}$.$0^{11,15}$]pentadecane-4,11-dicarboxylate	-141.464	-119.272	-22.1925
3	Fungalysin - Azadirachtin structure Derivative 56(SAR 3)	4,11-dimethyl (1S,4S,5R,6S,7S,8R,11S,12R,14S,15R)-12-ethoxy-4,7-dihydroxy-6-[(1S,2S,6S,8S,9R,11S)-2-hydroxy-11-methyl-5,7,10-trioxatetracyclo[6.3.1.$0^{2,6}$.$0^{9,11}$]dodec-3-en-9-yl]-6-methyl-14-{[(2E)-2-methylbut-2-enoyl]oxy}-3,9-dioxatetracyclo[6.6.1.$0^{1,5}$.$0^{11,15}$]pentadecane-4,11-dicarboxylate	-156.2	-141.775	-14.4259
4	Fungalysin - Azadirachtin structure Derivative 58(SAR 4)	4,11-dimethyl (1S,4S,5R,6S,7S,8R,11S,12R,14S,15R)-12-(ethanimidoyloxy)-4,7-dihydroxy-6-[(1S,2S,6S,8S,9R,11S)-2-hydroxy-11-methyl-5,7,10-trioxatetracyclo[6.3.1.$0^{2,6}$.$0^{9,11}$]dodec-3-en-9-yl]-6-methyl-14-{[(2E)-2-methylbut-2-enoyl]oxy}-3,9-dioxatetracyclo[6.6.1.$0^{1,5}$.$0^{11,15}$]pentadecane-4,11-dicarboxylate	-164.763	-124.717	-40.0461
5	Fungalysin - Azadirachtin structure Derivative 81(SAR 5)	4,11-dimethyl (1S,4S,5R,6S,7S,8R,11S,12R,14S,15R)-12-(acetyloxy)-14-{[(2Z)-2-(bromomethyl)but-2-enoyl]oxy}-4,7-dihydroxy-6-[(1S,2S,6S,8S,9R,11S)-2-hydroxy-11-methyl-5,7,10-trioxatetracyclo[6.3.1.$0^{2,6}$.$0^{9,11}$]dodec-3-en-9-yl]-6-methyl-3,9-dioxatetracyclo[6.6.1.$0^{1,5}$.$0^{11,15}$]pentadecane-4,11-dicarboxylate	-150.4	-126.465	-23.9348

Table22: The results of derivatives of Azadirachtin, a secondary metabolite of *A. indica*, with Homoserine dehydrogenase obtained from quick docking by using iGEMDOCK 2.0.

S no	Protein + Ligand derivative	Homoserine dehydrogenase with azadirachtin derivatives (IUPAC name)	Total Energy (Kcal per mol)	V D W (Kcal per mol)	H. Bond (Kcal per mol)
1	Homoserine dehydrogenase - Azadirachtin structure Derivative 02(SAR 1)	4,11-dimethyl (1S,4S,5R,6S,7S,8R,11S,12R,14S,15R)-12-(acetyloxy)-4,7-dihydroxy-6-[(1S,2S,6R,8S,9R,11S)-2-hydroxy-11-methyl-7,10-dioxatetracyclo[6.3.1.0^{2,6}.0^{9,11}]dodec-3-en-9-yl]-6-methyl-14-{[(2E)-2-methylbut-2-enoyl]oxy}-3,9-dioxatetracyclo[6.6.1.0^{1,5}.0^{11,15}]pentadecane-4,11-dicarboxylate	-211.691	-197.578	-14.1131
2	Homoserine dehydrogenase - Azadirachtin structure Derivative 19(SAR 2)	4,11-dimethyl (1S,4S,5R,6S,7S,8R,11S,12R,14S,15R)-12-(acetyloxy)-4,7-dihydroxy-6-[(1S,2S,6R,8S,9R,11S)-2-hydroxy-11-methyl-5,10-dioxa-7-azatetracyclo[6.3.1.0^{2,6}.0^{9,11}]dodec-3-en-9-yl]-6-methyl-14-{[(2E)-2-methylbut-2-enoyl]oxy}-3,9-dioxatetracyclo[6.6.1.0^{1,5}.0^{11,15}]pentadecane-4,11-dicarboxylate	-168.172	-138.77	-29.4023
3	Homoserine dehydrogenase - Azadirachtin structure Derivative 56(SAR 3)	4,11-dimethyl (1S,4S,5R,6S,7S,8R,11S,12R,14S,15R)-12-ethoxy-4,7-dihydroxy-6-[(1S,2S,6S,8S,9R,11S)-2-hydroxy-11-methyl-5,7,10-trioxatetracyclo[6.3.1.0^{2,6}.0^{9,11}]dodec-3-en-9-yl]-6-methyl-14-{[(2E)-2-methylbut-2-enoyl]oxy}-3,9-dioxatetracyclo[6.6.1.0^{1,5}.0^{11,15}]pentadecane-4,11-dicarboxylate	-155.378	-120.441	-34.9371
4	Homoserine dehydrogenase - Azadirachtin structure Derivative 58(SAR 4)	4,11-dimethyl (1S,4S,5R,6S,7S,8R,11S,12R,14S,15R)-12-(ethanimidoyloxy)-4,7-dihydroxy-6-[(1S,2S,6S,8S,9R,11S)-2-hydroxy-11-methyl-5,7,10-trioxatetracyclo[6.3.1.0^{2,6}.0^{9,11}]dodec-3-en-9-yl]-6-methyl-14-{[(2E)-2-methylbut-2-enoyl]oxy}-3,9-dioxatetracyclo[6.6.1.0^{1,5}.0^{11,15}]pentadecane-4,11-dicarboxylate	-227.028	-201.337	-25.6909
5	Homoserine dehydrogenase - Azadirachtin structure Derivative 81(SAR 5)	4,11-dimethyl (1S,4S,5R,6S,7S,8R,11S,12R,14S,15R)-12-(acetyloxy)-14-{[(2Z)-2-(bromomethyl)but-2-enoyl]oxy}-4,7-dihydroxy-6-[(1S,2S,6S,8S,9R,11S)-2-hydroxy-11-methyl-5,7,10-trioxatetracyclo[6.3.1.0^{2,6}.0^{9,11}]dodec-3-en-9-yl]-6-methyl-3,9-dioxatetracyclo[6.6.1.0^{1,5}.0^{11,15}]pentadecane-4,11-dicarboxylate	-226.658	-189.755	-36.9027

Table23: The results of derivatives of Azadirachtin, a secondary metabolite of *A. indica*, with Lumazine synthase obtained from quick docking by using iGEMDOCK 2.0.

S no	Protein + Ligand derivative	Lumazine synthase with azadirachtin derivatives (IUPAC name)	Total Energy (Kcal per mol)	V D W (Kcal per mol)	H. Bond (Kcal per mol)
1	Lumazine synthase - Azadirachtin structure Derivative 02(SAR 1)	4,11-dimethyl (1S,4S,5R,6S,7S,8R,11S,12R,14S,15R)-12-(acetyloxy)-4,7-dihydroxy-6-[(1S,2S,6R,8S,9R,11S)-2-hydroxy-11-methyl-7,10-dioxatetracyclo[6.3.1.0^{2},^{6}.0^{9},^{11}]dodec-3-en-9-yl]-6-methyl-14-{[(2E)-2-methylbut-2-enoyl]oxy}-3,9-dioxatetracyclo[6.6.1.0^{1},^{5}.0^{11},^{15}]pentadecane-4,11-dicarboxylate	-169.296	-153.889	-15.4064
2	Lumazine synthase - Azadirachtin structure Derivative 19(SAR 2)	4,11-dimethyl (1S,4S,5R,6S,7S,8R,11S,12R,14S,15R)-12-(acetyloxy)-4,7-dihydroxy-6-[(1S,2S,6R,8S,9R,11S)-2-hydroxy-11-methyl-5,10-dioxa-7-azatetracyclo[6.3.1.0^{2},^{6}.0^{9},^{11}]dodec-3-en-9-yl]-6-methyl-14-{[(2E)-2-methylbut-2-enoyl]oxy}-3,9-dioxatetracyclo[6.6.1.0^{1},^{5}.0^{11},^{15}]pentadecane-4,11-dicarboxylate	-171.633	-135.127	-36.5057
3	Lumazine synthase - Azadirachtin structure Derivative 56(SAR 3)	4,11-dimethyl (1S,4S,5R,6S,7S,8R,11S,12R,14S,15R)-12-ethoxy-4,7-dihydroxy-6-[(1S,2S,6S,8S,9R,11S)-2-hydroxy-11-methyl-5,7,10-trioxatetracyclo[6.3.1.0^{2},^{6}.0^{9},^{11}]dodec-3-en-9-yl]-6-methyl-14-{[(2E)-2-methylbut-2-enoyl]oxy}-3,9-dioxatetracyclo[6.6.1.0^{1},^{5}.0^{11},^{15}]pentadecane-4,11-dicarboxylate	-159.185	-150.133	-9.05174
4	Lumazine synthase - Azadirachtin structure Derivative 58(SAR 4)	4,11-dimethyl (1S,4S,5R,6S,7S,8R,11S,12R,14S,15R)-12-(ethanimidoyloxy)-4,7-dihydroxy-6-[(1S,2S,6S,8S,9R,11S)-2-hydroxy-11-methyl-5,7,10-trioxatetracyclo[6.3.1.0^{2},^{6}.0^{9},^{11}]dodec-3-en-9-yl]-6-methyl-14-{[(2E)-2-methylbut-2-enoyl]oxy}-3,9-dioxatetracyclo[6.6.1.0^{1},^{5}.0^{11},^{15}]pentadecane-4,11-dicarboxylate	-177.683	-163.707	-13.9761
5	Lumazine synthase - Azadirachtin structure Derivative 81(SAR 5)	4,11-dimethyl (1S,4S,5R,6S,7S,8R,11S,12R,14S,15R)-12-(acetyloxy)-14-{[(2Z)-2-(bromomethyl)but-2-enoyl]oxy}-4,7-dihydroxy-6-[(1S,2S,6S,8S,9R,11S)-2-hydroxy-11-methyl-5,7,10-trioxatetracyclo[6.3.1.0^{2},^{6}.0^{9},^{11}]dodec-3-en-9-yl]-6-methyl-3,9-dioxatetracyclo[6.6.1.0^{1},^{5}.0^{11},^{15}]pentadecane-4,11-dicarboxylate	-166.182	-154.113	-12.0688

Table24: **The results of derivatives of Azadirachtin, a secondary metabolite of *A. indica*, with Phosphoribosylaminoimidazole carboxylase obtained from quick docking by using iGEMDOCK 2.0.**

S no	Protein + Ligand derivative	Phosphoribosylaminoimidazole carboxylasewith azadirachtin derivatives (IUPAC name)	Total Energy (Kcal per mol)	V D W (Kcal per mol)	H. Bond (Kcal per mol)
1	Phosphoribosylaminoimidazole - Azadirachtin structure Derivative 02(SAR 1)	4,11-dimethyl (1S,4S,5R,6S,7S,8R,11S,12R,14S,15R)-12-(acetyloxy)-4,7-dihydroxy-6-[(1S,2S,6R,8S,9R,11S)-2-hydroxy-11-methyl-7,10-dioxatetracyclo[6.3.1.0^{2},^{6}.0^{9},^{11}]dodec-3-en-9-yl]-6-methyl-14-{[(2E)-2-methylbut-2-enoyl]oxy}-3,9-dioxatetracyclo[6.6.1.0^{1},^{5}.0^{11},^{15}]pentadecane-4,11-dicarboxylate	-181.62	-136.741	-44.8791
2	Phosphoribosylaminoimidazole - Azadirachtin structure Derivative 19(SAR 2)	4,11-dimethyl (1S,4S,5R,6S,7S,8R,11S,12R,14S,15R)-12-(acetyloxy)-4,7-dihydroxy-6-[(1S,2S,6R,8S,9R,11S)-2-hydroxy-11-methyl-5,10-dioxa-7-azatetracyclo[6.3.1.0^{2},^{6}.0^{9},^{11}]dodec-3-en-9-yl]-6-methyl-14-{[(2E)-2-methylbut-2-enoyl]oxy}-3,9-dioxatetracyclo[6.6.1.0^{1},^{5}.0^{11},^{15}]pentadecane-4,11-dicarboxylate	-158.863	-153.241	-5.62146
3	Phosphoribosylaminoimidazole - Azadirachtin structure Derivative 56(SAR 3)	4,11-dimethyl (1S,4S,5R,6S,7S,8R,11S,12R,14S,15R)-12-ethoxy-4,7-dihydroxy-6-[(1S,2S,6S,8S,9R,11S)-2-hydroxy-11-methyl-5,7,10-trioxatetracyclo[6.3.1.0^{2},^{6}.0^{9},^{11}]dodec-3-en-9-yl]-6-methyl-14-{[(2E)-2-methylbut-2-enoyl]oxy}-3,9-dioxatetracyclo[6.6.1.0^{1},^{5}.0^{11},^{15}]pentadecane-4,11-dicarboxylate	-164.876	-147.906	-16.9705
4	Phosphoribosylaminoimidazole - Azadirachtin structure Derivative 58(SAR 4)	4,11-dimethyl (1S,4S,5R,6S,7S,8R,11S,12R,14S,15R)-12-(ethanimidoyloxy)-4,7-dihydroxy-6-[(1S,2S,6S,8S,9R,11S)-2-hydroxy-11-methyl-5,7,10-trioxatetracyclo[6.3.1.0^{2},^{6}.0^{9},^{11}]dodec-3-en-9-yl]-6-methyl-14-{[(2E)-2-methylbut-2-enoyl]oxy}-3,9-dioxatetracyclo[6.6.1.0^{1},^{5}.0^{11},^{15}]pentadecane-4,11-dicarboxylate	21.8922	49.1707	-27.2785
5	Phosphoribosylaminoimidazole - Azadirachtin structure Derivative 81(SAR 5)	4,11-dimethyl (1S,4S,5R,6S,7S,8R,11S,12R,14S,15R)-12-(acetyloxy)-14-{[(2Z)-2-(bromomethyl)but-2-enoyl]oxy}-4,7-dihydroxy-6-[(1S,2S,6S,8S,9R,11S)-2-hydroxy-11-methyl-5,7,10-trioxatetracyclo[6.3.1.0^{2},^{6}.0^{9},^{11}]dodec-3-en-9-yl]-6-methyl-3,9-dioxatetracyclo[6.6.1.0^{1},^{5}.0^{11},^{15}]pentadecane-4,11-dicarboxylate	-173.228	-169.728	-3.5

Table 25: **The results of derivatives of Azadirachtin, a secondary metabolite of *A. indica*, with Protein elongation factor 3 obtained from quick docking by using iGEMDOCK 2.0.**

S no	Protein + Ligand derivative	Protein elongation factor 3with azadirachtin derivatives (IUPAC name)	Total Energy (Kcal per mol)	V D W (Kcal per mol)	H. Bond (Kcal per mol)
1	Protein elongation factor- Azadirachtin structure Derivative 02(SAR 1)	4,11-dimethyl (1S,4S,5R,6S,7S,8R,11S,12R,14S,15R)-12-(acetyloxy)-4,7-dihydroxy-6-[(1S,2S,6R,8S,9R,11S)-2-hydroxy-11-methyl-7,10-dioxatetracyclo[6.3.1.$0^{2,6}$.$0^{9,11}$]dodec-3-en-9-yl]-6-methyl-14-{[(2E)-2-methylbut-2-enoyl]oxy}-3,9-dioxatetracyclo[6.6.1.$0^{1,5}$.$0^{11,15}$]pentadecane-4,11-dicarboxylate	-155.138	-146.614	-8.52329
2	Protein elongation factor- Azadirachtin structure Derivative 19(SAR 2)	4,11-dimethyl (1S,4S,5R,6S,7S,8R,11S,12R,14S,15R)-12-(acetyloxy)-4,7-dihydroxy-6-[(1S,2S,6R,8S,9R,11S)-2-hydroxy-11-methyl-5,10-dioxa-7-azatetracyclo[6.3.1.$0^{2,6}$.$0^{9,11}$]dodec-3-en-9-yl]-6-methyl-14-{[(2E)-2-methylbut-2-enoyl]oxy}-3,9-dioxatetracyclo[6.6.1.$0^{1,5}$.$0^{11,15}$]pentadecane-4,11-dicarboxylate	-149.878	-128.104	-21.7746
3	Protein elongation factor- Azadirachtin structure Derivative 56(SAR 3)	4,11-dimethyl (1S,4S,5R,6S,7S,8R,11S,12R,14S,15R)-12-ethoxy-4,7-dihydroxy-6-[(1S,2S,6S,8S,9R,11S)-2-hydroxy-11-methyl-5,7,10-trioxatetracyclo[6.3.1.$0^{2,6}$.$0^{9,11}$]dodec-3-en-9-yl]-6-methyl-14-{[(2E)-2-methylbut-2-enoyl]oxy}-3,9-dioxatetracyclo[6.6.1.$0^{1,5}$.$0^{11,15}$]pentadecane-4,11-dicarboxylate	-141.14	-116.132	-25.0077
4	Protein elongation factor- Azadirachtin structure Derivative 58(SAR 4)	4,11-dimethyl (1S,4S,5R,6S,7S,8R,11S,12R,14S,15R)-12-(ethanimidoyloxy)-4,7-dihydroxy-6-[(1S,2S,6S,8S,9R,11S)-2-hydroxy-11-methyl-5,7,10-trioxatetracyclo[6.3.1.$0^{2,6}$.$0^{9,11}$]dodec-3-en-9-yl]-6-methyl-14-{[(2E)-2-methylbut-2-enoyl]oxy}-3,9-dioxatetracyclo[6.6.1.$0^{1,5}$.$0^{11,15}$]pentadecane-4,11-dicarboxylate	-136.594	-113.004	-23.5902
5	Protein elongation factor- Azadirachtin structure Derivative 81(SAR 5)	4,11-dimethyl (1S,4S,5R,6S,7S,8R,11S,12R,14S,15R)-12-(acetyloxy)-14-{[(2Z)-2-(bromomethyl)but-2-enoyl]oxy}-4,7-dihydroxy-6-[(1S,2S,6S,8S,9R,11S)-2-hydroxy-11-methyl-5,7,10-trioxatetracyclo[6.3.1.$0^{2,6}$.$0^{9,11}$]dodec-3-en-9-yl]-6-methyl-3,9-dioxatetracyclo[6.6.1.$0^{1,5}$.$0^{11,15}$]pentadecane-4,11-dicarboxylate	-156.875	-142.603	-14.2721

Table 26: **The results of derivatives of Azadirachtin, a secondary metabolite of *A. indica*, with Sulphite reductase obtained from quick docking by using iGEMDOCK 2.0.**

S no	Protein + Ligand derivative	Sulphite reductasewith azadirachtin derivatives (IUPAC name)	Total Energy (Kcal per mol)	V D W (Kcal per mol)	H. Bond (Kcal per mol)
1	Sulphite reductase-Azadirachtin structure Derivative 02(SAR 1)	4,11-dimethyl (1S,4S,5R,6S,7S,8R,11S,12R,14S,15R)-12-(acetyloxy)-4,7-dihydroxy-6-[(1S,2S,6R,8S,9R,11S)-2-hydroxy-11-methyl-7,10-dioxatetracyclo[6.3.1.$0^{2,6}$.$0^{9,11}$]dodec-3-en-9-yl]-6-methyl-14-{[(2E)-2-methylbut-2-enoyl]oxy}-3,9-dioxatetracyclo[6.6.1.$0^{1,5}$.$0^{11,15}$]pentadecane-4,11-dicarboxylate	-165.798	-149.368	-16.4302
2	Sulphite reductase-Azadirachtin structure Derivative 19(SAR 2)	4,11-dimethyl (1S,4S,5R,6S,7S,8R,11S,12R,14S,15R)-12-(acetyloxy)-4,7-dihydroxy-6-[(1S,2S,6R,8S,9R,11S)-2-hydroxy-11-methyl-5,10-dioxa-7-azatetracyclo[6.3.1.$0^{2,6}$.$0^{9,11}$]dodec-3-en-9-yl]-6-methyl-14-{[(2E)-2-methylbut-2-enoyl]oxy}-3,9-dioxatetracyclo[6.6.1.$0^{1,5}$.$0^{11,15}$]pentadecane-4,11-dicarboxylate	-161.921	-158.708	-3.21293
3	Sulphite reductase-Azadirachtin structure Derivative 56(SAR 3)	4,11-dimethyl (1S,4S,5R,6S,7S,8R,11S,12R,14S,15R)-12-ethoxy-4,7-dihydroxy-6-[(1S,2S,6S,8S,9R,11S)-2-hydroxy-11-methyl-5,7,10-trioxatetracyclo[6.3.1.$0^{2,6}$.$0^{9,11}$]dodec-3-en-9-yl]-6-methyl-14-{[(2E)-2-methylbut-2-enoyl]oxy}-3,9-dioxatetracyclo[6.6.1.$0^{1,5}$.$0^{11,15}$]pentadecane-4,11-dicarboxylate	-187.527	-151.95	-35.577
4	Sulphite reductase-Azadirachtin structure Derivative 58(SAR 4)	4,11-dimethyl (1S,4S,5R,6S,7S,8R,11S,12R,14S,15R)-12-(ethanimidoyloxy)-4,7-dihydroxy-6-[(1S,2S,6S,8S,9R,11S)-2-hydroxy-11-methyl-5,7,10-trioxatetracyclo[6.3.1.$0^{2,6}$.$0^{9,11}$]dodec-3-en-9-yl]-6-methyl-14-{[(2E)-2-methylbut-2-enoyl]oxy}-3,9-dioxatetracyclo[6.6.1.$0^{1,5}$.$0^{11,15}$]pentadecane-4,11-dicarboxylate	-158.826	-152.616	-6.20961
5	Sulphite reductase-Azadirachtin structure Derivative 81(SAR 5)	4,11-dimethyl (1S,4S,5R,6S,7S,8R,11S,12R,14S,15R)-12-(acetyloxy)-14-{[(2Z)-2-(bromomethyl)but-2-enoyl]oxy}-4,7-dihydroxy-6-[(1S,2S,6S,8S,9R,11S)-2-hydroxy-11-methyl-5,7,10-trioxatetracyclo[6.3.1.$0^{2,6}$.$0^{9,11}$]dodec-3-en-9-yl]-6-methyl-3,9-dioxatetracyclo[6.6.1.$0^{1,5}$.$0^{11,15}$]pentadecane-4,11-dicarboxylate	-167.613	-145.031	-22.5819

Table 27: The results of derivatives of Nimbin, a secondary metabolite of *A. indica*, with 1, 3 β Glucan synthase obtained from quick docking by using iGEMDOCK 2.0.

S no	Protein + Ligand derivative	1, 3 β Glucan synthase with Nimbin derivatives (IUPAC name)	Total Energy (Kcal per mol)	V D W (Kcal per mol)	H. Bond (Kcal per mol)
1	1,3 β Glucan synthase- Nimbin structure Derivative 01(SAR 1)	ethyl (1S,2R,3R,4R,8R,9S,10R,13R,15R)-2-(acetyloxy)-13-(furan-3-yl)-9-(2-methoxy-2-oxoethyl)-4,8,10,12-tetramethyl-7-oxo-16-oxatetracyclo[8.6.0.0^{3},^{8}.0^{11},^{15}]hexadeca-5,11-diene-4-carboxylate	-165.506	-162.006	-3.5
2	1,3 β Glucan synthase- Nimbin structure Derivative 41(SAR 2)	methyl (1S,2R,3R,4S,8R,9S,10R,13R,15R)-2-(acetyloxy)-13-(furan-3-yl)-9-(2-methoxy-2-oxoethyl)-4,5,8,10,12-pentamethyl-7-oxo-16-oxatetracyclo[8.6.0.0^{3},^{8}.0^{11},^{15}]hexadeca-5,11-diene-4-carboxylate	-154.186	-154.167	-0.01837
3	1,3 β Glucan synthase- Nimbin structure Derivative 50(SAR 3)	methyl (1S,2R,3R,4R,8R,9S,10R,13R,15R)-2-(acetyloxy)-13-(furan-3-yl)-9-(2-methoxy-2-oxoethyl)-4,6,8,10,12-pentamethyl-7-oxo-16-oxatetracyclo[8.6.0.0^{3},^{8}.0^{11},^{15}]hexadeca-5,11-diene-4-carboxylate	-166.67	-163.37	-3.29984
4	1,3 β Glucan synthase- Nimbin structure Derivative 63(SAR 4)	methyl (1S,2R,3R,4R,8R,9S,10R,13R,15R)-2-(acetyloxy)-13-(furan-3-yl)-9-(2-methoxy-2-oxoethyl)-4,8,10,12-tetramethyl-7-oxo-16-oxatetracyclo[8.6.0.0^{3},^{8}.0^{11},^{15}]hexadeca-5,11-diene-4-carboxylate	-165.653	-159.587	-6.06566
5	1,3 β Glucan synthase- Nimbin structure Derivative 107(SAR 5)	methyl (1S,2R,3R,4R,8R,9S,10R,13R,15R)-2-(acetyloxy)-13-(furan-3-yl)-9-(2-methoxy-2-oxoethyl)-4,8,10,12,14-pentamethyl-7-oxo-16-oxatetracyclo[8.6.0.0^{3},^{8}.0^{11},^{15}]hexadeca-5,11-diene-4-carboxylate	-175.83	-172.33	-3.5

Table 28: **The results of derivatives of Nimbin, a secondary metabolite of *A. indica*, with Chitin synthase obtained from quick docking by using iGEMDOCK 2.0.**

S no	Protein + Ligand derivative	Chitin synthase with Nimbin derivatives (IUPAC name)	Total Energy (Kcal per mol)	V D W (Kcal per mol)	H. Bond (Kcal per mol)
1	Chitin synthase - Nimbin structure Derivative 01 (SAR 1)	ethyl (1S,2R,3R,4R,8R,9S,10R,13R,15R)-2-(acetyloxy)-13-(furan-3-yl)-9-(2-methoxy-2-oxoethyl)-4,8,10,12-tetramethyl-7-oxo-16-oxatetracyclo[8.6.0.0^{3},^{8}.0^{11},^{15}]hexadeca-5,11-diene-4-carboxylate	-152.459	-135.417	-17.0414
2	Chitin synthase - Nimbin structure Derivative 41 (SAR 2)	methyl (1S,2R,3R,4S,8R,9S,10R,13R,15R)-2-(acetyloxy)-13-(furan-3-yl)-9-(2-methoxy-2-oxoethyl)-4,5,8,10,12-pentamethyl-7-oxo-16-oxatetracyclo[8.6.0.0^{3},^{8}.0^{11},^{15}]hexadeca-5,11-diene-4-carboxylate	-156.099	-134.315	-21.785
3	Chitin synthase - Nimbin structure Derivative 50 (SAR 3)	methyl (1S,2R,3R,4R,8R,9S,10R,13R,15R)-2-(acetyloxy)-13-(furan-3-yl)-9-(2-methoxy-2-oxoethyl)-4,6,8,10,12-pentamethyl-7-oxo-16-oxatetracyclo[8.6.0.0^{3},^{8}.0^{11},^{15}]hexadeca-5,11-diene-4-carboxylate	-149.458	-129.887	-19.5711
4	Chitin synthase - Nimbin structure Derivative 63 (SAR 4)	methyl (1S,2R,3R,4R,8R,9S,10R,13R,15R)-2-(acetyloxy)-13-(furan-3-yl)-9-(2-methoxy-2-oxoethyl)-4,8,10,12-tetramethyl-7-oxo-16-oxatetracyclo[8.6.0.0^{3},^{8}.0^{11},^{15}]hexadeca-5,11-diene-4-carboxylate	-143.853	-127.961	-15.8923
5	Chitin synthase - Nimbin structure Derivative 107 (SAR 5)	methyl (1S,2R,3R,4R,8R,9S,10R,13R,15R)-2-(acetyloxy)-13-(furan-3-yl)-9-(2-methoxy-2-oxoethyl)-4,8,10,12,14-pentamethyl-7-oxo-16-oxatetracyclo[8.6.0.0^{3},^{8}.0^{11},^{15}]hexadeca-5,11-diene-4-carboxylate	-186.32	-165.818	-20.5018

Table 29: **The results of derivatives of Nimbin, a secondary metabolite of *A. indica*, with Chitinase obtained from quick docking by using iGEMDOCK 2.0.**

S no	Protein + Ligand derivative	Chitinase with Nimbin derivatives (IUPAC name)	Total Energy (Kcal per mol)	V D W (Kcal per mol)	H. Bond (Kcal per mol)
1	Chitinase - Nimbin structure Derivative 01(SAR 1)	ethyl (1S,2R,3R,4R,8R,9S,10R,13R,15R)-2-(acetyloxy)-13-(furan-3-yl)-9-(2-methoxy-2-oxoethyl)-4,8,10,12-tetramethyl-7-oxo-16-oxatetracyclo[8.6.0.0^{3,8}.0^{11,15}]hexadeca-5,11-diene-4-carboxylate	-175.8	-167.844	-7.95629
2	Chitinase - Nimbin structure Derivative 41(SAR 2)	methyl (1S,2R,3R,4S,8R,9S,10R,13R,15R)-2-(acetyloxy)-13-(furan-3-yl)-9-(2-methoxy-2-oxoethyl)-4,5,8,10,12-pentamethyl-7-oxo-16-oxatetracyclo[8.6.0.0^{3,8}.0^{11,15}]hexadeca-5,11-diene-4-carboxylate	-168.806	-157.158	-11.6484
3	Chitinase - Nimbin structure Derivative 50(SAR 3)	methyl (1S,2R,3R,4R,8R,9S,10R,13R,15R)-2-(acetyloxy)-13-(furan-3-yl)-9-(2-methoxy-2-oxoethyl)-4,6,8,10,12-pentamethyl-7-oxo-16-oxatetracyclo[8.6.0.0^{3,8}.0^{11,15}]hexadeca-5,11-diene-4-carboxylate	-170.259	-159.273	-10.9859
4	Chitinase - Nimbin structure Derivative 63(SAR 4)	methyl (1S,2R,3R,4R,8R,9S,10R,13R,15R)-2-(acetyloxy)-13-(furan-3-yl)-9-(2-methoxy-2-oxoethyl)-4,8,10,12-tetramethyl-7-oxo-16-oxatetracyclo[8.6.0.0^{3,8}.0^{11,15}]hexadeca-5,11-diene-4-carboxylate	-170.738	-162.049	-8.68959
5	Chitinase - Nimbin structure Derivative 107(SAR 5)	methyl (1S,2R,3R,4R,8R,9S,10R,13R,15R)-2-(acetyloxy)-13-(furan-3-yl)-9-(2-methoxy-2-oxoethyl)-4,8,10,12,14-pentamethyl-7-oxo-16-oxatetracyclo[8.6.0.0^{3,8}.0^{11,15}]hexadeca-5,11-diene-4-carboxylate	-173.854	-165.244	-8.60952

Table 30: The results of derivatives of Nimbin, a secondary metabolite of *A. indica*, with Deuterolysin obtained from quick docking by using iGEMDOCK 2.0.

S no	Protein + Ligand derivative	Deuterolysin with Nimbin derivatives (IUPAC name)	Total Energy (Kcal per mol)	V D W (Kcal per mol)	H. Bond (Kcal per mol)
1	Deuterolysin - Nimbin structure Derivative 01(SAR 1)	ethyl (1S,2R,3R,4R,8R,9S,10R,13R,15R)-2-(acetyloxy)-13-(furan-3-yl)-9-(2-methoxy-2-oxoethyl)-4,8,10,12-tetramethyl-7-oxo-16-oxatetracyclo[8.6.0.0^{3},^{8}.0^{11},^{15}]hexadeca-5,11-diene-4-carboxylate	-149.349	-131.628	-17.7213
2	Deuterolysin – Nimbin structure Derivative 41(SAR 2)	methyl (1S,2R,3R,4S,8R,9S,10R,13R,15R)-2-(acetyloxy)-13-(furan-3-yl)-9-(2-methoxy-2-oxoethyl)-4,5,8,10,12-pentamethyl-7-oxo-16-oxatetracyclo[8.6.0.0^{3},^{8}.0^{11},^{15}]hexadeca-5,11-diene-4-carboxylate	-155.423	-144.083	-11.3402
3	Deuterolysin - Nimbin structure Derivative 50(SAR 3)	methyl (1S,2R,3R,4R,8R,9S,10R,13R,15R)-2-(acetyloxy)-13-(furan-3-yl)-9-(2-methoxy-2-oxoethyl)-4,6,8,10,12-pentamethyl-7-oxo-16-oxatetracyclo[8.6.0.0^{3},^{8}.0^{11},^{15}]hexadeca-5,11-diene-4-carboxylate	-154.074	-144.574	-9.5
4	Deuterolysin - Nimbin structure Derivative 63(SAR 4)	methyl (1S,2R,3R,4R,8R,9S,10R,13R,15R)-2-(acetyloxy)-13-(furan-3-yl)-9-(2-methoxy-2-oxoethyl)-4,8,10,12-tetramethyl-7-oxo-16-oxatetracyclo[8.6.0.0^{3},^{8}.0^{11},^{15}]hexadeca-5,11-diene-4-carboxylate	-149.24	-139.74	-9.5
5	Deuterolysin - Nimbin structure Derivative 107(SAR 5)	methyl (1S,2R,3R,4R,8R,9S,10R,13R,15R)-2-(acetyloxy)-13-(furan-3-yl)-9-(2-methoxy-2-oxoethyl)-4,8,10,12,14-pentamethyl-7-oxo-16-oxatetracyclo[8.6.0.0^{3},^{8}.0^{11},^{15}]hexadeca-5,11-diene-4-carboxylate	-167.941	-152.189	-15.7519

Table 31: **The results of derivatives of Nimbin, a secondary metabolite of *A. indica*, with Fungalysin obtained from quick docking by using iGEMDOCK 2.0.**

S no	Protein + Ligand derivative	Fungalysin with Nimbin derivatives (IUPAC name)	Total Energy (Kcal per mol)	V D W (Kcal per mol)	H. Bond (Kcal per mol)
1	Fungalysin - Nimbin structure Derivative 01(SAR 1)	ethyl (1S,2R,3R,4R,8R,9S,10R,13R,15R)-2-(acetyloxy)-13-(furan-3-yl)-9-(2-methoxy-2-oxoethyl)-4,8,10,12-tetramethyl-7-oxo-16-oxatetracyclo[8.6.0.0^{3},^{8}.0^{11},^{15}]hexadeca-5,11-diene-4-carboxylate	-140.588	-128.219	-12.3695
2	Fungalysin - Nimbin structure Derivative 41(SAR 2)	methyl (1S,2R,3R,4S,8R,9S,10R,13R,15R)-2-(acetyloxy)-13-(furan-3-yl)-9-(2-methoxy-2-oxoethyl)-4,5,8,10,12-pentamethyl-7-oxo-16-oxatetracyclo[8.6.0.0^{3},^{8}.0^{11},^{15}]hexadeca-5,11-diene-4-carboxylate	-136.145	-120.414	-15.7312
3	Fungalysin - Nimbin structure Derivative 50(SAR 3)	methyl (1S,2R,3R,4R,8R,9S,10R,13R,15R)-2-(acetyloxy)-13-(furan-3-yl)-9-(2-methoxy-2-oxoethyl)-4,6,8,10,12-pentamethyl-7-oxo-16-oxatetracyclo[8.6.0.0^{3},^{8}.0^{11},^{15}]hexadeca-5,11-diene-4-carboxylate	-137.746	-118.294	-19.4515
4	Fungalysin - Nimbin structure Derivative 63(SAR 4)	methyl (1S,2R,3R,4R,8R,9S,10R,13R,15R)-2-(acetyloxy)-13-(furan-3-yl)-9-(2-methoxy-2-oxoethyl)-4,8,10,12-tetramethyl-7-oxo-16-oxatetracyclo[8.6.0.0^{3},^{8}.0^{11},^{15}]hexadeca-5,11-diene-4-carboxylate	-127.048	-111.148	-15.8994
5	Fungalysin - Nimbin structure Derivative 107(SAR 5)	methyl (1S,2R,3R,4R,8R,9S,10R,13R,15R)-2-(acetyloxy)-13-(furan-3-yl)-9-(2-methoxy-2-oxoethyl)-4,8,10,12,14-pentamethyl-7-oxo-16-oxatetracyclo[8.6.0.0^{3},^{8}.0^{11},^{15}]hexadeca-5,11-diene-4-carboxylate	-132.593	-127.995	-4.59779

Table 32: The results of derivatives of Nimbin, a secondary metabolite of *A. indica*, with Homoserine dehydrogenase obtained from quick docking by using iGEMDOCK 2.0.

S no	Protein + Ligand derivative	Homoserine dehydrogenase with Nimbin derivatives (IUPAC name)	Total Energy (Kcal per mol)	V D W (Kcal per mol)	H. Bond (Kcal per mol)
1	Homoserine dehydrogenase - Nimbin structure Derivative 01(SAR 1)	ethyl (1S,2R,3R,4R,8R,9S,10R,13R,15R)-2-(acetyloxy)-13-(furan-3-yl)-9-(2-methoxy-2-oxoethyl)-4,8,10,12-tetramethyl-7-oxo-16-oxatetracyclo[8.6.0.0^{3},^{8}.0^{11},^{15}]hexadeca-5,11-diene-4-carboxylate	-186.36	-172.519	-13.8403
2	Homoserine dehydrogenase - Nimbin structure Derivative 41(SAR 2)	methyl (1S,2R,3R,4S,8R,9S,10R,13R,15R)-2-(acetyloxy)-13-(furan-3-yl)-9-(2-methoxy-2-oxoethyl)-4,5,8,10,12-pentamethyl-7-oxo-16-oxatetracyclo[8.6.0.0^{3},^{8}.0^{11},^{15}]hexadeca-5,11-diene-4-carboxylate	-146.099	-128.346	-17.7527
3	Homoserine dehydrogenase - Nimbin structure Derivative 50(SAR 3)	methyl (1S,2R,3R,4R,8R,9S,10R,13R,15R)-2-(acetyloxy)-13-(furan-3-yl)-9-(2-methoxy-2-oxoethyl)-4,6,8,10,12-pentamethyl-7-oxo-16-oxatetracyclo[8.6.0.0^{3},^{8}.0^{11},^{15}]hexadeca-5,11-diene-4-carboxylate	-177.369	-162.129	-15.2402
4	Homoserine dehydrogenase - Nimbin structure Derivative 63(SAR 4)	methyl (1S,2R,3R,4R,8R,9S,10R,13R,15R)-2-(acetyloxy)-13-(furan-3-yl)-9-(2-methoxy-2-oxoethyl)-4,8,10,12-tetramethyl-7-oxo-16-oxatetracyclo[8.6.0.0^{3},^{8}.0^{11},^{15}]hexadeca-5,11-diene-4-carboxylate	-180.155	-167.665	-12.4895
5	Homoserine dehydrogenase - Nimbin structure Derivative 107(SAR 5)	methyl (1S,2R,3R,4R,8R,9S,10R,13R,15R)-2-(acetyloxy)-13-(furan-3-yl)-9-(2-methoxy-2-oxoethyl)-4,8,10,12,14-pentamethyl-7-oxo-16-oxatetracyclo[8.6.0.0^{3},^{8}.0^{11},^{15}]hexadeca-5,11-diene-4-carboxylate	-183.078	-166.105	-16.9727

Table 33: The results of derivatives of Nimbin, a secondary metabolite of *A. indica*, with Lumazine synthase obtained from quick docking by using iGEMDOCK 2.0.

S no	Protein + Ligand derivative	Lumazine synthase with Nimbin derivatives (IUPAC name)	Total Energy (Kcal per mol)	V D W (Kcal per mol)	H. Bond (Kcal per mol)
1	Lumazine synthase - Nimbin structure Derivative 01(SAR 1)	ethyl (1S,2R,3R,4R,8R,9S,10R,13R,15R)-2-(acetyloxy)-13-(furan-3-yl)-9-(2-methoxy-2-oxoethyl)-4,8,10,12-tetramethyl-7-oxo-16-oxatetracyclo[8.6.0.0^{3},^{8}.0^{11},^{15}]hexadeca-5,11-diene-4-carboxylate	-183.994	-167.036	-16.9585
2	Lumazine synthase - Nimbin structure Derivative 41(SAR 2)	methyl (1S,2R,3R,4S,8R,9S,10R,13R,15R)-2-(acetyloxy)-13-(furan-3-yl)-9-(2-methoxy-2-oxoethyl)-4,5,8,10,12-pentamethyl-7-oxo-16-oxatetracyclo[8.6.0.0^{3},^{8}.0^{11},^{15}]hexadeca-5,11-diene-4-carboxylate	-173.105	-162.846	-10.2587
3	Lumazine synthase - Nimbin structure Derivative 50(SAR 3)	methyl (1S,2R,3R,4R,8R,9S,10R,13R,15R)-2-(acetyloxy)-13-(furan-3-yl)-9-(2-methoxy-2-oxoethyl)-4,6,8,10,12-pentamethyl-7-oxo-16-oxatetracyclo[8.6.0.0^{3},^{8}.0^{11},^{15}]hexadeca-5,11-diene-4-carboxylate	-157.793	-151.192	-6.60094
4	Lumazine synthase - Nimbin structure Derivative 63(SAR 4)	methyl (1S,2R,3R,4R,8R,9S,10R,13R,15R)-2-(acetyloxy)-13-(furan-3-yl)-9-(2-methoxy-2-oxoethyl)-4,8,10,12-tetramethyl-7-oxo-16-oxatetracyclo[8.6.0.0^{3},^{8}.0^{11},^{15}]hexadeca-5,11-diene-4-carboxylate	-174.055	-150.648	-23.4073
5	Lumazine synthase - Nimbin structure Derivative 107(SAR 5)	methyl (1S,2R,3R,4R,8R,9S,10R,13R,15R)-2-(acetyloxy)-13-(furan-3-yl)-9-(2-methoxy-2-oxoethyl)-4,8,10,12,14-pentamethyl-7-oxo-16-oxatetracyclo[8.6.0.0^{3},^{8}.0^{11},^{15}]hexadeca-5,11-diene-4-carboxylate	-173.198	-149.197	-24.0014

Table 34: The results of derivatives of Nimbin, a secondary metabolite of *A. indica*, with Phosphoribosylaminoimidazole obtained from quick docking by using iGEMDOCK 2.0.

S no	Protein + Ligand derivative	Phosphoribosylaminoimidazole carboxylase with Nimbin derivatives (IUPAC name)	Total Energy (Kcal per mol)	V D W (Kcal per mol)	H. Bond (Kcal per mol)
1	Phosphoribosylaminoimidazole - Nimbin structure Derivative 01(SAR 1)	ethyl (1S,2R,3R,4R,8R,9S,10R,13R,15R)-2-(acetyloxy)-13-(furan-3-yl)-9-(2-methoxy-2-oxoethyl)-4,8,10,12-tetramethyl-7-oxo-16-oxatetracyclo[8.6.0.0^{3},^{8}.0^{11},^{15}]hexadeca-5,11-diene-4-carboxylate	-170.048	-154.427	-15.6205
2	Phosphoribosylaminoimidazole - Nimbin structure Derivative 41(SAR 2)	methyl (1S,2R,3R,4S,8R,9S,10R,13R,15R)-2-(acetyloxy)-13-(furan-3-yl)-9-(2-methoxy-2-oxoethyl)-4,5,8,10,12-pentamethyl-7-oxo-16-oxatetracyclo[8.6.0.0^{3},^{8}.0^{11},^{15}]hexadeca-5,11-diene-4-carboxylate	-173.798	-160.798	-13
3	Phosphoribosylaminoimidazole - Nimbin structure Derivative 50(SAR 3)	methyl (1S,2R,3R,4R,8R,9S,10R,13R,15R)-2-(acetyloxy)-13-(furan-3-yl)-9-(2-methoxy-2-oxoethyl)-4,6,8,10,12-pentamethyl-7-oxo-16-oxatetracyclo[8.6.0.0^{3},^{8}.0^{11},^{15}]hexadeca-5,11-diene-4-carboxylate	-162.315	-154.155	-8.15976
4	Phosphoribosylaminoimidazole - Nimbin structure Derivative 63(SAR 4)	methyl (1S,2R,3R,4R,8R,9S,10R,13R,15R)-2-(acetyloxy)-13-(furan-3-yl)-9-(2-methoxy-2-oxoethyl)-4,8,10,12-tetramethyl-7-oxo-16-oxatetracyclo[8.6.0.0^{3},^{8}.0^{11},^{15}]hexadeca-5,11-diene-4-carboxylate	-166.201	-152.304	-13.8967
5	Phosphoribosylaminoimidazole - Nimbin structure Derivative 107(SAR 5)	methyl (1S,2R,3R,4R,8R,9S,10R,13R,15R)-2-(acetyloxy)-13-(furan-3-yl)-9-(2-methoxy-2-oxoethyl)-4,8,10,12,14-pentamethyl-7-oxo-16-oxatetracyclo[8.6.0.0^{3},^{8}.0^{11},^{15}]hexadeca-5,11-diene-4-carboxylate	-168.921	-147.439	-21.4817

Table 35: The results of derivatives of Nimbin, a secondary metabolite of *A. indica*, with Protein elongation factor 3 obtained from quick docking by using iGEMDOCK 2.0.

S no	Protein + Ligand derivative	Protein Elongation Factor 3 with Nimbin derivatives (IUPAC name)	Total Energy (Kcal per mol)	V D W (Kcal per mol)	H. Bond (Kcal per mol)
1	Protein elongation factor- Nimbin structure Derivative 01(SAR 1)	ethyl (1S,2R,3R,4R,8R,9S,10R,13R,15R)-2-(acetyloxy)-13-(furan-3-yl)-9-(2-methoxy-2-oxoethyl)-4,8,10,12-tetramethyl-7-oxo-16-oxatetracyclo[8.6.0.$0^{3,8}$.$0^{11,15}$]hexadeca-5,11-diene-4-carboxylate	-129.258	-113.308	-15.9503
2	Protein elongation factor- Nimbin structure Derivative 41(SAR 2)	methyl (1S,2R,3R,4S,8R,9S,10R,13R,15R)-2-(acetyloxy)-13-(furan-3-yl)-9-(2-methoxy-2-oxoethyl)-4,5,8,10,12-pentamethyl-7-oxo-16-oxatetracyclo[8.6.0.$0^{3,8}$.$0^{11,15}$]hexadeca-5,11-diene-4-carboxylate	-154.536	-142.693	-11.8429
3	Protein elongation factor- Nimbin structure Derivative 50(SAR 3)	methyl (1S,2R,3R,4R,8R,9S,10R,13R,15R)-2-(acetyloxy)-13-(furan-3-yl)-9-(2-methoxy-2-oxoethyl)-4,6,8,10,12-pentamethyl-7-oxo-16-oxatetracyclo[8.6.0.$0^{3,8}$.$0^{11,15}$]hexadeca-5,11-diene-4-carboxylate	-130.109	-118.86	-11.2492
4	Protein elongation factor- Nimbin structure Derivative 63(SAR 4)	methyl (1S,2R,3R,4R,8R,9S,10R,13R,15R)-2-(acetyloxy)-13-(furan-3-yl)-9-(2-methoxy-2-oxoethyl)-4,8,10,12-tetramethyl-7-oxo-16-oxatetracyclo[8.6.0.$0^{3,8}$.$0^{11,15}$]hexadeca-5,11-diene-4-carboxylate	-153.405	-142.923	-10.4813
5	Protein elongation factor- Nimbin structure Derivative 107(SAR 5)	methyl (1S,2R,3R,4R,8R,9S,10R,13R,15R)-2-(acetyloxy)-13-(furan-3-yl)-9-(2-methoxy-2-oxoethyl)-4,8,10,12,14-pentamethyl-7-oxo-16-oxatetracyclo[8.6.0.$0^{3,8}$.$0^{11,15}$]hexadeca-5,11-diene-4-carboxylate	-150.663	-136.748	-13.9146

Table 36: The results of derivatives of Nimbin, a secondary metabolite of *A. indica*, with Sulphite reductase obtained from quick docking by using iGEMDOCK 2.0.

S no	Protein + Ligand derivative	Sulphite reductase with Nimbin derivatives (IUPAC name)	Total Energy (Kcal per mol)	V D W (Kcal per mol)	H. Bond (Kcal per mol)
1	Sulphite reductase- Nimbin structure Derivative 01(SAR 1)	ethyl (1S,2R,3R,4R,8R,9S,10R,13R,15R)-2-(acetyloxy)-13-(furan-3-yl)-9-(2-methoxy-2-oxoethyl)-4,8,10,12-tetramethyl-7-oxo-16-oxatetracyclo[8.6.0.0^{3},^{8}.0^{11},^{15}]hexadeca-5,11-diene-4-carboxylate	-167.453	-156.883	-10.5707
2	Sulphite reductase- Nimbin structure Derivative 41(SAR 2)	methyl (1S,2R,3R,4S,8R,9S,10R,13R,15R)-2-(acetyloxy)-13-(furan-3-yl)-9-(2-methoxy-2-oxoethyl)-4,5,8,10,12-pentamethyl-7-oxo-16-oxatetracyclo[8.6.0.0^{3},^{8}.0^{11},^{15}]hexadeca-5,11-diene-4-carboxylate	-174.175	-144.661	-29.5138
3	Sulphite reductase- Nimbin structure Derivative 50(SAR 3)	methyl (1S,2R,3R,4R,8R,9S,10R,13R,15R)-2-(acetyloxy)-13-(furan-3-yl)-9-(2-methoxy-2-oxoethyl)-4,6,8,10,12-pentamethyl-7-oxo-16-oxatetracyclo[8.6.0.0^{3},^{8}.0^{11},^{15}]hexadeca-5,11-diene-4-carboxylate	-169.915	-146.941	-22.9745
4	Sulphite reductase- Nimbin structure Derivative 63(SAR 4)	methyl (1S,2R,3R,4R,8R,9S,10R,13R,15R)-2-(acetyloxy)-13-(furan-3-yl)-9-(2-methoxy-2-oxoethyl)-4,8,10,12-tetramethyl-7-oxo-16-oxatetracyclo[8.6.0.0^{3},^{8}.0^{11},^{15}]hexadeca-5,11-diene-4-carboxylate	-162.136	-132.153	-29.9829
5	Sulphite reductase- Nimbin structure Derivative 107(SAR 5)	methyl (1S,2R,3R,4R,8R,9S,10R,13R,15R)-2-(acetyloxy)-13-(furan-3-yl)-9-(2-methoxy-2-oxoethyl)-4,8,10,12,14-pentamethyl-7-oxo-16-oxatetracyclo[8.6.0.0^{3},^{8}.0^{11},^{15}]hexadeca-5,11-diene-4-carboxylate	-133.98	-103.817	-30.1629

Table 37: **The results of derivatives of Nimonol, a secondary metabolite of *A. indica*, with 1,3 β Glucan synthase obtained from quick docking by using iGEMDOCK 2.0.**

S no	Protein + Ligand derivative	1,3 β Glucan synthasewith Nimonol derivatives (IUPAC name)	Total Energy (Kcal per mol)	V D W (Kcal per mol)	H. Bond (Kcal per mol)
1	1,3 β Glucan synthase-Nimonol structure Derivative 01(SAR 1)	(1R,3bR,4S,5R,5aR,9aR,9bR,11aS)-5-hydroxy-3b,6,6,9a,11a-pentamethyl-1-(5-methylfuran-3-yl)-7-oxo-1H,2H,3bH,4H,5H,5aH,6H,7H,9aH,9bH,10H,11H,11aH-cyclopenta[a]phenanthren-4-yl acetate	-157.416	-157.416	0
2	1,3 β Glucan synthase-Nimonol structure Derivative 17(SAR 2)	(1R,3bR,4S,5R,5aR,9aR,9bR,11aS)-5-hydroxy-3b,6,6,9a,11a-pentamethyl-7-oxo-1-(1H-pyrrol-3-yl)-1H,2H,3bH,4H,5H,5aH,6H,7H,9aH,9bH,10H,11H,11aH-cyclopenta[a]phenanthren-4-yl acetate	-154.675	-154.675	0
3	1,3 β Glucan synthase-Nimonol structure Derivative 60(SAR 3)	(1R,3bR,4S,5R,5aR,9aR,9bR,11aS)-1-(furan-3-yl)-5-hydroxy-3,3b,6,6,9a,11a-hexamethyl-7-oxo-1H,2H,3bH,4H,5H,5aH,6H,7H,9aH,9bH,10H,11H,11aH-cyclopenta[a]phenanthren-4-yl acetate	-150.715	-147.215	-3.5
4	1,3 β Glucan synthase-Nimonol structure Derivative 96(SAR 4)	(1R,3bR,4S,5R,5aS,9aR,9bR,11aS)-1-(furan-3-yl)-5-hydroxy-3b,6,6,9a,11a-pentamethyl-1H,2H,3bH,4H,5H,5aH,6H,7H,9aH,9bH,10H,11H,11aH-cyclopenta[a]phenanthren-4-yl acetate	-140.671	-134.643	-6.02776
5	1,3 β Glucan synthase-Nimonol structure Derivative 136(SAR 5)	(1R,3bR,4S,5R,5aR,9aS,9bR,11aS)-1-(furan-3-yl)-5-hydroxy-3b,6,6,9a,9b,11a-hexamethyl-7-oxo-1H,2H,3bH,4H,5H,5aH,6H,7H,9aH,9bH,10H,11H,11aH-cyclopenta[a]phenanthren-4-yl acetate	-162.747	-162.747	0

Table 38: The results of derivatives of Nimonol, a secondary metabolite of *A. indica*, with Chitin synthase obtained from quick docking by using iGEMDOCK 2.0.

S no	Protein + Ligand derivative	Chitin synthasewith Nimonol derivatives (IUPAC name)	Total Energy (Kcal per mol)	V D W (Kcal per mol)	H. Bond (Kcal per mol)
1	Chitin synthase - Nimonol structure Derivative 01(SAR 1)	(1R,3bR,4S,5R,5aR,9aR,9bR,11aS)-5-hydroxy-3b,6,6,9a,11a-pentamethyl-1-(5-methylfuran-3-yl)-7-oxo-1H,2H,3bH,4H,5H,5aH,6H,7H,9aH,9bH,10H,11H,11aH-cyclopenta[a]phenanthren-4-yl acetate	-130.833	-126.297	-4.53579
2	Chitin synthase - Nimonol structure Derivative 17(SAR 2)	(1R,3bR,4S,5R,5aR,9aR,9bR,11aS)-5-hydroxy-3b,6,6,9a,11a-pentamethyl-7-oxo-1-(1H-pyrrol-3-yl)-1H,2H,3bH,4H,5H,5aH,6H,7H,9aH,9bH,10H,11H,11aH-cyclopenta[a]phenanthren-4-yl acetate	-125.706	-118.851	-6.85447
3	Chitin synthase - Nimonol structure Derivative 60(SAR 3)	(1R,3bR,4S,5R,5aR,9aR,9bR,11aS)-1-(furan-3-yl)-5-hydroxy-3,3b,6,6,9a,11a-hexamethyl-7-oxo-1H,2H,3bH,4H,5H,5aH,6H,7H,9aH,9bH,10H,11H,11aH-cyclopenta[a]phenanthren-4-yl acetate	-163.515	-144.761	-18.7538
4	Chitin synthase - Nimonol structure Derivative 96(SAR 4)	(1R,3bR,4S,5R,5aS,9aR,9bR,11aS)-1-(furan-3-yl)-5-hydroxy-3b,6,6,9a,11a-pentamethyl-1H,2H,3bH,4H,5H,5aH,6H,7H,9aH,9bH,10H,11H,11aH-cyclopenta[a]phenanthren-4-yl acetate	-129.336	-116.49	-12.8459
5	Chitin synthase - Nimonol structure Derivative 136(SAR 5)	(1R,3bR,4S,5R,5aR,9aS,9bR,11aS)-1-(furan-3-yl)-5-hydroxy-3b,6,6,9a,9b,11a-hexamethyl-7-oxo-1H,2H,3bH,4H,5H,5aH,6H,7H,9aH,9bH,10H,11H,11aH-cyclopenta[a]phenanthren-4-yl acetate	-173.153	-154.118	-19.0353

Table 39: The results of derivatives of Nimonol, a secondary metabolite of *A. indica*, with Chitinase obtained from quick docking by using iGEMDOCK 2.0.

S no	Protein + Ligand derivative	Chitinasewith Nimonol derivatives (IUPAC name)	Total Energy (Kcal per mol)	V D W (Kcal per mol)	H. Bond (Kcal per mol)
1	Chitinase - Nimonol structure Derivative 01(SAR 1)	(1R,3bR,4S,5R,5aR,9aR,9bR,11aS)-5-hydroxy-3b,6,6,9a,11a-pentamethyl-1-(5-methylfuran-3-yl)-7-oxo-1H,2H,3bH,4H,5H,5aH,6H,7H,9aH,9bH,10H,11H,11aH-cyclopenta[a]phenanthren-4-yl acetate	-142.101	-137.299	-4.80189
2	Chitinase - Nimonol structure Derivative 17(SAR 2)	(1R,3bR,4S,5R,5aR,9aR,9bR,11aS)-5-hydroxy-3b,6,6,9a,11a-pentamethyl-7-oxo-1-(1H-pyrrol-3-yl)-1H,2H,3bH,4H,5H,5aH,6H,7H,9aH,9bH,10H,11H,11aH-cyclopenta[a]phenanthren-4-yl acetate	-149.912	-136.26	-13.6529
3	Chitinase - Nimonol structure Derivative 60(SAR 3)	(1R,3bR,4S,5R,5aR,9aR,9bR,11aS)-1-(furan-3-yl)-5-hydroxy-3,3b,6,6,9a,11a-hexamethyl-7-oxo-1H,2H,3bH,4H,5H,5aH,6H,7H,9aH,9bH,10H,11H,11aH-cyclopenta[a]phenanthren-4-yl acetate	-152.052	-140.109	-11.9429
4	Chitinase - Nimonol structure Derivative 96(SAR 4)	(1R,3bR,4S,5R,5aS,9aR,9bR,11aS)-1-(furan-3-yl)-5-hydroxy-3b,6,6,9a,11a-pentamethyl-1H,2H,3bH,4H,5H,5aH,6H,7H,9aH,9bH,10H,11H,11aH-cyclopenta[a]phenanthren-4-yl acetate	-144.787	-136.395	-8.39255
5	Chitinase - Nimonol structure Derivative 136(SAR 5)	(1R,3bR,4S,5R,5aR,9aS,9bR,11aS)-1-(furan-3-yl)-5-hydroxy-3b,6,6,9a,9b,11a-hexamethyl-7-oxo-1H,2H,3bH,4H,5H,5aH,6H,7H,9aH,9bH,10H,11H,11aH-cyclopenta[a]phenanthren-4-yl acetate	-153.885	-148.885	-5

Table 40: The results of derivatives of Nimonol, a secondary metabolite of *A. indica*, with Deuterolysin obtained from quick docking by using iGEMDOCK 2.0.

S no	Protein + Ligand derivative	Deuterolysin with Nimonol derivatives (IUPAC name)	Total Energy (Kcal per mol)	V D W (Kcal per mol)	H. Bond (Kcal per mol)
1	Deuterolysin - Nimonol structure Derivative 01(SAR 1)	(1R,3bR,4S,5R,5aR,9aR,9bR,11aS)-5-hydroxy-3b,6,6,9a,11a-pentamethyl-1-(5-methylfuran-3-yl)-7-oxo-1H,2H,3bH,4H,5H,5aH,6H,7H,9aH,9bH,10H,11H,11aH-cyclopenta[a]phenanthren-4-yl acetate	-128.777	-125.676	-3.10065
2	Deuterolysin - Nimonol structure Derivative 17(SAR 2)	(1R,3bR,4S,5R,5aR,9aR,9bR,11aS)-5-hydroxy-3b,6,6,9a,11a-pentamethyl-7-oxo-1-(1H-pyrrol-3-yl)-1H,2H,3bH,4H,5H,5aH,6H,7H,9aH,9bH,10H,11H,11aH-cyclopenta[a]phenanthren-4-yl acetate	-154.534	-148.169	-6.36458
3	Deuterolysin - Nimonol structure Derivative 60(SAR 3)	(1R,3bR,4S,5R,5aR,9aR,9bR,11aS)-1-(furan-3-yl)-5-hydroxy-3,3b,6,6,9a,11a-hexamethyl-7-oxo-1H,2H,3bH,4H,5H,5aH,6H,7H,9aH,9bH,10H,11H,11aH-cyclopenta[a]phenanthren-4-yl acetate	-127.68	-126.299	-1.38091
4	Deuterolysin - Nimonol structure Derivative 96(SAR 4)	(1R,3bR,4S,5R,5aS,9aR,9bR,11aS)-1-(furan-3-yl)-5-hydroxy-3b,6,6,9a,11a-pentamethyl-1H,2H,3bH,4H,5H,5aH,6H,7H,9aH,9bH,10H,11H,11aH-cyclopenta[a]phenanthren-4-yl acetate	-151.926	-142.432	-9.49364
5	Deuterolysin - Nimonol structure Derivative 136(SAR 5)	(1R,3bR,4S,5R,5aR,9aS,9bR,11aS)-1-(furan-3-yl)-5-hydroxy-3b,6,6,9a,9b,11a-hexamethyl-7-oxo-1H,2H,3bH,4H,5H,5aH,6H,7H,9aH,9bH,10H,11H,11aH-cyclopenta[a]phenanthren-4-yl acetate	-141.487	-139.141	-2.34603

Table 41: The results of derivatives of Nimonol, a secondary metabolite of *A. indica*, with Fungalysin obtained from quick docking by using iGEMDOCK 2.0.

S no	Protein + Ligand derivative	Fungalysin with Nimonol derivatives (IUPAC name)	Total Energy (Kcal per mol)	V D W (Kcal per mol)	H. Bond (Kcal per mol)
1	Fungalysin - Nimonol structure Derivative 01(SAR 1)	(1R,3bR,4S,5R,5aR,9aR,9bR,11aS)-5-hydroxy-3b,6,6,9a,11a-pentamethyl-1-(5-methylfuran-3-yl)-7-oxo-1H,2H,3bH,4H,5H,5aH,6H,7H,9aH,9bH,10H,11H,11aH-cyclopenta[a]phenanthren-4-yl acetate	-131.468	-124.468	-7
2	Fungalysin - Nimonol structure Derivative 17(SAR 2)	(1R,3bR,4S,5R,5aR,9aR,9bR,11aS)-5-hydroxy-3b,6,6,9a,11a-pentamethyl-7-oxo-1-(1H-pyrrol-3-yl)-1H,2H,3bH,4H,5H,5aH,6H,7H,9aH,9bH,10H,11H,11aH-cyclopenta[a]phenanthren-4-yl acetate	-122.285	-119.777	-2.50823
3	Fungalysin - Nimonol structure Derivative 60(SAR 3)	(1R,3bR,4S,5R,5aR,9aR,9bR,11aS)-1-(furan-3-yl)-5-hydroxy-3,3b,6,6,9a,11a-hexamethyl-7-oxo-1H,2H,3bH,4H,5H,5aH,6H,7H,9aH,9bH,10H,11H,11aH-cyclopenta[a]phenanthren-4-yl acetate	-132.549	-124.143	-8.40529
4	Fungalysin - Nimonol structure Derivative 96(SAR 4)	(1R,3bR,4S,5R,5aS,9aR,9bR,11aS)-1-(furan-3-yl)-5-hydroxy-3b,6,6,9a,11a-pentamethyl-1H,2H,3bH,4H,5H,5aH,6H,7H,9aH,9bH,10H,11H,11aH-cyclopenta[a]phenanthren-4-yl acetate	-138.923	-138.923	0
5	Fungalysin - Nimonol structure Derivative 136(SAR 5)	(1R,3bR,4S,5R,5aR,9aS,9bR,11aS)-1-(furan-3-yl)-5-hydroxy-3b,6,6,9a,9b,11a-hexamethyl-7-oxo-1H,2H,3bH,4H,5H,5aH,6H,7H,9aH,9bH,10H,11H,11aH-cyclopenta[a]phenanthren-4-yl acetate	-128.457	-120.551	-7.9067

Table 42: The results of derivatives of Nimonol, a secondary metabolite of *A. indica*, with Homoserine dehydrogenase obtained from quick docking by using iGEMDOCK 2.0.

S no	Protein + Ligand derivative	Homoserine dehydrogenase with Nimonol derivatives (IUPAC name)	Total Energy (Kcal per mol)	V D W (Kcal per mol)	H. Bond (Kcal per mol)
1	Homoserine dehydrogenase - Nimonol structure Derivative 01(SAR 1)	(1R,3bR,4S,5R,5aR,9aR,9bR,11aS)-5-hydroxy-3b,6,6,9a,11a-pentamethyl-1-(5-methylfuran-3-yl)-7-oxo-1H,2H,3bH,4H,5H,5aH,6H,7H,9aH,9bH,10H,11H,11aH-cyclopenta[a]phenanthren-4-yl acetate	-172.497	-168.997	-3.5
2	Homoserine dehydrogenase - Nimonol structure Derivative 17(SAR 2)	(1R,3bR,4S,5R,5aR,9aR,9bR,11aS)-5-hydroxy-3b,6,6,9a,11a-pentamethyl-7-oxo-1-(1H-pyrrol-3-yl)-1H,2H,3bH,4H,5H,5aH,6H,7H,9aH,9bH,10H,11H,11aH-cyclopenta[a]phenanthren-4-yl acetate	-158.338	-148.232	-10.1065
3	Homoserine dehydrogenase - Nimonol structure Derivative 60(SAR 3)	(1R,3bR,4S,5R,5aR,9aR,9bR,11aS)-1-(furan-3-yl)-5-hydroxy-3,3b,6,6,9a,11a-hexamethyl-7-oxo-1H,2H,3bH,4H,5H,5aH,6H,7H,9aH,9bH,10H,11H,11aH-cyclopenta[a]phenanthren-4-yl acetate	-179.557	-166.112	-13.4448
4	Homoserine dehydrogenase - Nimonol structure Derivative 96(SAR 4)	(1R,3bR,4S,5R,5aS,9aR,9bR,11aS)-1-(furan-3-yl)-5-hydroxy-3b,6,6,9a,11a-pentamethyl-1H,2H,3bH,4H,5H,5aH,6H,7H,9aH,9bH,10H,11H,11aH-cyclopenta[a]phenanthren-4-yl acetate	-128.347	-124.847	-3.5
5	Homoserine dehydrogenase - Nimonol structure Derivative 136(SAR 5)	(1R,3bR,4S,5R,5aR,9aS,9bR,11aS)-1-(furan-3-yl)-5-hydroxy-3b,6,6,9a,9b,11a-hexamethyl-7-oxo-1H,2H,3bH,4H,5H,5aH,6H,7H,9aH,9bH,10H,11H,11aH-cyclopenta[a]phenanthren-4-yl acetate	-139.268	-126.417	-12.8509

Table 43: The results of derivatives of Nimonol, a secondary metabolite of *A. indica*, with Lumazine synthase obtained from quick docking by using iGEMDOCK 2.0.

S no	Protein + Ligand derivative	Lumazine synthase with Nimonol derivatives (IUPAC name)	Total Energy (Kcal per mol)	V D W (Kcal per mol)	H. Bond (Kcal per mol)
1	Lumazine synthase - Nimonol structure Derivative 01(SAR 1)	(1R,3bR,4S,5R,5aR,9aR,9bR,11aS)-5-hydroxy-3b,6,6,9a,11a-pentamethyl-1-(5-methylfuran-3-yl)-7-oxo-1H,2H,3bH,4H,5H,5aH,6H,7H,9aH,9bH,10H,11H,11aH-cyclopenta[a]phenanthren-4-yl acetate	-148.614	-141.872	-6.74152
2	Lumazine synthase - Nimonol structure Derivative 17(SAR 2)	(1R,3bR,4S,5R,5aR,9aR,9bR,11aS)-5-hydroxy-3b,6,6,9a,11a-pentamethyl-7-oxo-1-(1H-pyrrol-3-yl)-1H,2H,3bH,4H,5H,5aH,6H,7H,9aH,9bH,10H,11H,11aH-cyclopenta[a]phenanthren-4-yl acetate	-132.509	-128.677	-3.83202
3	Lumazine synthase - Nimonol structure Derivative 60(SAR 3)	(1R,3bR,4S,5R,5aR,9aR,9bR,11aS)-1-(furan-3-yl)-5-hydroxy-3,3b,6,6,9a,11a-hexamethyl-7-oxo-1H,2H,3bH,4H,5H,5aH,6H,7H,9aH,9bH,10H,11H,11aH-cyclopenta[a]phenanthren-4-yl acetate	-141.202	-127.202	-14
4	Lumazine synthase - Nimonol structure Derivative 96(SAR 4)	(1R,3bR,4S,5R,5aS,9aR,9bR,11aS)-1-(furan-3-yl)-5-hydroxy-3b,6,6,9a,11a-pentamethyl-1H,2H,3bH,4H,5H,5aH,6H,7H,9aH,9bH,10H,11H,11aH-cyclopenta[a]phenanthren-4-yl acetate	-146.859	-139.473	-7.38619
5	Lumazine synthase - Nimonol structure Derivative 136(SAR 5)	(1R,3bR,4S,5R,5aR,9aS,9bR,11aS)-1-(furan-3-yl)-5-hydroxy-3b,6,6,9a,9b,11a-hexamethyl-7-oxo-1H,2H,3bH,4H,5H,5aH,6H,7H,9aH,9bH,10H,11H,11aH-cyclopenta[a]phenanthren-4-yl acetate	-156.615	-146.955	-9.65985

Table 44: The results of derivatives of Nimonol, a secondary metabolite of *A. indica*, with Phosphoribosylaminoimidazole obtained from quick docking by using iGEMDOCK 2.0.

S no	Protein + Ligand derivative	Phosphoribosylaminoimidazole carboxylase with Nimonol derivatives (IUPAC name)	Total Energy (Kcal per mol)	V D W (Kcal per mol)	H. Bond (Kcal per mol)
1	Phosphoribosylaminoimidazole - Nimonol structure Derivative 01(SAR 1)	(1R,3bR,4S,5R,5aR,9aR,9bR,11aS)-5-hydroxy-3b,6,6,9a,11a-pentamethyl-1-(5-methylfuran-3-yl)-7-oxo-1H,2H,3bH,4H,5H,5aH,6H,7H,9aH,9bH,10H,11H,11aH-cyclopenta[a]phenanthren-4-yl acetate	-150.99	-141.749	-9.24178
2	Phosphoribosylaminoimidazole - Nimonol structure Derivative 17(SAR 2)	(1R,3bR,4S,5R,5aR,9aR,9bR,11aS)-5-hydroxy-3b,6,6,9a,11a-pentamethyl-7-oxo-1-(1H-pyrrol-3-yl)-1H,2H,3bH,4H,5H,5aH,6H,7H,9aH,9bH,10H,11H,11aH-cyclopenta[a]phenanthren-4-yl acetate	-130.919	-125.541	-5.37836
3	Phosphoribosylaminoimidazole - Nimonol structure Derivative 60(SAR 3)	(1R,3bR,4S,5R,5aR,9aR,9bR,11aS)-1-(furan-3-yl)-5-hydroxy-3,3b,6,6,9a,11a-hexamethyl-7-oxo-1H,2H,3bH,4H,5H,5aH,6H,7H,9aH,9bH,10H,11H,11aH-cyclopenta[a]phenanthren-4-yl acetate	-151.637	-149.137	-2.5
4	Phosphoribosylaminoimidazole - Nimonol structure Derivative 96(SAR 4)	(1R,3bR,4S,5R,5aS,9aR,9bR,11aS)-1-(furan-3-yl)-5-hydroxy-3b,6,6,9a,11a-pentamethyl-1H,2H,3bH,4H,5H,5aH,6H,7H,9aH,9bH,10H,11H,11aH-cyclopenta[a]phenanthren-4-yl acetate	-140.355	-123.872	-16.4826
5	Phosphoribosylaminoimidazole - Nimonol structure Derivative 136(SAR 5)	(1R,3bR,4S,5R,5aR,9aS,9bR,11aS)-1-(furan-3-yl)-5-hydroxy-3b,6,6,9a,9b,11a-hexamethyl-7-oxo-1H,2H,3bH,4H,5H,5aH,6H,7H,9aH,9bH,10H,11H,11aH-cyclopenta[a]phenanthren-4-yl acetate	-154.113	-145.331	-8.78157

Table 45: The results of derivatives of Nimonol, a secondary metabolite of *A. indica*, with Protein elongation factor 3 obtained from quick docking by using iGEMDOCK 2.0.

S no	Protein + Ligand derivative	Protein Elongation Factor 3 with Nimonol derivatives (IUPAC name)	Total Energy (Kcal per mol)	V DW (Kcal per mol)	H. Bond (Kcal per mol)
1	Protein elongation factor- Nimonol structure Derivative 01(SAR1)	(1R,3bR,4S,5R,5aR,9aR,9bR,11aS)-5-hydroxy-3b,6,6,9a,11a-pentamethyl-1-(5-methylfuran-3-yl)-7-oxo-1H,2H,3bH,4H,5H,5aH,6H,7H,9aH,9bH,10H,11H,11aH-cyclopenta[a]phenanthren-4-yl acetate	-122.828	-116.622	-6.2053
2	Protein elongation factor- Nimonol structure Derivative 17(SAR 2)	(1R,3bR,4S,5R,5aR,9aR,9bR,11aS)-5-hydroxy-3b,6,6,9a,11a-pentamethyl-7-oxo-1-(1H-pyrrol-3-yl)-1H,2H,3bH,4H,5H,5aH,6H,7H,9aH,9bH,10H,11H,11aH-cyclopenta[a]phenanthren-4-yl acetate	-129.298	-118.52	-10.778
3	Protein elongation factor- Nimonol structure Derivative 60(SAR 3)	(1R,3bR,4S,5R,5aR,9aR,9bR,11aS)-1-(furan-3-yl)-5-hydroxy-3,3b,6,6,9a,11a-hexamethyl-7-oxo-1H,2H,3bH,4H,5H,5aH,6H,7H,9aH,9bH,10H,11H,11aH-cyclopenta[a]phenanthren-4-yl acetate	-144.977	-135.293	-9.68485
4	Protein elongation factor- Nimonol structure Derivative 96(SAR 4)	(1R,3bR,4S,5R,5aS,9aR,9bR,11aS)-1-(furan-3-yl)-5-hydroxy-3b,6,6,9a,11a-pentamethyl-1H,2H,3bH,4H,5H,5aH,6H,7H,9aH,9bH,10H,11H,11aH-cyclopenta[a]phenanthren-4-yl acetate	-122.71	-118.251	-4.45882
5	Protein elongation factor- Nimonol structure Derivative 136(SAR 5)	(1R,3bR,4S,5R,5aR,9aS,9bR,11aS)-1-(furan-3-yl)-5-hydroxy-3b,6,6,9a,9b,11a-hexamethyl-7-oxo-1H,2H,3bH,4H,5H,5aH,6H,7H,9aH,9bH,10H,11H,11aH-cyclopenta[a]phenanthren-4-yl acetate	-146.776	-136.963	-9.8133

Table 46: The results of derivatives of Nimonol, a secondary metabolite of *A. indica*, with Sulphite reductase obtained from quick docking by using iGEMDOCK 2.0.

S no	Protein + Ligand derivative	Sulphite reductase with Nimonol derivatives (IUPAC name)	Total Energy (Kcal per mol)	V D W (Kcal per mol)	H. Bond (Kcal per mol)
1	Sulphite reductase-Nimonol structure Derivative 01(SAR 1)	(1R,3bR,4S,5R,5aR,9aR,9bR,11aS)-5-hydroxy-3b,6,6,9a,11a-pentamethyl-1-(5-methylfuran-3-yl)-7-oxo-1H,2H,3bH,4H,5H,5aH,6H,7H,9aH,9bH,10H,11H,11aH-cyclopenta[a]phenanthren-4-yl acetate	-155.159	-143.597	-11.5617
2	Sulphite reductase-Nimonol structure Derivative 17(SAR 2)	(1R,3bR,4S,5R,5aR,9aR,9bR,11aS)-5-hydroxy-3b,6,6,9a,11a-pentamethyl-7-oxo-1-(1H-pyrrol-3-yl)-1H,2H,3bH,4H,5H,5aH,6H,7H,9aH,9bH,10H,11H,11aH-cyclopenta[a]phenanthren-4-yl acetate	-146.079	-131.472	-14.6067
3	Sulphite reductase-Nimonol structure Derivative 60(SAR 3)	(1R,3bR,4S,5R,5aR,9aR,9bR,11aS)-1-(furan-3-yl)-5-hydroxy-3,3b,6,6,9a,11a-hexamethyl-7-oxo-1H,2H,3bH,4H,5H,5aH,6H,7H,9aH,9bH,10H,11H,11aH-cyclopenta[a]phenanthren-4-yl acetate	-149.398	-137.835	-11.5624
4	Sulphite reductase-Nimonol structure Derivative 96(SAR 4)	(1R,3bR,4S,5R,5aS,9aR,9bR,11aS)-1-(furan-3-yl)-5-hydroxy-3b,6,6,9a,11a-pentamethyl-1H,2H,3bH,4H,5H,5aH,6H,7H,9aH,9bH,10H,11H,11aH-cyclopenta[a]phenanthren-4-yl acetate	-146.333	-138.675	-7.65877
5	Sulphite reductase-Nimonol structure Derivative 136(SAR 5)	(1R,3bR,4S,5R,5aR,9aS,9bR,11aS)-1-(furan-3-yl)-5-hydroxy-3b,6,6,9a,9b,11a-hexamethyl-7-oxo-1H,2H,3bH,4H,5H,5aH,6H,7H,9aH,9bH,10H,11H,11aH-cyclopenta[a]phenanthren-4-yl acetate	-151.991	-142.547	-9.44414

Table 47: **The results of derivatives of Lawsone, a secondary metabolite of *L. inermis,* with 1, 3 β Glucan synthase obtained from quick docking by using iGEMDOCK 2.0.**

S no	Protein + Ligand derivative	1,3 β Glucan synthase with Lawsone derivatives (IUPAC name)	Total Energy (Kcal per mol)	V D W (Kcal per mol)	H. Bond (Kcal per mol)
1	1,3 β Glucan synthase- Lawsone structure Derivative 01(SAR 1)	4-hydroxy-8-methyl-1,2-dihydronaphthalene-1,2-dione	-84.4852	-82.5118	-1.97334
2	1,3 β Glucan synthase- Lawsone structure Derivative 57(SAR 2)	4-methoxy-1,2-dihydronaphthalene-1,2-dione	-82.7704	-79.2704	-3.5
3	1,3 β Glucan synthase- Lawsone structure Derivative 71(SAR 3)	4-hydroxy-3-methyl-1,2-dihydronaphthalene-1,2-dione	-85.6273	-83.1985	-2.42879
4	1,3 β Glucan synthase- Lawsone structure Derivative 87(SAR 4)	4-hydroxy-2-imino-1,2-dihydronaphthalen-1-one	-84.1084	-78.0642	-6.04421
5	1,3 β Glucan synthase- Lawsone structure Derivative 101(SAR 5)	4-hydroxy-1-imino-1,2-dihydronaphthalen-2-one	-84.374	-76.6578	-7.71619

Table 48: The results of derivatives of Lawsone, a secondary metabolite of *L. inermis*, with Chitin synthase obtained from quick docking by using iGEMDOCK 2.0.

S no	Protein + Ligand derivative	Chitin synthase with Lawsone derivatives (IUPAC name)	Total Energy (Kcal per mol)	V DW (Kcal per mol)	H. Bond (Kcal per mol)
1	Chitin synthase - Lawsone structure Derivative 01(SAR1)	4-hydroxy-8-methyl-1,2-dihydronaphthalene-1,2-dione	-95.4681	-81.6467	-13.8214
2	Chitin synthase - Lawsone structure Derivative57(SAR2)	4-methoxy-1,2-dihydronaphthalene-1,2-dione	-92.4669	-81.2986	-11.1683
3	Chitin synthase - Lawsone structure Derivative 71(SAR 3)	4-hydroxy-3-methyl-1,2-dihydronaphthalene-1,2-dione	-96.38	-83.6275	-12.7526
4	Chitin synthase - Lawsone structure Derivative87(SAR 4)	4-hydroxy-2-imino-1,2-dihydronaphthalen-1-one	-85.5668	-75.48	-10.0868
5	Chitin synthase - Lawsone structure Derivative 101(SAR 5)	4-hydroxy-1-imino-1,2-dihydronaphthalen-2-one	-93.5276	-78.7206	-14.8069

Table 49: The results of derivatives of Lawsone, a secondary metabolite of *L. inermis*, with Chitinase obtained from quick docking by using iGEMDOCK 2.0.

S no	Protein + Ligand derivative	Chitinasewith Lawsone derivatives (IUPAC name)	Total Energy (Kcal per mol)	V DW (Kcal per mol)	H. Bond (Kcal per mol)
1	Chitinase - Lawsone structure Derivative 01(SAR1)	4-hydroxy-8-methyl-1,2-dihydronaphthalene-1,2-dione	-96.6913	-72.5408	-24.1504
2	Chitinase - Lawsone structure Derivative57(SAR2)	4-methoxy-1,2-dihydronaphthalene-1,2-dione	-90.364	-83.4711	-6.89287
3	Chitinase - Lawsone structure Derivative 71(SAR 3)	4-hydroxy-3-methyl-1,2-dihydronaphthalene-1,2-dione	-94.5052	-86.1189	-8.38627
4	Chitinase - Lawsone structure Derivative 87(SAR 4)	4-hydroxy-2-imino-1,2-dihydronaphthalen-1-one	-99.1723	-78.3246	-20.8478
5	Chitinase - Lawsone structure Derivative 101(SAR 5)	4-hydroxy-1-imino-1,2-dihydronaphthalen-2-one	-96.9137	-79.6278	-17.2859

Table 50: The results of derivatives of Lawsone, a secondary metabolite of *L. inermis*, with Deuterolysin obtained from quick docking by using iGEMDOCK 2.0.

S no	Protein + Ligand derivative	Deuterolysinwith Lawsone derivatives (IUPAC name)	Total Energy (Kcal per mol)	V DW (Kcal per mol)	H. Bond (Kcal per mol)
1	Deuterolysin - Lawsone structure Derivative 01(SAR1)	4-hydroxy-8-methyl-1,2-dihydronaphthalene-1,2-dione	-91.6149	-79.6159	-11.999
2	Deuterolysin – Lawsone structure Derivative57(SAR2)	4-methoxy-1,2-dihydronaphthalene-1,2-dione	-87.9093	-78.1907	-9.71866
3	Deuterolysin - Lawsone structure Derivative 71(SAR 3)	4-hydroxy-3-methyl-1,2-dihydronaphthalene-1,2-dione	-91.5998	-85.6653	-5.93456
4	Deuterolysin - Lawsone structure Derivative 87(SAR 4)	4-hydroxy-2-imino-1,2-dihydronaphthalen-1-one	-89.8203	-73.5112	-16.309
5	Deuterolysin - Lawsone structure Derivative 101(SAR 5)	4-hydroxy-1-imino-1,2-dihydronaphthalen-2-one	-81.0473	-70.3087	-10.7386

Table 51: The results of derivatives of Lawsone, a secondary metabolite of *L. inermis*, with Fungalysin obtained from quick docking by using iGEMDOCK 2.0.

S no	Protein + Ligand derivative	Fungalysinwith Lawsone derivatives (IUPAC name)	Total Energy (Kcal per mol)	V DW (Kcal per mol)	H. Bond (Kcal per mol)
1	Fungalysin - Lawsone structure Derivative 01(SAR1)	4-hydroxy-8-methyl-1,2-dihydronaphthalene-1,2-dione	-77.915	-61.9015	-16.0136
2	Fungalysin - Lawsone structure Derivative57(SAR2)	4-methoxy-1,2-dihydronaphthalene-1,2-dione	-85.7222	-68.1006	-17.6216
3	Fungalysin - Lawsone structure Derivative 71(SAR 3)	4-hydroxy-3-methyl-1,2-dihydronaphthalene-1,2-dione	-83.4939	-67.4726	-16.0213
4	Fungalysin - Lawsone structure Derivative 87(SAR 4)	4-hydroxy-2-imino-1,2-dihydronaphthalen-1-one	-85.9281	-63.8544	-22.0737
5	Fungalysin - Lawsone structure Derivative 101(SAR 5)	4-hydroxy-1-imino-1,2-dihydronaphthalen-2-one	-88.6353	-65.4454	-23.1899

Table 52: The results of derivatives of Lawsone, a secondary metabolite of *L. inermis*, with Homoserine dehydrogenase obtained from quick docking by using iGEMDOCK 2.0.

S no	Protein + Ligand derivative	Homoserine dehydrogenasewith Lawsone derivatives (IUPAC name)	Total Energy (Kcal per mol)	V DW (Kcal per mol)	H. Bond (Kcal per mol)
1	Homoserine dehydrogenase - Lawsone structure Derivative 01(SAR1)	4-hydroxy-8-methyl-1,2-dihydronaphthalene-1,2-dione	-109.496	-83.244	-26.2517
2	Homoserine dehydrogenase - Lawsone structure Derivative57(SAR2)	4-methoxy-1,2-dihydronaphthalene-1,2-dione	-105.23	-86.3938	-18.8365
3	Homoserine dehydrogenase - Lawsone structure Derivative 71(SAR 3)	4-hydroxy-3-methyl-1,2-dihydronaphthalene-1,2-dione	-95.8102	-89.8789	-5.93129
4	Homoserine dehydrogenase - Lawsone structure Derivative 87(SAR 4)	4-hydroxy-2-imino-1,2-dihydronaphthalen-1-one	-95.2247	-86.5886	-8.6361
5	Homoserine dehydrogenase - Lawsone structure Derivative 101(SAR 5)	4-hydroxy-1-imino-1,2-dihydronaphthalen-2-one	-103.564	-87.9301	-15.6335

Table 53: The results of derivatives of Lawsone, a secondary metabolite of *L. inermis*, with Lumazine synthase obtained from quick docking by using iGEMDOCK 2.0.

S no	Protein + Ligand derivative	Lumazine synthase with Lawsone derivatives (IUPAC name)	Total Energy (Kcal per mol)	V DW (Kcal per mol)	H. Bond (Kcal per mol)
1	Lumazine synthase - Lawsone structure Derivative 01(SAR1)	4-hydroxy-8-methyl-1,2-dihydronaphthalene-1,2-dione	-93.5984	-62.0216	-31.5768
2	Lumazine synthase - Lawsone structure Derivative57(SAR2)	4-methoxy-1,2-dihydronaphthalene-1,2-dione	-90.5523	-66.4493	-24.103
3	Lumazine synthase - Lawsone structure Derivative 71(SAR 3)	4-hydroxy-3-methyl-1,2-dihydronaphthalene-1,2-dione	-102.582	-70.2286	-32.3535
4	Lumazine synthase - Lawsone structure Derivative 87(SAR 4)	4-hydroxy-2-imino-1,2-dihydronaphthalen-1-one	-99.0603	-82.9888	-16.0715
5	Lumazine synthase - Lawsone structure Derivative 101(SAR 5)	4-hydroxy-1-imino-1,2-dihydronaphthalen-2-one	-95.076	-83.388	-11.688

Table 54: **The results of derivatives of Lawsone, a secondary metabolite of *L. inermis*, with Phosphoribosylaminoimidazole obtained from quick docking by using iGEMDOCK 2.0.**

S no	Protein + Ligand derivative	Phosphoribosylaminoimidazole with Lawsone derivatives (IUPAC name)	Total Energy (Kcal per mol)	V DW (Kcal per mol)	H. Bond (Kcal per mol)
1	Phosphoribosylaminoimidazole- Lawsone structure Derivative 01(SAR1)	4-hydroxy-8-methyl-1,2-dihydronaphthalene-1,2-dione	-97.7377	-85.8562	-11.8814
2	Phosphoribosylaminoimidazole- Lawsone structure Derivative57(SAR2)	4-methoxy-1,2-dihydronaphthalene-1,2-dione	-97.2503	-90.5763	-6.67394
3	Phosphoribosylaminoimidazole- Lawsone structure Derivative 71(SAR 3)	4-hydroxy-3-methyl-1,2-dihydronaphthalene-1,2-dione	-98.6152	-90.7124	-7.9028
4	Phosphoribosylaminoimidazole - Lawsone structure Derivative 87(SAR 4)	4-hydroxy-2-imino-1,2-dihydronaphthalen-1-one	-94.3073	-84.4972	-9.81003
5	Phosphoribosylaminoimidazole - Lawsone structure Derivative 101(SAR 5)	4-hydroxy-1-imino-1,2-dihydronaphthalen-2-one	-86.7612	-67.6158	-19.1454

Table 55: The results of derivatives of Lawsone, a secondary metabolite of *L. inermis*, with Protein elongation factor 3 obtained from quick docking by using iGEMDOCK 2.0.

S no	Protein + Ligand derivative	Protein Elongation Factor 3 with Lawsone derivatives (IUPAC name)	Total Energy (Kcal per mol)	V DW (Kcal per mol)	H. Bond (Kcal per mol)
1	Protein elongation factor-Lawsone structure Derivative 01(SAR1)	4-hydroxy-8-methyl-1,2-dihydronaphthalene-1,2-dione	-72.7794	-59.5533	-13.2262
2	Protein elongation factor-Lawsone structure Derivative57(SAR2)	4-methoxy-1,2-dihydronaphthalene-1,2-dione	-77.5448	-67.9925	-9.55234
3	Protein elongation factor-Lawsone structure Derivative 71(SAR 3)	4-hydroxy-3-methyl-1,2-dihydronaphthalene-1,2-dione	-77.0963	-66.7435	-10.3528
4	Protein elongation factor-Lawsone structure Derivative 87(SAR 4)	4-hydroxy-2-imino-1,2-dihydronaphthalen-1-one	-74.4911	-67.8956	-6.59549
5	Protein elongation factor-Lawsone structure Derivative 101(SAR 5)	4-hydroxy-1-imino-1,2-dihydronaphthalen-2-one	-75.665	-67.9842	-7.68083

Table 56: The results of derivatives of Lawsone, a secondary metabolite of *L. inermis*, with Sulphite reductase obtained from quick docking by using iGEMDOCK 2.0.

S no	Protein + Ligand derivative	Sulphite reductasewith Lawsone derivatives (IUPAC name)	Total Energy (Kcal per mol)	V DW (Kcal per mol)	H. Bond (Kcal per mol)
1	Sulphite reductase- Lawsone structure Derivative 01(SAR1)	4-hydroxy-8-methyl-1,2-dihydronaphthalene-1,2-dione	-94.9317	-66.9371	-27.9946
2	Sulphite reductase- Lawsone structure Derivative 57(SAR2)	4-methoxy-1,2-dihydronaphthalene-1,2-dione	-83.2701	-72.7374	-10.5327
3	Sulphite reductase- Lawsone structure Derivative 71(SAR 3)	4-hydroxy-3-methyl-1,2-dihydronaphthalene-1,2-dione	-94.1968	-70.4458	-23.751
4	Sulphite reductase- Lawsone structure Derivative 87(SAR 4)	4-hydroxy-2-imino-1,2-dihydronaphthalen-1-one	-83.023	-65.9316	-17.0914
5	Sulphite reductase- Lawsone structure Derivative 101(SAR 5)	4-hydroxy-1-imino-1,2-dihydronaphthalen-2-one	-88.9001	-68.9001	-20

Table 57: The results of derivatives of Lawsoniaside, a secondary metabolite of *L. inermis*, with 1,3 β Glucan synthase obtained from quick docking by using iGEMDOCK 2.0.

S no	Protein + Ligand derivative	1,3 β Glucan synthasewith Lawsoniaside derivatives (IUPAC name)	Total Energy (Kcal per mol)	V D W (Kcal per mol)	H. Bond (Kcal per mol)
1	1,3 β Glucan synthase-Lawsoniaside structure Derivative 01(SAR 1)	(2S,3R,4S,5S,6R)-2-[(2-hydroxy-5-methyl-4-{[(2S,3R,4S,5S,6R)-3,4,5-trihydroxy-6-(hydroxymethyl)oxan-2-yl]oxy}naphthalen-1-yl)oxy]-6-(hydroxymethyl)oxane-3,4,5-triol	-145.119	-143.708	-1.41096
2	1,3 β Glucan synthase-Lawsoniaside structure Derivative 75(SAR 2)	(2S,3R,4S,5S,6R)-4,5-dihydroxy-2-[(2-hydroxy-4-{[(2S,3R,4S,5S,6R)-3,4,5-trihydroxy-6-(hydroxymethyl)oxan-2-yl]oxy}naphthalen-1-yl)oxy]-6-(hydroxymethyl)oxan-3-yl hypofluorite	-148.572	-145.072	-3.5
3	1,3 β Glucan synthase-Lawsoniaside structure Derivative 124(SAR 3)	(2S,3R,4S,5S,6R)-2-[(3-hydroperoxy-4-{[(2S,3R,4S,5S,6R)-3,4,5-trihydroxy-6-(hydroxymethyl)oxan-2-yl]oxy}naphthalen-1-yl)oxy]-6-(hydroxymethyl)oxane-3,4,5-triol	-145.133	-145.133	0
4	1,3 β Glucan synthase-Lawsoniaside structure Derivative 151(SAR 4)	(2R,3S,4S,5R,6S)-2-[(aminooxy)methyl]-6-[(3-hydroxy-4-{[(2S,3R,4S,5S,6R)-3,4,5-trihydroxy-6-(hydroxymethyl)oxan-2-yl]oxy}naphthalen-1-yl)oxy]oxane-3,4,5-triol	-140.244	-137.028	-3.21651
5	1,3 β Glucan synthase-Lawsoniaside structure Derivative 182(SAR 5)	(2S,3R,4S,5S,6R)-4,5-dihydroxy-2-[(3-hydroxy-4-{[(2S,3R,4S,5S,6R)-3,4,5-trihydroxy-6-(hydroxymethyl)oxan-2-yl]oxy}naphthalen-1-yl)oxy]-6-(hydroxymethyl)oxan-3-yl hypofluorite	-145.626	-139.343	-6.28282

Table 58: The results of derivatives of Lawsoniaside, a secondary metabolite of *L. inermis*, with Chitin synthase obtained from quick docking by using iGEMDOCK 2.0.

S no	Protein + Ligand derivative	Chitin synthasewith Lawsoniaside derivatives (IUPAC name)	Total Energy (Kcal per mol)	V D W (Kcal per mol)	H. Bond (Kcal per mol)
1	Chitin synthase - Lawsoniaside structure Derivative 01(SAR 1)	(2S,3R,4S,5S,6R)-2-[(2-hydroxy-5-methyl-4-{[(2S,3R,4S,5S,6R)-3,4,5-trihydroxy-6-(hydroxymethyl)oxan-2-yl]oxy}naphthalen-1-yl)oxy]-6-(hydroxymethyl)oxane-3,4,5-triol	-131.024	-106.427	-24.5973
2	Chitin synthase - Lawsoniaside structure Derivative 75(SAR 2)	(2S,3R,4S,5S,6R)-4,5-dihydroxy-2-[(2-hydroxy-4-{[(2S,3R,4S,5S,6R)-3,4,5-trihydroxy-6-(hydroxymethyl)oxan-2-yl]oxy}naphthalen-1-yl)oxy]-6-(hydroxymethyl)oxan-3-yl hypofluorite	-156.069	-138.35	-17.7182
3	Chitin synthase - Lawsoniaside structure Derivative 124(SAR 3)	(2S,3R,4S,5S,6R)-2-[(3-hydroperoxy-4-{[(2S,3R,4S,5S,6R)-3,4,5-trihydroxy-6-(hydroxymethyl)oxan-2-yl]oxy}naphthalen-1-yl)oxy]-6-(hydroxymethyl)oxane-3,4,5-triol	-130.987	-108.763	-22.2243
4	Chitin synthase - Lawsoniaside structure Derivative 151(SAR 4)	(2R,3S,4S,5R,6S)-2-[(aminooxy)methyl]-6-[(3-hydroxy-4-{[(2S,3R,4S,5S,6R)-3,4,5-trihydroxy-6-(hydroxymethyl)oxan-2-yl]oxy}naphthalen-1-yl)oxy]oxane-3,4,5-triol	-127.025	-103.749	-23.2759
5	Chitin synthase - Lawsoniaside structure Derivative 182(SAR 5)	(2S,3R,4S,5S,6R)-4,5-dihydroxy-2-[(3-hydroxy-4-{[(2S,3R,4S,5S,6R)-3,4,5-trihydroxy-6-(hydroxymethyl)oxan-2-yl]oxy}naphthalen-1-yl)oxy]-6-(hydroxymethyl)oxan-3-yl hypofluorite	-152.968	-134.38	-18.5884

Table 59: The results of derivatives of Lawsoniaside, a secondary metabolite of *L. inermis*, with Chitinase obtained from quick docking by using iGEMDOCK 2.0.

S no	Protein + Ligand derivative	Chitinasewith Lawsoniaside derivatives (IUPAC name)	Total Energy (Kcal per mol)	V D W (Kcal per mol)	H. Bond (Kcal per mol)
1	Chitinase - Lawsoniaside structure Derivative 01(SAR 1)	(2S,3R,4S,5S,6R)-2-[(2-hydroxy-5-methyl-4-{[(2S,3R,4S,5S,6R)-3,4,5-trihydroxy-6-(hydroxymethyl)oxan-2-yl]oxy}naphthalen-1-yl)oxy]-6-(hydroxymethyl)oxane-3,4,5-triol	-163.707	-145.586	-18.1207
2	Chitinase - Lawsoniaside structure Derivative 75(SAR 2)	(2S,3R,4S,5S,6R)-4,5-dihydroxy-2-[(2-hydroxy-4-{[(2S,3R,4S,5S,6R)-3,4,5-trihydroxy-6-(hydroxymethyl)oxan-2-yl]oxy}naphthalen-1-yl)oxy]-6-(hydroxymethyl)oxan-3-yl hypofluorite	-162.272	-147.428	-14.8434
3	Chitinase - Lawsoniaside structure Derivative 124(SAR 3)	(2S,3R,4S,5S,6R)-2-[(3-hydroperoxy-4-{[(2S,3R,4S,5S,6R)-3,4,5-trihydroxy-6-(hydroxymethyl)oxan-2-yl]oxy}naphthalen-1-yl)oxy]-6-(hydroxymethyl)oxane-3,4,5-triol	-162.16	-144.164	-17.9967
4	Chitinase - Lawsoniaside structure Derivative 151(SAR 4)	(2R,3S,4S,5R,6S)-2-[(aminooxy)methyl]-6-[(3-hydroxy-4-{[(2S,3R,4S,5S,6R)-3,4,5-trihydroxy-6-(hydroxymethyl)oxan-2-yl]oxy}naphthalen-1-yl)oxy]oxane-3,4,5-triol	-157.473	-136.212	-21.2614
5	Chitinase - Lawsoniaside structure Derivative 182(SAR 5)	(2S,3R,4S,5S,6R)-4,5-dihydroxy-2-[(3-hydroxy-4-{[(2S,3R,4S,5S,6R)-3,4,5-trihydroxy-6-(hydroxymethyl)oxan-2-yl]oxy}naphthalen-1-yl)oxy]-6-(hydroxymethyl)oxan-3-yl hypofluorite	-160.942	-149.929	-11.0133

Table 60: The results of derivatives of Lawsoniaside, a secondary metabolite of *L. inermis*, with Deuterolysin obtained from quick docking by using iGEMDOCK 2.0.

S no	Protein + Ligand derivative	Deuterolysinwith Lawsoniaside derivatives (IUPAC name)	Total Energy (Kcal per mol)	V D W (Kcal per mol)	H. Bond (Kcal per mol)
1	Deuterolysin - Lawsoniaside structure Derivative 01(SAR 1)	(2S,3R,4S,5S,6R)-2-[(2-hydroxy-5-methyl-4-{[(2S,3R,4S,5S,6R)-3,4,5-trihydroxy-6-(hydroxymethyl)oxan-2-yl]oxy}naphthalen-1-yl)oxy]-6-(hydroxymethyl)oxane-3,4,5-triol	-128.962	-122.228	-6.73413
2	Deuterolysin - Lawsoniaside structure Derivative 75(SAR 2)	(2S,3R,4S,5S,6R)-4,5-dihydroxy-2-[(2-hydroxy-4-{[(2S,3R,4S,5S,6R)-3,4,5-trihydroxy-6-(hydroxymethyl)oxan-2-yl]oxy}naphthalen-1-yl)oxy]-6-(hydroxymethyl)oxan-3-yl hypofluorite	-131.36	-111.254	-20.1052
3	Deuterolysin - Lawsoniaside structure Derivative 124(SAR 3)	(2S,3R,4S,5S,6R)-2-[(3-hydroperoxy-4-{[(2S,3R,4S,5S,6R)-3,4,5-trihydroxy-6-(hydroxymethyl)oxan-2-yl]oxy}naphthalen-1-yl)oxy]-6-(hydroxymethyl)oxane-3,4,5-triol	-130.373	-111.86	-18.513
4	Deuterolysin - Lawsoniaside structure Derivative 151(SAR 4)	(2R,3S,4S,5R,6S)-2-[(aminooxy)methyl]-6-[(3-hydroxy-4-{[(2S,3R,4S,5S,6R)-3,4,5-trihydroxy-6-(hydroxymethyl)oxan-2-yl]oxy}naphthalen-1-yl)oxy]oxane-3,4,5-triol	-141.325	-78.6451	-62.6802
5	Deuterolysin - Lawsoniaside structure Derivative 182(SAR 5)	(2S,3R,4S,5S,6R)-4,5-dihydroxy-2-[(3-hydroxy-4-{[(2S,3R,4S,5S,6R)-3,4,5-trihydroxy-6-(hydroxymethyl)oxan-2-yl]oxy}naphthalen-1-yl)oxy]-6-(hydroxymethyl)oxan-3-yl hypofluorite	-117.794	-95.148	-22.6455

Table 61: The results of derivatives of Lawsoniaside, a secondary metabolite of *L. inermis*, with Fungalysin obtained from quick docking by using iGEMDOCK 2.0.

S no	Protein + Ligand derivative	Fungalysinwith Lawsoniaside derivatives (IUPAC name)	Total Energy (Kcal per mol)	V D W (Kcal per mol)	H. Bond (Kcal per mol)
1	Fungalysin - Lawsoniaside structure Derivative 01(SAR 1)	(2S,3R,4S,5S,6R)-2-[(2-hydroxy-5-methyl-4-{[(2S,3R,4S,5S,6R)-3,4,5-trihydroxy-6-(hydroxymethyl)oxan-2-yl]oxy}naphthalen-1-yl)oxy]-6-(hydroxymethyl)oxane-3,4,5-triol	-124.855	-103.137	-21.7184
2	Fungalysin - Lawsoniaside structure Derivative 75(SAR 2)	(2S,3R,4S,5S,6R)-4,5-dihydroxy-2-[(2-hydroxy-4-{[(2S,3R,4S,5S,6R)-3,4,5-trihydroxy-6-(hydroxymethyl)oxan-2-yl]oxy}naphthalen-1-yl)oxy]-6-(hydroxymethyl)oxan-3-yl hypofluorite	-129.961	-109.14	-20.8205
3	Fungalysin - Lawsoniaside structure Derivative 124(SAR 3)	(2S,3R,4S,5S,6R)-2-[(3-hydroperoxy-4-{[(2S,3R,4S,5S,6R)-3,4,5-trihydroxy-6-(hydroxymethyl)oxan-2-yl]oxy}naphthalen-1-yl)oxy]-6-(hydroxymethyl)oxane-3,4,5-triol	-127.81	-104.074	-23.7358
4	Fungalysin - Lawsoniaside structure Derivative 151(SAR 4)	(2R,3S,4S,5R,6S)-2-[(aminooxy)methyl]-6-[(3-hydroxy-4-{[(2S,3R,4S,5S,6R)-3,4,5-trihydroxy-6-(hydroxymethyl)oxan-2-yl]oxy}naphthalen-1-yl)oxy]oxane-3,4,5-triol	-140.391	-113.187	-27.2037
5	Fungalysin - Lawsoniaside structure Derivative 182(SAR 5)	(2S,3R,4S,5S,6R)-4,5-dihydroxy-2-[(3-hydroxy-4-{[(2S,3R,4S,5S,6R)-3,4,5-trihydroxy-6-(hydroxymethyl)oxan-2-yl]oxy}naphthalen-1-yl)oxy]-6-(hydroxymethyl)oxan-3-yl hypofluorite	-120.284	-83.9387	-36.3452

Table 62: The results of derivatives of Lawsoniaside, a secondary metabolite of *L. inermis*, with Homoserine dehydrogenase obtained from quick docking by using iGEMDOCK 2.0.

S no	Protein + Ligand derivative	Homoserine dehydrogenasewith Lawsoniaside derivatives (IUPAC name)	Total Energy (Kcal per mol)	V D W (Kcal per mol)	H. Bond (Kcal per mol)
1	Homoserine dehydrogenase - Lawsoniaside structure Derivative 01(SAR 1)	(2S,3R,4S,5S,6R)-2-[(2-hydroxy-5-methyl-4-{[(2S,3R,4S,5S,6R)-3,4,5-trihydroxy-6-(hydroxymethyl)oxan-2-yl]oxy}naphthalen-1-yl)oxy]-6-(hydroxymethyl)oxane-3,4,5-triol	-180.278	-151.379	-28.899
2	Homoserine dehydrogenase - Lawsoniaside structure Derivative 75(SAR 2)	(2S,3R,4S,5S,6R)-4,5-dihydroxy-2-[(2-hydroxy-4-{[(2S,3R,4S,5S,6R)-3,4,5-trihydroxy-6-(hydroxymethyl)oxan-2-yl]oxy}naphthalen-1-yl)oxy]-6-(hydroxymethyl)oxan-3-yl hypofluorite	-121.477	-86.5718	-34.9054
3	Homoserine dehydrogenase - Lawsoniaside structure Derivative 124(SAR 3)	(2S,3R,4S,5S,6R)-2-[(3-hydroperoxy-4-{[(2S,3R,4S,5S,6R)-3,4,5-trihydroxy-6-(hydroxymethyl)oxan-2-yl]oxy}naphthalen-1-yl)oxy]-6-(hydroxymethyl)oxane-3,4,5-triol	-189.49	-156.482	-33.0086
4	Homoserine dehydrogenase - Lawsoniaside structure Derivative 151(SAR 4)	(2R,3S,4S,5R,6S)-2-[(aminooxy)methyl]-6-[(3-hydroxy-4-{[(2S,3R,4S,5S,6R)-3,4,5-trihydroxy-6-(hydroxymethyl)oxan-2-yl]oxy}naphthalen-1-yl)oxy]oxane-3,4,5-triol	-152.199	-129.093	-23.1068
5	Homoserine dehydrogenase - Lawsoniaside structure Derivative 182(SAR 5)	(2S,3R,4S,5S,6R)-4,5-dihydroxy-2-[(3-hydroxy-4-{[(2S,3R,4S,5S,6R)-3,4,5-trihydroxy-6-(hydroxymethyl)oxan-2-yl]oxy}naphthalen-1-yl)oxy]-6-(hydroxymethyl)oxan-3-yl hypofluorite	-138.222	-120.706	-17.5158

Table 63: The results of derivatives of Lawsoniaside, a secondary metabolite of *L. inermis*, with Lumazine synthase obtained from quick docking by using iGEMDOCK 2.0.

S no	Protein + Ligand derivative	Lumazine synthasewith Lawsoniaside derivatives (IUPAC name)	Total Energy (Kcal per mol)	V D W (Kcal per mol)	H. Bond (Kcal per mol)
1	Lumazine synthase - Lawsoniaside structure Derivative 01(SAR 1)	(2S,3R,4S,5S,6R)-2-[(2-hydroxy-5-methyl-4-{[(2S,3R,4S,5S,6R)-3,4,5-trihydroxy-6-(hydroxymethyl)oxan-2-yl]oxy}naphthalen-1-yl)oxy]-6-(hydroxymethyl)oxane-3,4,5-triol	-160.986	-130.842	-30.144
2	Lumazine synthase - Lawsoniaside structure Derivative 75(SAR 2)	(2S,3R,4S,5S,6R)-4,5-dihydroxy-2-[(2-hydroxy-4-{[(2S,3R,4S,5S,6R)-3,4,5-trihydroxy-6-(hydroxymethyl)oxan-2-yl]oxy}naphthalen-1-yl)oxy]-6-(hydroxymethyl)oxan-3-yl hypofluorite	-143.846	-126.526	-17.3202
3	Lumazine synthase - Lawsoniaside structure Derivative 124(SAR 3)	(2S,3R,4S,5S,6R)-2-[(3-hydroperoxy-4-{[(2S,3R,4S,5S,6R)-3,4,5-trihydroxy-6-(hydroxymethyl)oxan-2-yl]oxy}naphthalen-1-yl)oxy]-6-(hydroxymethyl)oxane-3,4,5-triol	-163.528	-144.909	-18.6181
4	Lumazine synthase - Lawsoniaside structure Derivative 151(SAR 4)	(2R,3S,4S,5R,6S)-2-[(aminooxy)methyl]-6-[(3-hydroxy-4-{[(2S,3R,4S,5S,6R)-3,4,5-trihydroxy-6-(hydroxymethyl)oxan-2-yl]oxy}naphthalen-1-yl)oxy]oxane-3,4,5-triol	-149.214	-125.419	-23.7954
5	Lumazine synthase - Lawsoniaside structure Derivative 182(SAR 5)	(2S,3R,4S,5S,6R)-4,5-dihydroxy-2-[(3-hydroxy-4-{[(2S,3R,4S,5S,6R)-3,4,5-trihydroxy-6-(hydroxymethyl)oxan-2-yl]oxy}naphthalen-1-yl)oxy]-6-(hydroxymethyl)oxan-3-yl hypofluorite	-153.13	-124.251	-28.879

Table 64: The results of derivatives of Lawsoniaside, a secondary metabolite of *L. inermis*, with Phosphoribosylaminoimidazole obtained from quick docking by using iGEMDOCK 2.0.

S no	Protein + Ligand derivative	Phosphoribosylaminoimidazolewith Lawsoniaside derivatives (IUPAC name)	Total Energy (Kcal per mol)	V D W (Kcal per mol)	H. Bond (Kcal per mol)
1	Phosphoribosylaminoimidazole - Lawsoniaside structure Derivative 01(SAR 1)	(2S,3R,4S,5S,6R)-2-[(2-hydroxy-5-methyl-4-{[(2S,3R,4S,5S,6R)-3,4,5-trihydroxy-6-(hydroxymethyl)oxan-2-yl]oxy}naphthalen-1-yl)oxy]-6-(hydroxymethyl)oxane-3,4,5-triol	-162.68	-136.896	-25.7838
2	Phosphoribosylaminoimidazole - Lawsoniaside structure Derivative 75(SAR 2)	(2S,3R,4S,5S,6R)-4,5-dihydroxy-2-[(2-hydroxy-4-{[(2S,3R,4S,5S,6R)-3,4,5-trihydroxy-6-(hydroxymethyl)oxan-2-yl]oxy}naphthalen-1-yl)oxy]-6-(hydroxymethyl)oxan-3-yl hypofluorite	-150.296	-124.144	-26.1522
3	Phosphoribosylaminoimidazole - Lawsoniaside structure Derivative 124(SAR 3)	(2S,3R,4S,5S,6R)-2-[(3-hydroperoxy-4-{[(2S,3R,4S,5S,6R)-3,4,5-trihydroxy-6-(hydroxymethyl)oxan-2-yl]oxy}naphthalen-1-yl)oxy]-6-(hydroxymethyl)oxane-3,4,5-triol	-134.162	-122.152	-12.01
4	Phosphoribosylaminoimidazole - Lawsoniaside structure Derivative 151(SAR 4)	(2R,3S,4S,5R,6S)-2-[(aminooxy)methyl]-6-[(3-hydroxy-4-{[(2S,3R,4S,5S,6R)-3,4,5-trihydroxy-6-(hydroxymethyl)oxan-2-yl]oxy}naphthalen-1-yl)oxy]oxane-3,4,5-triol	-135.003	-125.152	-9.85109
5	Phosphoribosylaminoimidazole - Lawsoniaside structure Derivative 182(SAR 5)	(2S,3R,4S,5S,6R)-4,5-dihydroxy-2-[(3-hydroxy-4-{[(2S,3R,4S,5S,6R)-3,4,5-trihydroxy-6-(hydroxymethyl)oxan-2-yl]oxy}naphthalen-1-yl)oxy]-6-(hydroxymethyl)oxan-3-yl hypofluorite	-166.142	-129.958	-36.1842

Table 65: **The results of derivatives of Lawsoniaside, a secondary metabolite of *L. inermis*, with Protein Elongation Factor 3 obtained from quick docking by using iGEMDOCK 2.0.**

S no	Protein + Ligand derivative	Protein Elongation Factor 3 with Lawsoniaside derivatives (IUPAC name)	Total Energy (Kcal per mol)	V D W (Kcal per mol)	H. Bond (Kcal per mol)
1	Protein elongation factor-Lawsoniaside structure Derivative 01(SAR 1)	(2S,3R,4S,5S,6R)-2-[(2-hydroxy-5-methyl-4-{[(2S,3R,4S,5S,6R)-3,4,5-trihydroxy-6-(hydroxymethyl)oxan-2-yl]oxy}naphthalen-1-yl)oxy]-6-(hydroxymethyl)oxane-3,4,5-triol	-115.528	-86.0427	-29.4849
2	Protein elongation factor-Lawsoniaside structure Derivative 75(SAR 2)	(2S,3R,4S,5S,6R)-4,5-dihydroxy-2-[(2-hydroxy-4-{[(2S,3R,4S,5S,6R)-3,4,5-trihydroxy-6-(hydroxymethyl)oxan-2-yl]oxy}naphthalen-1-yl)oxy]-6-(hydroxymethyl)oxan-3-yl hypofluorite	-123.1	-90.1738	-32.9265
3	Protein elongation factor-Lawsoniaside structure Derivative 124(SAR 3)	(2S,3R,4S,5S,6R)-2-[(3-hydroperoxy-4-{[(2S,3R,4S,5S,6R)-3,4,5-trihydroxy-6-(hydroxymethyl)oxan-2-yl]oxy}naphthalen-1-yl)oxy]-6-(hydroxymethyl)oxane-3,4,5-triol	-125.268	-91.7771	-33.491
4	Protein elongation factor-Lawsoniaside structure Derivative 151(SAR 4)	(2R,3S,4S,5R,6S)-2-[(aminooxy)methyl]-6-[(3-hydroxy-4-{[(2S,3R,4S,5S,6R)-3,4,5-trihydroxy-6-(hydroxymethyl)oxan-2-yl]oxy}naphthalen-1-yl)oxy]oxane-3,4,5-triol	-124.401	-91.0323	-33.3686
5	Protein elongation factor-Lawsoniaside structure Derivative 182(SAR 5)	(2S,3R,4S,5S,6R)-4,5-dihydroxy-2-[(3-hydroxy-4-{[(2S,3R,4S,5S,6R)-3,4,5-trihydroxy-6-(hydroxymethyl)oxan-2-yl]oxy}naphthalen-1-yl)oxy]-6-(hydroxymethyl)oxan-3-yl hypofluorite	-124.192	-91.0858	-33.1063

Table 66: The results of derivatives of Lawsoniaside, a secondary metabolite of *L. inermis*, with Sulphite reductase obtained from quick docking by using iGEMDOCK 2.0.

S no	Protein + Ligand derivative	Sulphite reductasewith Lawsoniaside derivatives (IUPAC name)	Total Energy (Kcal per mol)	V D W (Kcal per mol)	H. Bond (Kcal per mol)
1	Sulphite reductase-Lawsoniaside structure Derivative 01(SAR 1)	(2S,3R,4S,5S,6R)-2-[(2-hydroxy-5-methyl-4-{[(2S,3R,4S,5S,6R)-3,4,5-trihydroxy-6-(hydroxymethyl)oxan-2-yl]oxy}naphthalen-1-yl)oxy]-6-(hydroxymethyl)oxane-3,4,5-triol	-141.83	-91.8411	-49.9894
2	Sulphite reductase-Lawsoniaside structure Derivative 75(SAR 2)	(2S,3R,4S,5S,6R)-4,5-dihydroxy-2-[(2-hydroxy-4-{[(2S,3R,4S,5S,6R)-3,4,5-trihydroxy-6-(hydroxymethyl)oxan-2-yl]oxy}naphthalen-1-yl)oxy]-6-(hydroxymethyl)oxan-3-yl hypofluorite	-150.141	-107.959	-42.1825
3	Sulphite reductase-Lawsoniaside structure Derivative 124(SAR 3)	(2S,3R,4S,5S,6R)-2-[(3-hydroperoxy-4-{[(2S,3R,4S,5S,6R)-3,4,5-trihydroxy-6-(hydroxymethyl)oxan-2-yl]oxy}naphthalen-1-yl)oxy]-6-(hydroxymethyl)oxane-3,4,5-triol	-174.222	-122.808	-51.4136
4	Sulphite reductase-Lawsoniaside structure Derivative 151(SAR 4)	(2R,3S,4S,5R,6S)-2-[(aminooxy)methyl]-6-[(3-hydroxy-4-{[(2S,3R,4S,5S,6R)-3,4,5-trihydroxy-6-(hydroxymethyl)oxan-2-yl]oxy}naphthalen-1-yl)oxy]oxane-3,4,5-triol	-164.854	-123.926	-40.9282
5	Sulphite reductase-Lawsoniaside structure Derivative 182(SAR 5)	(2S,3R,4S,5S,6R)-4,5-dihydroxy-2-[(3-hydroxy-4-{[(2S,3R,4S,5S,6R)-3,4,5-trihydroxy-6-(hydroxymethyl)oxan-2-yl]oxy}naphthalen-1-yl)oxy]-6-(hydroxymethyl)oxan-3-yl hypofluorite	-168.151	-128.608	-39.5427

Table 67: The results of derivatives of Scopoletin, a secondary metabolite of *L. inermis*, with 1,3 β Glucan synthase obtained from quick docking by using iGEMDOCK 2.0

S no	Protein + Ligand derivative	1,3 β Glucan synthase with Scopoletin derivatives (IUPAC name)	Total Energy (Kcal per mol)	V D W (Kcal per mol)	H. Bond (Kcal per mol)
1	1,3 β Glucan synthase- Scopoletin structure Derivative 01(SAR 1)	6-ethoxy-7-hydroxy-2H-chromen-2-one	-88.3627	-82.2832	-6.0795
2	1,3 β Glucan synthase- Scopoletin structure Derivative 44(SAR 2)	4-amino-7-hydroxy-6-methoxy-2H-chromen-2-one	-89.8086	-86.3086	-3.5
3	1,3 β Glucan synthase- Scopoletin structure Derivative 60(SAR 3)	7-hydroxy-6-methoxy-3-sulfanyl-2H-chromen-2-one	-90.3056	-83.6764	-6.62917
4	1,3 β Glucan synthase- Scopoletin structure Derivative 114(SAR 4)	7-(aminooxy)-6-methoxy-2H-chromen-2-one	-88.8804	-81.6147	-7.26574
5	1,3 β Glucan synthase- Scopoletin structure Derivative 127(SAR 5)	6-ethoxy-7-hydroxy-2H-chromen-2-one	-88.1775	-81.2326	-6.94484

Table 68: The results of derivatives of Scopoletin, a secondary metabolite of *L. inermis*, with Chitin synthase obtained from quick docking by using iGEMDOCK 2.0.

S no	Protein + Ligand derivative	Chitin synthase with Scopoletin derivatives (IUPAC name)	Total Energy (Kcal per mol)	V DW (Kcal per mol)	H. Bond (Kcal per mol)
1	Chitin synthase - Scopoletin structure Derivative 01(SAR1)	6-ethoxy-7-hydroxy-2H-chromen-2-one	-101.177	-81.9534	-19.2235
2	Chitin synthase - Scopoletin structure Derivative 44(SAR 2)	4-amino-7-hydroxy-6-methoxy-2H-chromen-2-one	-94.6952	-76.2681	-18.4271
3	Chitin synthase - Scopoletin structure Derivative 60(SAR 3)	7-hydroxy-6-methoxy-3-sulfanyl-2H-chromen-2-one	-101.356	-80.0042	-21.3519
4	Chitin synthase - Scopoletin structure Derivative 114(SAR 4)	7-(aminooxy)-6-methoxy-2H-chromen-2-one	-101.051	-83.551	-17.5
5	Chitin synthase - Scopoletin structure Derivative 127(SAR 5)	6-ethoxy-7-hydroxy-2H-chromen-2-one	-87.0179	-77.5299	-9.48799

Table 69: The results of derivatives of Scopoletin, a secondary metabolite of *L. inermis*, with Chitinase obtained from quick docking by using iGEMDOCK 2.0.

S no	Protein + Ligand derivative	Chitinase with Scopoletin derivatives (IUPAC name)	Total Energy (Kcal per mol)	V DW (Kcal per mol)	H. Bond (Kcal per mol)
1	Chitinase - Scopoletin structure Derivative 01(SAR1)	6-ethoxy-7-hydroxy-2H-chromen-2-one	-92.8121	-78.8121	-14
2	Chitinase - Scopoletin structure Derivative 44(SAR 2)	4-amino-7-hydroxy-6-methoxy-2H-chromen-2-one	-101.045	-82.2182	-18.8269
3	Chitinase - Scopoletin structure Derivative 60(SAR 3)	7-hydroxy-6-methoxy-3-sulfanyl-2H-chromen-2-one	-102.486	-90.2147	-12.2709
4	Chitinase - Scopoletin structure Derivative 114(SAR 4)	7-(aminooxy)-6-methoxy-2H-chromen-2-one	-101.898	-86.1555	-15.7423
5	Chitinase - Scopoletin structure Derivative 127(SAR 5)	6-ethoxy-7-hydroxy-2H-chromen-2-one	-99.9323	-83.3279	-16.6044

Table 70: The results of derivatives of Scopoletin, a secondary metabolite of *L. inermis*, with Deuterolysin obtained from quick docking by using iGEMDOCK 2.0.

S no	Protein + Ligand derivative	Deuterolysin with Scopoletin derivatives (IUPAC name)	Total Energy (Kcal per mol)	V DW (Kcal per mol)	H. Bond (Kcal per mol)
1	Deuterolysin - Scopoletin structure Derivative 01(SAR1)	6-ethoxy-7-hydroxy-2H-chromen-2-one	-87.8215	-74.6937	-13.1278
2	Deuterolysin - Scopoletin structure Derivative 44(SAR 2)	4-amino-7-hydroxy-6-methoxy-2H-chromen-2-one	-87.7408	-65.1847	-22.5561
3	Deuterolysin - Scopoletin structure Derivative 60(SAR 3)	7-hydroxy-6-methoxy-3-sulfanyl-2H-chromen-2-one	-86.2803	-68.751	-17.5293
4	Deuterolysin - Scopoletin structure Derivative 114(SAR 4)	7-(aminooxy)-6-methoxy-2H-chromen-2-one	-94.29	-87.1514	-7.13864
5	Deuterolysin - Scopoletin structure Derivative 127(SAR 5)	6-ethoxy-7-hydroxy-2H-chromen-2-one	-95.8143	-89.8994	-5.91492

Table 71: **The results of derivatives of Scopoletin, a secondary metabolite of *L. inermis*, with Fungalysin obtained from quick docking by using iGEMDOCK 2.0.**

S no	Protein + Ligand derivative	Fungalysin with Scopoletin derivatives (IUPAC name)	Total Energy (Kcal per mol)	V DW (Kcal per mol)	H. Bond (Kcal per mol)
1	Fungalysin - Scopoletin structure Derivative 01(SAR1)	6-ethoxy-7-hydroxy-2H-chromen-2-one	-75.3357	-63.3905	-11.9452
2	Fungalysin - Scopoletin structure Derivative 44(SAR 2)	4-amino-7-hydroxy-6-methoxy-2H-chromen-2-one	-93.6776	-64.1106	-29.567
3	Fungalysin - Scopoletin structure Derivative 60(SAR 3)	7-hydroxy-6-methoxy-3-sulfanyl-2H-chromen-2-one	-85.7976	-69.5069	-16.2907
4	Fungalysin - Scopoletin structure Derivative 114(SAR 4)	7-(aminooxy)-6-methoxy-2H-chromen-2-one	-94.6138	-68.4959	-26.1179
5	Fungalysin - Scopoletin structure Derivative 127(SAR 5)	6-ethoxy-7-hydroxy-2H-chromen-2-one	-84.6706	-73.4533	-11.2173

Table 72: The results of derivatives of Scopoletin, a secondary metabolite of *L. inermis*, with Homoserine dehydrogenase obtained from quick docking by using iGEMDOCK 2.0.

S no	Protein + Ligand derivative	Homoserine dehydrogenase with Scopoletin derivatives (IUPAC name)	Total Energy (Kcal per mol)	V DW (Kcal per mol)	H. Bond (Kcal per mol)
1	Homoserine dehydrogenase - Scopoletin structure Derivative 01(SAR1)	6-ethoxy-7-hydroxy-2H-chromen-2-one	-101.553	-78.318	-23.2348
2	Homoserine dehydrogenase - Scopoletin structure Derivative 44(SAR 2)	4-amino-7-hydroxy-6-methoxy-2H-chromen-2-one	-102.702	-83.1345	-19.5677
3	Homoserine dehydrogenase - Scopoletin structure Derivative 60(SAR 3)	7-hydroxy-6-methoxy-3-sulfanyl-2H-chromen-2-one	-110.267	-84.8476	-25.4199
4	Homoserine dehydrogenase - Scopoletin structure Derivative 114(SAR 4)	7-(aminooxy)-6-methoxy-2H-chromen-2-one	-101.951	-83.7323	-18.2187
5	Homoserine dehydrogenase - Scopoletin structure Derivative 127(SAR 5)	6-ethoxy-7-hydroxy-2H-chromen-2-one	-103.514	-73.1225	-30.3916

Table 73: The results of derivatives of Scopoletin, a secondary metabolite of *L. inermis*, with Lumazine synthase obtained from quick docking by using iGEMDOCK 2.0.

S no	Protein + Ligand derivative	Lumazine synthase with Scopoletin derivatives (IUPAC name)	Total Energy (Kcal per mol)	V DW (Kcal per mol)	H. Bond (Kcal per mol)
1	Lumazine synthase - Scopoletin structure Derivative 01(SAR1)	6-ethoxy-7-hydroxy-2H-chromen-2-one	-95.5604	-78.0604	-17.5
2	Lumazine synthase - Scopoletin structure Derivative 44(SAR 2)	4-amino-7-hydroxy-6-methoxy-2H-chromen-2-one	-97.1444	-80.1161	-17.0283
3	Lumazine synthase - Scopoletin structure Derivative 60(SAR 3)	7-hydroxy-6-methoxy-3-sulfanyl-2H-chromen-2-one	-93.8581	-80.1444	-13.7137
4	Lumazine synthase - Scopoletin structure Derivative 114(SAR 4)	7-(aminooxy)-6-methoxy-2H-chromen-2-one	-96.5144	-70.9017	-25.6127
5	Lumazine synthase - Scopoletin structure Derivative 127(SAR 5)	6-ethoxy-7-hydroxy-2H-chromen-2-one	-93.5334	-77.7347	-15.7988

Table 74: The results of derivatives of Scopoletin, a secondary metabolite of *L. inermis*, with Phosphoribosylaminoimidazole obtained from quick docking by using iGEMDOCK 2.0.

S no	Protein + Ligand derivative	Phosphoribosylaminoimidazole with Scopoletin derivatives (IUPAC name)	Total Energy (Kcal per mol)	V DW (Kcal per mol)	H. Bond (Kcal per mol)
1	Phosphoribosylaminoimidazole-Scopoletin structure Derivative 01(SAR1)	6-ethoxy-7-hydroxy-2H-chromen-2-one	-94.4345	-74.6034	-19.8312
2	Phosphoribosylaminoimidazole-Scopoletin structure Derivative 44(SAR 2)	4-amino-7-hydroxy-6-methoxy-2H-chromen-2-one	-101.672	-79.4941	-22.1776
3	Phosphoribosylaminoimidazole - Scopoletin structure Derivative 60(SAR 3)	7-hydroxy-6-methoxy-3-sulfanyl-2H-chromen-2-one	-103.631	-89.966	-13.6647
4	Phosphoribosylaminoimidazole-Scopoletin structure Derivative 114(SAR 4)	7-(aminooxy)-6-methoxy-2H-chromen-2-one	-104.286	-86.494	-17.792
5	Phosphoribosylaminoimidazole-Scopoletin structure Derivative 127(SAR 5)	6-ethoxy-7-hydroxy-2H-chromen-2-one	-99.8464	-88.8957	-10.9507

Table 75: The results of derivatives of Scopoletin, a secondary metabolite of *L. inermis*, with Protein Elongation Factor 3 obtained from quick docking by using iGEMDOCK 2.0.

S no	Protein + Ligand derivative	Protein Elongation Factor 3 with Scopoletin derivatives (IUPAC name)	Total Energy (Kcal per mol)	V DW (Kcal per mol)	H. Bond (Kcal per mol)
1	Protein elongation factor-Scopoletin structure Derivative 01(SAR1)	6-ethoxy-7-hydroxy-2H-chromen-2-one	-79.7829	-68.7077	-11.0753
2	Protein elongation factor-Scopoletin structure Derivative 44(SAR 2)	4-amino-7-hydroxy-6-methoxy-2H-chromen-2-one	-82.9808	-69.5038	-13.477
3	Protein elongation factor-Scopoletin structure Derivative 60(SAR 3)	7-hydroxy-6-methoxy-3-sulfanyl-2H-chromen-2-one	-75.7691	-72.2691	-3.5
4	Protein elongation factor-Scopoletin structure Derivative 114(SAR 4)	7-(aminooxy)-6-methoxy-2H-chromen-2-one	-79.6442	-70.3828	-9.26134
5	Protein elongation factor-Scopoletin structure Derivative 127(SAR 5)	6-ethoxy-7-hydroxy-2H-chromen-2-one	-74.9207	-71.6968	-3.22387

Table 76: **The results of derivatives of Scopoletin, a secondary metabolite of *L. inermis*, with Sulphite reductase obtained from quick docking by using iGEMDOCK 2.0.**

S no	Protein + Ligand derivative	Sulphite reductase with Scopoletin derivatives (IUPAC name)	Total Energy (Kcal per mol)	V DW (Kcal per mol)	H. Bond (Kcal per mol)
1	Sulphite reductase- Scopoletin structure Derivative 01(SAR1)	6-ethoxy-7-hydroxy-2H-chromen-2-one	-84.5378	-73.6285	-10.9093
2	Sulphite reductase- Scopoletin structure Derivative 44(SAR 2)	4-amino-7-hydroxy-6-methoxy-2H-chromen-2-one	-107.662	-80.2991	-27.3627
3	Sulphite reductase- Scopoletin structure Derivative 60(SAR 3)	7-hydroxy-6-methoxy-3-sulfanyl-2H-chromen-2-one	-90.2403	-65.468	-24.7724
4	Sulphite reductase- Scopoletin structure Derivative 114(SAR 4)	7-(aminooxy)-6-methoxy-2H-chromen-2-one	-92.9368	-67.8052	-25.1315
5	Sulphite reductase- Scopoletin structure Derivative 127(SAR 5)	6-ethoxy-7-hydroxy-2H-chromen-2-one	-93.7862	-74.6855	-19.1008

Table 77: The results of derivatives of Stigmasterol, a secondary metabolite of *L. inermis*, with 1,3 β Glucan synthase obtained from quick docking by using iGEMDOCK 2.0.

S no	Protein + Ligand derivative	1,3 β Glucan synthase with Stigmasterol derivatives (IUPAC name)	Total Energy (Kcal per mol)	V D W (Kcal per mol)	H. Bond (Kcal per mol)
1	1,3 β Glucan synthase-Stigmasterol structure Derivative 16(SAR 1)	(1R,3aS,3bS,7S,9aR,9bS,11aR)-1-[(3E)-7-amino-5-ethyl-6-methylhept-3-en-2-yl]-9a,11a-dimethyl-1H,2H,3H,3aH,3bH,4H,6H,7H,8H,9H,9aH,9bH,10H,11H,11aH-cyclopenta[a]phenanthren-7-ol	-137.304	-137.304	0
2	1,3 β Glucan synthase-Stigmasterol structure Derivative 44(SAR 2)	(1R,3aS,3bS,7S,9aR,9bS,11aR)-1-[(3E)-6-amino-5-ethyl-6-methylhept-3-en-2-yl]-9a,11a-dimethyl-1H,2H,3H,3aH,3bH,4H,6H,7H,8H,9H,9aH,9bH,10H,11H,11aH-cyclopenta[a]phenanthren-7-ol	-116.826	-114.428	-2.39743
3	1,3 β Glucan synthase-Stigmasterol structure Derivative 89(SAR 3)	(1R,3aS,3bS,7S,9aR,9bS,11aR)-9a,11a-dimethyl-1-[(3E)-5-(propan-2-yl)oct-3-en-2-yl]-1H,2H,3H,3aH,3bH,4H,6H,7H,8H,9H,9aH,9bH,10H,11H,11aH-cyclopenta[a]phenanthren-7-ol	-141.835	-141.835	0
4	1,3 β Glucan synthase-Stigmasterol structure Derivative 145(SAR 4)	(1R,3aS,3bS,7S,9aR,9bS,11aR)-4-amino-1-[(3E)-5-ethyl-6-methylhept-3-en-2-yl]-9a,11a-dimethyl-1H,2H,3H,3aH,3bH,4H,6H,7H,8H,9H,9aH,9bH,10H,11H,11aH-cyclopenta[a]phenanthren-7-ol	-141.099	-141.099	0
5	1,3 β Glucan synthase-Stigmasterol structure Derivative 181(SAR 5)	(1R,3aS,3bS,7S,9aR,9bS,11aS)-1-[(3E)-1-amino-5-ethyl-6-methylhept-3-en-2-yl]-9a,11a-dimethyl-1H,2H,3H,3aH,3bH,4H,6H,7H,8H,9H,9aH,9bH,10H,11H,11aH-cyclopenta[a]phenanthren-7-ol	-123.805	-121.305	-2.5

Table 78: The results of derivatives of Stigmasterol, a secondary metabolite of *L. inermis*, with Chitin synthase obtained from quick docking by using iGEMDOCK 2.0.

S no	Protein + Ligand derivative	Chitin synthase with Stigmasterol derivatives (IUPAC name)	Total Energy (Kcal per mol)	V D W (Kcal per mol)	H. Bond (Kcal per mol)
1	Chitin synthase - Stigmasterol structure Derivative 16(SAR 1)	(1R,3aS,3bS,7S,9aR,9bS,11aR)-1-[(3E)-7-amino-5-ethyl-6-methylhept-3-en-2-yl]-9a,11a-dimethyl-1H,2H,3H,3aH,3bH,4H,6H,7H,8H,9H,9aH,9bH,10H,11H,11aH-cyclopenta[a]phenanthren-7-ol	-128.927	-125.427	-3.5
2	Chitin synthase - Stigmasterol structure Derivative 44(SAR 2)	(1R,3aS,3bS,7S,9aR,9bS,11aR)-1-[(3E)-6-amino-5-ethyl-6-methylhept-3-en-2-yl]-9a,11a-dimethyl-1H,2H,3H,3aH,3bH,4H,6H,7H,8H,9H,9aH,9bH,10H,11H,11aH-cyclopenta[a]phenanthren-7-ol	-119.063	-115.563	-3.5
3	Chitin synthase - Stigmasterol structure Derivative 89(SAR 3)	(1R,3aS,3bS,7S,9aR,9bS,11aR)-9a,11a-dimethyl-1-[(3E)-5-(propan-2-yl)oct-3-en-2-yl]-1H,2H,3H,3aH,3bH,4H,6H,7H,8H,9H,9aH,9bH,10H,11H,11aH-cyclopenta[a]phenanthren-7-ol	-113.798	-109.917	-3.88066
4	Chitin synthase - Stigmasterol structure Derivative 145(SAR 4)	(1R,3aS,3bS,7S,9aR,9bS,11aR)-4-amino-1-[(3E)-5-ethyl-6-methylhept-3-en-2-yl]-9a,11a-dimethyl-1H,2H,3H,3aH,3bH,4H,6H,7H,8H,9H,9aH,9bH,10H,11H,11aH-cyclopenta[a]phenanthren-7-ol	-119.994	-104.758	-15.2357
5	Chitin synthase - Stigmasterol structure Derivative 181(SAR 5)	(1R,3aS,3bS,7S,9aR,9bS,11aS)-1-[(3E)-1-amino-5-ethyl-6-methylhept-3-en-2-yl]-9a,11a-dimethyl-1H,2H,3H,3aH,3bH,4H,6H,7H,8H,9H,9aH,9bH,10H,11H,11aH-cyclopenta[a]phenanthren-7-ol	-143.725	-138.261	-5.46416

Table 79: **The results of derivatives of Stigmasterol, a secondary metabolite of *L. inermis*, with Chitinase obtained from quick docking by using iGEMDOCK 2.0.**

S no	Protein + Ligand derivative	Chitinase with Stigmasterol derivatives (IUPAC name)	Total Energy (Kcal per mol)	V D W (Kcal per mol)	H. Bond (Kcal per mol)
1	Chitinase - Stigmasterol structure Derivative 16(SAR 1)	(1R,3aS,3bS,7S,9aR,9bS,11aR)-1-[(3E)-7-amino-5-ethyl-6-methylhept-3-en-2-yl]-9a,11a-dimethyl-1H,2H,3H,3aH,3bH,4H,6H,7H,8H,9H,9aH,9bH,10H,11H,11aH-cyclopenta[a]phenanthren-7-ol	-148.059	-136.305	-11.7533
2	Chitinase - Stigmasterol structure Derivative 44(SAR 2)	(1R,3aS,3bS,7S,9aR,9bS,11aR)-1-[(3E)-6-amino-5-ethyl-6-methylhept-3-en-2-yl]-9a,11a-dimethyl-1H,2H,3H,3aH,3bH,4H,6H,7H,8H,9H,9aH,9bH,10H,11H,11aH-cyclopenta[a]phenanthren-7-ol	-145.681	-137.196	-8.48556
3	Chitinase - Stigmasterol structure Derivative 89(SAR 3)	(1R,3aS,3bS,7S,9aR,9bS,11aR)-9a,11a-dimethyl-1-[(3E)-5-(propan-2-yl)oct-3-en-2-yl]-1H,2H,3H,3aH,3bH,4H,6H,7H,8H,9H,9aH,9bH,10H,11H,11aH-cyclopenta[a]phenanthren-7-ol	-135.445	-131.624	-3.82142
4	Chitinase - Stigmasterol structure Derivative 145(SAR 4)	(1R,3aS,3bS,7S,9aR,9bS,11aR)-4-amino-1-[(3E)-5-ethyl-6-methylhept-3-en-2-yl]-9a,11a-dimethyl-1H,2H,3H,3aH,3bH,4H,6H,7H,8H,9H,9aH,9bH,10H,11H,11aH-cyclopenta[a]phenanthren-7-ol	-143.867	-140.367	-3.5
5	Chitinase - Stigmasterol structure Derivative 181(SAR 5)	(1R,3aS,3bS,7S,9aR,9bS,11aS)-1-[(3E)-1-amino-5-ethyl-6-methylhept-3-en-2-yl]-9a,11a-dimethyl-1H,2H,3H,3aH,3bH,4H,6H,7H,8H,9H,9aH,9bH,10H,11H,11aH-cyclopenta[a]phenanthren-7-ol	-144.452	-140.952	-3.5

Table 80: The results of derivatives of Stigmasterol, a secondary metabolite of *L. inermis*, with Deuterolysin obtained from quick docking by using iGEMDOCK 2.0.

S no	Protein + Ligand derivative	Deuterolysin with Stigmasterol derivatives (IUPAC name)	Total Energy (Kcal per mol)	V D W (Kcal per mol)	H- Bond (Kcal per mol)
1	Deuterolysin – Stigmasterol structure Derivative 16(SAR 1)	(1R,3aS,3bS,7S,9aR,9bS,11aR)-1-[(3E)-7-amino-5-ethyl-6-methylhept-3-en-2-yl]-9a,11a-dimethyl-1H,2H,3H,3aH,3bH,4H,6H,7H,8H,9H,9aH,9bH,10H,11H,11aH-cyclopenta[a]phenanthren-7-ol	-146.112	-138.643	-7.46839
2	Deuterolysin - Stigmasterol structure Derivative 44(SAR 2)	(1R,3aS,3bS,7S,9aR,9bS,11aR)-1-[(3E)-6-amino-5-ethyl-6-methylhept-3-en-2-yl]-9a,11a-dimethyl-1H,2H,3H,3aH,3bH,4H,6H,7H,8H,9H,9aH,9bH,10H,11H,11aH-cyclopenta[a]phenanthren-7-ol	-123.339	-121.233	-2.10606
3	Deuterolysin - Stigmasterol structure Derivative 89(SAR 3)	(1R,3aS,3bS,7S,9aR,9bS,11aR)-9a,11a-dimethyl-1-[(3E)-5-(propan-2-yl)oct-3-en-2-yl]-1H,2H,3H,3aH,3bH,4H,6H,7H,8H,9H,9aH,9bH,10H,11H,11aH-cyclopenta[a]phenanthren-7-ol	-143.068	-136.647	-6.42088
4	Deuterolysin - Stigmasterol structure Derivative 145(SAR 4)	(1R,3aS,3bS,7S,9aR,9bS,11aR)-4-amino-1-[(3E)-5-ethyl-6-methylhept-3-en-2-yl]-9a,11a-dimethyl-1H,2H,3H,3aH,3bH,4H,6H,7H,8H,9H,9aH,9bH,10H,11H,11aH-cyclopenta[a]phenanthren-7-ol	-116.522	-113.022	-3.5
5	Deuterolysin - Stigmasterol structure Derivative 181(SAR 5)	(1R,3aS,3bS,7S,9aR,9bS,11aS)-1-[(3E)-1-amino-5-ethyl-6-methylhept-3-en-2-yl]-9a,11a-dimethyl-1H,2H,3H,3aH,3bH,4H,6H,7H,8H,9H,9aH,9bH,10H,11H,11aH-cyclopenta[a]phenanthren-7-ol	-128.476	-124.976	-3.5

Table 81: The results of derivatives of Stigmasterol, a secondary metabolite of *L. inermis*, with Fungalysin obtained from quick docking by using iGEMDOCK 2.0.

S no	Protein + Ligand derivative	Fungalysin with Stigmasterol derivatives (IUPAC name)	Total Energy (Kcal per mol)	V D W (Kcal per mol)	H. Bond (Kcal per mol)
1	Fungalysin - Stigmasterol structure Derivative 16(SAR 1)	(1R,3aS,3bS,7S,9aR,9bS,11aR)-1-[(3E)-7-amino-5-ethyl-6-methylhept-3-en-2-yl]-9a,11a-dimethyl-1H,2H,3H,3aH,3bH,4H,6H,7H,8H,9H,9aH,9bH,10H,11H,11aH-cyclopenta[a]phenanthren-7-ol	-115.251	-111.751	-3.5
2	Fungalysin - Stigmasterol structure Derivative 44(SAR 2)	(1R,3aS,3bS,7S,9aR,9bS,11aR)-1-[(3E)-6-amino-5-ethyl-6-methylhept-3-en-2-yl]-9a,11a-dimethyl-1H,2H,3H,3aH,3bH,4H,6H,7H,8H,9H,9aH,9bH,10H,11H,11aH-cyclopenta[a]phenanthren-7-ol	-115.637	-108.292	-7.34529
3	Fungalysin - Stigmasterol structure Derivative 89(SAR 3)	(1R,3aS,3bS,7S,9aR,9bS,11aR)-9a,11a-dimethyl-1-[(3E)-5-(propan-2-yl)oct-3-en-2-yl]-1H,2H,3H,3aH,3bH,4H,6H,7H,8H,9H,9aH,9bH,10H,11H,11aH-cyclopenta[a]phenanthren-7-ol	-134.616	-129.699	-4.9176
4	Fungalysin - Stigmasterol structure Derivative 145(SAR 4)	(1R,3aS,3bS,7S,9aR,9bS,11aR)-4-amino-1-[(3E)-5-ethyl-6-methylhept-3-en-2-yl]-9a,11a-dimethyl-1H,2H,3H,3aH,3bH,4H,6H,7H,8H,9H,9aH,9bH,10H,11H,11aH-cyclopenta[a]phenanthren-7-ol	-124.17	-120.709	-3.46046
5	Fungalysin - Stigmasterol structure Derivative 181(SAR 5)	(1R,3aS,3bS,7S,9aR,9bS,11aS)-1-[(3E)-1-amino-5-ethyl-6-methylhept-3-en-2-yl]-9a,11a-dimethyl-1H,2H,3H,3aH,3bH,4H,6H,7H,8H,9H,9aH,9bH,10H,11H,11aH-cyclopenta[a]phenanthren-7-ol	-118.524	-111.524	-7

Table 82: The results of derivatives of Stigmasterol, a secondary metabolite of *L. inermis*, with Homoserine dehydrogenase obtained from quick docking by using iGEMDOCK 2.0.

S no	Protein + Ligand derivative	Homoserine dehydrogenase with Stigmasterol derivatives (IUPAC name)	Total Energy (Kcal per mol)	V D W (Kcal per mol)	H. Bond (Kcal per mol)
1	Homoserine dehydrogenase - Stigmasterol structure Derivative 16(SAR 1)	(1R,3aS,3bS,7S,9aR,9bS,11aR)-1-[(3E)-7-amino-5-ethyl-6-methylhept-3-en-2-yl]-9a,11a-dimethyl-1H,2H,3H,3aH,3bH,4H,6H,7H,8H,9H,9aH,9bH,10H,11H,11aH-cyclopenta[a]phenanthren-7-ol	-115.686	-104.859	-10.8265
2	Homoserine dehydrogenase - Stigmasterol structure Derivative 44(SAR 2)	(1R,3aS,3bS,7S,9aR,9bS,11aR)-1-[(3E)-6-amino-5-ethyl-6-methylhept-3-en-2-yl]-9a,11a-dimethyl-1H,2H,3H,3aH,3bH,4H,6H,7H,8H,9H,9aH,9bH,10H,11H,11aH-cyclopenta[a]phenanthren-7-ol	-149.749	-142.571	-7.17857
3	Homoserine dehydrogenase - Stigmasterol structure Derivative 89(SAR 3)	(1R,3aS,3bS,7S,9aR,9bS,11aR)-9a,11a-dimethyl-1-[(3E)-5-(propan-2-yl)oct-3-en-2-yl]-1H,2H,3H,3aH,3bH,4H,6H,7H,8H,9H,9aH,9bH,10H,11H,11aH-cyclopenta[a]phenanthren-7-ol	-143.828	-140.328	-3.5
4	Homoserine dehydrogenase - Stigmasterol structure Derivative 145(SAR 4)	(1R,3aS,3bS,7S,9aR,9bS,11aR)-4-amino-1-[(3E)-5-ethyl-6-methylhept-3-en-2-yl]-9a,11a-dimethyl-1H,2H,3H,3aH,3bH,4H,6H,7H,8H,9H,9aH,9bH,10H,11H,11aH-cyclopenta[a]phenanthren-7-ol	-151.418	-141.918	-9.5
5	Homoserine dehydrogenase - Stigmasterol structure Derivative 181(SAR 5)	(1R,3aS,3bS,7S,9aR,9bS,11aS)-1-[(3E)-1-amino-5-ethyl-6-methylhept-3-en-2-yl]-9a,11a-dimethyl-1H,2H,3H,3aH,3bH,4H,6H,7H,8H,9H,9aH,9bH,10H,11H,11aH-cyclopenta[a]phenanthren-7-ol	-121.676	-118.176	-3.5

Table 83: **The results of derivatives of Stigmasterol, a secondary metabolite of *L. inermis*, with Lumazine synthase obtained from quick docking by using iGEMDOCK 2.0.**

S no	Protein + Ligand derivative	Lumazine synthase with Stigmasterol derivatives (IUPAC name)	Total Energy (Kcal per mol)	V D W (Kcal per mol)	H. Bond (Kcal per mol)
1	Lumazine synthase - Stigmasterol structure Derivative 16(SAR 1)	(1R,3aS,3bS,7S,9aR,9bS,11aR)-1-[(3E)-7-amino-5-ethyl-6-methylhept-3-en-2-yl]-9a,11a-dimethyl-1H,2H,3H,3aH,3bH,4H,6H,7H,8H,9H,9aH,9bH,10H,11H,11aH-cyclopenta[a]phenanthren-7-ol	-129.967	-129.967	0
2	Lumazine synthase - Stigmasterol structure Derivative 44(SAR 2)	(1R,3aS,3bS,7S,9aR,9bS,11aR)-1-[(3E)-6-amino-5-ethyl-6-methylhept-3-en-2-yl]-9a,11a-dimethyl-1H,2H,3H,3aH,3bH,4H,6H,7H,8H,9H,9aH,9bH,10H,11H,11aH-cyclopenta[a]phenanthren-7-ol	-116.264	-111.517	-4.74743
3	Lumazine synthase - Stigmasterol structure Derivative 89(SAR 3)	(1R,3aS,3bS,7S,9aR,9bS,11aR)-9a,11a-dimethyl-1-[(3E)-5-(propan-2-yl)oct-3-en-2-yl]-1H,2H,3H,3aH,3bH,4H,6H,7H,8H,9H,9aH,9bH,10H,11H,11aH-cyclopenta[a]phenanthren-7-ol	-131.408	-127.908	-3.5
4	Lumazine synthase - Stigmasterol structure Derivative 145(SAR 4)	(1R,3aS,3bS,7S,9aR,9bS,11aR)-4-amino-1-[(3E)-5-ethyl-6-methylhept-3-en-2-yl]-9a,11a-dimethyl-1H,2H,3H,3aH,3bH,4H,6H,7H,8H,9H,9aH,9bH,10H,11H,11aH-cyclopenta[a]phenanthren-7-ol	-120.585	-113.831	-6.75424
5	Lumazine synthase - Stigmasterol structure Derivative 181(SAR 5)	(1R,3aS,3bS,7S,9aR,9bS,11aS)-1-[(3E)-1-amino-5-ethyl-6-methylhept-3-en-2-yl]-9a,11a-dimethyl-1H,2H,3H,3aH,3bH,4H,6H,7H,8H,9H,9aH,9bH,10H,11H,11aH-cyclopenta[a]phenanthren-7-ol	-147.791	-140.888	-6.90263

Table 84: **The results of derivatives of Stigmasterol, a secondary metabolite of *L. inermis*, with Phosphoribosylaminoimidazole obtained from quick docking by using iGEMDOCK 2.0.**

S no	Protein + Ligand derivative	Phosphoribosylaminoimidazole with Stigmasterol derivatives (IUPAC name)	Total Energy (Kcal per mol)	V D W (Kcal per mol)	H. Bond (Kcal per mol)
1	Phosphoribosylaminoimidazole - Stigmasterol structure Derivative 16(SAR 1)	(1R,3aS,3bS,7S,9aR,9bS,11aR)-1-[(3E)-7-amino-5-ethyl-6-methylhept-3-en-2-yl]-9a,11a-dimethyl-1H,2H,3H,3aH,3bH,4H,6H,7H,8H,9H,9aH,9bH,10H,11H,11aH-cyclopenta[a]phenanthren-7-ol	-127.69	-124.19	-3.5
2	Phosphoribosylaminoimidazole - Stigmasterol structure Derivative 44(SAR 2)	(1R,3aS,3bS,7S,9aR,9bS,11aR)-1-[(3E)-6-amino-5-ethyl-6-methylhept-3-en-2-yl]-9a,11a-dimethyl-1H,2H,3H,3aH,3bH,4H,6H,7H,8H,9H,9aH,9bH,10H,11H,11aH-cyclopenta[a]phenanthren-7-ol	-164.044	-156.046	-7.99889
3	Phosphoribosylaminoimidazole - Stigmasterol structure Derivative 89(SAR 3)	(1R,3aS,3bS,7S,9aR,9bS,11aR)-9a,11a-dimethyl-1-[(3E)-5-(propan-2-yl)oct-3-en-2-yl]-1H,2H,3H,3aH,3bH,4H,6H,7H,8H,9H,9aH,9bH,10H,11H,11aH-cyclopenta[a]phenanthren-7-ol	-140.935	-137.435	-3.5
4	Phosphoribosylaminoimidazole - Stigmasterol structure Derivative 145(SAR 4)	(1R,3aS,3bS,7S,9aR,9bS,11aR)-4-amino-1-[(3E)-5-ethyl-6-methylhept-3-en-2-yl]-9a,11a-dimethyl-1H,2H,3H,3aH,3bH,4H,6H,7H,8H,9H,9aH,9bH,10H,11H,11aH-cyclopenta[a]phenanthren-7-ol	-126.249	-119.181	-7.06768
5	Phosphoribosylaminoimidazole - Stigmasterol structure Derivative 181(SAR 5)	(1R,3aS,3bS,7S,9aR,9bS,11aS)-1-[(3E)-1-amino-5-ethyl-6-methylhept-3-en-2-yl]-9a,11a-dimethyl-1H,2H,3H,3aH,3bH,4H,6H,7H,8H,9H,9aH,9bH,10H,11H,11aH-cyclopenta[a]phenanthren-7-ol	-152.445	-148.945	-3.5

Table 85: The results of derivatives of Stigmasterol, a secondary metabolite of *L. inermis*, with Protein Elongation Factor 3 obtained from quick docking by using iGEMDOCK 2.0.

S no	Protein + Ligand derivative	Protein Elongation Factor 3 with Stigmasterol derivatives (IUPAC name)	Total Energy (Kcal per mol)	V D W (Kcal per mol)	H. Bond (Kcal per mol)
1	Protein elongation factor-Stigmasterol structure Derivative 16(SAR 1)	(1R,3aS,3bS,7S,9aR,9bS,11aR)-1-[(3E)-7-amino-5-ethyl-6-methylhept-3-en-2-yl]-9a,11a-dimethyl-1H,2H,3H,3aH,3bH,4H,6H,7H,8H,9H,9aH,9bH,10H,11H,11aH-cyclopenta[a]phenanthren-7-ol	-126.622	-123.122	-3.5
2	Protein elongation factor-Stigmasterol structure Derivative 44(SAR 2)	(1R,3aS,3bS,7S,9aR,9bS,11aR)-1-[(3E)-6-amino-5-ethyl-6-methylhept-3-en-2-yl]-9a,11a-dimethyl-1H,2H,3H,3aH,3bH,4H,6H,7H,8H,9H,9aH,9bH,10H,11H,11aH-cyclopenta[a]phenanthren-7-ol	-120.361	-116.009	-4.35265
3	Protein elongation factor-Stigmasterol structure Derivative 89(SAR 3)	(1R,3aS,3bS,7S,9aR,9bS,11aR)-9a,11a-dimethyl-1-[(3E)-5-(propan-2-yl)oct-3-en-2-yl]-1H,2H,3H,3aH,3bH,4H,6H,7H,8H,9H,9aH,9bH,10H,11H,11aH-cyclopenta[a]phenanthren-7-ol	-131.763	-128.61	-3.15338
4	Protein elongation factor-Stigmasterol structure Derivative 145(SAR 4)	(1R,3aS,3bS,7S,9aR,9bS,11aR)-4-amino-1-[(3E)-5-ethyl-6-methylhept-3-en-2-yl]-9a,11a-dimethyl-1H,2H,3H,3aH,3bH,4H,6H,7H,8H,9H,9aH,9bH,10H,11H,11aH-cyclopenta[a]phenanthren-7-ol	-126.24	-122.74	-3.5
5	Protein elongation factor-Stigmasterol structure Derivative 181(SAR 5)	(1R,3aS,3bS,7S,9aR,9bS,11aS)-1-[(3E)-1-amino-5-ethyl-6-methylhept-3-en-2-yl]-9a,11a-dimethyl-1H,2H,3H,3aH,3bH,4H,6H,7H,8H,9H,9aH,9bH,10H,11H,11aH-cyclopenta[a]phenanthren-7-ol	-124.951	-121.578	-3.37347

Table 86: The results of derivatives of Stigmasterol, a secondary metabolite of *L. inermis*, with Sulphite reductase obtained from quick docking by using iGEMDOCK 2.0.

S no	Protein + Ligand derivative	Sulphite reductase with Stigmasterol derivatives (IUPAC name)	Total Energy (Kcal per mol)	V D W (Kcal per mol)	H. Bond (Kcal per mol)
1	Sulphite reductase-Stigmasterol structure Derivative 16(SAR 1)	(1R,3aS,3bS,7S,9aR,9bS,11aR)-1-[(3E)-7-amino-5-ethyl-6-methylhept-3-en-2-yl]-9a,11a-dimethyl-1H,2H,3H,3aH,3bH,4H,6H,7H,8H,9H,9aH,9bH,10H,11H,11aH-cyclopenta[a]phenanthren-7-ol	-122.306	-122.306	0
2	Sulphite reductase-Stigmasterol structure Derivative 44(SAR 2)	(1R,3aS,3bS,7S,9aR,9bS,11aR)-1-[(3E)-6-amino-5-ethyl-6-methylhept-3-en-2-yl]-9a,11a-dimethyl-1H,2H,3H,3aH,3bH,4H,6H,7H,8H,9H,9aH,9bH,10H,11H,11aH-cyclopenta[a]phenanthren-7-ol	-115.018	-108.018	-7
3	Sulphite reductase-Stigmasterol structure Derivative 89(SAR 3)	(1R,3aS,3bS,7S,9aR,9bS,11aR)-9a,11a-dimethyl-1-[(3E)-5-(propan-2-yl)oct-3-en-2-yl]-1H,2H,3H,3aH,3bH,4H,6H,7H,8H,9H,9aH,9bH,10H,11H,11aH-cyclopenta[a]phenanthren-7-ol	-115.85	-108.985	-6.86482
4	Sulphite reductase-Stigmasterol structure Derivative 145(SAR 4)	(1R,3aS,3bS,7S,9aR,9bS,11aR)-4-amino-1-[(3E)-5-ethyl-6-methylhept-3-en-2-yl]-9a,11a-dimethyl-1H,2H,3H,3aH,3bH,4H,6H,7H,8H,9H,9aH,9bH,10H,11H,11aH-cyclopenta[a]phenanthren-7-ol	-138.956	-131.956	-7
5	Sulphite reductase-Stigmasterol structure Derivative 181(SAR 5)	(1R,3aS,3bS,7S,9aR,9bS,11aS)-1-[(3E)-1-amino-5-ethyl-6-methylhept-3-en-2-yl]-9a,11a-dimethyl-1H,2H,3H,3aH,3bH,4H,6H,7H,8H,9H,9aH,9bH,10H,11H,11aH-cyclopenta[a]phenanthren-7-ol	-133.042	-124.431	-8.611

5.8.7 Properties of best derivatives of ligands

The best derivatives are selected from the derivatives obtained by using SwissADME, and the toxicity profile was with the help of admetSAR was tabulated from table 87 to table 121.

The azadirachtin derivatives selected are derivatives 2, 19, 56, 58, and 81 which are named as structure-activity relative (SAR) molecules.

The azadirachtin derivative 2 (SAR 1 with IUPAC name: 4,11-dimethyl (1S,4S,5R,6S,7S,8R,11S,12R,14S,15R)-12-(acetyloxy)-4,7-dihydroxy-6-[(1S,2S,6R,8S,9R,11S)-2-hydroxy-11-methyl-7,10-dioxatetracyclo[6.3.1.$0^{2,6}$.$0^{9,11}$]dodec-3-en-9-yl]-6-methyl-14-{[(2E)-2-methylbut-2-enoyl]oxy}-3,9-dioxatetracyclo[6.6.1.$0^{1,5}$.$0^{11,15}$]pentadecane-4,11-dicarboxylate) shows more Lipophilicity, an inhibitor of CYP3A4, disobeys the Brenk filter in four parameters which was presented in table 87.

The azadirachtin derivative 19 (SAR 2 with IUPAC name: 4,11-dimethyl (1S,4S,5R,6S,7S,8R,11S,12R,14S,15R)-12-(acetyloxy)-4,7-dihydroxy-6-[(1S,2S,6R,8S,9R,11S)-2-hydroxy-11-methyl-5,10-dioxa-7-azatetracyclo[6.3.1.$0^{2,6}$.$0^{9,11}$]dodec-3-en-9-yl]-6-methyl-14-{[(2E)-2-methylbut-2-enoyl]oxy}-3,9-dioxatetracyclo[6.6.1.$0^{1,5}$.$0^{11,15}$]pentadecane-4,11-dicarboxylate), the hydrogen bond donors are 4, Ghose filter shows 4 violations, high lipophilic, acute oral toxicity shows category III, Acute rat toxicity was less, and TPT was also less with azadirachtin parent compound which was presented in table 88.

The azadirachtin derivative 56 (SAR 3 with IUPAC name: 4,11-dimethyl(1S,4S,5R,6S,7S,8R,11S,12R,14S,15R)-12-ethoxy-4,7-dihydroxy-6[(1S,2S,6S,8S,9R,11S)-2-hydroxy-11-methyl-5,7,10-

trioxatetracyclo[6.3.1.0^{2},^{6}.0^{9},^{11}]dodec-3-en-9-yl]-6-methyl-14-{[(2E)-2-methylbut-2-enoyl]oxy}-3,9-dioxatetracyclo[6.6.1.0^{1},^{5}.0^{11},^{15}]pentadecane-4,11-dicarboxylate), no of H-bond acceptors 15, more lipophilic, skin permeability was -9.6 cm/s, acute rat toxicity, 4.2870 mol/kg, fish toxicity, 0.6060 mg/L, TPT 0.7128 mcg/L which was presented in table 89.

The azadirachtin derivative 58 (SAR 4 with IUPAC name: 4,11-dimethyl (1S,4S,5R,6S,7S,8R,11S,12R,14S,15R)-12-(ethanimidoyloxy)-4,7-dihydroxy-6-[(1S,2S,6S,8S,9R,11S)-2-hydroxy-11-methyl-5,7,10-trioxatetracyclo[6.3.1.0^{2},^{6}.0^{9},^{11}]dodec-3-en-9-yl]-6-methyl-14-{[(2E)-2-methylbut-2-enoyl]oxy}-3,9-dioxatetracyclo[6.6.1.0^{1},^{5}.0^{11},^{15}]pentadecane-4,11-dicarboxylate), no of H-bond donors are 4, high lipophilic as consensus Log $P_{o/w}$ was 1.23, inhibitor of CYP3A4, skin permeability was -9.85 cm/s, Brenk filter was 4 violations, acute oral toxicity shows category III, acute rat toxicity was 3.3092 mol/kg, fish toxicity was 0.8499 mg/L, TPT was 0.5168 mcg/L which was presented in table 90.

The azadirachtin derivative 81 (SAR 5 with IUPAC name: 4,11-dimethyl (1S,4S,5R,6S,7S,8R,11S,12R,14S,15R)-12-(acetyloxy)-14-{[(2Z)-2-(bromomethyl)but-2-enoyl]oxy}-4,7-dihydroxy-6-[(1S,2S,6S,8S,9R,11S)-2-hydroxy-11-methyl-5,7,10-trioxatetracyclo[6.3.1.0^{2},^{6}.0^{9},^{11}]dodec-3-en-9-yl]-6-methyl-3,9-dioxatetracyclo[6.6.1.0^{1},^{5}.0^{11},^{15}]pentadecane-4,11-dicarboxylate), no of H-bond acceptors 16 and donors are 3, Veber filter shows 2 violations, highly lipophilic with consensus Log Po/w was 1.49, skin permeability was -10.27 cm/s, acute rat toxicity was 4.2446 mol/kg, fish toxicity was 0.4395 mg/L, TPT was 0.9296 mcg/L which was presented in table 91.

The nimbin derivatives selected are derivatives 1, 41, 50, 63, and 107 which are named as structure-activity relative (SAR) molecules.

The nimbin derivative 1 (SAR 1 with IUPAC name: ethyl (1S,2R,3R,4R,8R,9S,10R,13R,15R)-2-(acetyloxy)-13-(furan-3-yl)-9-(2-methoxy-2-oxoethyl)-4,8,10,12-tetramethyl-7-oxo-16-oxatetracyclo[8.6.0.0^{3},^{8}.0^{11},^{15}]hexadeca-5,11-diene-4-carboxylate), the no of heavy atoms are 40, the number of rotatable bonds was 9, molar refractivity was 143.61, highly lipophilic as consensus Log $P_{o/w}$ was 3.58, an inhibitor of CYP3A4, carcinogenicity (three class) was Danger which was presented in table 92.

The nimbin derivative 41 (SAR 2 with IUPAC name: methyl (1S,2R,3R,4S,8R,9S,10R,13R,15R)-2-(acetyloxy)-13-(furan-3-yl)-9-(2-methoxy-2-oxoethyl)-4,5,8,10,12-pentamethyl-7-oxo-16-oxatetracyclo[8.6.0.0^{3},^{8}.0^{11},^{15}]hexadeca-5,11-diene-4-carboxylate), the no of heavy atoms are 40; molar refractivity was 143.61, Log S (SILICOS-IT) was poorly soluble, skin permeability was -8.12 cm/s which was presented in table 93.

The nimbin derivative 50 (SAR 3 with IUPAC name: methyl (1S,2R,3R,4R,8R,9S,10R,13R,15R)-2-(acetyloxy)-13-(furan-3-yl)-9-(2-methoxy-2-oxoethyl)-4,6,8,10,12-pentamethyl-7-oxo-16-oxatetracyclo[8.6.0.0^{3},^{8}.0^{11},^{15}]hexadeca-5,11-diene-4-carboxylate), number of heavy atoms are 40; molar refractivity was 143.61, Log S (SILICOS-IT) was poorly soluble, highly lipophilic as consensus Log Po/w was 3.55, skin permeability was -7.79 cm/s, synthetic accessibility was 6.54 which was presented in table 94.

The nimbin derivative 63 (SAR 4 with IUPAC name: methyl (1S,2R,3R,4R,8R,9S,10R,13R,15R)-2-(acetyloxy)-13-(furan-3-yl)-9-(2-methoxy-2-oxoethyl)-4,8,10,12-tetramethyl-7-oxo-16-oxatetracyclo[8.6.0.0^{3},^{8}.0^{11},^{15}]hexadeca-5,11-diene-4-carboxylate), was which exactly as parent compound in all parameters which was presented in table 95.

The nimbin derivative 107 (SAR 5 with IUPAC name: methyl (1S,2R,3R,4R,8R,9S,10R,13R,15R)-2-(acetyloxy)-13-(furan-3-yl)-9-(2-methoxy-2-oxoethyl)-4,8,10,12,14-pentamethyl-7-oxo-16-oxatetracyclo[8.6.0.0^{3},^{8}.0^{11},^{15}]hexadeca-5,11-diene-4-carboxylate), the number of heavy atoms are 40, no of rotatable bonds are 9, molar refractivity was 143.61, Lipophilic with consensus Log $P_{o/w}$ was 3.44, P-gp substrate, acute rat toxicity was 2.8455 mol/kg, fish toxicity was -1.0643 mg/L, TPT was 1.0663 mcg/L which was presented in table 96.

The nimonol derivatives selected are derivative 1, 17, 60, 96, and 136 which are named as structure-activity relative (SAR) molecules.

The nimonol derivative 1 (SAR 1 with IUPAC name: (1R,3bR,4S,5R,5aR,9aR,9bR,11aS)-5-hydroxy-3b,6,6,9a,11a-pentamethyl-1-(5-methylfuran-3-yl)-7-oxo-1H,2H,3bH,4H,5H,5aH,6H,7H,9aH,9bH,10H,11H,11aH-cyclopenta[a]phenanthren-4-yl acetate), the number of heavy atoms are 34, molar refractivity was 131.40, Ghose filter shows 2 violations, Muegge observed as 1 violation, Lipophilic with consensus Log $P_{o/w}$ 4.57, skin permeability was -5.50 cm/s which was presented in table 97.

The nimonol derivative 17 (SAR 4 with IUPAC name: (1R,3bR,4S,5R,5aR,9aR,9bR,11aS)-5-hydroxy-3b,6,6,9a,11a-pentamethyl-

7-oxo-1-(1H-pyrrol-3-yl)-
1H,2H,3bH,4H,5H,5aH,6H,7H,9aH,9bH,10H,11H,11aH-cyclopenta[a]phenanthren-4-yl acetate), number of hydrogen bond acceptors are 4, number of hydrogen bond donors are 2, molar refractivity was 128.52, TPSA was 79.39 °A^2, Lipophilicity with consensus Log $P_{o/w}$ 4.02, Inhibits CYP3A4, skin permeability was -5.88 cm/s which was presented in table 98.

The nimonol derivative 60 (SAR 6 with IUPAC name: (1R,3bR,4S,5R,5aR,9aR,9bR,11aS)-1-(furan-3-yl)-5-hydroxy-3,3b,6,6,9a,11a-hexamethyl-7-oxo-1H,2H,3bH,4H,5H,5aH,6H,7H,9aH,9bH,10H,11H,11aH-cyclopenta[a]phenanthren-4-yl acetate), number of heavy atoms are 34, molar refractivity was 131.24, Log S (SILICOS-IT) was poorly soluble, Ghose was 2 violations, Lipophilic with consensus Log $P_{o/w}$ 4.46, Inhibits CYP3A4, skin permeability was -5.84 cm/s which was presented in table 99.

The nimonol derivative 96 (SAR 7 with IUPAC name: (1R,3bR,4S,5R,5aS,9aR,9bR,11aS)-1-(furan-3-yl)-5-hydroxy-3b,6,6,9a,11a-pentamethyl-1H,2H,3bH,4H,5H,5aH,6H,7H,9aH,9bH,10H,11H,11aH-cyclopenta[a]phenanthren-4-yl acetate), number of heavy atoms are 32, no of H-bond acceptors are 4, molar refractivity was 127.49, TPSA was 59.67 °A^2, Log S (ESOL) and Log S(Ali) are poorly soluble, Lipinski and Muegge shows 1 violation, Lipophilic with consensus Log $P_{o/w}$ 4.79, skin permeability was -4.82 cm/s, acute rat toxicity was 3.1127 mol/kg, fish toxicity was -0.3565 mg/L, TPT was 1.4869 mcg/L which was presented in table 100.

The nimonol derivative 136 (SAR 10 with IUPAC name: (1R,3bR,4S,5R,5aR,9aS,9bR,11aS)-1-(furan-3-yl)-5-hydroxy-3b,6,6,9a,9b,11a-hexamethyl-7-oxo-1H,2H,3bH,4H,5H,5aH,6H,7H,9aH,9bH,10H,11H,11aH-cyclopenta[a]phenanthren-4-yl acetate), number of heavy atoms are 34, molar refractivity was 130.98, Log S(Ali) and Log S (SILICOS-IT) are poorly soluble, Lipophilic with consensus Log $P_{o/w}$ 4.49, Ghose observed as 2 violations, Muegge shows 1 violation, skin permeability was -5.50 cm/s which was presented in table 101.

The Lawsone derivatives selected are derivative 1, 57, 71, 87, and 101 which are named as structure-activity relative (SAR) molecules.

The lawsone derivative 1 (SAR 1 with IUPAC name: 4-hydroxy-8-methyl-1,2-dihydronaphthalene-1,2-dione), the number of heavy atoms are 14, Fraction Csp3 was 0.09, molar refractivity was 51.35, Log S (ESOL) shows as soluble, Lipophilic with consensus as 1.29, Inhibits CYP1A2, skin permeability was -6.58 cm/s, AMES toxicity shows as toxic with 0.9107, acute rat toxicity was 2.9100 mol/kg, fish toxicity was -0.5112 mg/L, TPT was 1.3218 mcg/L which was presented in table 102.

The lawsone derivative 57 (SAR 2 with IUPAC name: 4-methoxy-1,2-dihydronaphthalene-1,2-dione), the number of heavy atoms are 14, Fraction Csp3 was 0.09, molar refractivity was 50.71, Log S (ESOL) shows as soluble, Lipophilic with consensus as 1.35, Inhibits CYP1A2, skin permeability was -6.76 cm/s, AMES toxicity shows as toxic with 0.9107, acute oral toxicity observed as category IV, acute rat toxicity was 2.3300 mol/kg, fish toxicity was -0.3902 mg/L, TPT was 1.3934 mcg/L which was presented in table 103.

The lawsone derivative 71 (SAR 3 with IUPAC name: 4-hydroxy-3-methyl-1,2-dihydronaphthalene-1,2-dione), the number of heavy atoms are 13, Fraction Csp3 was 0.09, molar refractivity was 51.19, Log S (ESOL) shows as soluble, obeys the Ghose filter, Lipophilic with consensus as 1.35, Inhibits CYP1A2 and CYP3A4, acute rat toxicity was 3.0215 mol/kg, fish toxicity was -0.7442 mg/L, TPT was 1.2824 mcg/L which was presented in table 104.

The lawsone derivative 87 (SAR 4 with IUPAC name: 4-hydroxy-2-imino-1,2-dihydronaphthalen-1-one), Num. H-bond donors are 2, molar refractivity was 49.78, TPSA was 61.15 $^{o}A^{2}$, Lipophilic with consensus as 1.16, Inhibits CYP3A4, synthetic accessibility observed as 6.16, HERG shows a weak inhibitor with 0.9187, HERG Inhibition shows as non-inhibitor with 0.8117, AMES Toxicity shows as toxicity with 0.6432, Carcinogens shows as non-carcinogen with 0.9344, acute oral toxicity shows category III with 0.5931, acute rat toxicity was 2.3414 mol/kg, fish toxicity was 0.7258 mg/L, TPT was 1.1964 mcg/L which was presented in table 105.

The lawsone derivative 101 (SAR 5 with IUPAC name: 4-hydroxy-1-imino-1,2-dihydronaphthalen-2-one), Num. H-bond donors are 2, molar refractivity was 49.55, TPSA was 61.15 $^{o}A^{2}$, obeys Ghose filter and Muegge filter, Lipophilic with consensus as 1.10, Inhibits CYP3A4, skin permeability was -6.69 cm/s, HERG shows a weak inhibitor with 0.9337, HERG Inhibition shows as non-inhibitor with 0.9036, AMES Toxicity shows as toxicity with 0.6464, Carcinogens shows as non-carcinogen with 0.8007, acute oral toxicity shows category III with 0.4742, Carcinogenicity (three class) shows 0.6159, acute rat toxicity was 2.5787 mol/kg, fish toxicity was 0.3500 mg/L, TPT was 1.5443 mcg/L which was presented in table 106.

The Lawsoniaside derivatives selected are derivative 1, 75, 124, 151, and 182 which are named as structure-activity relative (SAR) molecules.

The Lawsoniaside derivative 1 (SAR 1 with IUPAC name: (2S,3R,4S,5S,6R)-2-[(2-hydroxy-5-methyl-4-{[(2S,3R,4S,5S,6R)-3,4,5-trihydroxy-6-(hydroxymethyl)oxan-2-yl]oxy}naphthalen-1-yl)oxy]-6-(hydroxymethyl)oxane-3,4,5-triol), number of heavy atoms are 36, Fraction Csp3 was 0.57, molar refractivity was 119.23, hydrophilic with Log S (ESOL), Log S(Ali) and Log S (SILICOS-IT) are soluble, Lipophilicity with consensus as -1.52, skin permeability was -10.25 cm/s, HERG shows a weak inhibitor with 0.9181, HERG Inhibition shows as non-inhibitor with 0.6943, AMES Toxicity shows as toxicity with 0.6902, Carcinogens shows as non-carcinogen with 0.9573, acute oral toxicity shows category III with 0.5721, Carcinogenicity (three class) shows 0.6140, acute rat toxicity was 1.8761 mol/kg, fish toxicity was 1.3805 mg/L, TPT was 0.0716 mcg/L which was presented in table 107.

The Lawsoniaside derivative 75 (SAR 2 with IUPAC name: (2S,3R,4S,5S,6R)-4,5-dihydroxy-2-[(2-hydroxy-4-{[(2S,3R,4S,5S,6R)-3,4,5-trihydroxy-6-(hydroxymethyl)oxan-2-yl]oxy}naphthalen-1-yl)oxy]-6-(hydroxymethyl)oxan-3-yl hypofluorite), number of heavy atoms are 36, number of rotatable bonds is 7, number of H-bond acceptors are 14, number of H-bond donors are 8, molar refractivity was 114.24, TPSA was 207.99 $^{o}A^{2}$, hydrophilic with Log S (ESOL) was soluble, Lipophilicity with consensus as -1.19, skin permeability was -9.77 cm/s, HERG shows a weak inhibitor with 0.9365, HERG Inhibition shows as non-inhibitor with

0.6455, AMES Toxicity shows as toxicity with 0.5632, Carcinogens shows as non-carcinogen with 0.9277, acute oral toxicity shows category III with 0.4539, Carcinogenicity (three class) shows 0.5564, acute rat toxicity was 2.5256 mol/kg, fish toxicity was 1.0394 mg/L, TPT was 0.3185 mcg/L which was presented in table 108.

The Lawsoniaside derivative 124 (SAR 3 with IUPAC name: (2S,3R,4S,5S,6R)-2-[(3-hydroperoxy-4-{[(2S,3R,4S,5S,6R)-3,4,5-trihydroxy-6-(hydroxymethyl)oxan-2-yl]oxy}naphthalen-1-yl)oxy]-6-(hydroxymethyl)oxane-3,4,5-triol), number of heavy atoms are 36, Fraction Csp3 was 0.57, number of rotatable bonds are 7, number of H-bond acceptors are 14, molar refractivity was 115.50, TPSA was 228.22 $^{o}A^{2}$, Lipophilicity with consensus as -2.03, skin permeability was -10.64 cm/s, HERG shows as weak inhibitor with 0.8786, HERG Inhibition shows as non-inhibitor with 0.6283, AMES Toxicity shows as toxicity with 0.5764, Carcinogens shows as non-carcinogen with 0.9455, acute oral toxicity shows category III with 0.4532, Carcinogenicity (three class) shows 0.6085, acute rat toxicity was 2.1203 mol/kg, fish toxicity was 1.4080 mg/L, TPT was 0.1137 mcg/L which was presented in table 109.

The Lawsoniaside derivative 151 (SAR 4 with IUPAC name: (2R,3S,4S,5R,6S)-2-[(aminooxy)methyl]-6-[(3-hydroxy-4-{[(2S,3R,4S,5S,6R)-3,4,5-trihydroxy-6-(hydroxymethyl)oxan-2-yl]oxy}naphthalen-1-yl)oxy]oxane-3,4,5-triol), number of heavy atoms are 36, number of rotatable bonds are 7, number of H-bond acceptors are 14, molar refractivity was 116.89, TPSA was 234.01 $^{o}A^{2}$, Lipophilicity with consensus as -2.59, skin permeability was -11.05 cm/s, HERG shows a weak inhibitor with 0.8680, HERG Inhibition shows as non-inhibitor with 0.6076, AMES Toxicity shows as non-toxic with 0.5054, Carcinogens shows as non-carcinogen with 0.9043, acute oral toxicity shows category III with 0.5688, Carcinogenicity (three class) shows 0.5765, acute rat toxicity was 2.3788 mol/kg, fish toxicity was 1.5533 mg/L, TPT was 0.1668 mcg/L which was presented in table 110.

The Lawsoniaside derivative 182 (SAR 5 with IUPAC name: (2S,3R,4S,5S,6R)-4,5-dihydroxy-2-[(3-hydroxy-4-{[(2S,3R,4S,5S,6R)-3,4,5-trihydroxy-6-(hydroxymethyl)oxan-2-yl]oxy}naphthalen-1-yl)oxy]-6-(hydroxymethyl)oxan-3-yl hypofluorite), number of heavy atoms are 36, number of rotatable bonds is 7, number of H-bond acceptors are 14, number of H-bond donors are 8, molar refractivity was 114.24, TPSA was 207.99 $^{o}A^{2}$, hydrophilic with Log S (ESOL) was soluble, Lipophilicity with consensus as -1.25, skin permeability was -9.77 cm/s, HERG shows a weak inhibitor with 0.9365, HERG Inhibition shows as non-inhibitor with 0.6455, AMES Toxicity shows as toxicity with 0.5632, Carcinogens shows as non-carcinogen with 0.9277, acute oral toxicity shows category III with 0.4539, Carcinogenicity (three class) shows 0.5564, acute rat toxicity was 2.5256 mol/kg, fish toxicity was 1.0394 mg/L, TPT was 0.3185 mcg/L which was presented in table 111.

The Scopoletin derivatives selected are derivative 1, 44, 60, 114, and 127 which are named as structure-activity relative (SAR) molecules.

The Scopoletin derivative 1 (SAR 1 with IUPAC name: 6-ethoxy-7-hydroxy-2H-chromen-2-one), number of heavy atoms are 15, Fraction Csp3 was 0.18, number of rotatable bonds are 2, molar refractivity was 55.81, TPSA was 59.67 $^{o}A^{2}$, Hydrophilicity shows soluble for Log S (ESOL), Log S(Ali), and Log S (SILICOS-IT). Lipophilicity with consensus as 1.84, skin permeability was -6.22 cm/s, obeys Muegge filter,

HERG shows a weak inhibitor with 0.9674, HERG Inhibition shows as non-inhibitor with 0.8906, AMES Toxicity shows as Non-toxic with 0.5872, Carcinogens shows as non-carcinogen with 0.9245, acute oral toxicity shows category III with 0.5316, Carcinogenicity (three class) shows 0.6214, acute rat toxicity was 3.1340 mol/kg, fish toxicity was 0.4903 mg/L, TPT was 0.8978 mcg/L which was presented in table 112.

The Scopoletin derivative 44 (SAR 4 with IUPAC name: 4-amino-7-hydroxy-6-methoxy-2H-chromen-2-one), the number of heavy atoms are 15, number of H-bond donors are 2, molar refractivity was 55.4, TPSA was 85.69 $^{o}A^{2}$, Hydrophilicity shows very soluble for Log S (ESOL), and Log S(Ali), Lipophilicity with consensus as 0.91, inhibits CYP3A4,skin permeability was -7.17 cm/s, HERG shows a weak inhibitor with 0.9767, HERG Inhibition shows as non-inhibitor with 0.8803, AMES Toxicity shows toxic with 0.6538, Carcinogens shows as non-carcinogen with 0.9326, acute oral toxicity shows category III with 0.6283, Carcinogenicity (three class) shows 0.4534, acute rat toxicity was 2.1476 mol/kg, fish toxicity was 0.7708 mg/L, TPT was 0.9854 mcg/L which was presented in table 113.

The Scopoletin derivative 60 (SAR 5 with IUPAC name: 7-hydroxy-6-methoxy-3-sulfanyl-2H-chromen-2-one), number of heavy atoms are 15, molar refractivity was 58.25, TPSA was 98.47 $^{o}A^{2}$, Lipophilicity with consensus as 1.80, inhibits CYP1A2,skin permeability was -6.33 cm/s, Brenk filter shows 2 violations, HERG shows as weak inhibitor with 0.9910, HERG Inhibition shows as non-inhibitor with 0.8905, AMES Toxicity shows non-toxic with 0.5586, Carcinogens shows as non-carcinogen with 0.9299, acute oral toxicity shows category III with 0.7084, Carcinogenicity (three class) shows 0.5678, acute rat toxicity was 2.6208 mol/kg, fish toxicity was 0.7678 mg/L, TPT was 1.1931 mcg/L which was presented in table 114.

The Scopoletin derivative 114 (SAR 8 with IUPAC name: 7-(aminooxy)-6-methoxy-2H-chromen-2-one), number of heavy atoms are 15, number of rotatable bonds are 2, number of H-bond acceptors are 2, molar refractivity was 53.37, TPSA was 74.69 $^{o}A^{2}$, Lipophilicity with consensus as 1.20, skin permeability was -6.78 cm/s, Brenk filter shows 2 violations, HERG shows as weak inhibitor with 0.9264, HERG Inhibition shows as non-inhibitor with 0.8919, AMES Toxicity shows toxic with 0.5193, Carcinogens shows as non-carcinogen with 0.8855, acute oral toxicity shows category III with 0.6395, Carcinogenicity (three class) observed as Danger with 0.4893, acute rat toxicity was 2.3904 mol/kg, fish toxicity was 0.6495 mg/L, TPT was 0.3024 mcg/L which was presented in table 115.

The Scopoletin derivative 127 (SAR 10 with IUPAC name: 6-ethoxy-7-hydroxy-2H-chromen-2-one), number of heavy atoms are 15, Fraction Csp3 was 0.18, number of rotatable bonds are 2, molar refractivity was 55.81, TPSA was 59.67 $^{o}A^{2}$, Lipophilicity with consensus as 1.84, skin permeability was -6.22 cm/s, HERG shows as weak inhibitor with 0.9674, HERG Inhibition shows as non-inhibitor with 0.8906, AMES Toxicity shows non-toxic with 0.5872, Carcinogens shows as non-carcinogen with 0.9245, acute oral toxicity shows category III with 0.5316, Carcinogenicity (three class) observed as 0.6214, acute rat toxicity was 3.1340 mol/kg, fish toxicity was 0.4903 mg/L, TPT was 0.8978 mcg/L which was presented in table 116.

The Stigmasterol derivatives selected are derivative 16, 44, 89, 145, and 181 which are named as structure-activity relative (SAR) molecules.

The Stigmasterol derivative 16 (SAR 1 with IUPAC name: (1R,3aS,3bS,7S,9aR,9bS,11aR)-1-[(3E)-7-amino-5-ethyl-6-methylhept-3-en-2-yl]-9a,11a-dimethyl-1H,2H,3H,3aH,3bH,4H,6H,7H,8H,9H,9aH,9bH,10H,11H,11aH-cyclopenta[a]phenanthren-7-ol), number of heavy atoms are 31, number of rotatable bonds are 6, number of H-bond acceptors are 2, number of H-bond donors are 2, molar refractivity was 135.46, TPSA was 46.25 $^{o}A^{2}$, Lipophilicity with consensus as 6.06, Muegge filter shows 1 violation, skin permeability was -3.88 cm/s, HERG shows as weak inhibitor with 0.7489, HERG Inhibition shows as inhibitor with 0.5820, AMES Toxicity shows non-toxic with 0.8637, Carcinogens shows as non-carcinogen with 0.8839, acute oral toxicity shows category III with 0.6725, Carcinogenicity (three class) observed as 0.5295, acute rat toxicity was 2.3923 mol/kg, fish toxicity was 0.7669 mg/L, TPT was 0.7685 mcg/L which was presented in table 117.

The Stigmasterol derivative 44 (SAR 2 with IUPAC name: (1R,3aS,3bS,7S,9aR,9bS,11aR)-1-[(3E)-6-amino-5-ethyl-6-methylhept-3-en-2-yl]-9a,11a-dimethyl-1H,2H,3H,3aH,3bH,4H,6H,7H,8H,9H,9aH,9bH,10H,11H,11aH-cyclopenta[a]phenanthren-7-ol), number of heavy atoms are 31, number of H-bond acceptors are 2, number of H-bond donors are 2, molar refractivity was 135.50, TPSA was 46.25 $^{o}A^{2}$, Lipophilicity with consensus as 5.99, inhibits CYP2C9, Muegge filter shows 1 violation, skin permeability was -4.14 cm/s, HERG shows as weak inhibitor with 0.9095, HERG Inhibition shows as inhibitor with 0.6703, AMES Toxicity shows non-toxic with

0.8623, Carcinogens shows as non-carcinogen with 0.9187, acute oral toxicity shows category III with 0.4811, Carcinogenicity (three class) observed as 0.5198, acute rat toxicity was 2.9151 mol/kg, fish toxicity was 0.4480 mg/L, TPT was 0.8798 mcg/L which was presented in table 118.

The Stigmasterol derivative 89 (SAR 3 with IUPAC name: (1R,3aS,3bS,7S,9aR,9bS,11aR)-9a,11a-dimethyl-1-[(3E)-5-(propan-2-yl)oct-3-en-2-yl]-1H,2H,3H,3aH,3bH,4H,6H,7H,8H,9H,9aH,9bH,10H,11H,11aH-cyclopenta[a]phenanthren-7-ol), number of heavy atoms are 31, Fraction Csp3 was 0.87, number of rotatable bonds are 6, molar refractivity was 137.56, TPSA was 20.23 $^{o}A^{2}$, Lipophilicity with consensus as 7.31, not inhibits any CYP 450 enzymes, skin permeability was -2.44 cm/s, HERG shows as weak inhibitor with 0.8027, HERG Inhibition shows as inhibitor with 0.7104, AMES Toxicity shows non-toxic with 0.9132, Carcinogens shows as non-carcinogen with 0.9182, acute oral toxicity shows category I with 0.4287, Carcinogenicity (three class) observed as 0.5888, acute rat toxicity was 2.6561 mol/kg, fish toxicity was -0.2094 mg/L, TPT was 1.2496 mcg/L which was presented in table 119.

The Stigmasterol derivative 145 (SAR 4 with IUPAC name: (1R,3aS,3bS,7S,9aR,9bS,11aR)-4-amino-1-[(3E)-5-ethyl-6-methylhept-3-en-2-yl]-9a,11a-dimethyl-1H,2H,3H,3aH,3bH,4H,6H,7H,8H,9H,9aH,9bH,10H,11H,11aH-cyclopenta[a]phenanthren-7-ol), number of heavy atoms are 31, number of H-bond acceptors are 2, number of H-bond donors are 2, molar refractivity was 135.46, TPSA was 46.25 $^{o}A^{2}$, Lipophilicity with consensus as 6.02, not inhibits any CYP 450 enzymes, skin permeability was -3.80 cm/s, HERG shows as weak inhibitor with 0.9023, HERG Inhibition shows as inhibitor with 0.6819, AMES Toxicity shows non-toxic with 0.8533, Carcinogens shows as non-carcinogen with 0.9122, acute oral toxicity shows category III with 0.4146, Carcinogenicity (three class) observed as 0.5180, acute rat toxicity was 2.8110 mol/kg, fish toxicity was 0.4944 mg/L, TPT was 0.8489 mcg/L which was presented in table 120.

The Stigmasterol derivative 181 (SAR 5 with IUPAC name: (1R,3aS,3bS,7S,9aR,9bS,11aS)-1-[(3E)-1-amino-5-ethyl-6-methylhept-3-en-2-yl]-9a,11a-dimethyl-1H,2H,3H,3aH,3bH,4H,6H,7H,8H,9H,9aH,9bH,10H,11H,11aH-cyclopenta[a]phenanthren-7-ol), number of heavy atoms are 31, number of rotatable bonds are 6, number of H-bond acceptors are 2, number of H-bond donors are 2, molar refractivity was 135.46, TPSA was 46.25 $^{o}A^{2}$, Lipophilicity with consensus as 6.06, Muegge filter shows 1 violation, not inhibits any CYP 450 enzymes, skin permeability was -3.88 cm/s, HERG shows as weak inhibitor with 0.8122, HERG Inhibition shows as inhibitor with 0.5205, AMES Toxicity shows non-toxic with 0.8485, Carcinogens shows as non-carcinogen with 0.8856, acute oral toxicity shows category III with 0.6765, Carcinogenicity (three class) observed as 0.5623, acute rat toxicity was 2.5012 mol/kg, fish toxicity was 0.7579 mg/L, TPT was 0.8143 mcg/L which was presented in table 121.

Table 87: The canonical SMILE, IUPAC name, Physicochemical properties, Hydrophilicity, Lipophilicity, Pharmacokinetics, Druglikeliness, Medicinal Chemistry, and Toxicity profile showing the secondary metabolite of *A. indica*, Derivative, Azadirachtin Derivative 2

CANONICAL SMILES				
C/C=C(/C(=O)O[C@H]1C[C@@H](OC(=O)C)[C@@]2([C@H]3[C@@]41CO[C@]([C@H]4[C@@](C)([C@@H]([C@@H]3OC2)O)[C@@]12O[C@@]2(C)[C@H]2C[C@@H]1O[C@H]1[C@]2(O)C=C1)(O)C(=O)OC)C(=O)OC)\C				
IUPAC Name				
4,11-dimethyl (1S,4S,5R,6S,7S,8R,11S,12R,14S,15R)-12-(acetyloxy)-4,7-dihydroxy-6-[(1S,2S,6R,8S,9R,11S)-2-hydroxy-11-methyl-7,10-dioxatetracyclo[6.3.1.0^{2,6}.0^{9,11}]dodec-3-en-9-yl]-6-methyl-14-{[(2E)-2-methylbut-2-enoyl]oxy}-3,9-dioxatetracyclo[6.6.1.0^{1,5}.0^{11,15}]pentadecane-4,11-dicarboxylate				
Physicochemical Properties		**Lipophilicity**		
Formula	C36H46O15	Log $P_{o/w}$ (iLOGP)	4.44	
Molecular Weight	718.74 g/mol	Log $P_{o/w}$ (XLOGP3)	1.57	
Num. heavy atoms	51	Log $P_{o/w}$ (WLOGP)	0.26	
Num. arom. heavy atoms	0	Log $P_{o/w}$ (MLOGP)	0.04	
Fraction Csp3	0.78	Log $P_{o/w}$ (SILICOS-IT)	1.72	
Num. rotatable bonds	10	Consensus Log $P_{o/w}$	1.61	
Num. H-bond acceptors	15	**Pharmacokinetics**		
Num. H-bond donors	3	GI absorption	Low	
Molar Refractivity	169.64	BBB Permeability	No	
TPSA	206.11 $^{O}A^{2}$	P-gp Substrate	Yes	
Water Solubility		CYP 1A2 Inhibitor	No	
Log S (ESOL)	-4.63	CYP2C19 Inhibitor	No	
Solubility	1.70E-02 mg/ml; 2.37E-05 mol/l	CYP2C9 Inhibitor	No	
Class	Moderately soluble	CYP2D6 Inhibitor	No	
Log S(Ali)	-5.51	CYP3A4 Inhibitor	Yes	
Solubility	2.23E-03 mg/ml; 3.10E-06 mol/l	Log K_p (skin permeation)	-9.57 cm/s	
Class	Moderately soluble	**Medicinal chemistry**		
Log S (SILICOS-IT)	-1.94	Pains	0 alert	
Solubility	8.21E+00 mg/ml; 1.14E-02 mol/l	Brenk	4 alert	
Class	Soluble	Lead likeness	No; 2 violations	
Drug likeness		Synthetic accessibility	8.16	
Lipinski	No; 2 violations	**Toxicity**		
Ghose	No; 3 violations	HERG	Weak inhibitor	0.9919
Veber	No; 1 violations	HERG Inhibition	Non-inhibitor	0.5690
Egan	No; 1 violations	AMES Toxicity	Non AMES toxic	0.7563
Muegge	No; 4 violations	Carcinogens	Non-carcinogens	0.9455
Bioavailability score	0.17	Acute Oral Toxicity	I	0.6952
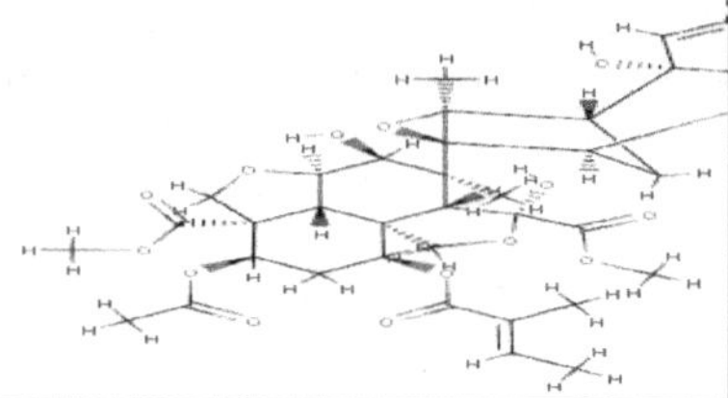		Carcinogenicity (three class)	Non-required	0.5886
		Acute rat toxicity	4.3477	LD50, mol/kg
		Fish Toxicity	0.5753	pLC50, mg/L
		TPT	0.6863	pIGC50, ug/L

Table 88: The canonical SMILE, IUPAC name, Physicochemical properties, Hydrophilicity, Lipophilicity, Pharmacokinetics, Druglikeliness, Medicinal Chemistry, and Toxicity profile showing the secondary metabolite of *A. indica*, Derivative, Azadirachtin Derivative 19.

CANONICAL SMILES				
C/C=C(/C(=O)O[C@H]1C[C@@H](OC(=O)C)[C@@]2([C@H]3[C@@]41CO[C@]([C@H]4[C@@](C)([C@@H]([C@@H]3OC2)O)[C@@]12O[C@@]2(C)[C@H]2C[C@@H]1N[C@H]1[C@]2(O)C=CO1)(O)C(=O)OC)C(=O)OC)\C				
IUPAC Name				
4,11-dimethyl (1S,4S,5R,6S,7S,8R,11S,12R,14S,15R)-12-(acetyloxy)-4,7-dihydroxy-6-[(1S,2S,6R,8S,9R,11S)-2-hydroxy-11-methyl-5,10-dioxa-7-azatetracyclo[6.3.1.0^{2},^{6}.0^{9},^{11}]dodec-3-en-9-yl]-6-methyl-14-{[(2E)-2-methylbut-2-enoyl]oxy}-3,9-dioxatetracyclo[6.6.1.0^{1},^{5}.0^{11},^{15}]pentadecane-4,11-dicarboxylate				
Physicochemical Properties		**Lipophilicity**		
Formula	C35H45NO15	Log $P_{o/w}$ (iLOGP)	3.24	
Molecular Weight	719.73 g/mol	Log $P_{o/w}$ (XLOGP3)	0.81	
Num. heavy atoms	51	Log $P_{o/w}$ (WLOGP)	-1.01	
Num. arom. heavy atoms	0	Log $P_{o/w}$ (MLOGP)	-0.47	
Fraction Csp3	0.77	Log $P_{o/w}$ (SILICOS-IT)	0.76	
Num. rotatable bonds	10	Consensus Log $P_{o/w}$	0.66	
Num. H-bond acceptors	16	**Pharmacokinetics**		
Num. H-bond donors	4	GI absorption	Low	
Molar Refractivity	171.55	BBB Permeability	No	
TPSA	218.14 $^{0}A^{2}$	P-gp Substrate	Yes	
Water Solubility		CYP 1A2 Inhibitor	No	
Log S (ESOL)	-4.15	CYP2C19 Inhibitor	No	
Solubility	5.06E-02 mg/ml; 7.04E-05 mol/l	CYP2C9 Inhibitor	No	
Class	Moderately soluble	CYP2D6 Inhibitor	No	
Log S(Ali)	-4.97	CYP3A4 Inhibitor	No	
Solubility	7.66E-03 mg/ml; 1.06E-05 mol/l	Log K_p (skin permeation)	-10.12 cm/s	
Class	Moderately soluble	**Medicinal chemistry**		
Log S (SILICOS-IT)	-1.71	Pains	0 alert	
Solubility	1.39E+01 mg/ml; 1.94E-02 mol/l	Brenk	3 alert	
Class	Soluble	Lead likeness	No; 2 violations	
Drug likeness		Synthetic accessibility	8.02	
Lipinski	No; 2 violations	**Toxicity**		
Ghose	No; 4 violations	HERG	Weak inhibitor	0.9972
Veber	No; 1 violations	HERG Inhibition	Non-inhibitor	0.6949
Egan	No; 1 violations	AMES Toxicity	Non AMES toxic	0.5171
Muegge	No; 4 violations	Carcinogens	Non-carcinogens	0.9455
Bioavailability score	0.17	Acute Oral Toxicity	III	0.4294
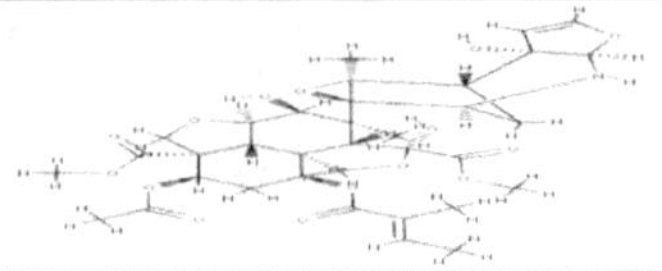		Carcinogenicity (three class)	Non-required	0.4818
		Acute rat toxicity	3.1422	LD50, mol/kg
		Fish Toxicity	1.0851	pLC50, mg/L
		TPT	0.4467	pIGC50, ug/L

Table 89: **The canonical SMILE, IUPAC name, Physicochemical properties, Hydrophilicity, Lipophilicity, Pharmacokinetics, Druglikeliness, Medicinal Chemistry, and Toxicity profile showing the secondary metabolite of *A. indica*, Derivative, Azadirachtin Derivative 56.**

CANONICAL SMILES				
CCO[C@@H]1C[C@H](OC(=O)/C(=C/C)/C)[C@]23[C@@H]4[C@@]1(CO[C@H]4[C@H]([C@@]([C@@H]3[C@@](OC2)(O)C(=O)OC)(C)[C@@]12O[C@@]2(C)[C@H]2C[C@@H]1O[C@H]1[C@]2(O)C=CO1)O)C(=O)OC				
IUPAC Name				
4,11-dimethyl (1S,4S,5R,6S,7S,8R,11S,12R,14S,15R)-12-ethoxy-4,7-dihydroxy-6-[(1S,2S,6S,8S,9R,11S)-2-hydroxy-11-methyl-5,7,10-trioxatetracyclo[$6.3.1.0^{2,6}.0^{9,11}$]dodec-3-en-9-yl]-6-methyl-14-{[(2E)-2-methylbut-2-enoyl]oxy}-3,9-dioxatetracyclo[$6.6.1.0^{1,5}.0^{11,15}$]pentadecane-4,11-dicarboxylate				
Physicochemical Properties		**Lipophilicity**		
Formula	C35H45O15	Log $P_{o/w}$ (iLOGP)	3.76	
Molecular Weight	705.72 g/mol	Log $P_{o/w}$ (XLOGP3)	1.42	
Num. heavy atoms	50	Log $P_{o/w}$ (WLOGP)	0.06	
Num. arom. heavy atoms	0	Log $P_{o/w}$ (MLOGP)	-0.55	
Fraction Csp3	0.77	Log $P_{o/w}$ (SILICOS-IT)	1.51	
Num. rotatable bonds	10	Consensus Log $P_{o/w}$	1.24	
Num. H-bond acceptors	15	**Pharmacokinetics**		
Num. H-bond donors	3	GI absorption	Low	
Molar Refractivity	166.98	BBB Permeability	No	
TPSA	198.27 ${}^{O}A^{2}$	P-gp Substrate	No	
Water Solubility		CYP 1A2 Inhibitor	No	
Log S (ESOL)	-4.45	CYP2C19 Inhibitor	No	
Solubility	2.50E-02 mg/ml; 3.55E-05 mol/l	CYP2C9 Inhibitor	No	
Class	Moderately soluble	CYP2D6 Inhibitor	No	
Log S(Ali)	-5.19	CYP3A4 Inhibitor	Yes	
Solubility	4.57E-03 mg/ml; 6.48E-06 mol/l	Log K_p (skin permeation)	-9.6 cm/s	
Class	Moderately soluble	**Medicinal chemistry**		
Log S (SILICOS-IT)	-1.88	Pains	0 alert	
Solubility	9.35E+00 mg/ml; 1.32E-02 mol/l	Brenk	3 alert	
Class	Soluble	Lead likeness	No; 2 violations	
Drug likeness		Synthetic accessibility	8.10	
Lipinski	No; 2 violations	**Toxicity**		
Ghose	No; 3 violations	HERG	Weak inhibitor	0.9887
Veber	No; 1 violations	HERG Inhibition	Non-inhibitor	0.5145
Egan	No; 1 violations	AMES Toxicity	Non AMES toxic	0.6849
Muegge	No; 4 violations	Carcinogens	Non-carcinogens	0.9393
Bioavailability score	0.17	Acute Oral Toxicity	I	0.6161
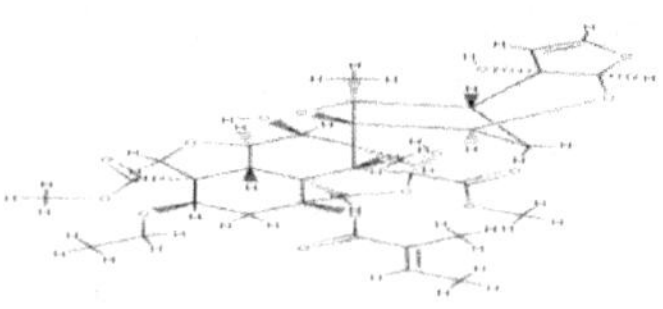		Carcinogenicity (three class)	Non-required	0.5993
		Acute rat toxicity	4.2870	LD50, mol/kg
		Fish Toxicity	0.6060	pLC50, mg/L
		TPT	0.7128	pIGC50, ug/L

Table 90: **The canonical SMILE, IUPAC name, Physicochemical properties, Hydrophilicity, Lipophilicity, Pharmacokinetics, Druglikeliness, Medicinal Chemistry, and Toxicity profile showing the secondary metabolite of *A. indica*, Derivative, Azadirachtin Derivative 58.**

CANONICAL SMILES				
C/C=C(/C(=O)O[C@H]1C[C@@H](OC(=N)C)[C@@]2([C@H]3[C@@]41CO[C@]([C@H]4[C@@](C)([C@@H]([C@@H]3OC2)O)[C@@]12O[C@@]2(C)[C@H]2C[C@@H]1O[C@H]1[C@]2(O)C=CO1)(O)C(=O)OC)C(=O)OC)\C				
IUPAC Name				
4,11-dimethyl (1S,4S,5R,6S,7S,8R,11S,12R,14S,15R)-12-(ethanimidoyloxy)-4,7-dihydroxy-6-[(1S,2S,6S,8S,9R,11S)-2-hydroxy-11-methyl-5,7,10-trioxatetracyclo[6.3.1.0²,⁶.0⁹,¹¹]dodec-3-en-9-yl]-6-methyl-14-{[(2E)-2-methylbut-2-enoyl]oxy}-3,9-dioxatetracyclo[6.6.1.0¹,⁵.0¹¹,¹⁵]pentadecane-4,11-dicarboxylate				
Physicochemical Properties		**Lipophilicity**		
Formula	C35H45NO15	Log $P_{o/w}$ (iLOGP)	3.99	
Molecular Weight	719.73 g/mol	Log $P_{o/w}$ (XLOGP3)	1.18	
Num. heavy atoms	51	Log $P_{o/w}$ (WLOGP)	0.25	
Num. arom. heavy atoms	0	Log $P_{o/w}$ (MLOGP)	-0.47	
Fraction Csp3	0.77	Log $P_{o/w}$ (SILICOS-IT)	1.20	
Num. rotatable bonds	10	Consensus Log $P_{o/w}$	1.23	
Num. H-bond acceptors	16	**Pharmacokinetics**		
Num. H-bond donors	4	GI absorption	Low	
Molar Refractivity	169.31	BBB Permeability	No	
TPSA	222.12 $^{O}A^{2}$	P-gp Substrate	Yes	
Water Solubility		CYP 1A2 Inhibitor	No	
Log S (ESOL)	-4.39	CYP2C19 Inhibitor	No	
Solubility	2.96E-02 mg/ml; 4.11E-05 mol/l	CYP2C9 Inhibitor	No	
Class	Moderately soluble	CYP2D6 Inhibitor	No	
Log S(Ali)	-5.44	CYP3A4 Inhibitor	Yes	
Solubility	2.61E-03 mg/ml; 3.63E-06 mol/l	Log K_p (skin permeation)	-9.85 cm/s	
Class	Moderately soluble	**Medicinal chemistry**		
Log S (SILICOS-IT)	-1.55	Pains	0 alert	
Solubility	2.04E+01 mg/ml; 2.84E-02 mol/l	Brenk	5 alert	
Class	Soluble	Lead likeness	No; 2 violations	
Drug likeness		Synthetic accessibility	8.20	
Lipinski	No; 2 violations	**Toxicity**		
Ghose	No; 3 violations	HERG	Weak inhibitor	0.9988
Veber	No; 1 violations	HERG Inhibition	Non-inhibitor	0.6722
Egan	No; 1 violations	AMES Toxicity	Non AMES toxic	0.6087
Muegge	No; 4 violations	Carcinogens	Non-carcinogens	0.9133
Bioavailability score	0.17	Acute Oral Toxicity	III	0.3976
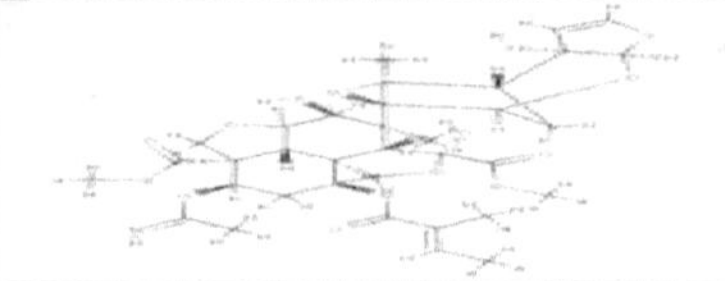		Carcinogenicity (three class)	Non-required	0.5669
		Acute rat toxicity	3.3092	LD50, mol/kg
		Fish Toxicity	0.8499	pLC50, mg/L
		TPT	0.5168	pIGC50, ug/L

Table 91: The canonical SMILE, IUPAC name, Physicochemical properties, Hydrophilicity, Lipophilicity, Pharmacokinetics, Druglikeliness, Medicinal Chemistry, and Toxicity profile showing the secondary metabolite of *A. indica*, Derivative, Azadirachtin Derivative 81.

CANONICAL SMILES				
BrC/C(=C\C)/C(=O)O[C@H]1C[C@@H](OC(=O)C)[C@@]2([C@H]3[C@@]41CO[C@]([C@H]4[C@@](C)([C@@H]([C@@H]3OC2)O)[C@@]12O[C@@]2(C)[C@H]2C[C@@H]1O[C@H]1[C@]2(O)C=CO1)(O)C(=O)OC)C(=O)OC				
IUPAC Name				
4,11-dimethyl (1S,4S,5R,6S,7S,8R,11S,12R,14S,15R)-12-(acetyloxy)-14-{[(2Z)-2-(bromomethyl)but-2-enoyl]oxy}-4,7-dihydroxy-6-[(1S,2S,6S,8S,9R,11S)-2-hydroxy-11-methyl-5,7,10-trioxatetracyclo[6.3.1.$0^{2,6}$.$0^{9,11}$]dodec-3-en-9-yl]-6-methyl-3,9-dioxatetracyclo[6.6.1.$0^{1,5}$.$0^{11,15}$]pentadecane-4,11-dicarboxylate				
Physicochemical Properties		**Lipophilicity**		
Formula	C35H43BrO16	Log $P_{o/w}$ (iLOGP)	4.55	
Molecular Weight	799.61 g/mol	Log $P_{o/w}$ (XLOGP3)	1.28	
Num. heavy atoms	52	Log $P_{o/w}$ (WLOGP)	0.17	
Num. arom. heavy atoms	0	Log $P_{o/w}$ (MLOGP)	-0.2	
Fraction Csp3	0.77	Log $P_{o/w}$ (SILICOS-IT)	1.64	
Num. rotatable bonds	11	Consensus Log $P_{o/w}$	1.49	
Num. H-bond acceptors	16	**Pharmacokinetics**		
Num. H-bond donors	3	GI absorption	Low	
Molar Refractivity	173.79	BBB Permeability	No	
TPSA	215.34 $^{O}A^{2}$	P-gp Substrate	Yes	
Water Solubility		CYP 1A2 Inhibitor	No	
Log S (ESOL)	-4.88	CYP2C19 Inhibitor	No	
Solubility	1.06E-02 mg/ml; 1.32E-05 mol/l	CYP2C9 Inhibitor	No	
Class	Moderately soluble	CYP2D6 Inhibitor	No	
Log S(Ali)	-5.40	CYP3A4 Inhibitor	No	
Solubility	3.17E-03 mg/ml; 3.97E-06 mol/l	Log K_p (skin permeation)	-10.27 cm/s	
Class	Moderately soluble	**Medicinal chemistry**		
Log S (SILICOS-IT)	-2.15	Pains	0 alert	
Solubility	5.71E+00 mg/ml; 7.14E-03 mol/l	Brenk	4 alert	
Class	Soluble	Lead likeness	No; 2 violations	
Drug likeness		Synthetic accessibility	8.24	
Lipinski	No; 2 violations	**Toxicity**		
Ghose	No; 3 violations	HERG	Weak inhibitor	0.9907
Veber	No; 2 violations	HERG Inhibition	Non-inhibitor	0.5451
Egan	No; 1 violations	AMES Toxicity	Non AMES toxic	0.6846
Muegge	No; 4 violations	Carcinogens	Non-carcinogens	0.9346
Bioavailability score	0.17	Acute Oral Toxicity	I	0.6098
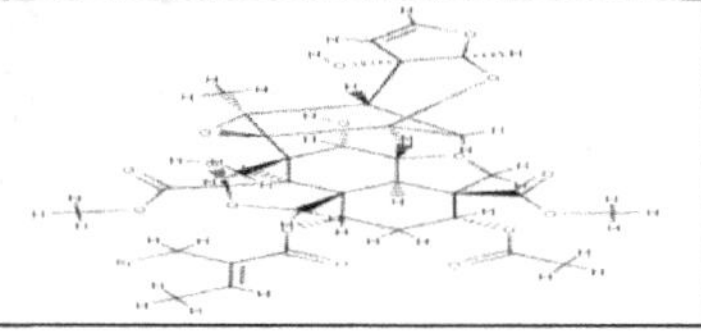		Carcinogenicity (three class)	Non-required	0.5266
		Acute rat toxicity	4.2446	LD50, mol/kg
		Fish Toxicity	0.4395	pLC50, mg/L
		TPT	0.9296	pIGC50, ug/L

Table92: **The canonical SMILE, IUPAC name, Physicochemical properties, Hydrophilicity, Lipophilicity, Pharmacokinetics, Druglikeliness, Medicinal Chemistry, and Toxicity profile showing the secondary metabolite of *A. indica*, Derivative, Nimbin Derivative 1.**

CANONICAL SMILESCCOC(=O)[C@]1(C)C=CC(=O)[C@]2([C@H]1[C@@H](OC(=O)C)[C@H]1O[C@H]3C(=C([C@@H](C3)c3ccoc3)C)[C@]1([C@@H]2CC(=O)OC)C)C				
IUPAC Name				
ethyl (1S,2R,3R,4R,8R,9S,10R,13R,15R)-2-(acetyloxy)-13-(furan-3-yl)-9-(2-methoxy-2-oxoethyl)-4,8,10,12-tetramethyl-7-oxo-16-oxatetracyclo[8.6.0.0^{3,8}.0^{11,15}]hexadeca-5,11-diene-4-carboxylate				
Physicochemical Properties		**Lipophilicity**		
Formula	C31H38O9	Log $P_{o/w}$ (iLOGP)	4.34	
Molecular Weight	554.63 g/mol	Log $P_{o/w}$ (XLOGP3)	2.65	
Num. heavy atoms	40	Log $P_{o/w}$ (WLOGP)	4.31	
Num. arom. heavy atoms	5	Log $P_{o/w}$ (MLOGP)	2.23	
Fraction Csp3	0.61	Log $P_{o/w}$ (SILICOS-IT)	4.37	
Num. rotatable bonds	9	Consensus Log $P_{o/w}$	3.58	
Num. H-bond acceptors	9	**Pharmacokinetics**		
Num. H-bond donors	0	GI absorption	High	
Molar Refractivity	143.61	BBB Permeability	No	
TPSA	118.34 $^{O}A^{2}$	P-gp Substrate	No	
Water Solubility		CYP 1A2 Inhibitor	No	
Log S (ESOL)	-4.45	CYP2C19 Inhibitor	No	
Solubility	1.98E-02 mg/ml; 3.58E-05 mol/l	CYP2C9 Inhibitor	No	
Class	Moderately soluble	CYP2D6 Inhibitor	No	
Log S(Ali)	-4.79	CYP3A4 Inhibitor	Yes	
Solubility	9.07E-03 mg/ml; 1.64E-05 mol/l	Log K_p (skin permeation)	-7.8 cm/s	
Class	Moderately soluble	**Medicinal chemistry**		
Log S (SILICOS-IT)	-5.83	Pains	0 alert	
Solubility	8.26E-04 mg/ml; 1.49E-06 mol/l	Brenk	2 alert	
Class	Moderately Soluble	Lead likeness	No; 2 violations	
Drug likeness		Synthetic accessibility	6.66	
Lipinski	No; 1 violations	**Toxicity**		
Ghose	No; 3 violations	HERG	Weak inhibitor	0.9843
Veber	Yes	HERG Inhibition	Non-inhibitor	0.7374
Egan	Yes	AMES Toxicity	Non AMES toxic	0.8570
Muegge	Yes	Carcinogens	Non-carcinogens	0.8960
Bioavailability score	0.55	Acute Oral Toxicity	III	0.7376
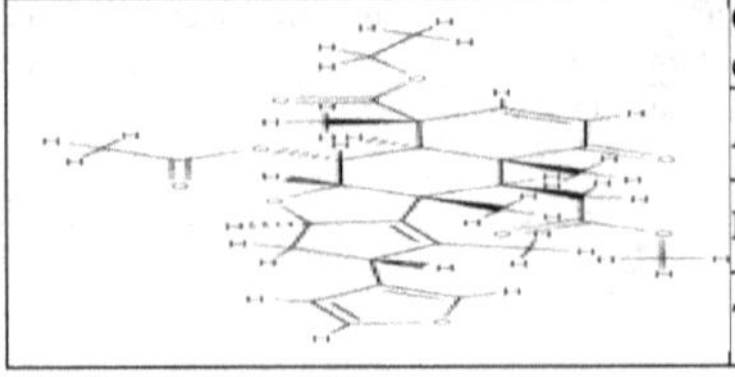		Carcinogenicity (three class)	Non-required	0.4317
		Acute rat toxicity	2.9188	LD50, mol/kg
		Fish Toxicity	-0.6150	pLC50, mg/L
		TPT	0.9078	pIGC50, ug/L

Table 93: The canonical SMILE, IUPAC name, Physicochemical properties, Hydrophilicity, Lipophilicity, Pharmacokinetics, Druglikeliness, Medicinal Chemistry, and Toxicity profile showing the secondary metabolite of *A. indica*, Derivative, Nimbin Derivative 41.

CANONICAL SMILES				
COC(=O)C[C@H]1[C@@]2(C)[C@H](O[C@H]3C2=C(C)[C@@H](C3)c2cocc2)[C@@H]([C@@H]2[C@]1(C)C(=O)C=C([C@@]2(C)C(=O)OC)C)OC(=O)C				
IUPAC Name				
methyl (1S,2R,3R,4S,8R,9S,10R,13R,15R)-2-(acetyloxy)-13-(furan-3-yl)-9-(2-methoxy-2-oxoethyl)-4,5,8,10,12-pentamethyl-7-oxo-16-oxatetracyclo[8.6.0.$0^{3,8}$.$0^{11,15}$]hexadeca-5,11-diene-4-carboxylate				
Physicochemical Properties		**Lipophilicity**		
Formula	C31H38O9	Log $P_{o/w}$ (iLOGP)	3.93	
Molecular Weight	554.63 g/mol	Log $P_{o/w}$ (XLOGP3)	2.20	
Num. heavy atoms	40	Log $P_{o/w}$ (WLOGP)	4.31	
Num. arom. heavy atoms	5	Log $P_{o/w}$ (MLOGP)	2.23	
Fraction Csp3	0.61	Log $P_{o/w}$ (SILICOS-IT)	4.48	
Num. rotatable bonds	8	Consensus Log $P_{o/w}$	3.43	
Num. H-bond acceptors	9	**Pharmacokinetics**		
Num. H-bond donors	0	GI absorption	High	
Molar Refractivity	143.61	BBB Permeability	No	
TPSA	118.34 $^{O}A^{2}$	P-gp Substrate	No	
Water Solubility		CYP 1A2 Inhibitor	No	
Log S (ESOL)	-4.23	CYP2C19 Inhibitor	No	
Solubility	3.27E-02 mg/ml; 5.90E-05 mol/l	CYP2C9 Inhibitor	No	
Class	Moderately soluble	CYP2D6 Inhibitor	No	
Log S(Ali)	-4.32	CYP3A4 Inhibitor	No	
Solubility	2.66E-03 mg/ml; 4.79E-05 mol/l	Log K_p (skin permeation)	-8.12 cm/s	
Class	Moderately soluble	**Medicinal chemistry**		
Log S (SILICOS-IT)	-6.03	Pains	0 alert	
Solubility	5.20E-04 mg/ml; 9.38E-07 mol/l	Brenk	2 alert	
Class	Poorly Soluble	Lead likeness	No; 2 violations	
Drug likeness		Synthetic accessibility	6.66	
Lipinski	No; 1 violations	**Toxicity**		
Ghose	No; 3 violations	HERG	Weak inhibitor	0.9755
Veber	Yes	HERG Inhibition	Non-inhibitor	0.8199
Egan	Yes	AMES Toxicity	Non AMES toxic	0.9132
Muegge	Yes	Carcinogens	Non-carcinogens	0.9131
Bioavailability score	0.55	Acute Oral Toxicity	III	0.7700
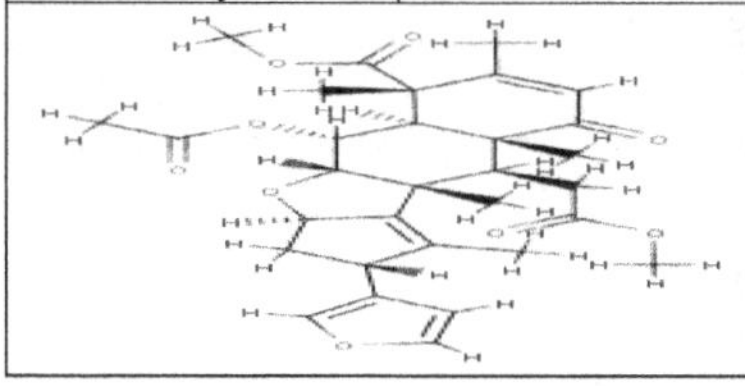		Carcinogenicity (three class)	Danger	0.5004
		Acute rat toxicity	2.9220	LD50, mol/kg
		Fish Toxicity	-0.7411	pLC50, mg/L
		TPT	1.0169	pIGC50, ug/L

Table 94: **The canonical SMILE, IUPAC name, Physicochemical properties, Hydrophilicity, Lipophilicity, Pharmacokinetics, Druglikeliness, Medicinal Chemistry, and Toxicity profile showing the secondary metabolite of *A. indica*, Derivative, Nimbin Derivative 50.**

CANONICAL SMILES				
COC(=O)C[C@H]1[C@@]2(C)[C@H](O[C@H]3C2=C(C)[C@@H](C3)c2cocc2)[C@@H]([C@@H]2[C@]1(C)C(=O)C(=C[C@@]2(C)C(=O)OC)C)OC(=O)C				
IUPAC Name				
methyl (1S,2R,3R,4R,8R,9S,10R,13R,15R)-2-(acetyloxy)-13-(furan-3-yl)-9-(2-methoxy-2-oxoethyl)-4,6,8,10,12-pentamethyl-7-oxo-16-oxatetracyclo[8.6.0.0^{3,8}.0^{11,15}]hexadeca-5,11-diene-4-carboxylate				
Physicochemical Properties		**Lipophilicity**		
Formula	C31H38O9	Log $P_{o/w}$ (iLOGP)	4.07	
Molecular Weight	554.63 g/mol	Log $P_{o/w}$ (XLOGP3)	2.66	
Num. heavy atoms	40	Log $P_{o/w}$ (WLOGP)	4.31	
Num. arom. heavy atoms	5	Log $P_{o/w}$ (MLOGP)	2.23	
Fraction Csp3	0.61	Log $P_{o/w}$ (SILICOS-IT)	4.48	
Num. rotatable bonds	8	Consensus Log $P_{o/w}$	3.55	
Num. H-bond acceptors	9	**Pharmacokinetics**		
Num. H-bond donors	0	GI absorption	High	
Molar Refractivity	143.61	BBB Permeability	No	
TPSA	$118.34\ ^{O}A^{2}$	P-gp Substrate	Yes	
Water Solubility		CYP 1A2 Inhibitor	No	
Log S (ESOL)	-4.52	CYP2C19 Inhibitor	No	
Solubility	1.68E-02 mg/ml; 3.03E-05 mol/l	CYP2C9 Inhibitor	No	
Class	Moderately soluble	CYP2D6 Inhibitor	No	
Log S(Ali)	-4.80	CYP3A4 Inhibitor	No	
Solubility	8.86E-03 mg/ml; 1.60E-05 mol/l	Log K_p (skin permeation)	-7.79 cm/s	
Class	Moderately soluble	**Medicinal chemistry**		
Log S (SILICOS-IT)	-6.03	Pains	0 alert	
Solubility	5.20E-04 mg/ml; 9.38E-07 mol/l	Brenk	2 alert	
Class	Poorly Soluble	Lead likeness	No; 2 violations	
Drug likeness		Synthetic accessibility	6.66	
Lipinski	No; 1 violations	**Toxicity**		
Ghose	No; 3 violations	HERG	Weak inhibitor	0.9755
Veber	Yes	HERG Inhibition	Non-inhibitor	0.8199
Egan	Yes	AMES Toxicity	Non AMES toxic	0.9132
Muegge	Yes	Carcinogens	Non-carcinogens	0.9131
Bioavailability score	0.55	Acute Oral Toxicity	III	0.7700
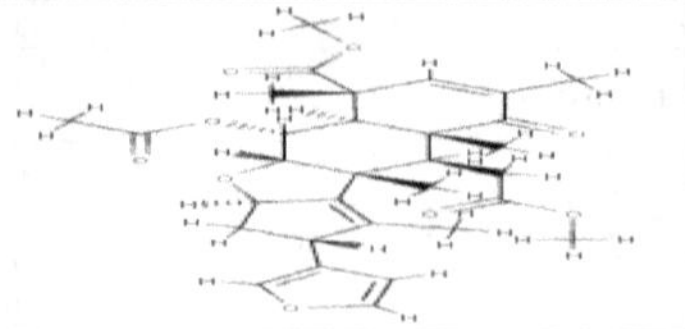		Carcinogenicity (three class)	Danger	0.5004
		Acute rat toxicity	2.9220	LD50, mol/kg
		Fish Toxicity	-0.7411	pLC50, mg/L
		TPT	1.0169	pIGC50, ug/L

Table 95: **The canonical SMILE, IUPAC name, Physicochemical properties, Hydrophilicity, Lipophilicity, Pharmacokinetics, Druglikeliness, Medicinal Chemistry, and Toxicity profile showing the secondary metabolite of *A. indica*, Derivative, Nimbin Derivative 63.**

CANONICAL SMILES				
COC(=O)C[C@H]1[C@@]2(C)[C@H](O[C@H]3C2=C(C)[C@@H](C3)c2cocc2)[C@@H]([C@@H]2[C@]1(C)C(=O)C=C[C@@]2(C)C(=O)OC)OC(=O)C				
IUPAC Name				
methyl (1S,2R,3R,4R,8R,9S,10R,13R,15R)-2-(acetyloxy)-13-(furan-3-yl)-9-(2-methoxy-2-oxoethyl)-4,8,10,12-tetramethyl-7-oxo-16-oxatetracyclo[8.6.0.0³,⁸.0¹¹,¹⁵]hexadeca-5,11-diene-4-carboxylate				
Physicochemical Properties		**Lipophilicity**		
Formula	C30H36O9	Log $P_{o/w}$ (iLOGP)	3.84	
Molecular Weight	540.6 g/mol	Log $P_{o/w}$ (XLOGP3)	2.28	
Num. heavy atoms	39	Log $P_{o/w}$ (WLOGP)	3.92	
Num. arom. heavy atoms	5	Log $P_{o/w}$ (MLOGP)	2.04	
Fraction Csp3	0.6	Log $P_{o/w}$ (SILICOS-IT)	3.96	
Num. rotatable bonds	8	Consensus Log $P_{o/w}$	3.21	
Num. H-bond acceptors	9	**Pharmacokinetics**		
Num. H-bond donors	0	GI absorption	High	
Molar Refractivity	138.81	BBB Permeability	No	
TPSA	118.34 $^{O}A^2$	P-gp Substrate	No	
Water Solubility		CYP 1A2 Inhibitor	No	
Log S (ESOL)	-4.20	CYP2C19 Inhibitor	No	
Solubility	3.45E-02 mg/ml; 6.38E-05 mol/l	CYP2C9 Inhibitor	No	
Class	Moderately soluble	CYP2D6 Inhibitor	No	
Log S(Ali)	-4.40	CYP3A4 Inhibitor	No	
Solubility	2.14E-03 mg/ml; 3.96E-05 mol/l	Log K_p (skin permeation)	-7.98 cm/s	
Class	Moderately soluble	**Medicinal chemistry**		
Log S (SILICOS-IT)	-5.44	Pains	0 alert	
Solubility	1.97E-04 mg/ml; 3.64E-06 mol/l	Brenk	2 alert	
Class	Moderately Soluble	Lead likeness	No; 2 violations	
Drug likeness		Synthetic accessibility	6.54	
Lipinski	No; 1 violations	**Toxicity**		
Ghose	No; 3 violations	HERG	Weak inhibitor	0.9755
Veber	Yes	HERG Inhibition	Non-inhibitor	0.8199
Egan	Yes	AMES Toxicity	Non AMES toxic	0.9132
Muegge	Yes	Carcinogens	Non-carcinogens	0.9131
Bioavailability score	0.55	Acute Oral Toxicity	III	0.7700
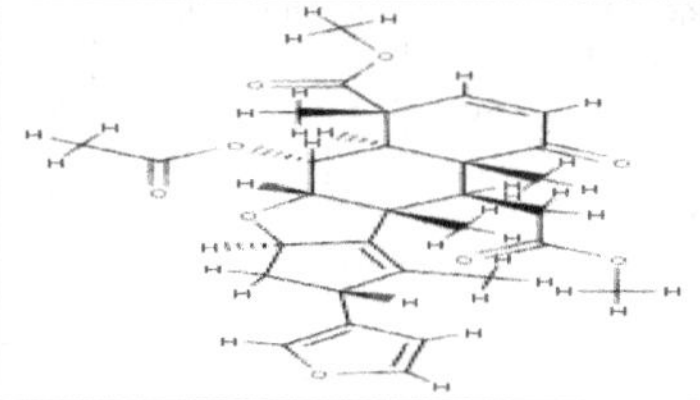		Carcinogenicity (three class)	Danger	0.5004
		Acute rat toxicity	2.9220	LD50, mol/kg
		Fish Toxicity	-0.7411	pLC50, mg/L
		TPT	1.0169	pIGC50, ug/L

Table 96: The canonical SMILE, IUPAC name, Physicochemical properties, Hydrophilicity, Lipophilicity, Pharmacokinetics, Druglikeliness, Medicinal Chemistry, and Toxicity profile showing the secondary metabolite of *A. indica*, Derivative, Nimbin Derivative 107.

CANONICAL SMILESCOC(=O)C[C@H]1[C@@]2(C)[C@H](O[C@H]3C2=C(C)[C@@H](C3C)c2cocc2)[C@@H]([C@@H]2[C@]1(C)C(=O)C=C[C@@]2(C)C(=O)OC)OC(=O)C				
IUPAC Name				
methyl (1S,2R,3R,4R,8R,9S,10R,13R,15R)-2-(acetyloxy)-13-(furan-3-yl)-9-(2-methoxy-2-oxoethyl)-4,8,10,12,14-pentamethyl-7-oxo-16-oxatetracyclo[8.6.0.0³,⁸.0¹¹,¹⁵]hexadeca-5,11-diene-4-carboxylate				
Physicochemical Properties		**Lipophilicity**		
Formula	C31H38O9	Log $P_{o/w}$ (iLOGP)	3.99	
Molecular Weight	554.63 g/mol	Log $P_{o/w}$ (XLOGP3)	2.72	
Num. heavy atoms	40	Log $P_{o/w}$ (WLOGP)	4.17	
Num. arom. heavy atoms	5	Log $P_{o/w}$ (MLOGP)	2.23	
Fraction Csp3	0.61	Log $P_{o/w}$ (SILICOS-IT)	4.09	
Num. rotatable bonds	9	Consensus Log $P_{o/w}$	3.44	
Num. H-bond acceptors	9	**Pharmacokinetics**		
Num. H-bond donors	0	GI absorption	High	
Molar Refractivity	143.61	BBB Permeability	No	
TPSA	118.34 $^{O}A^{2}$	P-gp Substrate	Yes	
Water Solubility		CYP 1A2 Inhibitor	No	
Log S (ESOL)	-4.56	CYP2C19 Inhibitor	No	
Solubility	1.54E-02 mg/ml; 2.77E-05 mol/l	CYP2C9 Inhibitor	No	
Class	Moderately soluble	CYP2D6 Inhibitor	No	
Log S(Ali)	-4.86	CYP3A4 Inhibitor	Yes	
Solubility	7.68E-03 mg/ml; 1.38E-05 mol/l	Log K_p (skin permeation)	-7.75 cm/s	
Class	Moderately soluble	**Medicinal chemistry**		
Log S (SILICOS-IT)	-5.58	Pains	0 alert	
Solubility	1.46E-03 mg/ml; 2.64E-06 mol/l	Brenk	2 alert	
Class	Moderately Soluble	Lead likeness	No; 2 violations	
Drug likeness		Synthetic accessibility	6.72	
Lipinski	No; 1 violations	**Toxicity**		
Ghose	No; 3 violations	HERG	Weak inhibitor	0.9743
Veber	Yes	HERG Inhibition	Non-inhibitor	0.8772
Egan	Yes	AMES Toxicity	Non AMES toxic	0.8698
Muegge	Yes	Carcinogens	Non-carcinogens	0.9124
Bioavailability score	0.55	Acute Oral Toxicity	III	0.7442
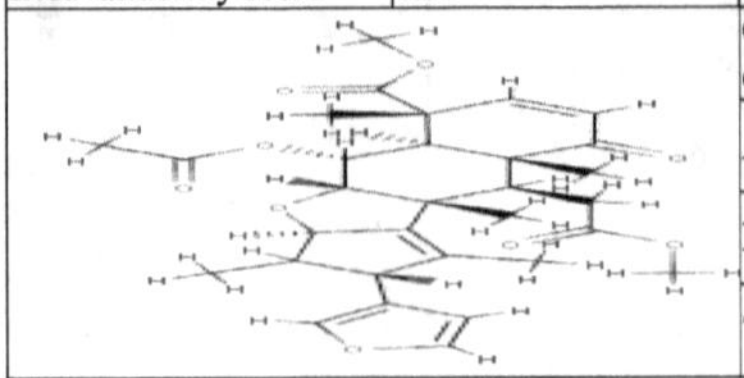		Carcinogenicity (three class)	Danger	0.5049
		Acute rat toxicity	2.8455	LD50, mol/kg
		Fish Toxicity	-1.0643	pLC50, mg/L
		TPT	1.0663	pIGC50, ug/L

Table 97: The canonical SMILE, IUPAC name, Physicochemical properties, Hydrophilicity, Lipophilicity, Pharmacokinetics, Druglikeliness, Medicinal Chemistry, and Toxicity profile showing the secondary metabolite of *A. indica*, Derivative, Nimonol Derivative 1.

CANONICAL SMILES				
CC(=O)O[C@@H]1[C@H](O)[C@@H]2[C@]([C@@H]3[C@]1(C)C1=CC[C@H]([C@@]1(CC3)C)c1coc(c1)C)(C)C=CC(=O)C2(C)C				
IUPAC Name				
(1R,3bR,4S,5R,5aR,9aR,9bR,11aS)-5-hydroxy-3b,6,6,9a,11a-pentamethyl-1-(5-methylfuran-3-yl)-7-oxo-1H,2H,3bH,4H,5H,5aH,6H,7H,9aH,9bH,10H,11H,11aH-cyclopenta[a]phenanthren-4-yl acetate				
Physicochemical Properties		**Lipophilicity**		
Formula	C29H38O5	Log $P_{o/w}$ (iLOGP)	3.70	
Molecular Weight	466.61 g/mol	Log $P_{o/w}$ (XLOGP3)	5.14	
Num. heavy atoms	34	Log $P_{o/w}$ (WLOGP)	5.52	
Num. arom. heavy atoms	5	Log $P_{o/w}$ (MLOGP)	3.55	
Fraction Csp3	0.66	Log $P_{o/w}$ (SILICOS-IT)	4.95	
Num. rotatable bonds	3	Consensus Log $P_{o/w}$	4.57	
Num. H-bond acceptors	5	**Pharmacokinetics**		
Num. H-bond donors	1	GI absorption	High	
Molar Refractivity	131.4	BBB Permeability	No	
TPSA	76.74 $^{O}A^{2}$	P-gp Substrate	Yes	
Water Solubility		CYP 1A2 Inhibitor	No	
Log S (ESOL)	-5.88	CYP2C19 Inhibitor	No	
Solubility	6.12E-04 mg/ml; 1.31E-06 mol/l	CYP2C9 Inhibitor	No	
Class	Moderately soluble	CYP2D6 Inhibitor	No	
Log S(Ali)	-6.5	CYP3A4 Inhibitor	No	
Solubility	1.49E-04 mg/ml; 3.19E-07 mol/l	Log K_p (skin permeation)	-5.5 cm/s	
Class	Poorly soluble	**Medicinal chemistry**		
Log S (SILICOS-IT)	-5.98	Pains	0 alert	
Solubility	4.85E-04 mg/ml; 1.04E-06 mol/l	Brenk	1 alert	
Class	Moderately Soluble	Lead likeness	No; 2 violations	
Drug likeness		Synthetic accessibility	6.15	
Lipinski	Yes	**Toxicity**		
Ghose	No; 2 violations	HERG	Weak inhibitor	0.9707
Veber	Yes	HERG Inhibition	Non-inhibitor	0.6719
Egan	Yes	AMES Toxicity	Non AMES toxic	0.9315
Muegge	No; 1 violations	Carcinogens	Non-carcinogens	0.9231
Bioavailability score	0.55	Acute Oral Toxicity	III	0.5415
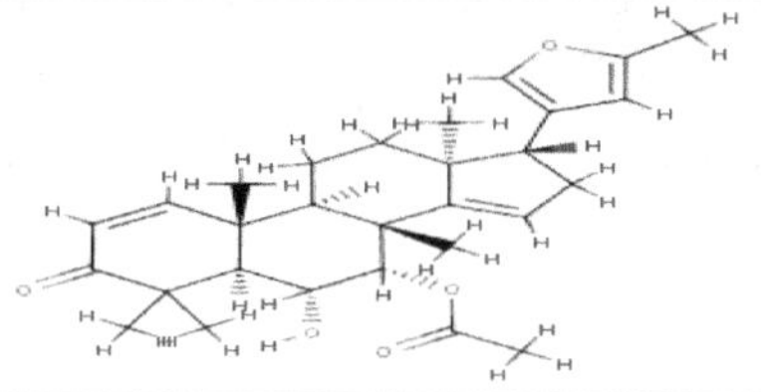		Carcinogenicity (three class)	Non-required	0.4755
		Acute rat toxicity	2.9784	LD50, mol/kg
		Fish Toxicity	-0.4640	pLC50, mg/L
		TPT	1.5116	pIGC50, ug/L

Table 98: **The canonical SMILE, IUPAC name, Physicochemical properties, Hydrophilicity, Lipophilicity, Pharmacokinetics, Druglikeliness, Medicinal Chemistry, and Toxicity profile showing the secondary metabolite of *A. indica*, Derivative, Nimonol Derivative 17.**

CANONICAL SMILES				
CC(=O)O[C@@H]1[C@H](O)[C@@H]2[C@]([C@@H]3[C@]1(C)C1=CC[C@H]([C@@]1(CC3)C)c1cc[nH]c1)(C)C=CC(=O)C2(C)C				
IUPAC Name				
(1R,3bR,4S,5R,5aR,9aR,9bR,11aS)-5-hydroxy-3b,6,6,9a,11a-pentamethyl-7-oxo-1-(1H-pyrrol-3-yl)-1H,2H,3bH,4H,5H,5aH,6H,7H,9aH,9bH,10H,11H,11aH-cyclopenta[a]phenanthren-4-yl acetate				
Physicochemical Properties		**Lipophilicity**		
Formula	C28H37NO4	Log $P_{o/w}$ (iLOGP)	2.76	
Molecular Weight	451.60 g/mol	Log $P_{o/w}$ (XLOGP3)	4.47	
Num. heavy atoms	33	Log $P_{o/w}$ (WLOGP)	4.94	
Num. arom. heavy atoms	5	Log $P_{o/w}$ (MLOGP)	3.36	
Fraction Csp3	0.64	Log $P_{o/w}$ (SILICOS-IT)	4.54	
Num. rotatable bonds	3	Consensus Log $P_{o/w}$	4.02	
Num. H-bond acceptors	4	**Pharmacokinetics**		
Num. H-bond donors	2	GI absorption	High	
Molar Refractivity	128.52	BBB Permeability	No	
TPSA	79.39 $^{O}A^{2}$	P-gp Substrate	Yes	
Water Solubility		CYP 1A2 Inhibitor	No	
Log S (ESOL)	-5.37	CYP2C19 Inhibitor	No	
Solubility	1.93E-03 mg/ml; 4.26E-05 mol/l	CYP2C9 Inhibitor	No	
Class	Moderately soluble	CYP2D6 Inhibitor	No	
Log S(Ali)	-5.86	CYP3A4 Inhibitor	Yes	
Solubility	6.28E-03 mg/ml; 1.39E-05 mol/l	Log K_p (skin permeation)	-5.88 cm/s	
Class	Moderately soluble	**Medicinal chemistry**		
Log S (SILICOS-IT)	-5.61	Pains	0 alert	
Solubility	1.12E-03 mg/ml; 2.47E-06 mol/l	Brenk	1 alert	
Class	Moderately Soluble	Lead likeness	2 violations	
Drug likeness		Synthetic accessibility	5.72	
Lipinski	Yes	**Toxicity**		
Ghose	Yes	HERG	Weak inhibitor	0.9757
Veber	Yes	HERG Inhibition	Non-inhibitor	0.6599
Egan	Yes	AMES Toxicity	Non AMES toxic	0.8227
Muegge	Yes	Carcinogens	Non-carcinogens	0.9372
Bioavailability score	0.55	Acute Oral Toxicity	III	0.5868
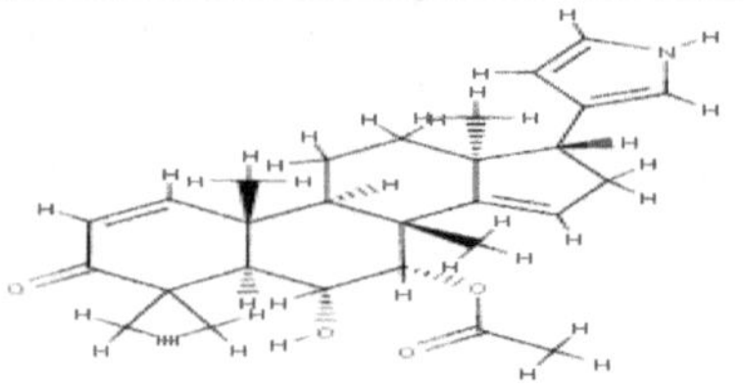		Carcinogenicity (three class)	Non-required	0.4969
		Acute rat toxicity	2.9545	LD50, mol/kg
		Fish Toxicity	0.1879	pLC50, mg/L
		TPT	1.2269	pIGC50, ug/L

Table 99: The canonical SMILE, IUPAC name, Physicochemical properties, Hydrophilicity, Lipophilicity, Pharmacokinetics, Druglikeliness, Medicinal Chemistry, and Toxicity profile showing the secondary metabolite of *A. indica*, Derivative, Nimonol Derivative 60.

CANONICAL SMILES				
CC(=O)O[C@@H]1[C@H](O)[C@@H]2[C@]([C@@H]3[C@]1(C)C1=C(C)C[C@H]([C@@]1(CC3)C)c1ccoc1)(C)C=CC(=O)C2(C)C				
IUPAC Name				
(1R,3bR,4S,5R,5aR,9aR,9bR,11aS)-1-(furan-3-yl)-5-hydroxy-3,3b,6,6,9a,11a-hexamethyl-7-oxo-1H,2H,3bH,4H,5H,5aH,6H,7H,9aH,9bH,10H,11H,11aH-cyclopenta[a]phenanthren-4-yl acetate				
Physicochemical Properties		**Lipophilicity**		
Formula	C29H38O5	Log $P_{o/w}$ (iLOGP)	3.55	
Molecular Weight	466.61 g/mol	Log $P_{o/w}$ (XLOGP3)	4.66	
Num. heavy atoms	34	Log $P_{o/w}$ (WLOGP)	5.6	
Num. arom. heavy atoms	5	Log $P_{o/w}$ (MLOGP)	3.55	
Fraction Csp3	0.66	Log $P_{o/w}$ (SILICOS-IT)	4.93	
Num. rotatable bonds	3	Consensus Log $P_{o/w}$	4.46	
Num. H-bond acceptors	5	**Pharmacokinetics**		
Num. H-bond donors	1	GI absorption	High	
Molar Refractivity	131.24	BBB Permeability	No	
TPSA	76.74 $^{O}A^{2}$	P-gp Substrate	Yes	
Water Solubility		CYP 1A2 Inhibitor	No	
Log S (ESOL)	-5.58	CYP2C19 Inhibitor	No	
Solubility	1.23E-03 mg/ml; 2.63E-06 mol/l	CYP2C9 Inhibitor	No	
Class	Moderately soluble	CYP2D6 Inhibitor	No	
Log S(Ali)	-6.00	CYP3A4 Inhibitor	Yes	
Solubility	4.68E-04 mg/ml; 1.00E-06 mol/l	Log K_p (skin permeation)	-5.84 cm/s	
Class	Moderately soluble	**Medicinal chemistry**		
Log S (SILICOS-IT)	-6.20	Pains	0 alert	
Solubility	2.93E-04 mg/ml; 6.28E-07 mol/l	Brenk	1 alert	
Class	Poorly Soluble	Lead likeness	No; 2 violations	
Drug likeness		Synthetic accessibility	6.16	
Lipinski	Yes	**Toxicity**		
Ghose	No; 2 violations	HERG	Weak inhibitor	0.9707
Veber	Yes	HERG Inhibition	Non-inhibitor	0.6719
Egan	Yes	AMES Toxicity	Non AMES toxic	0.9315
Muegge	Yes	Carcinogens	Non-carcinogens	0.9231
Bioavailability score	0.55	Acute Oral Toxicity	III	0.5415
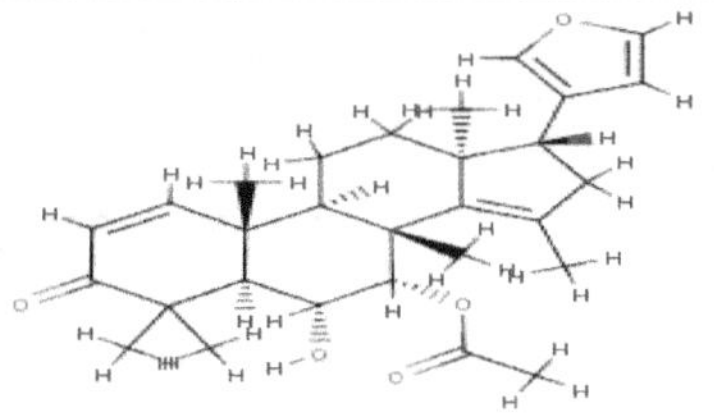		Carcinogenicity (three class)	Non-required	0.4755
		Acute rat toxicity	2.9784	LD50, mol/kg
		Fish Toxicity	-0.4640	pLC50, mg/L
		TPT	1.5116	pIGC50, ug/L

Table 100: **The canonical SMILE, IUPAC name, Physicochemical properties, Hydrophilicity, Lipophilicity, Pharmacokinetics, Druglikeliness, Medicinal Chemistry, and Toxicity profile showing the secondary metabolite of *A. indica*, Derivative, Nimonol Derivative 96.**

CANONICAL SMILES				
CC(=O)O[C@@H]1[C@H](O)[C@H]2C(C)(C)CC=C[C@@]2([C@@H]2[C@]1(C)C1=CC[C@H]([C@@]1(CC2)C)c1coccl)C				
IUPAC Name				
(1R,3bR,4S,5R,5aS,9aR,9bR,11aS)-1-(furan-3-yl)-5-hydroxy-3b,6,6,9a,11a-pentamethyl-1H,2H,3bH,4H,5H,5aH,6H,7H,9aH,9bH,10H,11H,11aH-cyclopenta[a]phenanthren-4-yl acetate				
Physicochemical Properties		**Lipophilicity**		
Formula	C28H37O4	Log $P_{o/w}$ (iLOGP)	3.73	
Molecular Weight	437.59 g/mol	Log $P_{o/w}$ (XLOGP3)	5.84	
Num. heavy atoms	32	Log $P_{o/w}$ (WLOGP)	5.47	
Num. arom. heavy atoms	5	Log $P_{o/w}$ (MLOGP)	4.19	
Fraction Csp3	0.64	Log $P_{o/w}$ (SILICOS-IT)	4.72	
Num. rotatable bonds	3	Consensus Log $P_{o/w}$	4.79	
Num. H-bond acceptors	4	**Pharmacokinetics**		
Num. H-bond donors	1	GI absorption	High	
Molar Refractivity	127.49	BBB Permeability	Yes	
TPSA	59.67 $^{O}A^{2}$	P-gp Substrate	No	
Water Solubility		CYP 1A2 Inhibitor	No	
Log S (ESOL)	-6.15	CYP2C19 Inhibitor	No	
Solubility	3.10E-04 mg/ml; 7.08E-07 mol/l	CYP2C9 Inhibitor	No	
Class	Poorly soluble	CYP2D6 Inhibitor	No	
Log S(Ali)	-6.86	CYP3A4 Inhibitor	No	
Solubility	5.98E-05 mg/ml; 1.37E-07 mol/l	Log K_p (skin permeation)	-4.82 cm/s	
Class	Poorly soluble	**Medicinal chemistry**		
Log S (SILICOS-IT)	-5.74	Pains	0 alert	
Solubility	8.06E-04 mg/ml; 1.84E-06 mol/l	Brenk	1 alert	
Class	Moderately Soluble	Lead likeness	No; 2 violations	
Drug likeness		Synthetic accessibility	6.03	
Lipinski	No; 1 violations	**Toxicity**		
Ghose	Yes	HERG	Weak inhibitor	0.9769
Veber	Yes	HERG Inhibition	Non-inhibitor	0.6516
Egan	Yes	AMES Toxicity	Non AMES toxic	0.9062
Muegge	No; 1 violations	Carcinogens	Non-carcinogens	0.9286
Bioavailability score	0.55	Acute Oral Toxicity	III	0.5504
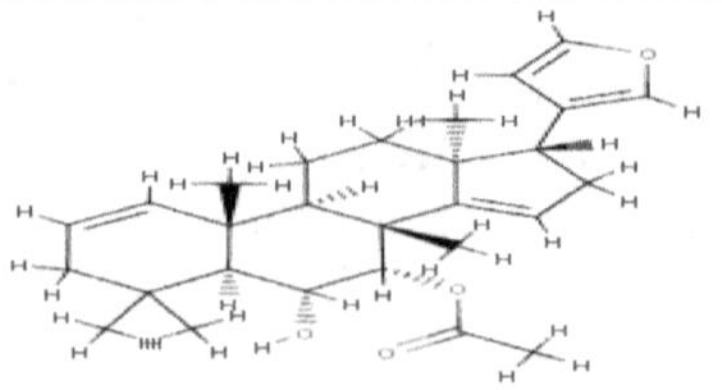		Carcinogenicity (three class)	Non-required	0.4810
		Acute rat toxicity	3.1127	LD50, mol/kg
		Fish Toxicity	-0.3565	pLC50, mg/L
		TPT	1.4869	pIGC50, ug/L

Table 101: The canonical SMILE, IUPAC name, Physicochemical properties, Hydrophilicity, Lipophilicity, Pharmacokinetics, Druglikeliness, Medicinal Chemistry, and Toxicity profile showing the secondary metabolite of *A. indica*, Derivative, Nimonol Derivative 136.

CANONICAL SMILES				
CC(=O)O[C@@H]1[C@H](O)[C@H]2C(C)(C)C(=O)C=C[C@@]2([C@@]2([C@]1(C)C1=CC[C@H]([C@]1(C)CC2)c1ccoc1)C)C				
IUPAC Name				
(1R,3bR,4S,5R,5aR,9aS,9bR,11aS)-1-(furan-3-yl)-5-hydroxy-3b,6,6,9a,9b,11a-hexamethyl-7-oxo-1H,2H,3bH,4H,5H,5aH,6H,7H,9aH,9bH,10H,11H,11aH-cyclopenta[a]phenanthren-4-yl acetate				
Physicochemical Properties		**Lipophilicity**		
Formula	C29H38O5	Log $P_{o/w}$ (iLOGP)	3.24	
Molecular Weight	466.61 g/mol	Log $P_{o/w}$ (XLOGP3)	5.14	
Num. heavy atoms	34	Log $P_{o/w}$ (WLOGP)	5.60	
Num. arom. heavy atoms	5	Log $P_{o/w}$ (MLOGP)	3.55	
Fraction Csp3	0.66	Log $P_{o/w}$ (SILICOS-IT)	4.93	
Num. rotatable bonds	3	Consensus Log $P_{o/w}$	4.49	
Num. H-bond acceptors	5	**Pharmacokinetics**		
Num. H-bond donors	1	GI absorption	High	
Molar Refractivity	130.98	BBB Permeability	No	
TPSA	76.74 $^{O}A^{2}$	P-gp Substrate	Yes	
Water Solubility		CYP 1A2 Inhibitor	No	
Log S (ESOL)	-5.88	CYP2C19 Inhibitor	No	
Solubility	6.12E-04 mg/ml; 1.31E-06 mol/l	CYP2C9 Inhibitor	No	
Class	Moderately soluble	CYP2D6 Inhibitor	No	
Log S(Ali)	-6.50	CYP3A4 Inhibitor	No	
Solubility	1.49E-04 mg/ml; 3.19E-07 mol/l	Log K_p (skin permeation)	-5.50 cm/s	
Class	Poorly soluble	**Medicinal chemistry**		
Log S (SILICOS-IT)	-6.2	Pains	0 alert	
Solubility	2.93E-04 mg/ml; 6.28E-07 mol/l	Brenk	1 alert	
Class	Poorly Soluble	Lead likeness	No; 2 violations	
Drug likeness		Synthetic accessibility	6.16	
Lipinski	Yes	**Toxicity**		
Ghose	No; 2 violations	HERG	Weak inhibitor	0.9707
Veber	Yes	HERG Inhibition	Non-inhibitor	0.6719
Egan	Yes	AMES Toxicity	Non AMES toxic	0.9315
Muegge	No; 1 violations	Carcinogens	Non-carcinogens	0.9231
Bioavailability score	0.55	Acute Oral Toxicity	III	0.5415
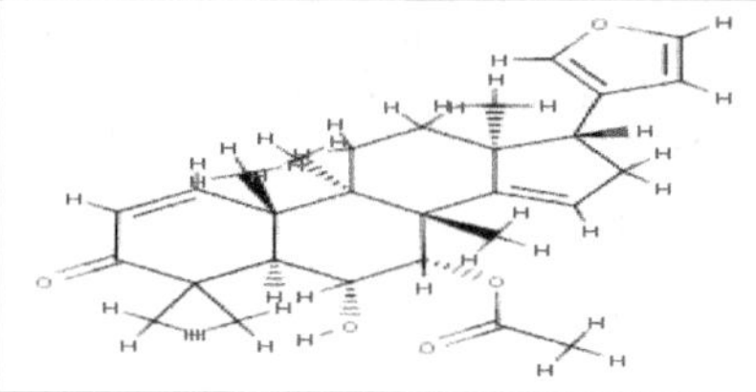		Carcinogenicity (three class)	Non-required	0.4755
		Acute rat toxicity	2.9784	LD50, mol/kg
		Fish Toxicity	-0.4640	pLC50, mg/L
		TPT	1.5116	pIGC50, ug/L

Table 102: The canonical SMILE, IUPAC name, Physicochemical properties, Hydrophilicity, Lipophilicity, Pharmacokinetics, Druglikeliness, Medicinal Chemistry, and Toxicity profile showing the secondary metabolite of *L. inermis*, Derivative, Lawsone Derivative 1.

CANONICAL SMILES: OC1=CC(=O)C(=O)c2c1cccc2C				
IUPAC Name: 4-hydroxy-8-methyl-1,2-dihydronaphthalene-1,2-dione				
Physicochemical Properties		**Lipophilicity**		
Formula	C11H8O3	Log $P_{o/w}$ (iLOGP)	1.04	
Molecular Weight	188.18 g/mol	Log $P_{o/w}$ (XLOGP3)	1.22	
Num. heavy atoms	14	Log $P_{o/w}$ (WLOGP)	1.66	
Num. arom. heavy atoms	6	Log $P_{o/w}$ (MLOGP)	0.32	
Fraction Csp3	0.09	Log $P_{o/w}$ (SILICOS-IT)	2.22	
Num. rotatable bonds	0	Consensus Log $P_{o/w}$	1.29	
Num. H-bond acceptors	3	**Pharmacokinetics**		
Num. H-bond donors	1	GI absorption	High	
Molar Refractivity	51.35	BBB Permeability	Yes	
TPSA	54.37 $^{O}A^2$	P-gp Substrate	No	
Water Solubility		CYP 1A2 Inhibitor	Yes	
Log S (ESOL)	-2.09	CYP2C19 Inhibitor	No	
Solubility	1.52E-00 mg/ml; 8.08E-03 mol/l	CYP2C9 Inhibitor	No	
Class	Soluble	CYP2D6 Inhibitor	No	
Log S(Ali)	-1.96	CYP3A4 Inhibitor	No	
Solubility	2.07E-00 mg/ml; 1.10E-02 mol/l	Log K_p (skin permeation)	-6.58 cm/s	
Class	Very soluble	**Medicinal chemistry**		
Log S (SILICOS-IT)	-2.85	Pains	2 alert	
Solubility	2.66E-01 mg/ml; 1.42E-03 mol/l	Brenk	1 alert	
Class	Soluble	Lead likeness	No; 1 violations	
Drug likeness		Synthetic accessibility	2.57	
Lipinski	Yes	**Toxicity**		
Ghose	Yes	HERG	Weak inhibitor	0.9475
Veber	Yes	HERG Inhibition	Non-inhibitor	0.9212
Egan	Yes	AMES Toxicity	AMES toxic	0.9030
Muegge	No; 1 violations	Carcinogens	Non-carcinogens	0.8973
Bioavailability score	0.56	Acute Oral Toxicity	II	0.5224
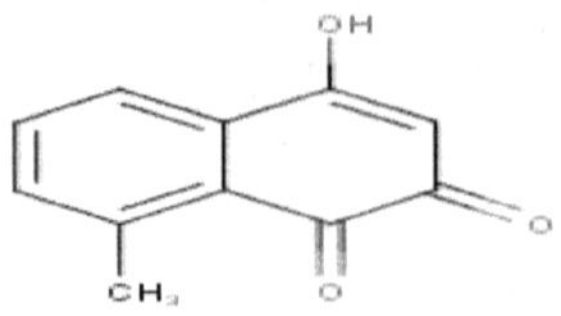		Carcinogenicity (three class)	Non-required	0.5063
		Acute rat toxicity	2.9100	LD50, mol/kg
		Fish Toxicity	-0.5112	pLC50, mg/L
		TPT	1.3218	pIGC50, ug/L

Table 103: The canonical SMILE, IUPAC name, Physicochemical properties, Hydrophilicity, Lipophilicity, Pharmacokinetics, Druglikeliness, Medicinal Chemistry, and Toxicity profile showing the secondary metabolite of *L. inermis*, Derivative, Lawsone Derivative 57.

CANONICAL SMILES: COC1=CC(=O)C(=O)c2c1cccc2				
IUPAC Name: 4-methoxy-1,2-dihydronaphthalene-1,2-dione				
Physicochemical Properties		**Lipophilicity**		
Formula	C11H8O3	Log $P_{o/w}$ (iLOGP)	1.56	
Molecular Weight	188.18 g/mol	Log $P_{o/w}$ (XLOGP3)	1.18	
Num. heavy atoms	14	Log $P_{o/w}$ (WLOGP)	1.44	
Num. arom. heavy atoms	6	Log $P_{o/w}$ (MLOGP)	0.32	
Fraction Csp3	0.09	Log $P_{o/w}$ (SILICOS-IT)	2.23	
Num. rotatable bonds	1	Consensus Log $P_{o/w}$	1.35	
Num. H-bond acceptors	3	**Pharmacokinetics**		
Num. H-bond donors	0	GI absorption	High	
Molar Refractivity	50.71	BBB Permeability	Yes	
TPSA	43.37 $^{O}A^{2}$	P-gp Substrate	No	
Water Solubility		CYP 1A2 Inhibitor	Yes	
Log S (ESOL)	-2.00	CYP2C19 Inhibitor	No	
Solubility	1.88E-00 mg/ml; 9.97E-03 mol/l	CYP2C9 Inhibitor	No	
Class	Soluble	CYP2D6 Inhibitor	No	
Log S(Ali)	-1.69	CYP3A4 Inhibitor	No	
Solubility	3.87E-00 mg/ml; 2.06E-02 mol/l	Log K_p (skin permeation)	-6.61 cm/s	
Class	Very soluble	**Medicinal chemistry**		
Log S (SILICOS-IT)	-3.16	Pains	2 alert	
Solubility	1.29E-01 mg/ml; 6.85E-04 mol/l	Brenk	1 alert	
Class	Soluble	Lead likeness	No; 1 violations	
Drug likeness		Synthetic accessibility	2.62	
Lipinski	Yes	**Toxicity**		
Ghose	Yes	HERG	Weak inhibitor	0.9406
Veber	Yes	HERG Inhibition	Non-inhibitor	0.9009
Egan	Yes	AMES Toxicity	AMES toxic	0.7340
Muegge	No; 1 violations	Carcinogens	Non-carcinogens	0.9126
Bioavailability score	0.56	Acute Oral Toxicity	IV	0.3570
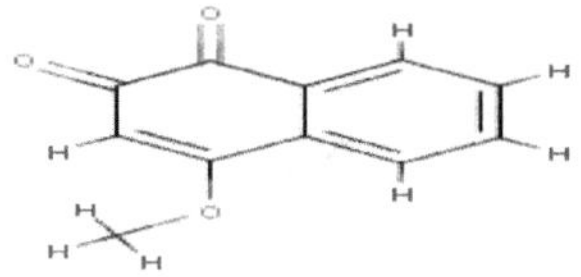		Carcinogenicity (three class)	Non-required	0.4748
		Acute rat toxicity	2.3300	LD50, mol/kg
		Fish Toxicity	-0.3902	pLC50, mg/L
		TPT	1.3934	pIGC50, ug/L

Table 104: **The canonical SMILE, IUPAC name, Physicochemical properties, Hydrophilicity, Lipophilicity, Pharmacokinetics, Druglikeliness, Medicinal Chemistry, and Toxicity profile showing the secondary metabolite of *L. inermis*, Derivative, Lawsone Derivative 71.**

CANONICAL SMILES: O=C1C(=O)C(=C(c2c1cccc2)O)C				
IUPAC Name: 4-hydroxy-3-methyl-1,2-dihydronaphthalene-1,2-dione				
Physicochemical Properties		**Lipophilicity**		
Formula	C11H8O3	Log $P_{o/w}$ (iLOGP)	1.29	
Molecular Weight	188.18 g/mol	Log $P_{o/w}$ (XLOGP3)	1.22	
Num. heavy atoms	14	Log $P_{o/w}$ (WLOGP)	1.74	
Num. arom. heavy atoms	6	Log $P_{o/w}$ (MLOGP)	0.32	
Fraction Csp3	0.09	Log $P_{o/w}$ (SILICOS-IT)	2.19	
Num. rotatable bonds	0	Consensus Log $P_{o/w}$	1.35	
Num. H-bond acceptors	3	**Pharmacokinetics**		
Num. H-bond donors	1	GI absorption	High	
Molar Refractivity	51.19	BBB Permeability	Yes	
TPSA	54.37 $^{O}A^{2}$	P-gp Substrate	No	
Water Solubility		CYP 1A2 Inhibitor	Yes	
Log S (ESOL)	-2.09	CYP2C19 Inhibitor	No	
Solubility	1.52E-00 mg/ml; 8.08E-03 mol/l	CYP2C9 Inhibitor	No	
Class	Soluble	CYP2D6 Inhibitor	No	
Log S(Ali)	-1.96	CYP3A4 Inhibitor	Yes	
Solubility	2.07E-00 mg/ml; 1.10E-02 mol/l	Log K_p (skin permeation)	-6.58 cm/s	
Class	Very soluble	**Medicinal chemistry**		
Log S (SILICOS-IT)	-3.07	Pains	2 alert	
Solubility	1.61E-01 mg/ml; 8.55E-04 mol/l	Brenk	1 alert	
Class	Soluble	Lead likeness	1 violations	
Drug likeness		Synthetic accessibility	2.54	
Lipinski	Yes	**Toxicity**		
Ghose	Yes	HERG	Weak inhibitor	0.9395
Veber	Yes	HERG Inhibition	Non-inhibitor	0.9082
Egan	Yes	AMES Toxicity	AMES toxic	0.8425
Muegge	No; 1 violations	Carcinogens	Non-carcinogens	0.9033
Bioavailability score	0.56	Acute Oral Toxicity	II	0.5017
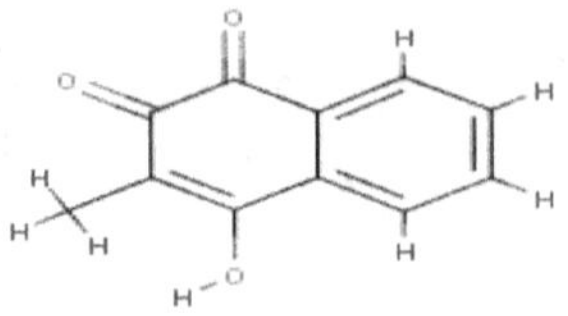		Carcinogenicity (three class)	Non-required	0.5232
		Acute rat toxicity	2.8967	LD50, mol/kg
		Fish Toxicity	-0.7442	pLC50, mg/L
		TPT	1.1149	pIGC50, ug/L

Table 105: The canonical SMILE, IUPAC name, Physicochemical properties, Hydrophilicity, Lipophilicity, Pharmacokinetics, Druglikeliness, Medicinal Chemistry, and Toxicity profile showing the secondary metabolite of *L. inermis*, Derivative, Lawsone Derivative 87.

CANONICAL SMILES: N=C1C=C(O)c2c(C1=O)cccc2				
IUPAC Name: 4-hydroxy-2-imino-1,2-dihydronaphthalen-1-one				
Physicochemical Properties		**Lipophilicity**		
Formula	C10H7NO2	Log $P_{o/w}$ (iLOGP)	1.16	
Molecular Weight	173.17 g/mol	Log $P_{o/w}$ (XLOGP3)	0.94	
Num. heavy atoms	13	Log $P_{o/w}$ (WLOGP)	1.80	
Num. arom. heavy atoms	6	Log $P_{o/w}$ (MLOGP)	0.03	
Fraction Csp3	0	Log $P_{o/w}$ (SILICOS-IT)	1.88	
Num. rotatable bonds	0	Consensus Log $P_{o/w}$	1.16	
Num. H-bond acceptors	3	**Pharmacokinetics**		
Num. H-bond donors	2	GI absorption	High	
Molar Refractivity	49.78	BBB Permeability	Yes	
TPSA	61.15 $^{O}A^{2}$	P-gp Substrate	No	
Water Solubility		CYP 1A2 Inhibitor	No	
Log S (ESOL)	-1.85	CYP2C19 Inhibitor	No	
Solubility	2.46E-00 mg/ml; 1.42E-02 mol/l	CYP2C9 Inhibitor	No	
Class	Very soluble	CYP2D6 Inhibitor	No	
Log S(Ali)	-1.81	CYP3A4 Inhibitor	Yes	
Solubility	2.68E-00 mg/ml; 1.55E-02 mol/l	Log K_p (skin permeation)	-6.69 cm/s	
Class	Very soluble	**Medicinal chemistry**		
Log S (SILICOS-IT)	-2.6	Pains	0 alert	
Solubility	4.35E-01 mg/ml; 2.51E-03 mol/l	Brenk	1 alert	
Class	Soluble	Lead likeness	No; 2 violations	
Drug likeness		Synthetic accessibility	6.16	
Lipinski	Yes	**Toxicity**		
Ghose	No; 2 violations	HERG	Weak inhibitor	0.9187
Veber	Yes	HERG Inhibition	Non-inhibitor	0.8117
Egan	Yes	AMES Toxicity	AMES toxic	0.6432
Muegge	Yes	Carcinogens	Non-carcinogens	0.9344
Bioavailability score	0.55	Acute Oral Toxicity	III	0.5931
		Carcinogenicity (three class)	Non-required	0.6440
		Acute rat toxicity	2.3414	LD50, mol/kg
		Fish Toxicity	0.7258	pLC50, mg/L
		TPT	1.1964	pIGC50, ug/L

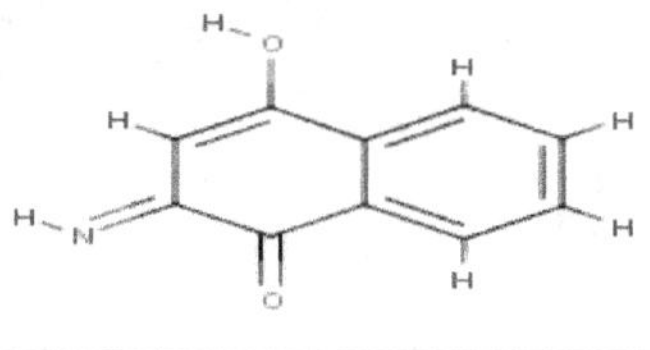

Table 106: **The canonical SMILE, IUPAC name, Physicochemical properties, Hydrophilicity, Lipophilicity, Pharmacokinetics, Druglikeliness, Medicinal Chemistry, and Toxicity profile showing the secondary metabolite of *L. inermis*, Derivative, Lawsone Derivative 101.**

CANONICAL SMILES: O=C1C=C(O)c2c(C1=N)cccc2				
IUPAC Name: 4-hydroxy-1-imino-1,2-dihydronaphthalen-2-one				
Physicochemical Properties		**Lipophilicity**		
Formula	C10H7NO2	Log $P_{o/w}$ (iLOGP)	1.11	
Molecular Weight	173.17 g/mol	Log $P_{o/w}$ (XLOGP3)	0.94	
Num. heavy atoms	13	Log $P_{o/w}$ (WLOGP)	1.54	
Num. arom. heavy atoms	6	Log $P_{o/w}$ (MLOGP)	0.03	
Fraction Csp3	0	Log $P_{o/w}$ (SILICOS-IT)	1.88	
Num. rotatable bonds	0	Consensus Log $P_{o/w}$	1.10	
Num. H-bond acceptors	3	**Pharmacokinetics**		
Num. H-bond donors	2	GI absorption	High	
Molar Refractivity	49.55	BBB Permeability	Yes	
TPSA	61.15 $^{O}A^{2}$	P-gp Substrate	No	
Water Solubility		CYP 1A2 Inhibitor	No	
Log S (ESOL)	-1.85	CYP2C19 Inhibitor	No	
Solubility	2.46E-00 mg/ml; 1.42E-02 mol/l	CYP2C9 Inhibitor	No	
Class	Very soluble	CYP2D6 Inhibitor	No	
Log S(Ali)	-1.81	CYP3A4 Inhibitor	Yes	
Solubility	2.68E-00 mg/ml; 1.55E-02 mol/l	Log K_p (skin permeation)	-6.69 cm/s	
Class	Very soluble	**Medicinal chemistry**		
Log S (SILICOS-IT)	-2.6	Pains	2 alert	
Solubility	4.35E-01 mg/ml; 2.51E-03 mol/l	Brenk	1 alert	
Class	Soluble	Lead likeness	No; 1 violations	
Drug likeness		Synthetic accessibility	2.59	
Lipinski	Yes	**Toxicity**		
Ghose	Yes	HERG	Weak inhibitor	0.9337
Veber	Yes	HERG Inhibition	Non-inhibitor	0.9036
Egan	Yes	AMES Toxicity	AMES toxic	0.6464
Muegge	Yes	Carcinogens	Non-carcinogens	0.8007
Bioavailability score	0.56	Acute Oral Toxicity	III	0.4742
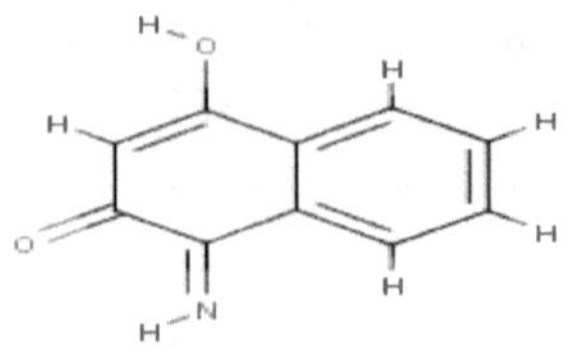		Carcinogenicity (three class)	Non-required	0.6159
		Acute rat toxicity	2.5787	LD50, mol/kg
		Fish Toxicity	0.3500	pLC50, mg/L
		TPT	1.5443	pIGC50, ug/L

Table 107: The canonical SMILE, IUPAC name, Physicochemical properties, Hydrophilicity, Lipophilicity, Pharmacokinetics, Druglikeliness, Medicinal Chemistry, and Toxicity profile showing the secondary metabolite of *L. inermis*, Derivative, Lawsoniside Derivative 1.

CANONICAL SMILES				
OC[C@H]1O[C@@H](Oc2c(O)cc(c3c2cccc3C)O[C@@H]2O[C@H](CO)[C@H]([C@@H]([C@H]2O)O)O)[C@@H]([C@H]([C@@H]1O)O)O				
IUPAC Name				
(2S,3R,4S,5S,6R)-2-[(2-hydroxy-5-methyl-4-{[(2S,3R,4S,5S,6R)-3,4,5-trihydroxy-6-(hydroxymethyl)oxan-2-yl]oxy}naphthalen-1-yl)oxy]-6-(hydroxymethyl)oxane-3,4,5-triol				
Physicochemical Properties		**Lipophilicity**		
Formula	C23H30O13	Log $P_{o/w}$ (iLOGP)	1.57	
Molecular Weight	514.48g/mol	Log $P_{o/w}$ (XLOGP3)	-1.14	
Num. heavy atoms	36	Log $P_{o/w}$ (WLOGP)	-2.79	
Num. arom. heavy atoms	10	Log $P_{o/w}$ (MLOGP)	-2.99	
Fraction Csp3	0.57	Log $P_{o/w}$ (SILICOS-IT)	-2.25	
Num. rotatable bonds	6	Consensus Log $P_{o/w}$	-1.52	
Num. H-bond acceptors	13	**Pharmacokinetics**		
Num. H-bond donors	9	GI absorption	Low	
Molar Refractivity	119.23	BBB Permeability	No	
TPSA	218.99 $^{O}A^{2}$	P-gp Substrate	No	
Water Solubility		CYP 1A2 Inhibitor	No	
Log S (ESOL)	-2.12	CYP2C19 Inhibitor	No	
Solubility	1.52E-00 mg/ml; 8.08E-03 mol/l	CYP2C9 Inhibitor	No	
Class	Soluble	CYP2D6 Inhibitor	No	
Log S(Ali)	-2.97	CYP3A4 Inhibitor	No	
Solubility	5.55E-01 mg/ml; 1.08E-03 mol/l	Log K_p (skin permeation)	-10.25 cm/s	
Class	Soluble	**Medicinal chemistry**		
Log S (SILICOS-IT)	0.67	Pains	0 alert	
Solubility	2.38E+03 mg/ml; 4.63E+00 mol/l	Brenk	0 alert	
Class	Soluble	Lead likeness	No; 1 violations	
Drug likeness		Synthetic accessibility	5.76	
Lipinski	No; 3 violations	**Toxicity**		
Ghose	No; 2 violations	HERG	Weak inhibitor	0.9181
Veber	No; 1 violations	HERG Inhibition	Non-inhibitor	0.6943
Egan	No; 1 violations	AMES Toxicity	AMES toxic	0.6902
Muegge	No; 3 violations	Carcinogens	Non-carcinogens	0.9573
Bioavailability score	0.17	Acute Oral Toxicity	III	0.5721
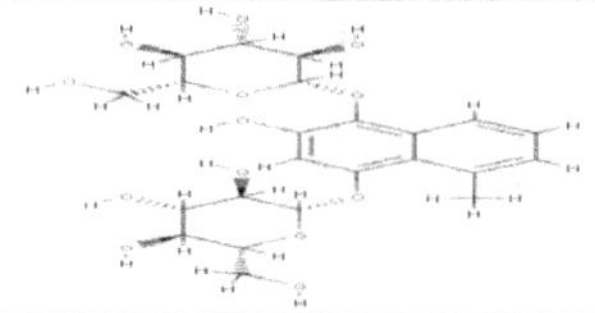		Carcinogenicity (three class)	Non-required	0.6140
		Acute rat toxicity	1.8761	LD50, mol/kg
		Fish Toxicity	1.3805	pLC50, mg/L
		TPT	0.0716	pIGC50, ug/L

Table 108: The canonical SMILE, IUPAC name, Physicochemical properties, Hydrophilicity, Lipophilicity, Pharmacokinetics, Druglikeliness, Medicinal Chemistry, and Toxicity profile showing the secondary metabolite of *L. inermis*, Derivative, Lawsoniside Derivative 75.

CANONICAL SMILES				
FO[C@H]1[C@@H](O[C@@H]([C@H]([C@@H]1O)O)CO)Oc1c(O)cc(c2c1cccc2)O[C@@H]1O[C@H](CO)[C@H]([C@@H]([C@H]1O)O)O				
IUPAC Name				
(2S,3R,4S,5S,6R)-4,5-dihydroxy-2-[(2-hydroxy-4-{[(2S,3R,4S,5S,6R)-3,4,5-trihydroxy-6-(hydroxymethyl)oxan-2-yl]oxy}naphthalen-1-yl)oxy]-6-(hydroxymethyl)oxan-3-yl hypofluorite				
Physicochemical Properties		**Lipophilicity**		
Formula	C22H27FO13	Log $P_{o/w}$ (iLOGP)	1.65	
Molecular Weight	518.44 g/mol	Log $P_{o/w}$ (XLOGP3)	-0.43	
Num. heavy atoms	36	Log $P_{o/w}$ (WLOGP)	-1.77	
Num. arom. heavy atoms	10	Log $P_{o/w}$ (MLOGP)	-3.1	
Fraction Csp3	0.55	Log $P_{o/w}$ (SILICOS-IT)	-2.32	
Num. rotatable bonds	7	Consensus Log $P_{o/w}$	-1.19	
Num. H-bond acceptors	14	**Pharmacokinetics**		
Num. H-bond donors	8	GI absorption	Low	
Molar Refractivity	114.24	BBB Permeability	No	
TPSA	207.99 $^{O}A^{2}$	P-gp Substrate	No	
Water Solubility		CYP 1A2 Inhibitor	No	
Log S (ESOL)	-2.53	CYP2C19 Inhibitor	No	
Solubility	1.54E+00 mg/ml; 2.97E-03 mol/l	CYP2C9 Inhibitor	No	
Class	Soluble	CYP2D6 Inhibitor	No	
Log S(Ali)	-3.47	CYP3A4 Inhibitor	No	
Solubility	1.75E-01 mg/ml; 3.37E-04 mol/l	Log K_p (skin permeation)	-9.77 cm/s	
Class	Soluble	**Medicinal chemistry**		
Log S (SILICOS-IT)	0.46	Pains	0 alert	
Solubility	1.51E+03 mg/ml; 2.90E+00 mol/l	Brenk	0 alert	
Class	Soluble	Lead likeness	No; 1 violations	
Drug likeness		Synthetic accessibility	5.99	
Lipinski	No; 3 violations	**Toxicity**		
Ghose	No; 2 violations	HERG	Weak inhibitor	0.9365
Veber	No; 1 violations	HERG Inhibition	Non-inhibitor	0.6455
Egan	No; 1 violations	AMES Toxicity	AMES toxic	0.5632
Muegge	No; 3 violations	Carcinogens	Non-carcinogens	0.9277
Bioavailability score	0.17	Acute Oral Toxicity	III	0.4539
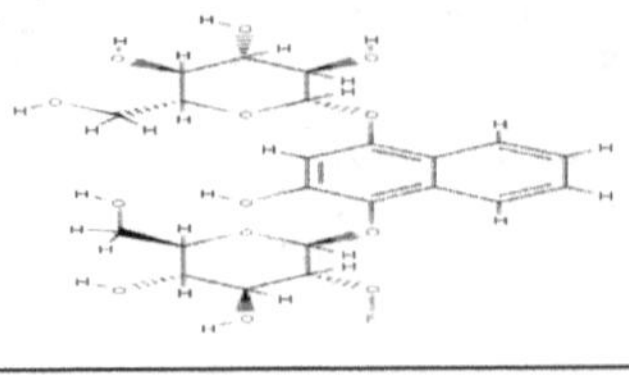		Carcinogenicity (three class)	Non-required	0.5564
		Acute rat toxicity	2.5256	LD50, mol/kg
		Fish Toxicity	1.0394	pLC50, mg/L
		TPT	0.3185	pIGC50, ug/L

Table 109: The canonical SMILE, IUPAC name, Physicochemical properties, Hydrophilicity, Lipophilicity, Pharmacokinetics, Druglikeliness, Medicinal Chemistry, and Toxicity profile showing the secondary metabolite of *L. inermis*, Derivative, Lawsoniside Derivative 124.

CANONICAL SMILES				
OC[C@H]1O[C@@H](Oc2cc(OO)c(c3c2cccc3)O[C@@H]2O[C@H](CO)[C@H]([C@@H]([C@H]2O)O)O)[C@@H]([C@H]([C@@H]1O)O)O				
IUPAC Name				
(2S,3R,4S,5S,6R)-2-[(3-hydroperoxy-4-{[(2S,3R,4S,5S,6R)-3,4,5-trihydroxy-6-(hydroxymethyl)oxan-2-yl]oxy}naphthalen-1-yl)oxy]-6-(hydroxymethyl)oxane-3,4,5-triol				
Physicochemical Properties		**Lipophilicity**		
Formula	C22H28O14	Log $P_{o/w}$ (iLOGP)	0.85	
Molecular Weight	516.45g/mol	Log $P_{o/w}$ (XLOGP3)	-1.67	
Num. heavy atoms	36	Log $P_{o/w}$ (WLOGP)	-2.95	
Num. arom. heavy atoms	10	Log $P_{o/w}$ (MLOGP)	-3.14	
Fraction Csp3	0.55	Log $P_{o/w}$ (SILICOS-IT)	-3.22	
Num. rotatable bonds	7	Consensus Log $P_{o/w}$	-2.03	
Num. H-bond acceptors	14	**Pharmacokinetics**		
Num. H-bond donors	9	GI absorption	Low	
Molar Refractivity	115.50	BBB Permeability	No	
TPSA	$228.22\ ^{O}A^{2}$	P-gp Substrate	No	
Water Solubility		CYP 1A2 Inhibitor	No	
Log S (ESOL)	-1.73	CYP2C19 Inhibitor	No	
Solubility	9.54E+00 mg/ml; 1.85E-02 mol/l	CYP2C9 Inhibitor	No	
Class	Very Soluble	CYP2D6 Inhibitor	No	
Log S(Ali)	-2.61	CYP3A4 Inhibitor	No	
Solubility	1.27E+00 mg/ml; 2.45E-03 mol/l	Log K_p (skin permeation)	-10.64 cm/s	
Class	Soluble	**Medicinal chemistry**		
Log S (SILICOS-IT)	1.31	Pains	0 alert	
Solubility	1.07E+04 mg/ml; 2.07E+01 mol/l	Brenk	1 alert	
Class	Soluble	Lead likeness	No; 1 violations	
Drug likeness		Synthetic accessibility	6.1	
Lipinski	No; 3 violations	**Toxicity**		
Ghose	No; 2 violations	HERG	Weak inhibitor	0.8786
Veber	No; 1 violations	HERG Inhibition	Non-inhibitor	0.6283
Egan	No; 1 violations	AMES Toxicity	AMES toxic	0.5764
Muegge	No; 3 violations	Carcinogens	Non-carcinogens	0.9455
Bioavailability score	0.17	Acute Oral Toxicity	III	0.4532
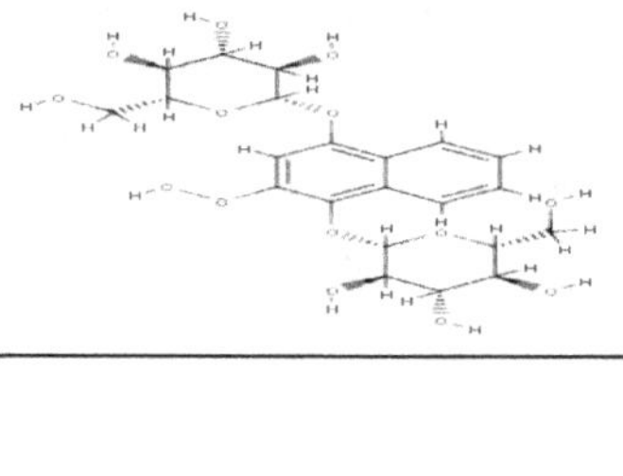		Carcinogenicity (three class)	Non-required	0.6085
		Acute rat toxicity	2.1203	LD50, mol/kg
		Fish Toxicity	1.4080	pLC50, mg/L
		TPT	0.1137	pIGC50, ug/L

Table 110: The canonical SMILE, IUPAC name, Physicochemical properties, Hydrophilicity, Lipophilicity, Pharmacokinetics, Druglikeliness, Medicinal Chemistry, and Toxicity profile showing the secondary metabolite of *L. inermis*, Derivative, Lawsoniside Derivative 151.

CANONICAL SMILES				
NOC[C@H]1O[C@@H](Oc2cc(O)c(c3c2cccc3)O[C@@H]2O[C@H](CO)[C@H]([C@@H]([C@H]2O)O)O)[C@@H]([C@H]([C@@H]1O)O)O				
IUPAC Name				
(2R,3S,4S,5R,6S)-2-[(aminooxy)methyl]-6-[(3-hydroxy-4-{[(2S,3R,4S,5S,6R)-3,4,5-trihydroxy-6-(hydroxymethyl)oxan-2-yl]oxy}naphthalen-1-yl)oxy]oxane-3,4,5-triol				
Physicochemical Properties		**Lipophilicity**		
Formula	C22H29NO13	Log $P_{o/w}$ (iLOGP)	-0.91	
Molecular Weight	515.46g/mol	Log $P_{o/w}$ (XLOGP3)	-2.26	
Num. heavy atoms	36	Log $P_{o/w}$ (WLOGP)	-3.2	
Num. arom. heavy atoms	10	Log $P_{o/w}$ (MLOGP)	-3.14	
Fraction Csp3	0.55	Log $P_{o/w}$ (SILICOS-IT)	-3.46	
Num. rotatable bonds	7	Consensus Log $P_{o/w}$	-2.59	
Num. H-bond acceptors	14	**Pharmacokinetics**		
Num. H-bond donors	9	GI absorption	Low	
Molar Refractivity	116.89	BBB Permeability	No	
TPSA	234.01 $^{O}A^{2}$	P-gp Substrate	No	
Water Solubility		CYP 1A2 Inhibitor	No	
Log S (ESOL)	-1.36	CYP2C19 Inhibitor	No	
Solubility	2.27E+01 mg/ml; 4.41E-02 mol/l	CYP2C9 Inhibitor	No	
Class	Very soluble	CYP2D6 Inhibitor	No	
Log S(Ali)	-2.12	CYP3A4 Inhibitor	No	
Solubility	3.91E+00 mg/ml; 7.58E-03 mol/l	Log K_p (skin permeation)	-11.05 cm/s	
Class	Soluble	**Medicinal chemistry**		
Log S (SILICOS-IT)	1.1	Pains	0 alert	
Solubility	6.46E+03 mg/ml; 1.25E+01 mol/l	Brenk	1 alert	
Class	Soluble	Lead likeness	No; 1 violations	
Drug likeness		Synthetic accessibility	5.98	
Lipinski	No; 3 violations	**Toxicity**		
Ghose	No; 2 violations	HERG	Weak inhibitor	0.8680
Veber	No; 1 violations	HERG Inhibition	Non-inhibitor	0.6076
Egan	No; 1 violations	AMES Toxicity	Non AMES toxic	0.5054
Muegge	No; 4 violations	Carcinogens	Non-carcinogens	0.9043
Bioavailability score	0.17	Acute Oral Toxicity	III	0.5688
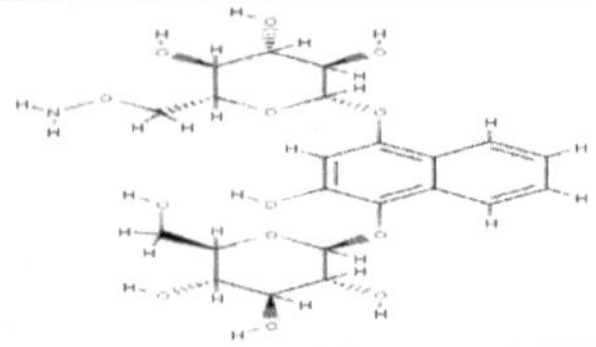		Carcinogenicity (three class)	Non-required	0.5765
		Acute rat toxicity	2.3788	LD50, mol/kg
		Fish Toxicity	1.5533	pLC50, mg/L
		TPT	0.1668	pIGC50, ug/L

Table 111: The canonical SMILE, IUPAC name, Physicochemical properties, Hydrophilicity, Lipophilicity, Pharmacokinetics, Druglikeliness, Medicinal Chemistry, and Toxicity profile showing the secondary metabolite of *L. inermis*, Derivative, Lawsoniside Derivative 182.

CANONICAL SMILES				
FO[C@H]1[C@@H](O[C@@H]([C@H]([C@@H]1O)O)CO)Oc1cc(O)c(c2c1cccc2)O[C@@H]1O[C@H](CO)[C@H]([C@@H]([C@H]1O)O)O				
IUPAC name				
(2S,3R,4S,5S,6R)-4,5-dihydroxy-2-[(3-hydroxy-4-{[(2S,3R,4S,5S,6R)-3,4,5-trihydroxy-6-(hydroxymethyl)oxan-2-yl]oxy}naphthalen-1-yl)oxy]-6-(hydroxymethyl)oxan-3-yl hypofluorite				
Physicochemical Properties		**Lipophilicity**		
Formula	C22H27FO13	Log $P_{o/w}$ (iLOGP)	1.36	
Molecular Weight	518.44 g/mol	Log $P_{o/w}$ (XLOGP3)	-0.43	
Num. heavy atoms	36	Log $P_{o/w}$ (WLOGP)	-1.77	
Num. arom. heavy atoms	10	Log $P_{o/w}$ (MLOGP)	-3.1	
Fraction Csp3	0.55	Log $P_{o/w}$ (SILICOS-IT)	-2.32	
Num. rotatable bonds	7	Consensus Log $P_{o/w}$	-1.25	
Num. H-bond acceptors	14	**Pharmacokinetics**		
Num. H-bond donors	8	GI absorption	Low	
Molar Refractivity	114.24	BBB Permeability	No	
TPSA	207.99 $^{O}A^{2}$	P-gp Substrate	No	
Water Solubility		CYP 1A2 Inhibitor	No	
Log S (ESOL)	-2.53	CYP2C19 Inhibitor	No	
Solubility	1.54E+00 mg/ml; 2.97E-03 mol/l	CYP2C9 Inhibitor	No	
Class	Soluble	CYP2D6 Inhibitor	No	
Log S(Ali)	-3.47	CYP3A4 Inhibitor	No	
Solubility	1.75E-01 mg/ml; 3.37E-04 mol/l	Log K_p (skin permeation)	-9.77 cm/s	
Class	Soluble	**Medicinal chemistry**		
Log S (SILICOS-IT)	0.46	Pains	0 alert	
Solubility	1.51E+03 mg/ml; 2.90E+00 mol/l	Brenk	0 alert	
Class	Soluble	Lead likeness	No; 1 violations	
Drug likeness		Synthetic accessibility	5.99	
Lipinski	No; 3 violations	**Toxicity**		
Ghose	No; 2 violations	HERG	Weak inhibitor	0.9365
Veber	No; 1 violations	HERG Inhibition	Non-inhibitor	0.6455
Egan	No; 1 violations	AMES Toxicity	AMES toxic	0.5632
Muegge	No; 3 violations	Carcinogens	Non-carcinogens	0.9277
Bioavailability score	0.17	Acute Oral Toxicity	III	0.4539
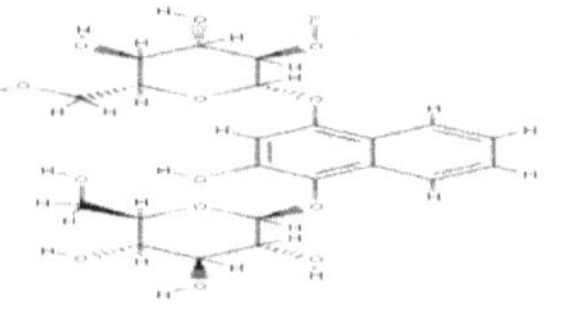		Carcinogenicity (three class)	Non-required	0.5564
		Acute rat toxicity	2.5256	LD50, mol/kg
		Fish Toxicity	1.0394	pLC50, mg/L
		TPT	0.3185	pIGC50, ug/L

Table 112: **The canonical SMILE, IUPAC name, Physicochemical properties, Hydrophilicity, Lipophilicity, Pharmacokinetics, Druglikeliness, Medicinal Chemistry, and Toxicity profile showing the secondary metabolite of *L. inermis*, Derivative, Scopoletin Derivative 1.**

CANONICAL SMILES: CCOc1cc2ccc(=O)oc2cc1O				
IUPAC Name: 6-ethoxy-7-hydroxy-2H-chromen-2-one				
Physicochemical Properties		**Lipophilicity**		
Formula	C11H10O4	Log $P_{o/w}$ (iLOGP)	2.11	
Molecular Weight	206.19g/mol	Log $P_{o/w}$ (XLOGP3)	1.89	
Num. heavy atoms	15	Log $P_{o/w}$ (WLOGP)	1.90	
Num. arom. heavy atoms	10	Log $P_{o/w}$ (MLOGP)	1.05	
Fraction Csp3	0.18	Log $P_{o/w}$ (SILICOS-IT)	2.27	
Num. rotatable bonds	2	Consensus Log $P_{o/w}$	1.84	
Num. H-bond acceptors	4	**Pharmacokinetics**		
Num. H-bond donors	1	GI absorption	High	
Molar Refractivity	55.81	BBB Permeability	Yes	
TPSA	59.67 $^{O}A^{2}$	P-gp Substrate	No	
Water Solubility		CYP 1A2 Inhibitor	Yes	
Log S (ESOL)	-2.67	CYP2C19 Inhibitor	No	
Solubility	4.40E-01 mg/ml; 2.14E-03 mol/l	CYP2C9 Inhibitor	No	
Class	Soluble	CYP2D6 Inhibitor	No	
Log S(Ali)	-2.77	CYP3A4 Inhibitor	No	
Solubility	3.54E-01 mg/ml; 1.72E-03 mol/l	Log K_p (skin permeation)	-6.22 cm/s	
Class	Soluble	**Medicinal chemistry**		
Log S (SILICOS-IT)	-3.58	Pains	0 alert	
Solubility	5.49E-02 mg/ml; 2.66E-04 mol/l	Brenk	1 alert	
Class	Soluble	Lead likeness	No; 1 violations	
Drug likeness		Synthetic accessibility	2.68	
Lipinski	Yes	**Toxicity**		
Ghose	Yes	HERG	Weak inhibitor	0.9674
Veber	Yes	HERG Inhibition	Non-inhibitor	0.8906
Egan	Yes	AMES Toxicity	Non AMES toxic	0.5872
Muegge	Yes	Carcinogens	Non-carcinogens	0.9245
Bioavailability score	0.55	Acute Oral Toxicity	III	0.5316
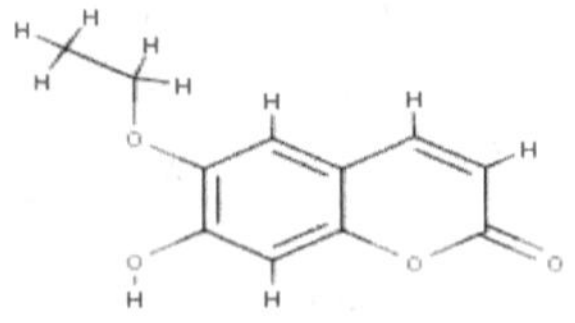		Carcinogenicity (three class)	Non-required	0.6214
		Acute rat toxicity	3.1340	LD50, mol/kg
		Fish Toxicity	0.4903	pLC50, mg/L
		TPT	0.8978	pIGC50, ug/L

Table 113: The canonical SMILE, IUPAC name, Physicochemical properties, Hydrophilicity, Lipophilicity, Pharmacokinetics, Druglikeliness, Medicinal Chemistry, and Toxicity profile showing the secondary metabolite of *L. inermis*, Derivative, Scopoletin Derivative 44.

CANONICAL SMILES: COc1cc2c(N)cc(=O)oc2cc1O				
IUPAC Name: 4-amino-7-hydroxy-6-methoxy-2H-chromen-2-one				
Physicochemical Properties		**Lipophilicity**		
Formula	C10H9NO4	Log $P_{o/w}$ (iLOGP)	1.51	
Molecular Weight	207.18 g/mol	Log $P_{o/w}$ (XLOGP3)	056	
Num. heavy atoms	15	Log $P_{o/w}$ (WLOGP)	1.1	
Num. arom. heavy atoms	10	Log $P_{o/w}$ (MLOGP)	0.2	
Fraction Csp3	0.1	Log $P_{o/w}$ (SILICOS-IT)	1.21	
Num. rotatable bonds	1	Consensus Log $P_{o/w}$	0.91	
Num. H-bond acceptors	4	**Pharmacokinetics**		
Num. H-bond donors	2	GI absorption	High	
Molar Refractivity	55.4	BBB Permeability	No	
TPSA	85.69 $^{O}A^{2}$	P-gp Substrate	No	
Water Solubility		CYP 1A2 Inhibitor	Yes	
Log S (ESOL)	-1.9	CYP2C19 Inhibitor	No	
Solubility	2.58E+00 mg/ml; 1.25E-02 mol/l	CYP2C9 Inhibitor	No	
Class	Very Soluble	CYP2D6 Inhibitor	No	
Log S(Ali)	-1.93	CYP3A4 Inhibitor	Yes	
Solubility	2.42E+00 mg/ml; 1.17E-02 mol/l	Log K_p (skin permeation)	-7.17 cm/s	
Class	Very soluble	**Medicinal chemistry**		
Log S (SILICOS-IT)	-2.81	Pains	0 alert	
Solubility	3.20E-01 mg/ml; 1.55E-03 mol/l	Brenk	1 alert	
Class	Soluble	Lead likeness	1 violations	
Drug likeness		Synthetic accessibility	2.67	
Lipinski	Yes	**Toxicity**		
Ghose	Yes	HERG	Weak inhibitor	0.9767
Veber	Yes	HERG Inhibition	Non-inhibitor	0.8803
Egan	Yes	AMES Toxicity	AMES toxic	0.6538
Muegge	Yes	Carcinogens	Non-carcinogens	0.9191
Bioavailability score	0.55	Acute Oral Toxicity	III	0.6283
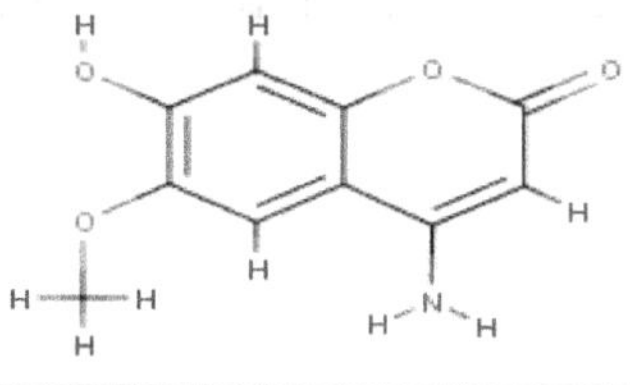		Carcinogenicity (three class)	Non-required	0.4534
		Acute rat toxicity	2.1476	LD50, mol/kg
		Fish Toxicity	0.7708	pLC50, mg/L
		TPT	0.9854	pIGC50, ug/L

Table 114: The canonical SMILE, IUPAC name, Physicochemical properties, Hydrophilicity, Lipophilicity, Pharmacokinetics, Druglikeliness, Medicinal Chemistry, and Toxicity profile showing the secondary metabolite of *L. inermis*, Derivative, Scopoletin Derivative 60.

CANONICAL SMILES: COc1cc2cc(S)c(=O)oc2cc1O				
IUPAC Name: 7-hydroxy-6-methoxy-3-sulfanyl-2H-chromen-2-one				
Physicochemical Properties		**Lipophilicity**		
Formula	C10H8O4S	Log $P_{o/w}$ (iLOGP)	2.09	
Molecular Weight	224.23 g/mol	Log $P_{o/w}$ (XLOGP3)	1.89	
Num. heavy atoms	15	Log $P_{o/w}$ (WLOGP)	1.8	
Num. arom. heavy atoms	10	Log $P_{o/w}$ (MLOGP)	1.03	
Fraction Csp3	0.1	Log $P_{o/w}$ (SILICOS-IT)	2.21	
Num. rotatable bonds	1	Consensus Log $P_{o/w}$	1.8	
Num. H-bond acceptors	4	**Pharmacokinetics**		
Num. H-bond donors	1	GI absorption	High	
Molar Refractivity	58.25	BBB Permeability	No	
TPSA	98.47 $^{O}A^{2}$	P-gp Substrate	No	
Water Solubility		CYP 1A2 Inhibitor	Yes	
Log S (ESOL)	-2.85	CYP2C19 Inhibitor	No	
Solubility	3.18E-01 mg/ml; 1.42E-03 mol/l	CYP2C9 Inhibitor	No	
Class	Soluble	CYP2D6 Inhibitor	No	
Log S(Ali)	-3.58	CYP3A4 Inhibitor	No	
Solubility	5.89E-02 mg/ml; 2.63E-04 mol/l	Log K_p (skin permeation)	-6.33 cm/s	
Class	Soluble	**Medicinal chemistry**		
Log S (SILICOS-IT)	-3.28	Pains	0 alert	
Solubility	1.17E-01 mg/ml; 5.22E-04 mol/l	Brenk	2 alert	
Class	Soluble	Lead likeness	No; 1 violations	
Drug likeness		Synthetic accessibility	2.65	
Lipinski	Yes	**Toxicity**		
Ghose	Yes	HERG	Weak inhibitor	0.9910
Veber	Yes	HERG Inhibition	Non-inhibitor	0.8905
Egan	Yes	AMES Toxicity	Non AMES toxic	0.5586
Muegge	Yes	Carcinogens	Non-carcinogens	0.9299
Bioavailability score	0.55	Acute Oral Toxicity	III	0.7084
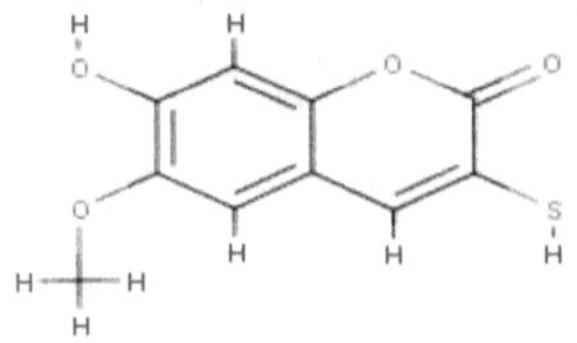		Carcinogenicity (three class)	Non-required	0.5678
		Acute rat toxicity	2.6208	LD50, mol/kg
		Fish Toxicity	0.7678	pLC50, mg/L
		TPT	1.1931	pIGC50, ug/L

Table 115: The canonical SMILE, IUPAC name, Physicochemical properties, Hydrophilicity, Lipophilicity, Pharmacokinetics, Druglikeliness, Medicinal Chemistry, and Toxicity profile showing the secondary metabolite of *L. inermis*, Derivative, Scopoletin Derivative 114.

CANONICAL SMILES: NOc1cc2oc(=O)ccc2cc1OC				
IUPAC Name: 7-(aminooxy)-6-methoxy-2H-chromen-2-one				
Physicochemical Properties		**Lipophilicity**		
Formula	C10H9NO4	Log $P_{o/w}$ (iLOGP)	1.87	
Molecular Weight	207.18 g/mol	Log $P_{o/w}$ (XLOGP3)	1.11	
Num. heavy atoms	15	Log $P_{o/w}$ (WLOGP)	1.05	
Num. arom. heavy atoms	10	Log $P_{o/w}$ (MLOGP)	0.74	
Fraction Csp3	0.1	Log $P_{o/w}$ (SILICOS-IT)	1.22	
Num. rotatable bonds	2	Consensus Log $P_{o/w}$	1.2	
Num. H-bond acceptors	5	**Pharmacokinetics**		
Num. H-bond donors	1	GI absorption	High	
Molar Refractivity	53.37	BBB Permeability	No	
TPSA	74.69 $^{O}A^{2}$	P-gp Substrate	No	
Water Solubility		CYP 1A2 Inhibitor	Yes	
Log S (ESOL)	-2.19	CYP2C19 Inhibitor	No	
Solubility	1.35E+00 mg/ml; 6.53E-03 mol/l	CYP2C9 Inhibitor	No	
Class	Soluble	CYP2D6 Inhibitor	No	
Log S(Ali)	-2.27	CYP3A4 Inhibitor	No	
Solubility	1.11E+00 mg/ml; 5.35E-03 mol/l	Log K_p (skin permeation)	-6.78 cm/s	
Class	Soluble	**Medicinal chemistry**		
Log S (SILICOS-IT)	-3.13	Pains	0 alert	
Solubility	1.55E-01 mg/ml; 7.46E-04 mol/l	Brenk	2 alert	
Class	Soluble	Lead likeness	No; 1 violations	
Drug likeness		Synthetic accessibility	2.85	
Lipinski	Yes	**Toxicity**		
Ghose	Yes	HERG	Weak inhibitor	0.9264
Veber	Yes	HERG Inhibition	Non-inhibitor	0.8919
Egan	Yes	AMES Toxicity	AMES toxic	0.5193
Muegge	Yes	Carcinogens	Non-carcinogens	0.8855
Bioavailability score	0.55	Acute Oral Toxicity	III	0.6395
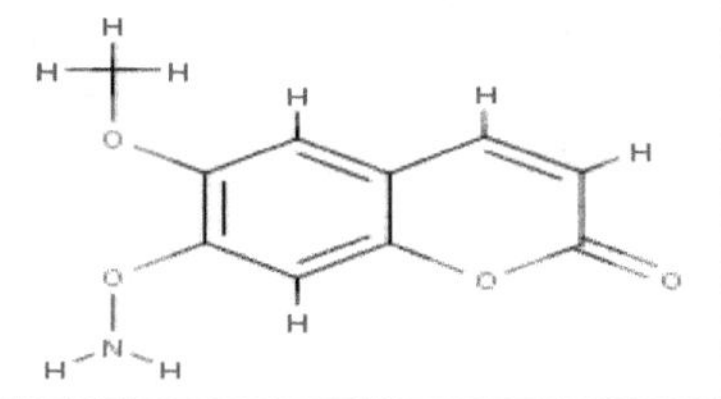		Carcinogenicity (three class)	Non-required	0.4893
		Acute rat toxicity	2.3904	LD50, mol/kg
		Fish Toxicity	0.6495	pLC50, mg/L
		TPT	0.3024	pIGC50, ug/L

Table 116: The canonical SMILE, IUPAC name, Physicochemical properties, Hydrophilicity, Lipophilicity, Pharmacokinetics, Druglikeliness, Medicinal Chemistry, and Toxicity profile showing the secondary metabolite of *L. inermis*, Derivative, Scopoletin Derivative 127.

CANONICAL SMILES: CCOc1cc2ccc(=O)oc2cc1O				
IUPAC Name: 6-ethoxy-7-hydroxy-2H-chromen-2-one				
Physicochemical Properties		**Lipophilicity**		
Formula	C11H10O4	Log $P_{o/w}$ (iLOGP)	2.11	
Molecular Weight	206.19 g/mol	Log $P_{o/w}$ (XLOGP3)	1.89	
Num. heavy atoms	15	Log $P_{o/w}$ (WLOGP)	1.90	
Num. arom. heavy atoms	10	Log $P_{o/w}$ (MLOGP)	1.05	
Fraction Csp3	0.18	Log $P_{o/w}$ (SILICOS-IT)	2.27	
Num. rotatable bonds	2	Consensus Log $P_{o/w}$	1.84	
Num. H-bond acceptors	4	**Pharmacokinetics**		
Num. H-bond donors	1	GI absorption	High	
Molar Refractivity	55.81	BBB Permeability	Yes	
TPSA	59.67 $^{O}A^{2}$	P-gp Substrate	No	
Water Solubility		CYP 1A2 Inhibitor	Yes	
Log S (ESOL)	-2.67	CYP2C19 Inhibitor	No	
Solubility	4.40E-01 mg/ml; 2.14E-03 mol/l	CYP2C9 Inhibitor	No	
Class	Soluble	CYP2D6 Inhibitor	No	
Log S(Ali)	-2.77	CYP3A4 Inhibitor	No	
Solubility	3.54E-01 mg/ml; 1.72E-03 mol/l	Log K_p (skin permeation)	-6.22 cm/s	
Class	Soluble	**Medicinal chemistry**		
Log S (SILICOS-IT)	-3.58	Pains	0 alert	
Solubility	5.49E-02 mg/ml; 2.66E-04 mol/l	Brenk	1 alert	
Class	Soluble	Lead likeness	No; 1 violations	
Drug likeness		Synthetic accessibility	2.68	
Lipinski	Yes	**Toxicity**		
Ghose	Yes	HERG	Weak inhibitor	0.9674
Veber	Yes	HERG Inhibition	Non-inhibitor	0.8906
Egan	Yes	AMES Toxicity	Non AMES toxic	0.5872
Muegge	Yes	Carcinogens	Non-carcinogens	0.9245
Bioavailability score	0.55	Acute Oral Toxicity	III	0.5316
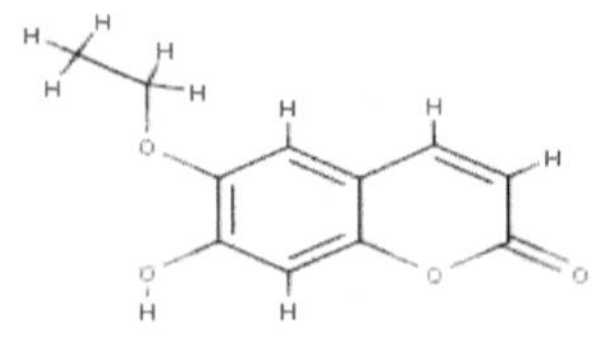		Carcinogenicity (three class)	Non-required	0.6214
		Acute rat toxicity	3.1340	LD50, mol/kg
		Fish Toxicity	0.4903	pLC50, mg/L
		TPT	0.8978	pIGC50, ug/L

Table 117: The canonical SMILE, IUPAC name, Physicochemical properties, Hydrophilicity, Lipophilicity, Pharmacokinetics, Druglikeliness, Medicinal Chemistry, and Toxicity profile showing the secondary metabolite of *L. inermis*, Derivative, Stigmasterol Derivative 16.

CANONICAL SMILES: NCC([C@H](/C=C/[C@H]([C@H]1CC[C@@H]2[C@]1(C)CC[C@H]1[C@H]2CC=C2[C@]1(C)CC[C@@H](C2)O)C)CC)C				
IUPAC Name (1R,3aS,3bS,7S,9aR,9bS,11aR)-1-[(3E)-7-amino-5-ethyl-6-methylhept-3-en-2-yl]-9a,11a-dimethyl-1H,2H,3H,3aH,3bH,4H,6H,7H,8H,9H,9aH,9bH,10H,11H,11aH-cyclopenta[a]phenanthren-7-ol				
Physicochemical Properties		**Lipophilicity**		
Formula	C29H49NO	Log $P_{o/w}$ (iLOGP)	4.76	
Molecular Weight	427.71 g/mol	Log $P_{o/w}$ (XLOGP3)	7.08	
Num. heavy atoms	31	Log $P_{o/w}$ (WLOGP)	6.74	
Num. arom. heavy atoms	0	Log $P_{o/w}$ (MLOGP)	5.7	
Fraction Csp3	0.86	Log $P_{o/w}$ (SILICOS-IT)	6.02	
Num. rotatable bonds	6	Consensus Log $P_{o/w}$	6.06	
Num. H-bond acceptors	2	**Pharmacokinetics**		
Num. H-bond donors	2	GI absorption	High	
Molar Refractivity	135.46	BBB Permeability	No	
TPSA	46.25 $^{O}A^{2}$	P-gp Substrate	No	
Water Solubility		CYP 1A2 Inhibitor	No	
Log S (ESOL)	-6.56	CYP2C19 Inhibitor	No	
Solubility	1.19E-04 mg/ml; 2.78E-07 mol/l	CYP2C9 Inhibitor	No	
Class	Poorly soluble	CYP2D6 Inhibitor	No	
Log S(Ali)	-7.87	CYP3A4 Inhibitor	No	
Solubility	5.78E-06 mg/ml; 1.35E-08 mol/l	Log K_p (skin permeation)	-3.88 cm/s	
Class	Poorly soluble	**Medicinal chemistry**		
Log S (SILICOS-IT)	-5.12	Pains	0 alert	
Solubility	3.28E-03 mg/ml; 7.67E-06 mol/l	Brenk	1 alert	
Class	Moderately Soluble	Lead likeness	No; 2 violations	
Drug likeness		Synthetic accessibility	6.10	
Lipinski	No; 1 violations	**Toxicity**		
Ghose	No; 3 violations	HERG	Weak inhibitor	0.7489
Veber	Yes	HERG Inhibition	Inhibitor	0.5820
Egan	No; 1 violations	AMES Toxicity	Non AMES toxic	0.8637
Muegge	No; 1 violations	Carcinogens	Non-carcinogens	0.8839
Bioavailability score	0.55	Acute Oral Toxicity	III	0.6725
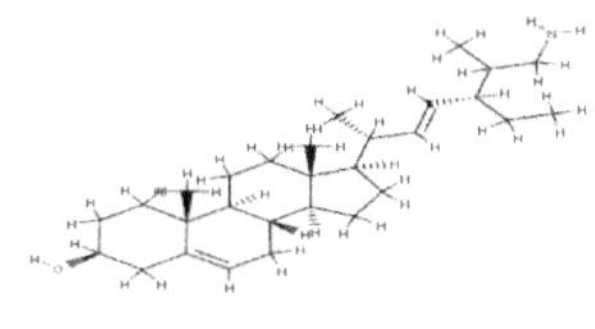		Carcinogenicity (three class)	Non-required	0.5295
		Acute rat toxicity	2.3923	LD50, mol/kg
		Fish Toxicity	0.7669	pLC50, mg/L
		TPT	0.7685	pIGC50, ug/L

Table 118: The canonical SMILE, IUPAC name, Physicochemical properties, Hydrophilicity, Lipophilicity, Pharmacokinetics, Druglikeliness, Medicinal Chemistry, and Toxicity profile showing the secondary metabolite of *L. inermis*, Derivative, Stigmasterol Derivative 44.

CANONICAL SMILES: CC[C@H](C(N)(C)C)/C=C/[C@H]([C@H]1CC[C@@H]2[C@]1(C)CC[C@H]1[C@H]2CC=C2[C@]1(C)CC[C@@H](C2)O)C				
IUPAC Name (1R,3aS,3bS,7S,9aR,9bS,11aR)-1-[(3E)-6-amino-5-ethyl-6-methylhept-3-en-2-yl]-9a,11a-dimethyl-1H,2H,3H,3aH,3bH,4H,6H,7H,8H,9H,9aH,9bH,10H,11H,11aH-cyclopenta[a]phenanthren-7-ol				
Physicochemical Properties		**Lipophilicity**		
Formula	C29H49NO	Log $P_{o/w}$ (iLOGP)	4.78	
Molecular Weight	427.71 g/mol	Log $P_{o/w}$ (XLOGP3)	6.72	
Num. heavy atoms	31	Log $P_{o/w}$ (WLOGP)	6.88	
Num. arom. heavy atoms	0	Log $P_{o/w}$ (MLOGP)	5.70	
Fraction Csp3	0.86	Log $P_{o/w}$ (SILICOS-IT)	5.87	
Num. rotatable bonds	5	Consensus Log $P_{o/w}$	5.99	
Num. H-bond acceptors	2	**Pharmacokinetics**		
Num. H-bond donors	2	GI absorption	Low	
Molar Refractivity	135.50	BBB Permeability	No	
TPSA	46.25 $^{O}A^{2}$	P-gp Substrate	No	
Water Solubility		CYP 1A2 Inhibitor	No	
Log S (ESOL)	-6.4	CYP2C19 Inhibitor	No	
Solubility	1.72E-04 mg/ml; 4.02E-07 mol/l	CYP2C9 Inhibitor	No	
Class	Poorly soluble	CYP2D6 Inhibitor	No	
Log S(Ali)	-7.5	CYP3A4 Inhibitor	No	
Solubility	1.37E-05 mg/ml; 3.19E-08 mol/l	Log K_p (skin permeation)	-4.14 cm/s	
Class	Poorly soluble	**Medicinal chemistry**		
Log S (SILICOS-IT)	-5.10	Pains	0 alert	
Solubility	3.42E-03 mg/ml; 8.00E-06 mol/l	Brenk	1 alert	
Class	Moderately Soluble	Lead likeness	No; 2 violations	
Drug likeness		Synthetic accessibility	6.27	
Lipinski	No; 1 violations	**Toxicity**		
Ghose	No; 3 violations	HERG	Weak inhibitor	0.9095
Veber	Yes	HERG Inhibition	Non-inhibitor	0.6703
Egan	No; 1 violations	AMES Toxicity	Non AMES toxic	0.8623
Muegge	No; 1 violations	Carcinogens	Non-carcinogens	0.9187
Bioavailability score	0.55	Acute Oral Toxicity	III	0.4811
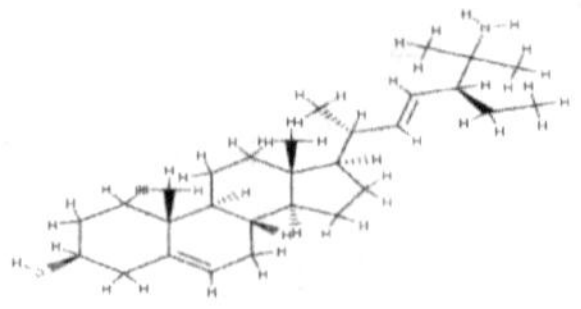		Carcinogenicity (three class)	Non-required	0.5198
		Acute rat toxicity	2.9151	LD50, mol/kg
		Fish Toxicity	0.4480	pLC50, mg/L
		TPT	0.8798	pIGC50, ug/L

Table 119: **The canonical SMILE, IUPAC name, Physicochemical properties, Hydrophilicity, Lipophilicity, Pharmacokinetics, Druglikeliness, Medicinal Chemistry, and Toxicity profile showing the secondary metabolite of *L. inermis*, Derivative, Stigmasterol Derivative 89.**

CANONICAL SMILES: CCC[C@H](C(C)C)/C=C/[C@H]([C@H]1CC[C@@H]2[C@]1(C)CC[C@H]1[C@H]2CC=C2[C@]1(C)CC[C@@H](C2)O)C				
IUPAC Name (1R,3aS,3bS,7S,9aR,9bS,11aR)-9a,11a-dimethyl-1-[(3E)-5-(propan-2-yl)oct-3-en-2-yl]-1H,2H,3H,3aH,3bH,4H,6H,7H,8H,9H,9aH,9bH,10H,11H,11aH-cyclopenta[a]phenanthren-7-ol				
Physicochemical Properties		**Lipophilicity**		
Formula	C30H50O	Log $P_{o/w}$ (iLOGP)	5.19	
Molecular Weight	426.75 g/mol	Log $P_{o/w}$ (XLOGP3)	9.10	
Num. heavy atoms	31	Log $P_{o/w}$ (WLOGP)	8.19	
Num. arom. heavy atoms	0	Log $P_{o/w}$ (MLOGP)	6.82	
Fraction Csp3	0.87	Log $P_{o/w}$ (SILICOS-IT)	7.27	
Num. rotatable bonds	6	Consensus Log $P_{o/w}$	7.31	
Num. H-bond acceptors	1	**Pharmacokinetics**		
Num. H-bond donors	1	GI absorption	Low	
Molar Refractivity	137.56	BBB Permeability	No	
TPSA	20.23 $^{O}A^{2}$	P-gp Substrate	No	
Water Solubility		CYP 1A2 Inhibitor	No	
Log S (ESOL)	-7.82	CYP2C19 Inhibitor	No	
Solubility	6.42E-06 mg/ml; 1.50E-08 mol/l	CYP2C9 Inhibitor	No	
Class	Poorly soluble	CYP2D6 Inhibitor	No	
Log S(Ali)	-9.42	CYP3A4 Inhibitor	No	
Solubility	1.63E-07 mg/ml; 3.81E-10 mol/l	Log K_p (skin permeation)	-2.44 cm/s	
Class	Poorly soluble	**Medicinal chemistry**		
Log S (SILICOS-IT)	-5.86	Pains	0 alert	
Solubility	5.86E-04 mg/ml; 1.37E-06 mol/l	Brenk	1 alert	
Class	Moderately Soluble	Lead likeness	No; 2 violations	
Drug likeness		Synthetic accessibility	6.34	
Lipinski	No; 1 violations	**Toxicity**		
Ghose	No; 3 violations	HERG	Weak inhibitor	0.8027
Veber	Yes	HERG Inhibition	Non-inhibitor	0.7104
Egan	No; 1 violations	AMES Toxicity	Non AMES toxic	0.9132
Muegge	No; 2 violations	Carcinogens	Non-carcinogens	0.9182
Bioavailability score	0.55	Acute Oral Toxicity	I	0.4287
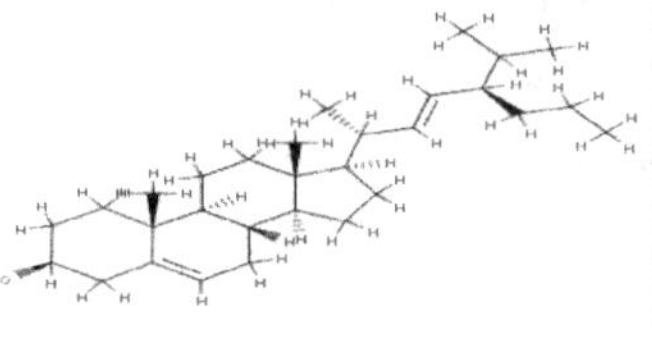		Carcinogenicity (three class)	Non-required	0.5888
		Acute rat toxicity	2.6561	LD50, mol/kg
		Fish Toxicity	-0.2094	pLC50, mg/L
		TPT	1.2496	pIGC50, ug/L

Table 120: The canonical SMILE, IUPAC name, Physicochemical properties, Hydrophilicity, Lipophilicity, Pharmacokinetics, Druglikeliness, Medicinal Chemistry, and Toxicity profile showing the secondary metabolite of *L. inermis*, Derivative, Stigmasterol Derivative 145.

CANONICAL SMILES:				
CC[C@H](C(C)C)/C=C/[C@H]([C@H]1CC[C@@H]2[C@]1(C)CC[C@H]1[C@H]2C(N)C=C2[C@]1(C)CC[C@@H](C2)O)C				
IUPAC Name				
(1R,3aS,3bS,7S,9aR,9bS,11aR)-4-amino-1-[(3E)-5-ethyl-6-methylhept-3-en-2-yl]-9a,11a-dimethyl-1H,2H,3H,3aH,3bH,4H,6H,7H,8H,9H,9aH,9bH,10H,11H,11aH-cyclopenta[a]phenanthren-7-ol				
Physicochemical Properties		**Lipophilicity**		
Formula	C29H49NO	Log $P_{o/w}$ (iLOGP)	4.74	
Molecular Weight	427.71 g/mol	Log $P_{o/w}$ (XLOGP3)	7.19	
Num. heavy atoms	31	Log $P_{o/w}$ (WLOGP)	6.74	
Num. arom. heavy atoms	0	Log $P_{o/w}$ (MLOGP)	5.70	
Fraction Csp3	0.86	Log $P_{o/w}$ (SILICOS-IT)	5.74	
Num. rotatable bonds	5	Consensus Log $P_{o/w}$	6.02	
Num. H-bond acceptors	2	**Pharmacokinetics**		
Num. H-bond donors	2	GI absorption	High	
Molar Refractivity	135.46	BBB Permeability	No	
TPSA	46.25 $^{O}A^{2}$	P-gp Substrate	No	
Water Solubility		CYP 1A2 Inhibitor	No	
Log S (ESOL)	-6.69	CYP2C19 Inhibitor	No	
Solubility	8.70E-05 mg/ml; 2.03E-07 mol/l	CYP2C9 Inhibitor	No	
Class	Poorly soluble	CYP2D6 Inhibitor	No	
Log S(Ali)	-7.98	CYP3A4 Inhibitor	No	
Solubility	4.44E-06 mg/ml; 1.04E-08 mol/l	Log K_p (skin permeation)	-3.8 cm/s	
Class	Poorly soluble	**Medicinal chemistry**		
Log S (SILICOS-IT)	-4.87	Pains	0 alert	
Solubility	5.81E-03 mg/ml; 1.36E-05 mol/l	Brenk	1 alert	
Class	Moderately Soluble	Lead likeness	No; 2 violations	
Drug likeness		Synthetic accessibility	6.20	
Lipinski	No; 1 violations	**Toxicity**		
Ghose	No; 3 violations	HERG	Weak inhibitor	0.9023
Veber	Yes	HERG Inhibition	Non-inhibitor	0.6819
Egan	No; 1 violations	AMES Toxicity	Non AMES toxic	0.8533
Muegge	No; 1 violations	Carcinogens	Non-carcinogens	0.9122
Bioavailability score	0.55	Acute Oral Toxicity	III	0.6146
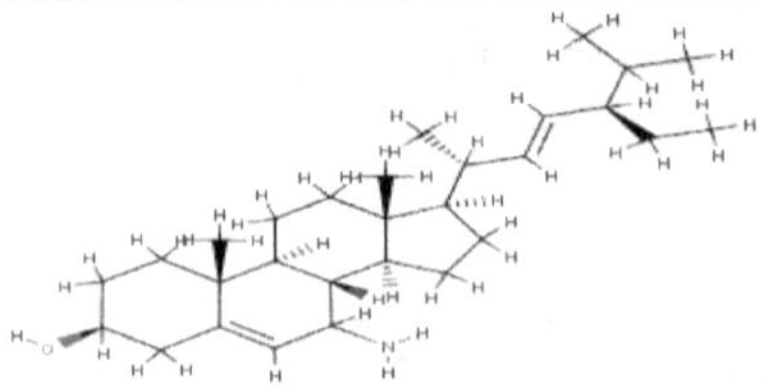		Carcinogenicity (three class)	Non-required	0.5180
		Acute rat toxicity	2.8110	LD50, mol/kg
		Fish Toxicity	0.4944	pLC50, mg/L
		TPT	0.8489	pIGC50, ug/L

Table 121: The canonical SMILE, IUPAC name, Physicochemical properties, Hydrophilicity, Lipophilicity, Pharmacokinetics, Druglikeliness, Medicinal Chemistry, and Toxicity profile showing the secondary metabolite of *L. inermis*, Derivative, Stigmasterol Derivative 181.

CANONICAL SMILES: NC[C@@H]([C@H]1CC[C@@H]2[C@]1(C)CC[C@H]1[C@H]2CC=C2[C@]1(C)CC[C@@H](C2)O)/C=C/[C@@H](C(C)C)CC				
IUPAC Name (1R,3aS,3bS,7S,9aR,9bS,11aS)-1-[(3E)-1-amino-5-ethyl-6-methylhept-3-en-2-yl]-9a,11a-dimethyl-1H,2H,3H,3aH,3bH,4H,6H,7H,8H,9H,9aH,9bH,10H,11H,11aH-cyclopenta[a]phenanthren-7-ol				
Physicochemical Properties		**Lipophilicity**		
Formula	C29H49NO	Log $P_{o/w}$ (iLOGP)	4.74	
Molecular Weight	427.71 g/mol	Log $P_{o/w}$ (XLOGP3)	7.08	
Num. heavy atoms	31	Log $P_{o/w}$ (WLOGP)	6.74	
Num. arom. heavy atoms	0	Log $P_{o/w}$ (MLOGP)	5.70	
Fraction Csp3	0.86	Log $P_{o/w}$ (SILICOS-IT)	6.02	
Num. rotatable bonds	6	Consensus Log $P_{o/w}$	6.06	
Num. H-bond acceptors	2	**Pharmacokinetics**		
Num. H-bond donors	2	GI absorption	High	
Molar Refractivity	135.46	BBB Permeability	No	
TPSA	46.25 $^{O}A^2$	P-gp Substrate	No	
Water Solubility		CYP 1A2 Inhibitor	No	
Log S (ESOL)	-6.56	CYP2C19 Inhibitor	No	
Solubility	1.19E-04 mg/ml; 2.78E-07 mol/l	CYP2C9 Inhibitor	No	
Class	Poorly soluble	CYP2D6 Inhibitor	No	
Log S(Ali)	-7.78	CYP3A4 Inhibitor	No	
Solubility	5.78E-06 mg/ml; 1.35E-08 mol/l	Log K_p (skin permeation)	-3.88 cm/s	
Class	Poorly soluble	**Medicinal chemistry**		
Log S (SILICOS-IT)	-5.12	Pains	0 alert	
Solubility	3.28E-03 mg/ml; 7.67E-06 mol/l	Brenk	1 alert	
Class	Moderately Soluble	Lead likeness	No; 2 violations	
Drug likeness		Synthetic accessibility	6.22	
Lipinski	No; 1 violations	**Toxicity**		
Ghose	No; 3 violations	HERG	Weak inhibitor	0.8122
Veber	Yes	HERG Inhibition	Inhibitor	0.5205
Egan	No; 1 violations	AMES Toxicity	Non AMES toxic	0.8485
Muegge	No; 1 violations	Carcinogens	Non-carcinogens	0.8856
Bioavailability score	0.55	Acute Oral Toxicity	III	0.6765
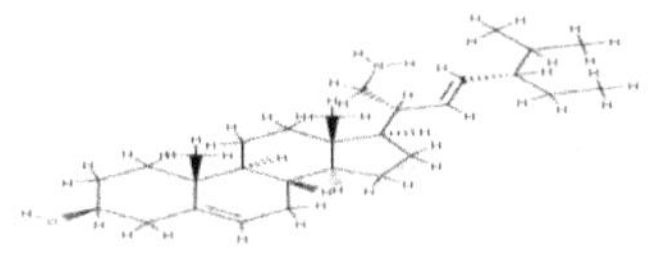		Carcinogenicity (three class)	Non-required	0.5623
		Acute rat toxicity	2.5012	LD50, mol/kg
		Fish Toxicity	0.7579	pLC50, mg/L
		TPT	0.8143	pIGC50, ug/L

5.9 Discussion

The protein that is present constitutively are acted as a drug target which is docked with the ligand, a secondary metabolite selected from *A. indica* and *L. inermis*, and it shows as good targets that impair the metabolic functions of the fungal organism. The binding affinity, total energy, Van der Waals forces between the protein and ligand showed that these are useful as a fungal target by binding and modulating the activity of the protein.

The target, 1, 3-β Glucan synthase was observed an excellent binding affinity in all the ligands. In a study by Sawistowska-Schriider, it was observed that the echinocandin group of anti-fungal drugs which are cyclic peptides that inhibit 1, 3-β Glucan synthase present in a mixed membrane fraction from *C. albicans* (259). In another study by Liu J, the inhibition of 1, 3-β glucan synthase enzyme by lipopeptide anti-fungal drugs trigger the cell cycle specific feedback mechanism which leads to cell arrest(133). In a study by Jimenez-Ortigosa, the drugs belong to echinocandins are first-line agents for severe invasive fungal infections, yeast was observed as cidal and molds as static by suppressing the synthesis of β-1,3-D-glucan, the vital ingredient of the cell wall of fungal organism (260). In research by Scott S. Walker, a novel class of a piperazinyl-pyridazinone group of Glucan Synthase inhibitor with oral efficacy in a murine model on *Candida glabrata* infection predicts as more potent than echinocandin with peroral administration (261). As per Jeyam et al., there was a functional interaction between 1, 3-Beta glucan synthase with 20 phytoconstituents present in the naturally obtained plants and the inhibition of this enzyme, 1, 3-β glucan synthase was better than Echinocandins (262). In a study by Juan et al., homoallylamines exhibit similar and stronger antifungal activity in inhibiting the 1, 3-β glucan synthase against *E.floccosum* and *M.canis* in comparison with polyene antibiotics and imidazoles (263). In a statement by Onishi that lipopeptide antifungal agents are more potent drugs against aspergillosis spp. and candidiasis spp. by inhibiting 1, 3-β glucan synthase (264).

The chitin synthase, another drug target for fungal growth inhibition observed as having higher binding affinity than Clotrimazole with azadirachtin, nimbin, nimonol, lawsoniaside, and stigmasterol. In a study by Joann P. Gaughran, the effectiveness of nikkomycins and polyoxins group of drugs depends to some extent on peptide transport systems and intracellular proteases which may degrade these agents. The Minimum Inhibitory Concentration (MIC) of nikkomycin for ECY36-3C is significantly more than 50 percent inhibitory concentration for the Chs3 enzyme, *Saccharomyces cerevisiae* cells exhibiting only Chs3 activity are sensitive to nikkomycin Z, while the cells showing Chs2 enzyme are not sensitive (265).

The binding affinity of the drug target Chitinase is observed as good with all the ligands as azadirachtin, nimbin, nimonol, lawsoniaside, and stigmasterol was more than with the standard drug Clotrimazole. According to Pocsi et al., chitinases are the most potential antifungal target as his findings exhibited that allosamandin inhibits hyphal fragments and the distribution of hyphal elements of various morphological forms and autolysis of mycelium of *Penicillium chrysogenum*(266). In a study by Arlorio M, the composite of chitinase and Beta-1, 3-glucanase extracted from pea pods was identified to inhibit the surge of various fungi. These enzymes inhibited the growth of the *Trichoderma longibrachiatum* is the consequence of a thinning of the cell wall in the hyphal apex which leads to an asymmetry of turgor pressure and wall tension that experienced to swell and burst the hyphal tip (267). According to Pranav Vyas, Chitinases can digest chitin the vital constituent of the cell wall in many of the phytopathogens such as *R.solani*, Bipolaris spp. *A. raphani*, *A. brassicicola* (268).

The deuterolysin is a member of Zn^{+2} metalloendopeptidases family, the binding affinity of the deuterolysin with the ligands has been observed great affinity as azadirachtin, nimbin, nimonol, lawsoniaside, and stigmasterol was more than the standard Clotrimazole. Metalloproteases are the enzymes secreted by peptidases with their capability to downgrade the *Matrix Extracellularis* proteins like elastin and collagen, and these are found to be acting like virulence factors in fungal organisms. According to Sharpton et al., the deuterolysin (M35) family genes are interestingly expanded in both the Coccidioides genus organisms and *Uncinocarpus reesii* organisms and that Coccidioides was found that they acquired three more M35 family genes with than of *Uncinocarpus reesii*(269).

Fungalysin is the other targeted protein that also observed very excellent binding affinity towards the ligands to modulate the mechanism of protein action which is a unique family of zinc-dependent peptidases. The Fungalysin is M36 metallopeptidase which functions as like as Deuterolysin (M35) to prevent the degradation of *Matrix Extracellularis* proteins on inhibition. The binding affinity was observed as more than Clotrimazole for azadirachtin, nimbin, nimonol, lawsoniaside, and stigmasterol. According to Anne Mathy, the actin gene was transcribed in the four tested strains of *Microsporum canis* in experiments of arthroconidia, adherence, invasion and observed undetectable transcription of fungalysin genes in arthroconidia or during adherence or invasion lead to the suggestion of the proteolytic activity of fungalysin including the keratolytic activity of Mep3 gene. In a study by Olivier Jousson, it was observed that the growth of the *T. rubrum*, *Trichophyton mentagrophytes,* and *Microsporum canis* are inhibited by 55–75% with o-phenanthroline may be inhibition of proteolytic activity (270).

Another protein, homoserine dehydrogenase is also employed as a drug target for modifying by binding with the ligand. The homoserine dehydrogenase is helpful in the synthesis of non-essential amino acids where it catalyzes the intermediate step of aspartate metabolic pathway involved in both storages of asparagine and the synthesis of the aspartate family of amino acids. The binding affinity obtained to hamper the activity of this enzyme by the ligands involved is observed as more than with Clotrimazole. In a study by Skwarecki AS, the dipeptide antifungal chemicals like 5-hydroxy-4-oxo-l-norvaline (HONV) observed that inhibition of the outgrowth of human pathogenic yeast of Candida genus in the RPMI-1640 medium, with MIC values in between 32 and 64 mcg per mL (271). According to Hiroshi Yamaki, it was observed that an antibiotic 2-amino-4-oxo-5-hydroxypentanoic acid inhibits the biosynthesis of aspartate family of amino acids leads to inhibition of protein biosynthesis in *S.cerevisae* which was affected by blocking the biosynthesis of homoserine attributed by inactivation of homoserine dehydrogenase (272). In a study by Mariane C. Bagatin, it was identified as the two new amino acid derivative compounds, HS1 and HS2, are potential antifungal molecules that may affect the growth of paracoccidioidomycosis by inhibiting the homoserine dehydrogenase(273). According to Yamaki, RI-331 is a chemical entity which observed as an antifungal agent by inhibiting homoserine dehydrogenase which is based on the interfering with amino acid synthesis (241). In a study by Konishi, Oki, and Capobianco, cispentacin, a new antifungal drug with excellent *in vivo* activity that targets many cellular proteins that elevated the probability of interrupting with amino acid synthesis (274–276).

The lumazine synthase is vital in riboflavin metabolic pathway in many organisms, including the pathogens caused to human beings and many plants where the enzyme involved in their metabolic pathway. The binding affinity observed as more with all the ligands except scopoletin with lumazine synthase. In a study by Manish S. Bhatia, the 3Dimentional QSAR models observed as positive correlation of electronic descriptors with the antifungal activity of Lumazine synthase while the steric and hydrophobic descriptors observed as a negative correlation with the fungicidal activity of lumazine synthase(277). In research by Pankaj Kumar, the cloned Lumazine synthase from *Salmonella typhimurium* (sLS) contains an N-terminal proline residue (Pro11) which is considered to be found as the one to disorganize the formation of the icosahedral assembly. Along with the resemblance of the structure of sLS with orthologous lumazine synthase, structures allowed for the identification of the amino acid residues responsible for substrate binding and catalysis to serve as the earliest point for the production of species-specific agents (278).According to Ekaterina Morgunova, the knowledge of structural analysis, thermodynamics , molecular docking of proteins, and mechanistic force between them suggests as a four new drug entities known as 1,3,7-trihydro-9-D-ribityl-2,4,8-purinetrione-7-yl (TS13), 3-(1,3-dihydro-9-D-ribityl-2,4,8 purinetrione-7-yl)butane-1-phosphate (TS44), 4-(6,7(5H,8H)-dioxo-8-D-ribityllumazine-5-yl)butane 1-phosphate(GJ43), and [4-(6-chloro-2,4-

dioxo-1,2,3,4-tetrahydropyrimidin-5-yl)butyl] phosphate (JC33)) to inhibit the lumazine synthase in *C. albicans* (279).

Phosphoribosylaminoimidazole carboxylase is an enzyme affected the nucleotides by purine biosynthesis. The ligands which was found to be bound to this enzyme suggests that having the binding affinity more than the standard for azadirachtin, nimbin, nimonol, lawsoniaside, and stigmasterol which suggests as these are right small molecules to modulate the receptor. According to Matthew Donovan, the potentiality of the Phosphoribosylaminoimidazole carboxylase was proved by inhibiting the *ade2* allele gene that ameliorates the virulence and pathogenicity of *C. albicans* (280). In a study by John R. Perfect, the glucocorticoid-induced cryptococcal meningitis induced in rabbits was used to assess the role of the Phosphoribosylaminoimidazole gene (*4DE2*) for virulence of *C. neoformans*, in his research an *ade2* auxotroph, wild-type strain of H99, and a randomly selected prototrophic transforming of MOO1 which had received the cloned *ADE2* cDNA copy (242).

Protein elongation factor is a vital protein which catalyzes the ribosomal translocation process in protein synthesis cascade in eukaryotic organisms. It was observed that the ligands are bound to the protein elongation factor and modulate the function of that protein. The binding affinity and total energy are helpful to decide the function of the protein. The ligands which are involved are showing excellent binding affinity compared with standard drug except for lawsone. According to Moldave, the cells of fungal organism and mammalian cells demand two soluble protein elongation factors, elongation factor 1 (EF-1a) and elongation factor 2 (EF-2) but for polypeptide chain elongation reactions of protein synthesis in fungal organism, an additional elongation factor 3 is required which is a good target and safe to the host (281,282). According to Juan Manuel Dominguez, the newer class of antifungal drugs, the sordarin group of molecules was observed to inhibit the protein synthesis. The sordarin was observed as 1%, 100% and 94 % protein synthesis inhibition against *C. albicans*, *Candida krusei*, *Candida parapsilosis* respectively in a 1 mcg per ml concentration (283). In a study by Shastry, the sordarin group of anti-fungal agents acts by hampering the function of eukaryotic elongation factor (eEF2). Mutations observed in this protein leads to resistance to a sordarin group of antibiotics. The amino acid residues that cross-linked with 521, 523, and 524 positions of *S. cerevisiae* eEF2 are the major contributor for sordarin pharmacological actions. They mapped fungal selectivity of anti-fungal drug sordarin as an eight-amino-acid region within eEF2 (284). In a study by Michael C. Justice, the *In-vitro* assays demonstrate that the sordarin sensitivity is dependent on the fungal*EF2* gene. In genomic studies of sordarin-resistant mutants of *S. cerevisiae* demonstrates that resistance to the drugs that inhibit are linked to the genes *EFT1* and *EFT2* that encodes the fungal *EF2*. The compound Sordarin inhibits the ribosomal translocation by stabilizing the fungal *EF2*-ribosome complex as like as fusidic acid (203). In a study by Laura Capa, the ribosomal protein in protein synthesis is observed to be significantly conserved in eukaryotic organisms except for fungi which present a soluble elongation factor (EF3). The translation elongation factor 2 (EF2), present in *S. cerevisiae* is translated from the *EFT1* and *EFT2* genes, which is a target for natural product sordarin. Mutations on EF2 clustered protein leads to loss of the capacity to bind to the agents by modulating the expected drug binding pocket on a virtual model of EF2 and mutant cell extracts (285).

The Sulphite reductase is an enzyme of iron protein that involves in sulphur metabolism which catalyzes sulphite to hydrogen sulphide and water. The binding affinity of the ligands and with sulphite reductase is to modulate the protein which observes as that these are having more affinity than conventional Clotrimazole except lawsone and scopoletin. According to Yuhko Aoki, the drug Azoxybacillin, antifungal drug produced by *B. cereus* in methionine-free medium which is due to the inhibition of sulfite fixation by the inclusion of [35S] sulfate into fractions of *S.cerevisae* which are acid-insoluble in nature under circumstances in which almost nearly zero inhibition was showed for DNA, RNA, or protein synthesis but by the involvement of the activity of enzymes for sulfate assimilation means that it inhibits the induction of those enzymes when *S. cerevisiae* cells are transplanted from a rich medium to synthetic methionine-free medium (286). In a study by Jessica Noble, the investigation on the kinetics of Sulphur dioxide (SO2) by two strains, one high and another low sulphite producer which shows as these strains exhibited common profiles, but only the high-sulfite strain continued to produce Sulphur dioxide in the stationary phase. In the transcriptomic studies, the data suggests as low-sulfite producer strain over expressed genes of the sulfur assimilation pathway. The Quantitative trait locus (QTL) mapping strategy used to establish MET2 and SKP2 genes accountable for phenotypic differences between strains which curb the activity of both branches of the sulphur amino acid synthesis and modulate sulfite/sulfide production (287). In a study by Fujji, the drug Azoxybacillin is chemically [(3S)-3-Amino-4-hydroxy-4-oxobutyl]-methyliminooxidoazanium isolated from *Bacillus cereus* is observed as to impede the five enzymes that are induced in Sulphate Assimilation Pathway due to the inhibition sulfite reductase enzyme in a minimum inhibition concentration (MIC) <10 mcg per ml. (212).

5.10 Conclusion

The infections caused by eukaryotic fungal organisms in this world are over 300 million, and 25 million are at jeopardy of severe infections in a 2012 epidemiology status. Fungal diseases are systemic infections and topical infections while the invasions of fungal infections are common and life-threatening such as cryptococcosis infection, candidiasis infection, aspergillosis infection, and pneumocystosis infection, while dermatophytosis caused by dermatophytes (Trichophyton spp., Microsporum spp., Epidermophyton spp.) are not so severe. The opportunistic infections caused by the injudicious use of corticosteroids and AIDS are more dangerous. The currently marked formulations in the treatment of fungal infections are majorly azoles for systemic infections, and others also can be used cautiously as these are well known for untoward effects. The newer drugs with a newer approach to mitigate the growth of the fungal organism are essential. In this view, the *in-silico* drug discovery is a boon in this period to get a safer and highly efficacious agent. Here in this research, we identified the most promising proteins which modulate their structure when it binds with a small molecule. The proteins subjected in this study are 1, 3-Beta Glucan synthase, chitinase, chitin synthase, deuterolysin, fungalysin, homoserine dehydrogenase, lumazine synthase, Phosphoribosylaminoimidazole carboxylase, protein elongation factor 3, and sulphite reductase. The ligands or small molecules are taken from two plants secondary metabolites that are well known for their antimicrobial properties. The plants are *A. indica*, and *L. inermis* and their secondary metabolites are azadirachtin, nimbin, nimonol, are from neem plant, and lawsone, lawsoniaside, scopoletin, stigmasterol are from henna plant. The standard drug, Clotrimazole is also subjected to this study. The software used for this study is Modeller for performing homology model as the protein 3 D structure was not available in the RCSB database, procheck for validation of the homology modeled protein, iGEMDOCK 2.0 for making rough docking to get the energy values of docked protein and ligand, Autodock is for accurate docking, SwissADME online tool for getting the derivatives of the ligands, admetSAR also an online tool used to know the pharmacokinetic and toxicity profile of the ligand and their derivatives. For visualization of the docked poses was with the help of Pymol software. In the *in-silico* analysis, the ligand was bound to the protein and modulates the function which can be analyzed by the binding affinity observed between the two. The ligands which are selected for this study was analyzed and found that they have almost all the properties that obey for a Hit molecule or Lead molecule of new drug entity with minimum violations. The Derivatives or structure-activity relative molecules (SAR) of the ligands like azadirachtin 105 derivatives; nimbin with 124 derivatives; nimonol of 144 derivatives; lawsone with 112 derivatives; lawsoniaside of 191 derivatives; scopoletin of 140 derivatives and stigmasterol with 193 derivatives are successfully derived with a software which are also having similar properties that are obeys Hit or Lead. Out of these derivatives, the most best-suited one in each was selected for docking which is tested for total energy, Van der Waals force and H-bond between them. The ligands and their best-suited molecules are observed as excellent small molecules for modulating the protein which may be useful in mitigating the virulence of fungal organisms and making the recipient a disease-free by further proceeding the research with these Hit or Lead molecules for *in-vivo* studies.

Finally the secondary metabolite of *L. inermis*, Lawsoniaside derivatives are showing very excellent interaction among all the selected proteins; the secondary metabolite of *A. indica*, Azadirachtin derivatives are showing very excellent interaction among all the selected proteins and the sulphite reductase as an excellent drug target as it is exhibiting best interaction with many ligands and their derivatives.

The lawsoniaside derivative 151 (SAR 4) with IUPAC no: (2R,3S,4S,5R,6S)-2-[(aminooxy)methyl]-6-[(3-hydroxy-4-{[(2S,3R,4S,5S,6R)-3,4,5-trihydroxy-6-(hydroxymethyl)oxan-2-yl]oxy}naphthalen-1-yl)oxy]oxane-3,4,5-triol which presented in figure 27 with the protein Deuterolysin (exhibited as total energy between the protein and ligand as -141.325 Kcal per mol, Van der Waals force between them as -78.6451 Kcal per mol, and H-bond between them as -62.6802 Kcal per mol).

The lawsoniaside derivative 124 (SAR 3) with IUPAC no: (2S,3R,4S,5S,6R)-2-[(3-hydroperoxy-4-{[(2S,3R,4S,5S,6R)-3,4,5-trihydroxy-6-(hydroxymethyl)oxan-2-yl]oxy}naphthalen-1-yl)oxy]-6-(hydroxymethyl)oxane-3,4,5-triol which presented in figure 27 with an enzyme Sulphite reductase (exhibited as total energy between the protein and ligand as -174.222 Kcal per mol, Van der Waals force between them as -122.808 Kcal per mol, and H-bond between them as -51.4136 Kcal per mol).

The lawsoniaside derivative 1 (SAR 1) with IUPAC no: (2S,3R,4S,5S,6R)-2-[(2-hydroxy-5-methyl-4-{[(2S,3R,4S,5S,6R)-3,4,5-trihydroxy-6-(hydroxymethyl)oxan-2-yl]oxy}naphthalen-1-yl)oxy]-6-(hydroxymethyl)oxane-3,4,5-triol which presented in figure 27 with an enzyme Sulphite reductase (exhibited as total energy between the protein and ligand as -141.83 Kcal per mol, Van der Waals force between them as -91.8411 Kcal per mol, and H-bond between them as -49.9894 Kcal per mol).

The azadirachtin structure derivative 2 (SAR 1) with IUPAC no: 4,11-dimethyl (1S,4S,5R,6S,7S,8R,11S,12R,14S,15R)-12-(acetyloxy)-4,7-dihydroxy-6-[(1S,2S,6R,8S,9R,11S)-2-hydroxy-11-methyl-7,10-dioxatetracyclo[6.3.1.$0^{2},^{6}$.$0^{9},^{11}$]dodec-3-en-9-yl]-6-methyl-14-{[(2E)-2-methylbut-2-enoyl]oxy}-3,9-dioxatetracyclo[6.6.1.$0^{1},^{5}$.$0^{11},^{15}$]pentadecane-4,11-dicarboxylate which presented in figure 28 with Phosphoribosylaminoimidazole carboxylase (exhibited total energy between the protein and ligand as -181.62 Kcal per mol, Van der Waals force between them as -136.741 Kcal per mol, and H-bond between them as -44.8791 Kcal per mol).

The Lawsoniaside structure Derivative 75(SAR 2) with IUPAC no: (2S,3R,4S,5S,6R)-4,5-dihydroxy-2-[(2-hydroxy-4-{[(2S,3R,4S,5S,6R)-3,4,5-trihydroxy-6-(hydroxymethyl)oxan-2-yl]oxy}naphthalen-1-yl)oxy]-6-(hydroxymethyl)oxan-3-yl hypofluorite which presented in figure 27 with sulphite reductase (exhibited as total energy between the protein and ligand as -150.141 Kcal per mol, Van der Waals force between them as -107.959 Kcal per mol, and H-bond between them as -42.1825 Kcal per mol).

The Lawsoniaside structure Derivative 151(SAR 4) with IUPAC no: (2R,3S,4S,5R,6S)-2-[(aminooxy)methyl]-6-[(3-hydroxy-4-{[(2S,3R,4S,5S,6R)-3,4,5-trihydroxy-6-(hydroxymethyl)oxan-2-yl]oxy}naphthalen-1-yl)oxy]oxane-3,4,5-triol which presented in figure 27 with sulphite reductase (exhibited as total energy between the protein and ligand as -164.854 Kcal per mol, Van der Waals force between them as -123.926 Kcal per mol, and H-bond between them as -40.9282 Kcal per mol).

The Azadirachtin structure Derivative 58(SAR 4) with IUPAC no: 4,11-dimethyl (1S,4S,5R,6S,7S,8R,11S,12R,14S,15R)-12-(ethanimidoyloxy)-4,7-dihydroxy-6-[(1S,2S,6S,8S,9R,11S)-2-hydroxy-11-methyl-5,7,10-trioxatetracyclo[6.3.1.$0^{2,6}$.$0^{9,11}$]dodec-3-en-9-yl]-6-methyl-14-{[(2E)-2-methylbut-2-enoyl]oxy}-3,9-dioxatetracyclo[6.6.1.$0^{1,5}$.$0^{11,15}$]pentadecane-4,11-dicarboxylate which presented in figure 28 with fungalysin (exhibited as total energy between the protein and ligand as -164.763 Kcal per mol, Van der Waals force between them as -124.717 Kcal per mol, and H-bond between them as -40.0461 Kcal per mol).

The Lawsoniaside structure Derivative 182(SAR 5) with IUPAC no: (2S,3R,4S,5S,6R)-4,5-dihydroxy-2-[(3-hydroxy-4-{[(2S,3R,4S,5S,6R)-3,4,5-trihydroxy-6-(hydroxymethyl)oxan-2-yl]oxy}naphthalen-1-yl)oxy]-6-(hydroxymethyl)oxan-3-yl hypofluorite which presented in figure 27 with sulphite reductase (exhibited as total energy between the protein and ligand as -168.151 Kcal per mol, Van der Waals force between them as -128.608 Kcal per mol, and H-bond between them as -39.5427 Kcal per mol).

The Azadirachtin structure Derivative 81(SAR 5) with IUPAC no: 4,11-dimethyl (1S,4S,5R,6S,7S,8R,11S,12R,14S,15R)-12-(acetyloxy)-14-{[(2Z)-2-(bromomethyl)but-2-enoyl]oxy}-4,7-dihydroxy-6-[(1S,2S,6S,8S,9R,11S)-2-hydroxy-11-methyl-5,7,10-

trioxatetracyclo[6.3.1.$0^{2,6}$.$0^{9,11}$]dodec-3-en-9-yl]-6-methyl-3,9-dioxatetracyclo[6.6.1.$0^{1,5}$.$0^{11,15}$]pentadecane-4,11-dicarboxylate which presented in figure 28 with sulphite reductase (exhibited as total energy between the protein and ligand as -226.658 Kcal per mol, Van der Waals force between them as -189.755 Kcal per mol, and H-bond between them as -36.9027 Kcal per mol).

The Azadirachtin structure Derivative 19(SAR 2) with IUPAC no: 4,11-dimethyl (1S,4S,5R,6S,7S,8R,11S,12R,14S,15R)-12-(acetyloxy)-4,7-dihydroxy-6-[(1S,2S,6R,8S,9R,11S)-2-hydroxy-11-methyl-5,10-dioxa-7-azatetracyclo[6.3.1.$0^{2,6}$.$0^{9,11}$]dodec-3-en-9-yl]-6-methyl-14-{[(2E)-2-methylbut-2-enoyl]oxy}-3,9-dioxatetracyclo[6.6.1.$0^{1,5}$.$0^{11,15}$]pentadecane-4,11-dicarboxylate which presented in figure 28 with Lumazine synthase (exhibited as total energy between the protein and ligand as -171.633 Kcal per mol, Van der Waals force between them as -135.127 Kcal per mol, and H-bond between them as -36.5057 Kcal per mol).

A plausible hypothesis is that the derivatives of lawsoniaside (*L.inermis*) and azadirachtin (*A.indica*) are observed as excellent ligands for all the drug targets in the fungal organism and sulphite reductase is an enzyme observed as a suitable drug target as it allows to bind all the derivatives of the ligands of *A.indica* and *L.inermis* as presented above.

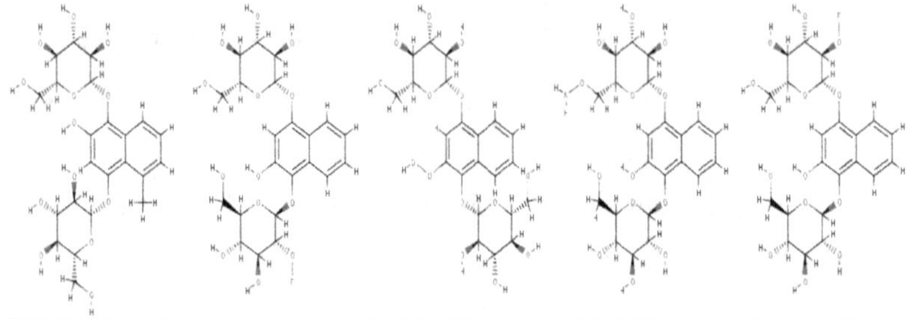

(2S,3R,4S,5S,6R)-2-[(2-hydroxy-5-methyl-4-{[(2S,3R,4S,5S,6R)-3,4,5-trihydroxy-6-(hydroxymethyl)oxan-2-yl]oxy}naphthalen-1-yl)oxy]-6-(hydroxymethyl)oxane-3,4,5-triol

(2S,3R,4S,5S,6R)-4,5-dihydroxy-2-[(2-hydroxy-4-{[(2S,3R,4S,5S,6R)-3,4,5-trihydroxy-6-(hydroxymethyl)oxan-2-yl]oxy}naphthalen-1-yl)oxy]-6-(hydroxymethyl)oxan-3-yl hypofluorite

(2S,3R,4S,5S,6R)-2-[(3-hydroperoxy-4-{[(2S,3R,4S,5S,6R)-3,4,5-trihydroxy-6-(hydroxymethyl)oxan-2-yl]oxy}naphthalen-1-yl)oxy]-6-(hydroxymethyl)oxane-3,4,5-triol

(2R,3S,4S,5R,6S)-2-[(aminooxy)methyl]-6-[(3-hydroxy-4-{[(2S,3R,4S,5S,6R)-3,4,5-trihydroxy-6-(hydroxymethyl)oxan-2-yl]oxy}naphthalen-1-yl)oxy]oxane-3,4,5-triol

(2S,3R,4S,5S,6R)-4,5-dihydroxy-2-[(3-hydroxy-4-{[(2S,3R,4S,5S,6R)-3,4,5-trihydroxy-6-(hydroxymethyl)oxan-2-yl]oxy}naphthalen-1-yl)oxy]-6-(hydroxymethyl)oxan-3-yl hypofluorite

Figure 27: The chemical structures with IUPAC name of the derivatives of lawsoniaside.

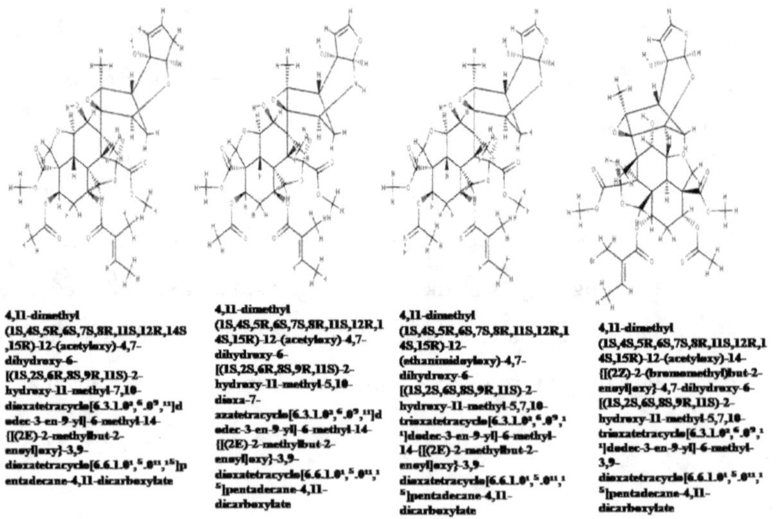

4,11-dimethyl (1S,4S,5R,6S,7S,8R,11S,12R,14S,15R)-12-(acetyloxy)-4,7-dihydroxy-6-[(1S,2S,6R,8S,9R,11S)-2-hydroxy-11-methyl-7,10-dioxatetracyclo[6.3.1.0^{2,6}.0^{9,13}]dodec-3-en-9-yl]-6-methyl-14-{[(2E)-2-methylbut-2-enoyl]oxy}-3,9-dioxatetracyclo[6.6.1.0^{1,5}.0^{11,15}]pentadecane-4,11-dicarboxylate

4,11-dimethyl (1S,4S,5R,6S,7S,8R,11S,12R,14S,15R)-12-(acetyloxy)-4,7-dihydroxy-6-[(1S,2S,6R,8S,9R,11S)-2-hydroxy-11-methyl-5,10-dioxa-7-azatetracyclo[6.3.1.0^{2,6}.0^{9,13}]dodec-3-en-9-yl]-6-methyl-14-{[(2E)-2-methylbut-2-enoyl]oxy}-3,9-dioxatetracyclo[6.6.1.0^{1,5}.0^{11,15}]pentadecane-4,11-dicarboxylate

4,11-dimethyl (1S,4S,5R,6S,7S,8R,11S,12R,14S,15R)-12-(ethanimidoyloxy)-4,7-dihydroxy-6-[(1S,2S,6S,8S,9R,11S)-2-hydroxy-11-methyl-5,7,10-trioxatetracyclo[6.3.1.0^{2,6}.0^{9,11}]dodec-3-en-9-yl]-6-methyl-14-{[(2E)-2-methylbut-2-enoyl]oxy}-3,9-dioxatetracyclo[6.6.1.0^{1,5}.0^{11,15}]pentadecane-4,11-dicarboxylate

4,11-dimethyl (1S,4S,5R,6S,7S,8R,11S,12R,14S,15R)-12-(acetyloxy)-14-{[(2Z)-2-(bromomethyl)but-2-enoyl]oxy}-4,7-dihydroxy-6-[(1S,2S,6S,8S,9R,11S)-2-hydroxy-11-methyl-5,7,10-trioxatetracyclo[6.3.1.0^{2,6}.0^{9,11}]dodec-3-en-9-yl]-6-methyl-3,9-dioxatetracyclo[6.6.1.0^{1,5}.0^{11,15}]pentadecane-4,11-dicarboxylate

Figure 28: The chemical structures with IUPAC name of the derivatives of azadirachtin.

6. References

1. Dixon DM, McNeil MM, Cohen ML, Gellin BG, La Montagne JR. Fungal infections: a growing threat. Public Health Rep. 1996;111(3):226–35.

2. Ravikant KT, Gupte S, Kaur M. A Review on Emerging Fungal Infections and Their Significance. J Bacteriol Mycol. 2015;1:9–11.

3. Ellis D, Marriott D, Hajjeh RA, Warnock D, Meyer W, Barton R. Epidemiology: surveillance of fungal infections. Med Mycol. 2000;38 Suppl 1:173–82.

4. Pappas PG, Alexander BD, Andes DR, Hadley S, Kauffman CA, Freifeld A, et al. Invasive fungal infections among organ transplant recipients: results of the Transplant-Associated Infection Surveillance Network (TRANSNET). Clin Infect Dis. 2010;50(8):1101–1111.

5. Brooks GF, Carroll KC, Butel JS, Morse SA. The growth, survival, & death of microorganisms. Jawetz Melnick Adelbergs Med Microbiol 24th Ed Mc Graw Hill N Y. 2007;52–61.

6. Das K, Basak S, Ray S. A study on superficial fungal infection from West Bengal: A brief report. J Life Sci. 2009;1(1):51–55.

7. Chopra RN, Nayar SL, Chopra IC, Asolkar LV, Kakkar KK, Chakre OJ, et al. Glossary of Indian medicinal plants ; [with] Supplement. New Delhi: Council of Scientific & Industrial Research; 1956.

8. Rao VS, Srinivas K. Modern drug discovery process: an in silico approach. J Bioinforma Seq Anal. 2011;3(5):89–94.

9. DiMasi JA, Hansen RW, Grabowski HG, Lasagna L. Cost of innovation in the pharmaceutical industry. J Health Econ. 1991 Jul;10(2):107–42.

10. Accounting For R&D | June 19, 2006 Issue - Vol. 84 Issue 25 | Chemical & Engineering News [Internet]. [cited 2018 Dec 30]. Available from: https://cen.acs.org/articles/84/i25/Accounting-RD.html

11. Taft CA, Da Silva VB. Current topics in computer-aided drug design. J Pharm Sci. 2008;97(3):1089–1098.

12. Bernard D, Coop A, MacKerell J, Alexander D. Computer-aided drug design: Structure-activity relationships of delta opioid ligands. Drug Des Rev-Online. 2005;2(4):277–291.

13. Chothia C, Lesk AM. The relation between the divergence of sequence and structure in proteins. EMBO J. 1986 Apr;5(4):823–6.

14. Saxena A. Reverse Pharmacology: A New Approach To Drug Development. Innoriginal Int J Sci. 2015;

15. Takenaka T. Classical vs reverse pharmacology in drug discovery. BJU Int. 2001;88:7–10.

16. Patwardhan B, Vaidya AD, Chorghade M, Joshi SP. Reverse pharmacology and systems approaches for drug discovery and development. Curr Bioact Compd. 2008;4(4):201–212.

17. Hube B, Hay R, Brasch J, Veraldi S, Schaller M. Dermatomycoses and inflammation: The adaptive balance between growth, damage, and survival. J Mycol Medicale. 2015;25(1):e44–e58.

18. Romani L. Immunity to fungal infections. Nat Rev Immunol. 2011;11(4):275.

19. Brasch J, Zaldua M. Enzyme patterns of dermatophytes: Enzymmuster von Dermatophyten. Mycoses. 1994;37(1–2):11–16.

20. Monod M. Secreted proteases from dermatophytes. Mycopathologia. 2008;166(5–6):285.

21. Brock M. Fungal metabolism in host niches. Curr Opin Microbiol. 2009;12(4):371–376.

22. Nenoff P, Krüger C, Ginter-Hanselmayer G, Tietz H-J. Dermatomycoses: causative agents, epidemiology and pathogenesis. J Dtsch Dermatol Ges J Ger Soc Dermatol JDDG. 2014 Mar;12(3):188–209; quiz 210, 188–211; 212.

23. Rodwell GE, Bayles CL, Towersey L, Aly R. The prevalence of dermatophyte infection in patients infected with human immunodeficiency virus. Int J Dermatol. 2008;47(4):339–343.

24. Peres NT de A, Maranhão FCA, Rossi A, Martinez-Rossi NM. Dermatophytes: host-pathogen interaction and antifungal resistance. An Bras Dermatol. 2010;85(5):657–667.

25. Ogawa H, Summerbell RC, Clemons KV, Koga T, Ran YP, Rashid A, et al. Dermatophytes and host defence in cutaneous mycoses. Med Mycol. 1998;36:166–173.

26. Martinez-Rossi NM, Persinoti GF, Peres NT, Rossi A. Role of pH in the pathogenesis of dermatophytoses. Mycoses. 2012;55(5):381–387.

27. Zurita J, Hay RJ. Adherence of dermatophyte microconidia and arthroconidia to human keratinocytes in vitro. J Invest Dermatol. 1987;89(5).

28. Duek L, Kaufman G, Ulman Y, Berdicevsky I. The pathogenesis of dermatophyte infections in human skin sections. J Infect. 2004;48(2):175–180.

29. Kaufman G, Horwitz BA, Duek L, Ullman Y, Berdicevsky I. Infection stages of the dermatophyte pathogen Trichophyton: microscopic characterization and proteolytic enzymes. Med Mycol. 2007;45(2):149–155.

30. Esquenazi D, De Souza W, Sales Alviano C, Rozental S. The role of surface carbohydrates on the interaction of microconidia of Trichophyton mentagrophytes with epithelial cells. FEMS Immunol Med Microbiol. 2003;35(2):113–123.

31. Baldo A, Mathy A, Tabart J, Camponova P, Vermout S, Massart L, et al. Secreted subtilisin Sub3 from Microsporum canis is required for adherence to but not for invasion of the epidermis. Br J Dermatol. 2010;162(5):990–997.

32. Hung C-Y, Yu J-J, Seshan KR, Reichard U, Cole GT. A parasitic phase-specific adhesin of Coccidioides immitis contributes to the virulence of this respiratory fungal pathogen. Infect Immun. 2002;70(7):3443–3456.

33. Peres NT de A, Silva LG da, Santos R da S, Jacob TR, Persinoti GF, Rocha LB, et al. In vitro and ex vivo infection models help assess the molecular aspects of the interaction of Trichophyton rubrum with the host milieu. Sabouraudia. 2016;54(4):420–427.

34. Shiraki Y, Ishibashi Y, Hiruma M, Nishikawa A, Ikeda S. Cytokine secretion profiles of human keratinocytes during Trichophyton tonsurans and Arthroderma benhamiae infections. J Med Microbiol. 2006;55(9):1175–1185.

35. Li H, Wu S, Mao L, Lei G, Zhang L, Lu A, et al. Human pathogenic fungus Trichophyton schoenleinii activates the NLRP3 inflammasome. Protein Cell. 2013;4(7):529–538.

36. Mao L, Zhang L, Li H, Chen W, Wang H, Wu S, et al. Pathogenic fungus Microsporum canis activates the NLRP3 inflammasome. Infect Immun. 2014;82(2):882–892.

37. Yoshikawa FSY, Ferreira LG, de Almeida SR. IL-1 signaling inhibits Trichophyton rubrum conidia development and modulates the IL-17 response in vivo. Virulence. 2015;6(5):449–457.

38. Joly S, Sutterwala FS. Fungal pathogen recognition by the NLRP3 inflammasome. Virulence. 2010;1(4):276–280.

39. Lorenz MC, Fink GR. The glyoxylate cycle is required for fungal virulence. Nature. 2001;412(6842):83.

40. Staib P, Zaugg C, Mignon B, Weber J, Grumbt M, Pradervand S, et al. Differential gene expression in the pathogenic dermatophyte Arthroderma benhamiaein vitro versus during infection. Microbiology. 2010;156(3):884–895.

41. Maranhão FC, Paião FG, Martinez-Rossi NM. Isolation of transcripts over-expressed in human pathogen Trichophyton rubrum during growth in keratin. Microb Pathog. 2007;43(4):166–172.

42. Silveira HC, Gras DE, Cazzaniga RA, Sanches PR, Rossi A, Martinez-Rossi NM. Transcriptional profiling reveals genes in the human pathogen Trichophyton rubrum that are expressed in response to pH signaling. Microb Pathog. 2010;48(2):91–96.

43. De Maio A. Extracellular heat shock proteins, cellular export vesicles, and the Stress Observation System: a form of communication during injury, infection, and cell damage. It is never known how far a controversial finding will go! Dedicated to Ferruccio Ritossa. Cell Stress Chaperones. 2011 May;16(3):235–49.

44. Garrido C, Gurbuxani S, Ravagnan L, Kroemer G. Heat shock proteins: endogenous modulators of apoptotic cell death. Biochem Biophys Res Commun. 2001;286(3):433–442.

45. Sorger PK, Pelham HR. Yeast heat shock factor is an essential DNA-binding protein that exhibits temperature-dependent phosphorylation. Cell. 1988;54(6):855–864.

46. Wiederrecht G, Seto D, Parker CS. Isolation of the gene encoding the S. cerevisiae heat shock transcription factor. Cell. 1988;54(6):841–853.

47. Martinez-Pastor MT, Marchler G, Schüller C, Marchler-Bauer A, Ruis H, Estruch F. The Saccharomyces cerevisiae zinc finger proteins Msn2p and Msn4p are required for transcriptional induction through the stress response element (STRE). EMBO J. 1996;15(9):2227–2235.

48. Schmitt AP, McEntee K. Msn2p, a zinc finger DNA-binding protein, is the transcriptional activator of the multistress response in Saccharomyces cerevisiae. Proc Natl Acad Sci. 1996;93(12):5777–5782.

49. Ghosh A. Small heat shock proteins (HSP12, HSP20 and HSP30) play a role in Ustilago maydis pathogenesis. FEMS Microbiol Lett. 2014;361(1):17–24.

50. Monahan IM, Betts J, Banerjee DK, Butcher PD. Differential expression of mycobacterial proteins following phagocytosis by macrophages. Microbiology. 2001;147(2):459–471.

51. Becherelli M, Tao J, Ryder NS. Involvement of heat shock proteins in Candida albicans biofilm formation. J Mol Microbiol Biotechnol. 2013;23(6):396–400.

52. Baeza LC, Bailão AM, Borges CL, Pereira M, de Almeida Soares CM, Giannini MJSM. cDNA representational difference analysis used in the identification of genes expressed by Trichophyton rubrum during contact with keratin. Microbes Infect. 2007;9(12–13):1415–1421.

53. Jacob TR, Peres NT, Martins MP, Lang EA, Sanches PR, Rossi A, et al. Heat shock protein 90 (Hsp90) as a molecular target for the development of novel drugs against the dermatophyte Trichophyton rubrum. Front Microbiol. 2015;6:1241.

54. Noble SM, French S, Kohn LA, Chen V, Johnson AD. Systematic screens of a Candida albicans homozygous deletion library decouple morphogenetic switching and pathogenicity. Nat Genet. 2010;42(7):590.

55. Singh-Babak SD, Babak T, Diezmann S, Hill JA, Xie JL, Chen Y-L, et al. Global analysis of the evolution and mechanism of echinocandin resistance in Candida glabrata. PLoS Pathog. 2012;8(5):e1002718.

56. Eid A, Jaradat N, Elmarzugi N. A Review of chemical constituents and traditional usage of Neem plant (Azadirachta Indica). Palest Med Pharm J. 2017;2:75–81.

57. Ley SV. Development of methods suitable for natural product synthesis: The azadirachtin story. Pure Appl Chem. 2005;77(7):1115–1130.

58. Alzohairy MA. Therapeutics role of Azadirachta indica (Neem) and their active constituents in diseases prevention and treatment. Evid Based Complement Alternat Med. 2016;2016.

59. Govindachari TR, Suresh G, Gopalakrishnan G, Banumathy B, Masilamani S. Identification of antifungal compounds from the seed oil ofAzadirachta indica. Phytoparasitica. 1998;26(2):109–116.

60. Siddiqui BS, Ali ST, Rajput MT, Gulzar T, Rasheed M, Mehmood R. GC-based analysis of insecticidal constituents of the flowers of Azadirachta indica A. Juss. Nat Prod Res. 2009;23(3):271–283.

61. Nisbet AJ. Azadirachtin from the neem tree Azadirachta indica: its action against insects. An Soc Entomológica Bras. 2000;29(4):615–632.

62. Sarmiento WC, Maramba CC, Gonzales MLM. An in-vitro study on the antibacterial effect of neem (Azadirachta indica) leaf extract on methicillin-sensitive and Methicillin-resistant Staphylococcus aureus. PIDSP J. 2011;12(1):40–45.

63. Hossain MA, Al-Toubi WA, Weli AM, Al-Riyami QA, Al-Sabahi JN. Identification and characterization of chemical compounds in different crude extracts from leaves of Omani neem. J Taibah Univ Sci. 2013;7(4):181–188.

64. Mitra CR, Garg HS, Pandey GN. Identification of nimbidic acid and nimbidinin from Azadirachta indica. Phytochemistry. 1971;10(4):857–864.

65. Siddiqui S. A note on the isolation of three new bitter principles from the nim oil. Curr Sci. 1942;11(7):278–279.

66. Bhargava KP, Gupta MB, Gupta GP, Mitra CR. Anti-inflammatory activity of saponins and ot-her natural products. Indian J Med Res. 1970 Jun;58(6):724–30.

67. Pillai NR, Santhakumari G. Anti-arthritic and anti-inflammatory actions of nimbidin. Planta Med. 1981;43(09):59–63.

68. Pillai NR, Santhakumari G. Hypoglycaemic activity of Melia azadirachta Linn (neem). Indian J Med Res. 1981;

69. Pillai NR, Santhakumari G. Toxicity studies on nimbidin, a potential antiulcer drug. Planta Med. 1984;50(02):146–148.

70. Radhakrishna NP, Suganthan D, Seshadri C, Santhakumari G. Anti-gastric ulcer activity of nimbidin. Indian J Med Res. 1978;68:169–175.

71. Pillai NR, Santhakumari G. Effect of nimbidin on gastric acid secretion. Anc Sci Life. 1985;5(2):91.

72. Biswas K, Chattopadhyay I, Banerjee RK, Bandyopadhyay U. Biological activities and medicinal properties of neem (Azadirachta indica). Curr Sci-BANGALORE-. 2002;82(11):1336–1345.

73. Raman RP. Applicability, Feasibility and Efficacy of Phytotherapy in Aquatic Animal Health Management. Am J Plant Sci. 2017 Jan 19;08:257.

74. Bhide NK, Mehta DJ, Altekar WW, Lewis RA. Toxicity of sodium nimbidinate. Indian J Med Sci. 1958 Mar;12(3):146–9.

75. Rojanapo W, Suwanno S, Somaree R, Glinsukon T, Thebtaranonth Y. Screening of Antioxidants from some Thia vegetables and herbs. J Sci Thail. 1985;11:177–188.

76. Khalid SA, Duddeck H, Gonzalez-Sierra M. Isolation and characterization of an antimalarial agent of the neem tree Azadirachta indica. J Nat Prod. 1989;52(5):922–927.

77. Butterworth JH, Morgan ED. Isolation of a substance that suppresses feeding in locusts. Chem Commun Lond. 1968;(1):23–24.

78. Jones IW, Denholm AA, Ley SV, Lovell H, Wood A, Sinden RE. Sexual development of malaria parasites is inhibited in vitro by the Neem extract Azadirachtin, and its semi-synthetic analogues. FEMS Microbiol Lett. 1994 Jul 1;120(3):267–73.

79. Van der Nat JM, Van der Sluis WG, Van Dijk H, De Silva KTD, Labadie RP. Activity-guided isolation and identification of Azadirachta indica bark extract constituents which specifically inhibit chemiluminescence production by activated human polymorphonuclear leukocytes. Planta Med. 1991;57(01):65–68.

80. Ara I, Siddiqui BS, Faizi S, Siddiqui S. Structurally novel diterpenoid constituents from the stem bark of Azadirachta indica(meliaceae). J Chem Soc Perkin 1. 1989 Jan 1;0(2):343–5.

81. Pant N, Garg HS, Madhusudanan KP, Bhakuni DS. Sulfurous compounds from Azadirachta indica leaves. Fitoterapia. 1986;

82. Tewari A, Tiwari S. Synthesis of Medicinal Agents from Plants. Elsevier; 2018. 384 p.

83. Natarajan V. Effect of azadirachta indica (neem) on the growth pattern of dermatophytes. Indian J Med Microbiol. 2003 Apr 1;21(2):98.

84. Bajaj YPS. Medicinal and Aromatic Plants XI. Springer Science & Business Media; 2013. 438 p.

85. Van der Nat JM, Klerx J, Van Dijk H, De Silva KTD, Labadie RP. Immunomodulatory activity of an aqueous extract of Azadirachta indica stem bark. J Ethnopharmacol. 1987;19(2):125–131.

86. Van der Nat JM, Van Der Sluis WG, Van Dijk H, Van den Berg AJJ, De Silva KTD, Labadie RP. Characterization of anti-complement compounds from Azadirachta indica. J Ethnopharmacol. 1989;27(1–2):15–24.

87. Moursi SH, AL-KHATIB IM. Effect of Melia azedarach fruits on gipsing-restraint stress-induced ulcers in rats. Jpn J Pharmacol. 1984;36(4):527–533.

88. Muhammad HS, Muhammad S. The use of Lawsonia inermis Linn.(henna) in the management of burn wound infections. Afr J Biotechnol. 2005;4(9).

89. Bailey LH, Bailey EZ. Hortus third: A concise dictionary of plants cultivated in the United States and Canada. Macmillan New York; 1976.

90. Varghese KJ, Silvipriya KS, Resmi S, Jolly CI. Lawsonia inermis (henna): a natural Dye of various therapeutic uses-a review. Inven Impact Cosmeceuticals. 2010;

91. Rahmoun N, Boucherit-Otmani Z, Boucherit K, Benabdallah M, Choukchou-Braham N. Antifungal activity of the Algerian Lawsonia inermis (henna). Pharm Biol. 2013 Jan 1;51(1):131–5.

92. Khare CP. Indian medicinal plants: an illustrated dictionary. Springer Science & Business Media; 2008.

93. Ahmed S, Rahman A, Alam A, Saleem M, Athar M, Sultana S. Evaluation of the efficacy of Lawsonia alba in the alleviation of carbon tetrachloride-induced oxidative stress. J Ethnopharmacol. 2000 Feb;69(2):157–64.

94. Rosenberg NM. Antibacterial deodorizing compositions containing extracts of Lawsonia inermis. PCT Int Appl. 1999;

95. Vardamides JC, Dongo E, Nkengfack AE, Fomum ZT, Ngando TM, Vogler B, et al. Diterpenoid and limonoids from the stem of Pterorhachis zenkeri. Fitoterapia. 2001;72(4):386–393.

96. Chaudhary G, Goyal S, Poonia P. Lawsonia inermis Linnaeus: a phytopharmacological review. Int J Pharm Sci Drug Res. 2010;2(2):91–98.

97. Krishnaraju AV, Rao TV, Sundararaju D, Vanisree M, Tsay H-S, Subbaraju GV. Assessment of bioactivity of Indian medicinal plants using brine shrimp (Artemia salina) lethality assay. Int J Appl Sci Eng. 2005;3(2):125–34.

98. Debprasad C, Hemanta M, Paromita B, Durbadal O, Kumar KA, Shanta D, et al. Inhibition of NO 2 , PGE 2 , TNF- α, and *i* NOS EXpression by *Shorea robusta* L.: An Ethnomedicine Used for Anti-Inflammatory and Analgesic Activity. Evid Based Complement Alternat Med. 2012;2012:1–14.

99. Naikodi MAR, Nagaiah K, Waheed MA. Phytochemical Standardization of Oleo Resin of Shorea robusta Gaertn (Dipterocarpaceae) with modern analytical technique. Int J Phytomedicine. 2013;4(4):503–510.

100. Kaur S, Dayal R, Varshney VK, Bartley JP. GC-MS analysis of essential oils of heartwood and resin of Shorea robusta. Planta Med. 2001;67(09):883–886.

101. Patra A, Dey AK, Kundu AB, Saraswathy A, Purushothaman KK. Shoreaphenol, a polyphenol from Shorea robusta. Phytochemistry. 1992;31(7):2561–2562.

102. Pullaiah T, Rani SS. Trees of Andhra Pradesh, India. Daya Books; 1999.

103. Upadhyay OP, Kumar K, Tiwari RK. Ethnobotanical study of skin treatment uses of medicinal plants of Bihar. Pharm Biol. 1998;36(3):167–172.

104. Misra LN, Ahmad A. Triterpenoids from Shorea robusta resin. Phytochemistry. 1997;45(3):575–578.

105. Warrier PK, Nambiar VPK. Indian medicinal plants: a compendium of 500 species. Vol. 5. Orient Blackswan; 1993.

106. Wani TA, Chandrashekara HH, Kumar D, Prasad R, Gopal A, Sardar KK, et al. Wound healing activity of ethanolic extract of Shorea robusta Gaertn. f. resin. 2012;

107. Uthamarayan KS, Thirattu SV. India; Directorate of Indian Medicine and Homeopathy Publications. Chennai; 1998.

108. Datta HS, Mitra SK, Patwardhan B. Wound Healing Activity of Topical Application Forms Based on Ayurveda. Evid-Based Complement Altern Med ECAM [Internet]. 2011 [cited 2018 Dec 30];2011. Available from: https://www.ncbi.nlm.nih.gov/pmc/articles/PMC3136177/

109. Hota RK, Bapuji M. Triterpenoids from the resin of Shorea robusta. Phytochemistry. 1993;32(2):466–468.

110. Harborne JB. Recent advances in chemical ecology. Nat Prod Rep. 1999 Jan 1;16(4):509–23.

111. Prakash EO, Rao JT. A new flavone glycoside from the seeds of Shorea robusta. Fitoterapia. 1999;70(6):539–541.

112. Chauhan SMS, Singh M, Narayan L. Isolation of 3β-hydroxyolean-12-ene,friedelin and 7-methoxy-4' -5-dihydroxyisoflavone from dry and fresh leaves of *Shorea robusta*. IJC-B Vol41B05 May 2002 [Internet]. 2002 May [cited 2018 Dec 31]; Available from: http://nopr.niscair.res.in/handle/123456789/21929

113. Duddukuri GR, Rao DE, Rao K, Chaitanya KK, Sireesha C. Preliminary studies on in vitro antibacterial activity and phytochemical. Int J Curr Res. 2011;3:4.

114. Nainwal P, Bhatt R, Nanda D, Saini P. Screening of in vitro anti-inflammatory activity of aqueous extract of leaves of Shorea robusta. Int J Pharmacol Screen Method. 2013;3(2):43–45.

115. Jyothi G, Carey WM, Kumar RB, Mohan KG. Antinociceptive and antiinflammatory activity of methanolic extract of leaves of Shorea robusta. Pharmacol Online. 2008;1:9–19.

116. Wani TA, Kumar D, Prasad R, Verma PK, Sardar KK, Tandan SK, et al. Analgesic activity of the ethanolic extract of Shorea robusta resin in experimental animals. Indian J Pharmacol. 2012;44(4):493.

117. Murthy KSR. Biological activity and phytochemical screening of the oleoresin of Shorea robusta Gaertn. f. Trop Subtrop Agroecosystems. 2011;14(3).

118. Kalaiselvan A, Gokulakrishnan K, Anand T, Akhilesh U, Velavan S. Preventive effect of Shorea robusta bark extract against diethylnitrosamine-induced hepatocellular carcinoma in rats. Int Res J Med Sci. 2013;1(1):2–9.

119. Lakshmamma P, Prayaga L. Identifying the sources of tolerance for drought in castor, Ricinus communis L. J Oilseeds Res. 2006;23(2):348.

120. Raoof MA, Yasmeen M. Etiology, epidemiology and management of Botrytis grey mold of castor, Ricinus communis L.-A review. J Oilseeds Res. 2006;23(2):144.

121. Evans WC, Evans D, Trease GE. Trease and Evans Pharmacognosy. Saunders/Elsevier; 2009. 603 p.

122. Bhakta S, Das SK. In praise of the medicinal plant ricinus communis l.: A review. 2015;4(5):12.

123. Khogali A, Barakat S, Abou-Zeid H. Isolation and identification of the phenolics from Ricinus communis L. Delta J Sci. 1992;16(1):198–211.

124. Kang SS, Cordell GA, Soejarto DD, Fong HH. Alkaloids and flavonoids from Ricinus communis. J Nat Prod. 1985;48(1):155–156.

125. Kadri A, Gharsallah N, Damak M, Gdoura R. Chemical composition and in vitro antioxidant properties of essential oil of Ricinus communis L. J Med Plants Res. 2011;5(8):1466–1470.

126. Thompson MJ, Bowers WS. Lupeol and 30-norlupan-3β-ol-20-one from the coating of the castor bean (Ricinus communi L.). Phytochemistry. 1968;7(5):845–847.

127. Isha D, Milind P. Eat til and protect dil. Int Res J Pharm. 2012;3(5457):16.

128. Kim KS, Park SH. Anthrasesamone F from the seeds of black Sesamum indicum. Biosci Biotechnol Biochem. 2008;72(6):1626–1627.

129. Hasan AFMF, Begum S, Furumoto T, Fukui H. A New Chlorinated Red Naphthoquinone from Roots of Sesamum indicum. Biosci Biotechnol Biochem. 2000 Jan 1;64(4):873–4.

130. Furumoto T, Takeuchi A, Fukui H. Anthrasesamones D and E from Sesamum indicum roots. Biosci Biotechnol Biochem. 2006;70(7):1784–1785.

131. Furumoto T, Ohara T, Kubo T, Kawanami Y, Fukui H. 2-Geranyl-1, 4-naphthoquinone, a possible intermediate of anthraquinones in a Sesamum indicum hairy root culture. Biosci Biotechnol Biochem. 2007;71(10):2600–2602.

132. Milder IEJ, Arts ICW, van de Putte B, Venema DP, Hollman PCH. Lignan contents of Dutch plant foods: a database including lariciresinol, pinoresinol, secoisolariciresinol and matairesinol. Br J Nutr. 2005 Mar;93(3):393–402.

133. Liu J, Balasubramanian MK. 1, 3-beta-Glucan synthase: a useful target for antifungal drugs. Curr Drug Targets-Infect Disord. 2001;1(2):159–169.

134. Barnett JA, Robinow CF. A history of research on yeasts 4: cytology part II, 1950-1990. Yeast. 2002 Jun 30;19(9):745–72.

135. Kapteyn JC, Van Den Ende H, Klis FM. The contribution of cell wall proteins to the organization of the yeast cell wall. Biochim Biophys Acta BBA-Gen Subj. 1999;1426(2):373–383.

136. Bernard M, Latgé J-P. Aspergillus fumigatus cell wall: composition and biosynthesis. Med Mycol. 2001;39(1):9–17.

137. Klis FM, Groot PD, Hellingwerf K. Molecular organization of the cell wall of Candida albicans. Med Mycol. 2001;39(1):1–8.

138. Grün CH, Hochstenbach F, Humbel BM, Verkleij AJ, Sietsma JH, Klis FM, et al. The structure of cell wall alpha-glucan from fission yeast. Glycobiology. 2005 Mar;15(3):245–57.

139. Cabib E, Bowers B, Sburlati A, Silverman SJ. Fungal cell wall synthesis: the construction of a biological structure. Microbiol Sci. 1988;5(12):370–375.

140. Borkovich KA, Alex LA, Yarden O, Freitag M, Turner GE, Read ND, et al. Lessons from the genome sequence of Neurospora crassa: tracing the path from genomic blueprint to multicellular organism. Microbiol Mol Biol Rev. 2004;68(1):1–108.

141. Fontaine T, Simenel C, Dubreucq G, Adam O, Delepierre M, Lemoine J, et al. Molecular organization of the alkali-insoluble fraction of Aspergillus fumigatus cell wall. J Biol Chem. 2000 Sep 8;275(36):27594–607.

142. Manners DJ, Masson AJ, Patterson JC. The structure of a β-(1→ 3)-D-glucan from yeast cell walls. Biochem J. 1973;135(1):19–30.

143. Kollár R, Reinhold BB, Petráková E, Yeh HJ, Ashwell G, Drgonová J, et al. Architecture of the yeast cell wall β (1→ 6)-glucan interconnects mannoprotein, β (1→ 3)-glucan, and chitin. J Biol Chem. 1997;272(28):17762–17775.

144. Qadota H, Python CP, Inoue SB, Arisawa M, Anraku Y, Zheng Y, et al. Identification of yeast Rho1p GTPase as a regulatory subunit of 1, 3-β-glucan synthase. Science. 1996;272(5259):279–281.

145. Douglas CM, Foor F, Marrinan JA, Morin N, Nielsen JB, Dahl AM, et al. The Saccharomyces cerevisiae FKS1 (ETG1) gene encodes an integral membrane protein which is a subunit of 1, 3-beta-D-glucan synthase. Proc Natl Acad Sci. 1994;91(26):12907–12911.

146. Mazur P, Morin N, Baginsky W, El-Sherbeini M, Clemas JA, Nielsen JB, et al. Differential expression and function of two homologous subunits of yeast 1, 3-beta-D-glucan synthase. Mol Cell Biol. 1995;15(10):5671–5681.

147. Bartnicki-Garcia S. Cell wall chemistry, morphogenesis, and taxonomy of fungi. Annu Rev Microbiol. 1968;22(1):87–108.

148. Hartland RP, Vermeulen CA, Sietsma JH, Wessels JG, Klis FM. The linkage of (1–3)-β-glucan to chitin during cell wall assembly in Saccharomyces cerevisiae. Yeast. 1994;10(12):1591–1599.

149. Klis FM, Mol P, Hellingwerf K, Brul S. Dynamics of cell wall structure in Saccharomyces cerevisiae. FEMS Microbiol Rev. 2002;26(3):239–256.

150. Silverman SJ, Sburlati A, Slater ML, Cabib E. Chitin synthase 2 is essential for septum formation and cell division in Saccharomyces cerevisiae. Proc Natl Acad Sci. 1988;85(13):4735–4739.

151. Bulawa CE, Slater M, Cabib E, Au-Young J, Sburlati A, Adair Jr WL, et al. The S. cerevisiae structural gene for chitin synthase is not required for chitin synthesis in vivo. Cell. 1986;46(2):213–225.

152. Shaw JA, Mol PC, Bowers B, Silverman SJ, Valdivieso MH, Durán A, et al. The function of chitin synthases 2 and 3 in the Saccharomyces cerevisiae cell cycle. J Cell Biol. 1991;114(1):111–123.

153. Cabib E, Mol PC, Shaw JA, Choi WJ. Biosynthesis of cell wall and septum during yeast growth. Arch Med Res. 1993;24(3):301–303.

154. Munro CA, Gow NAR. Chitin synthesis in human pathogenic fungi. Med Mycol. 2001;39(1):41–53.

155. Arellano M, Cartagena-Lirola H, Nasser Hajibagheri MA, Durán A, Henar Valdivieso M. Proper ascospore maturation requires the chs1+ chitin synthase gene in Schizosaccharomyces pombe. Mol Microbiol. 2000;35(1):79–89.

156. Mata J, Lyne R, Burns G, Bähler J. The transcriptional program of meiosis and sporulation in fission yeast. Nat Genet. 2002;32(1):143.

157. Bhattacharya D, Nagpure A, Gupta RK. Bacterial chitinases: properties and potential. Crit Rev Biotechnol. 2007 Mar;27(1):21–8.

158. Yuli PE, Suhartono MT, Rukayadi Y, Hwang JK, Pyun YR. Characteristics of thermostable chitinase enzymes from the indonesian Bacillus sp. 13.26. Enzyme Microb Technol. 2004;35(2–3):147–153.

159. Kasprzewska A. Plant chitinases-regulation and function. Cell Mol Biol Lett. 2003;8(3):809–824.

160. Matsumiya M, Karasuda S, Miyauchi K, Mochizuki A. Substrate specificity and partial amino acid sequence of a Chitinase from the stomach of coelacanth Latimeria chalumnae. Fish Sci. 2008;74(6):1360.

161. Yamanaka S, Tsuyoshi N, Kikuchi R, Takayama S, Sakuda S, Yamada Y. Effect of demethylallosamidin, a chitinase inhibitor, on morphology of fungus Geotrichum candidum. J Gen Appl Microbiol. 1994;40(2):171–174.

162. Sándor E, Pusztahelyi T, Karaffa L, Karányi Z, Pócsi I, Biró S, et al. Allosamidin inhibits the fragmentation of Acremonium chrysogenum but does not influence the cephalosporin-C production of the fungus. FEMS Microbiol Lett. 1998;164(2):231–236.

163. Horsch M, Mayer C, Sennhauser U, Rast DM. Beta-N-acetylhexosaminidase: a target for the design of antifungal agents. Pharmacol Ther. 1997 Dec;76(1–3):187–218.

164. Tatsumi H, Murakami S, Tsuji RF, Ishida Y, Murakami K, Masaki A, et al. Cloning and expression in yeast of a cDNA clone encoding Aspergillus oryzae neutral protease II, a unique metalloprotease. Mol Gen Genet MGG. 1991;228(1–2):97–103.

165. Fushimi N, Nakajima T, Ichishima E. Aspzincin, a Family of Metalloendopeptidases with a New Zinc-binding Motif Identification of new zinc-binding sites (His128, His132, and Asp164) and three catalytically crucial residues (Glu129, Asp143, and Tyr106) of deuterolysin from *Aspergillus oryzae* by site-directed mutagenesis. J Biol Chem. 1999;274(34):24195–24201.

166. Creighton TE. Proteins : structures and molecular properties /. 2nd ed. New York : W.H. Freeman,; c1993.

167. Vallee BL, Auld DS. Zinc coordination, function, and structure of zinc enzymes and other proteins. Biochemistry. 1990;29(24):5647–5659.

168. Hooper NM. Families of zinc metalloproteases. FEBS Lett. 1994;354(1):1–6.

169. Sekine H. Neutral Proteinases I and II of Aspergillus sojae: Isolation in Homogeneous Form. Agric Biol Chem. 1972;36(2):198–206.

170. Gripon JC, Hermier J. The proteolytic system of Penicillium roqueforti. III. - Purification, properties and specificity of a protease inhibited by E.D.T.A]. Biochimie. 1974;56(10):1323–32.

171. Monod M, Paris S, Sanglard D, Jaton-Ogay K, Bille J, Latge JP. Isolation and characterization of a secreted metalloprotease of Aspergillus fumigatus. Infect Immun. 1993;61(10):4099–4104.

172. Sirakova TD, Markaryan A, Kolattukudy PE. Molecular cloning and sequencing of the cDNA and gene for a novel elastinolytic metalloproteinase from Aspergillus fumigatus and its expression in Escherichia coli. Infect Immun. 1994;62(10):4208–4218.

173. Fernández D, Russi S, Vendrell J, Monod M, Pallarès I. A functional and structural study of the major metalloprotease secreted by the pathogenic fungus Aspergillus fumigatus. Acta Crystallogr D Biol Crystallogr. 2013;69(10):1946–1957.

174. Azevedo RA. Analysis of the aspartic acid metabolic pathway using mutant genes. Amino Acids. 2002;22(3):217–230.

175. Zhu-Shimoni JX, Galili G. Expression of an Arabidopsis aspartate kinase/homoserine dehydrogenase gene is metabolically regulated by photosynthesis-related signals but not by nitrogenous compounds. Plant Physiol. 1998;116(3):1023–1028.

176. Jacques SL, Mirza IA, Ejim L, Koteva K, Hughes DW, Green K, et al. Enzyme-assisted suicide: molecular basis for the antifungal activity of 5-hydroxy-4-oxonorvaline by potent inhibition of homoserine dehydrogenase. Chem Biol. 2003;10(10):989–995.

177. Kis K, Bacher A. Substrate channeling in the lumazine synthase/riboflavin synthase complex of Bacillus subtilis. J Biol Chem. 1995;270(28):16788–16795.

178. Bacher A, Baur R, Eggers U, Harders HD, Otto MK, Schnepple H. Riboflavin synthases of Bacillus subtilis. Purification and properties. J Biol Chem. 1980;255(2):632–637.

179. Bacher A, Eberhardt S, Fischer M, Mörtl S, Kis K, Kugelbrey K, et al. Biosynthesis of riboflavin: Lumazine synthase and riboflavin synthase. In: Methods in Enzymology [Internet]. Academic Press; 1997 [cited 2018 Dec 30]. p. 389–99. (Vitamins and Coenzymes Part J; vol. 280). Available from: http://www.sciencedirect.com/science/article/pii/S0076687997801309

180. Bacher A, Fischer M, Kis K, Kugelbrey K, Mörtl S, Scheuring J, et al. Biosynthesis of riboflavin: structure and mechanism of lumazine synthase. Biochem Soc Trans. 1996 Feb;24(1):89–94.

181. Plaut GWE, Beach R, Aogaichi T. Mechanism of elimination of protons from the methyl groups of 6, 7-dimethyl-8-ribityllumazine by riboflavine synthetase. Biochemistry. 1970;9(4):771–785.

182. Plaut GWE, Harvey RA. The enzymatic synthesis of riboflavin. In: Methods in Enzymology [Internet]. Academic Press; 1971 [cited 2018 Dec 30]. p. 515–38. (Vitamins and Coenzymes; vol. 18). Available from: http://www.sciencedirect.com/science/article/pii/S0076687971181141

183. Ladenstein R, Meyer B, Huber R, Labischinski H, Bartels K, Bartunik H-D, et al. Heavy riboflavin synthase from Bacillus subtilis: Particle dimensions, crystal packing and molecular symmetry. J Mol Biol. 1986;187(1):87–100.

184. Bacher A. Heavy riboflavin synthase from Bacillus subtilis. In: Methods in Enzymology [Internet]. Academic Press; 1986 [cited 2018 Dec 31]. p. 192–9. (Vitamins and Coenzymes Part G; vol. 122). Available from: http://www.sciencedirect.com/science/article/pii/0076687986221709

185. Bacher A, Mailänder B. Biosynthesis of riboflavin in Bacillus subtilis: function and genetic control of the riboflavin synthase complex. J Bacteriol. 1978;134(2):476–482.

186. BACHER A, LUDWIG HC. Ligand-Binding Studies on Heavy Riboflavin Synthase of Bacillus subtilis. Eur J Biochem. 1982;127(3):539–545.

187. Elion GB. An overview of the role of nucleosides in chemotherapy. Adv Enzyme Regul. 1985;24:323–334.

188. Elion GB. The purine path to chemotherapy (nobel lecture). Angew Chem Int Ed Engl. 1989;28(7):870–878.

189. Hitchings GH, Elion GB, Vanderwerff H. 2-Aminopurine as a purine antagonist. Fed Proc. 1948 Mar;7(1 Pt 1):160.

190. Fasoli MOF, Kerridge D, Ryley JF. Pathogenicity of 5-fluorocytosine resistant strains of Candida albicans. J Med Vet Mycol. 1990;28(1):27–34.

191. Kirsch DR, Whitney RR. Pathogenicity of Candida albicans auxotrophic mutants in experimental infections. Infect Immun. 1991;59(9):3297–3300.

192. Kwon-Chung KJ, Hill WB. Studies on the pink, adenine-deficient strains of Candida albicans: I. Cultural and morphological characteristics. Sabouraudia J Med Vet Mycol. 1970;8(1):48–59.

193. McFarland WC, Stocker BA. Effect of different purine auxotrophic mutations on mouse-virulence of a Vi-positive strain of Salmonella dublin and of two strains of Salmonella typhimurium. Microb Pathog. 1987;3(2):129–141.

194. Bennett JE. Flucytosine. Ann Intern Med. 1977;86(3):319–322.

195. Bacon GA, Burrows TW, Yates M. The effects of biochemical mutation on the virulence of Bacterium typhosum: the virulence of mutants. Br J Exp Pathol. 1950;31(6):714.

196. Garber ED, Hackett AJ, Franklin R. The virulence of biochemical mutants of Klebsiella pneumoniae. Proc Natl Acad Sci. 1952;38(8):693–697.

197. Ivanovics G, Marjai E, Dobozy A. The growth of purine mutants of Bacillus anthracis in the body of the mouse. Microbiology. 1968;53(2):147–162.

198. Burrows TW, Bacon GA. The Basis of Virulence in Pasteurella pestis: Comparative Behaviour of Virulent and Avirulent Strains in vivo. Br J Exp Pathol. 1954 Apr;35(2):134–43.

199. Straley SC, Harmon PA. Growth in mouse peritoneal macrophages of Yersinia pestis lacking established virulence determinants. Infect Immun. 1984;45(3):649–654.

200. Bacon GA, Burrows TW, Yates M. The Effects of Biochemical Mutation on the Virulence of Bacterium typhosum: The Loss of Virulence of Certain Mutants. Br J Exp Pathol. 1951 Apr;32(2):85–96.

201. Sarachek A. Promotion or retardation of the growth of adenine auxotrophs ofCandida albicans by purines, pyrimidines and nucleosides. Antonie Van Leeuwenhoek. 1964;30(1):289–302.

202. Skogerson L, Wakatama E. A ribosome-dependent GTPase from yeast distinct from elongation factor 2. Proc Natl Acad Sci. 1976;73(1):73–76.

203. Justice MC, Hsu M-J, Tse B, Ku T, Balkovec J, Schmatz D, et al. Elongation factor 2 as a novel target for selective inhibition of fungal protein synthesis. J Biol Chem. 1998;273(6):3148–3151.

204. Triana-Alonso FJ, Chakraburtty K, Nierhaus KH. The Elongation Factor 3 Unique in Higher Fungi and Essential for Protein Biosynthesis Is an E Site Factor. J Biol Chem. 1995 Sep 1;270(35):20473–8.

205. Parey K, Warkentin E, Kroneck PM, Ermler U. Reaction cycle of the dissimilatory sulfite reductase from Archaeoglobus fulgidus. Biochemistry. 2010;49(41):8912–8921.

206. Pinto R, Harrison JS, Hsu T, Jacobs WR, Leyh TS. Sulfite reduction in mycobacteria. J Bacteriol. 2007;189(18):6714–6722.

207. Siegel LM, Murphy MJ, Kamin H. Reduced nicotinamide adenine dinucleotide phosphate-sulfite reductase of enterobacteria I. The Escherichia coli hemoflavoprotein: molecular parameters and prosthetic groups. J Biol Chem. 1973;248(1):251–264.

208. Thomas D, Surdin-kerjan Y. Metabolism of Sulfur Amino Acids in Saccharomyces cerevisiae. 1997.

209. Cherest H, Surdin-Kerjan Y. Genetic analysis of a new mutation conferring cysteine auxotrophy in Saccharomyces cerevisiae: updating of the sulfur metabolism pathway. Genetics. 1992 Jan;130(1):51–8.

210. Kerjan P, Cherest H, Surdin-Kerjan Y. Nucleotide sequence of the Saccharomyces cerevisiae MET25 gene. Nucleic Acids Res. 1986 Oct 1;14(20):7861–71.

211. Marchenko GN, Marchenko ND, Tsygankov YD, Chistoserdov AY. Organization of threonine biosynthesis genes from the obligate methylotroph Methylobacillus flagellatus. Microbiology. 1999;145(11):3273–82.

212. Fujiu M, Sawairi S, Shimada H, Takaya H, Aoki Y, Okuda T, et al. Azoxybacilin, a novel antifungal agent produced by Bacillus cereus NR2991. Production, isolation and structure elucidation. J Antibiot (Tokyo). 1994 Jul;47(7):833–5.

213. Bauer AW, Kirby WMM, Sherris JC, Turck M. Antibiotic susceptibility testing by a standardized single disk method. Am J Clin Pathol. 1966;45(4_ts):493–496.

214. Ericsson HM, Sherris JC. Antibiotic sensitivity testing. Report of an international collaborative study. Acta Pathol Microbiol Scand. 1971;(Suppl. 217).

215. Bueno C, Villegas ML, Bertolotti SG, Previtali CM, Neumann MG, Encinas MV. The Excited-State Interaction of Resazurin and Resorufin with Aminesin Aqueous Solutions. Photophysics and Photochemical Reaction¶. Photochem Photobiol. 2002;76(4):385–90.

216. Kreft S, Kreft M. Quantification of dichromatism: a characteristic of color in transparent materials. JOSA A. 2009;26(7):1576–1581.

217. Pesch KL, Simmert U. Combined assays for lactose and galactose by enzymatic reactions. Kiel Milchw Forsch. 1929;8:551.

218. Anoopkumar-Dukie S, Carey JB, Conere T, O'sullivan E, Van Pelt FN, Allshire A. Resazurin assay of radiation response in cultured cells. Br J Radiol. 2005;78(934):945–947.

219. González-Pinzón R, Haggerty R, Myrold DD. Measuring aerobic respiration in stream ecosystems using the resazurin-resorufin system. J Geophys Res Biogeosciences. 2012;117(G3).

220. Koona S, Budida S. Antibacterial Potential of the Extracts of the Leaves of Azadirachta indica Linn. Not Sci Biol. 2011;3(1):65–69.

221. Patil RC, Kulkarni CP, Pandey A. Antifungal and phytochemical properties of Tinospora cordifolia, Azadirachta indica and Ocimum sanctum leaves extract. J Med Plants. 2017;5(5):23–26.

222. Arumugam PA, Mohamad I, Salim R, Mohamed Z. Antifungal effect of Malaysian neem leaf extract on selected fungal species causing Otomycosis in in-vitro culture medium. Malays J Med Health Sci. 2015;11(2):69–84.

223. Mahmoud DA, Hassanein NM, Youssef KA, Zeid A. Antifungal activity of different neem leaf extracts and the nimonol against some important human pathogens. Braz J Microbiol. 2011;42(3):1007–1016.

224. Fariba B, Hassan R, Homeyra E. In vitro study of the effects of henna extracts (Lawsonia inermis) on Malassezia species. Jundishapur J Microbiol. 2010;2010(3, Summer):125–128.

225. Sowjanya NC, Chary CM. Effect of plant extracts on the growth of Microsporum gypseum. J Phytol. 2012;

226. Sagar K, Vidyasagar GM. Anti-dermatophytic activity of some traditionally used medicinal plants of North Karnataka Region. J Appl Pharm Sci. 2013;3(2):77.

227. Jain N, Sharma M. Screening of *Lawsonia inermis* essential oil against fungi causing dermatophytic infection in human. Asian J Pharm Clin Res. 2016 Jul 1;9(4):67–9.

228. Islam T, Bakshi H, Sam S, Sharma E, Hameed B, Rathore B, et al. Assessment of antibacterial potential of leaves of Ricinus communis against pathogenic and dermatophytic bacteria. Int J Pharma Res Dev. 2010;1(12):1–7.

229. Mathur A, Verma SK, Yousuf S, Singh SK, Prasad G, Dua VK. Antimicrobial potential of roots of Riccinus communis against pathogenic microorganisms. Int J Pharm BioL Sci. 2011;1(2):545–548.

230. Saleem TM. Anti-microbial activity of sesame oil. Int J Res Phytochem Pharmacol. 2011;1(1):21–23.

231. Anand TD, Pothiraj C, Gopinath RM, Kayalvizhi B. Effect of oil-pulling on dental caries causing bacteria. Afr J Microbiol Res. 2008;2(3):63–66.

232. Fukuda Y, Nagata M, Osawa T, Namiki M. Contribution of lignan analogues to antioxidative activity of refined unroasted sesame seed oil. J Am Oil Chem Soc. 1986;63(8):1027–1031.

233. Pascoe GA, FARISS MW, OLAFSDOTTIR K, REED DJ. A role of vitamin E in protection against cell injury: maintenance of intracellular glutathione precursors and biosynthesis. Eur J Biochem. 1987;166(1):241–247.

234. Kiran K, Asad M. Wound healing activity of Sesamum indicum L seed and oil in rats. Indian J Exp Biol. 2008 Nov;46(11):777–82.

235. Salih KA. Synergistic Effects of Plant Extracts and Antifungal Drugs on C. albicans. J Dev Drugs [Internet]. 2016 [cited 2018 Dec 30];05(03). Available from: https://www.omicsgroup.org/journals/synergistic-effects-of-plant-extracts-and-antifungal-drugs-on-c-albicans-2329-6631-1000165.php?aid=82799

236. Khosravi-Darani K, Khaksar R, Esmaeili S, Seyed-Reihani F, Zoghi A, Shahbazizadeh S. Antifungal and anti-bacterial synergistic effects of mixture of honey and herbal extracts. Zahedan J Res Med Sci. 2013;15(8):30–33.

237. Hawksworth DL. The magnitude of fungal diversity: the 1.5 million species estimate revisited. Mycol Res. 2001 Dec;105(12):1422–32.

238. Tkacz JS. Glucan biosynthesis in fungi and its inhibition. In: Emerging targets in antibacterial and antifungal chemotherapy. Springer; 1992. p. 495–523.

239. Bulawa CE. Genetics and molecular biology of chitin synthesis in fungi. Annu Rev Microbiol. 1993;47(1):505–534.

240. Sakuda S, Nishimoto Y, Ohi M, Watanabe M, Takayama S, Isogai A, et al. Effects of demethylallosamidin, a potent yeast chitinase inhibitor, on the cell division of yeast. Agric Biol Chem. 1990;54(5):1333–1335.

241. Yamaki H, Yamaguchi M, Imamura H, Suzuki H, Nishimura T, Saito H, et al. The mechanism of antifungal action of (S)-2-amino-4-oxo-5-hydroxypentanoic acid, RI-331: the inhibition of homoserine dehydrogenase in Saccharomyces cerevisiae. Biochem Biophys Res Commun. 1990;168(2):837–843.

242. Perfect JR, Toffaletti DL, Rude TH. The gene encoding phosphoribosylaminoimidazole carboxylase (ADE2) is essential for growth of Cryptococcus neoformans in cerebrospinal fluid. Infect Immun. 1993;61(10):4446–4451.

243. Skogerson L, Engelhardt D. Dissimilarity in protein chain elongation factor requirements between yeast and rat liver ribosomes. J Biol Chem. 1977;252(4):1471–1475.

244. Qin SL, Xie AG, Bonato MC, McLaughlin CS. Sequence analysis of the translational elongation factor 3 from Saccharomyces cerevisiae. J Biol Chem. 1990;265(4):1903–1912.

245. Colthurst DR, Santos M, Grant CM, Tuite MF. Candida albicans and three other Candida species contain an elongation factor structurally and functionally analogous to elongation factor 3. FEMS Microbiol Lett. 1991 May 1;64(1):45–9.

246. Trott O, Olson AJ. AutoDock Vina: improving the speed and accuracy of docking with a new scoring function, efficient optimization, and multithreading. J Comput Chem. 2010;31(2):455–461.

247. Lipinski CA, Lombardo F, Dominy BW, Feeney PJ. Experimental and computational approaches to estimate solubility and permeability in drug discovery and development settings. Adv Drug Deliv Rev. 1997;23(1–3):3–25.

248. Lipinski CA. Lead-and drug-like compounds: the rule-of-five revolution. Drug Discov Today Technol. 2004;1(4):337–341.

249. Richardson JS. The anatomy and taxonomy of protein structure. In: Advances in protein chemistry. Elsevier; 1981. p. 167–339.

250. Ramchandran GN, Ramakrishnan C, Sasisekharan V. Streochemistry of polypeptide chain configuration. J Mol Biol. 1963;7:95–99.

251. Daina A, Michielin O, Zoete V. SwissADME: a free web tool to evaluate pharmacokinetics, drug-likeness and medicinal chemistry friendliness of small molecules. Sci Rep. 2017 03;7:42717.

252. Ghose AK, Viswanadhan VN, Wendoloski JJ. A knowledge-based approach in designing combinatorial or medicinal chemistry libraries for drug discovery. 1. A qualitative and quantitative characterization of known drug databases. J Comb Chem. 1999;1(1):55–68.

253. Veber DF, Johnson SR, Cheng H-Y, Smith BR, Ward KW, Kopple KD. Molecular properties that influence the oral bioavailability of drug candidates. J Med Chem. 2002;45(12):2615–2623.

254. Egan WJ, Merz KM, Baldwin JJ. Prediction of drug absorption using multivariate statistics. J Med Chem. 2000;43(21):3867–3877.

255. Muegge I, Heald SL, Brittelli D. Simple selection criteria for drug-like chemical matter. J Med Chem. 2001;44(12):1841–1846.

256. Cheng F, Li W, Zhou Y, Shen J, Wu Z, Liu G, et al. admetSAR: A Comprehensive Source and Free Tool for Assessment of Chemical ADMET Properties. J Chem Inf Model. 2012 Nov 26;52(11):3099–105.

257. Mortelmans K, Zeiger E. The Ames Salmonella/microsome mutagenicity assay. Mutat Res Mol Mech Mutagen. 2000;455(1):29–60.

258. McCann J, Choi E, Yamasaki E, Ames BN. Detection of carcinogens as mutagens in the Salmonella/microsome test: assay of 300 chemicals. Proc Natl Acad Sci. 1975;72(12):5135–5139.

259. Sawistowska-Schröder ET, Kerridge D, Perry H. Echinocandin inhibition of 1, 3-β-D-glucan synthase from Candida albicans. FEBS Lett. 1984;173(1):134–138.

260. Jiménez-Ortigosa C, Paderu P, Motyl MR, Perlin DS. Enfumafungin derivative MK-3118 shows increased in vitro potency against clinical echinocandin-resistant Candida species and Aspergillus species isolates. Antimicrob Agents Chemother. 2014;58(2):1248–1251.

261. Walker SS, Xu Y, Triantafyllou I, Waldman MF, Mendrick C, Brown N, et al. Discovery of a novel class of orally active antifungal β-1, 3-d-glucan synthase inhibitors. Antimicrob Agents Chemother. 2011;AAC–00432.

262. Jeyam M, Arangaraj M, Ravikumar P, Shalini G. Computational analysis of phytocompounds with 1, 3-[beta]-D-Glucan synthase for antidermatophytic activity. J Appl Pharm Sci. 2014;4(2):64.

263. Urbina JM, Cortés JC, Palma A, López SN, Zacchino SA, Enriz RD, et al. Inhibitors of the fungal cell wall. Synthesis of 4-aryl-4-N-arylamine-1-butenes and related compounds with inhibitory activities on β (1–3) glucan and chitin synthases. Bioorg Med Chem. 2000;8(4):691–698.

264. Onishi J, Meinz M, Thompson J, Curotto J, Dreikorn S, Rosenbach M, et al. Discovery of novel antifungal (1, 3)-β-D-glucan synthase inhibitors. Antimicrob Agents Chemother. 2000;44(2):368–377.

265. Gaughran JP, Lai MH, Kirsch DR, Silverman SJ. Nikkomycin Z is a specific inhibitor of Saccharomyces cerevisiae chitin synthase isozyme Chs3 in vitro and in vivo. J Bacteriol. 1994;176(18):5857–5860.

266. Pócsi I, Emri T, Varecza Z, Sámi L, Pusztahelyi T. Allosamidin inhibits the fragmentation and autolysis of Penicillium chrysogenum. Adv Chitin Sci. 2000;4:558–564.

267. Arlorio M, Ludwig A, Boller T, Bonfante P. Inhibition of fungal growth by plant chitinases andβ-1, 3-glucanases. Protoplasma. 1992;171(1–2):34–43.

268. Zarei M, Aminzadeh S, Zolgharnein H, Safahieh A, Daliri M, Noghabi KA, et al. Characterization of a chitinase with antifungal activity from a native Serratia marcescens B4A. Braz J Microbiol. 2011;42(3):1017–1029.

269. Sharpton TJ, Stajich JE, Rounsley SD, Gardner MJ, Wortman JR, Jordar VS, et al. Comparative genomic analyses of the human fungal pathogens Coccidioides and their relatives. Genome Res. 2009;

270. Jousson O, Lechenne B, Bontems O, Capoccia S, Mignon B, Barblan J, et al. Multiplication of an ancestral gene encoding secreted fungalysin preceded species differentiation in the dermatophytes Trichophyton and Microsporum. Microbiology. 2004;150(2):301–310.

271. Skwarecki AS, Schielmann M, Martynow D, Kawczyński M, Wiśniewska A, Milewska MJ, et al. Antifungal dipeptides incorporating an inhibitor of homoserine dehydrogenase. J Pept Sci. 2018;24(1):e3060.

272. Yamaki H, Yamaguchi M, Tsuruo T, Yamaguchi H. Mechanism of action of an antifungal antibiotic, RI-331,(S) 2-amino-4-oxo-5-hydroxypentanoic acid; kinetics of inactivation of homoserine dehydrogenase from Saccharomyces cerevisiae. J Antibiot (Tokyo). 1992;45(5):750–755.

273. Bagatin MC, Pimentel AL, Biavatti DC, Basso EA, Kioshima ES, Seixas FA, et al. Targeting the homoserine dehydrogenase from Paracoccidioides Genus against systemic fungal infections. Antimicrob Agents Chemother. 2017;AAC–00165.

274. Konishi M, Nishio M, Saitoh K, Miyaki T, Oki T, Kawaguchi H. Cispentacin, A new antifungal antibiotic I. Production, isolation, physico-chemical properties and structure. J Antibiot (Tokyo). 1989;42(12):1749–55.

275. Oki T, Hirano M, Tomatsu K, Numata K-I, Kamei H. Cispentacin, A new antifungal antibiotic. J Antibiot (Tokyo). 1989;42(12):1756–1762.

276. Capobianco JO, Zakula D, Coen ML, Goldman RC. Anti-Candida activity of cispentacin: the active transport by amino acid permeases and possible mechanisms of action. Biochem Biophys Res Commun. 1993;190(3):1037–1044.

277. Bhatia MS, Pakhare KD, Choudhari PB, Jadhav SD, Dhavale RP, Bhatia NM. Pharmacophore modeling and 3D QSAR studies of aryl amine derivatives as potential lumazine synthase inhibitors. Arab J Chem. 2017;10:S100–S104.

278. Kumar P, Singh M, Karthikeyan S. Crystal structure analysis of icosahedral lumazine synthase from Salmonella typhimurium, an antibacterial drug target. Acta Crystallogr D Biol Crystallogr. 2011;67(2):131–139.

279. Morgunova E, Saller S, Haase I, Cushman M, Bacher A, Fischer M, et al. Lumazine synthase from Candida albicans as an anti-fungal target enzyme: structural and biochemical basis for drug design. J Biol Chem. 2007;

280. Donovan M, Schumuke JJ, Fonzi WA, Bonar SL, Gheesling-Mullis K, Jacob GS, et al. Virulence of a Phosphoribosylaminoimidazole Carboxylase-DeficientCandida albicans Strain in an Immunosuppressed Murine Model of Systemic Candidiasis. Infect Immun. 2001;69(4):2542–2548.

281. Kamath A, Chakraburtty K. Role of yeast elongation factor 3 in the elongation cycle. J Biol Chem. 1989;264(26):15423–15428.

282. Moldave K. Eukaryotic protein synthesis. Annu Rev Biochem. 1985;54(1):1109–1149.

283. Domínguez JM, Kelly VA, Kinsman OS, Marriott MS, de las Heras FG, Martín JJ. Sordarins: a new class of antifungals with selective inhibition of the protein synthesis elongation cycle in yeasts. Antimicrob Agents Chemother. 1998;42(9):2274–2278.

284. Shastry M, Nielsen J, Ku T, Hsu M-J, Liberator P, Anderson J, et al. Species-specific inhibition of fungal protein synthesis by sordarin: identification of a sordarin-specificity region in eukaryotic elongation factor 2. Microbiology. 2001;147(2):383–90.

285. Capa L, Mendoza A, Lavandera JL, de las Heras FG, García-Bustos JF. Translation elongation factor 2 is part of the target for a new family of antifungals. Antimicrob Agents Chemother. 1998;42(10):2694–2699.

286. Aoki Y, Yamamoto M, Hosseini-Mazinani SM, Koshikawa N, Sugimoto K, Arisawa M. Antifungal azoxybacilin exhibits activity by inhibiting gene expression of sulfite reductase. Antimicrob Agents Chemother. 1996;40(1):127–132.

287. Noble J, Sanchez I, Blondin B. Identification of new Saccharomyces cerevisiae variants of the MET2 and SKP2 genes controlling the sulfur assimilation pathway and the production of undesirable sulfur compounds during alcoholic fermentation. Microb Cell Factories. 2015;14(1):68.

www.ingramcontent.com/pod-product-compliance
Lightning Source LLC
LaVergne TN
LVHW011928070526
838202LV00054B/4535